HIGH PERFORMANCE
PARALLEL I/O

Chapman & Hall/CRC
Computational Science Series

SERIES EDITOR

Horst Simon
Deputy Director
Lawrence Berkeley National Laboratory
Berkeley, California, U.S.A.

PUBLISHED TITLES

COMBINATORIAL SCIENTIFIC COMPUTING
Edited by Uwe Naumann and Olaf Schenk

CONTEMPORARY HIGH PERFORMANCE COMPUTING: FROM PETASCALE
TOWARD EXASCALE
Edited by Jeffrey S. Vetter

DATA-INTENSIVE SCIENCE
Edited by Terence Critchlow and Kerstin Kleese van Dam

PETASCALE COMPUTING: ALGORITHMS AND APPLICATIONS
Edited by David A. Bader

FUNDAMENTALS OF MULTICORE SOFTWARE DEVELOPMENT
Edited by Victor Pankratius, Ali-Reza Adl-Tabatabai, and Walter Tichy

THE GREEN COMPUTING BOOK: TACKLING ENERGY EFFICIENCY AT LARGE SCALE
Edited by Wu-chun Feng

GRID COMPUTING: TECHNIQUES AND APPLICATIONS
Barry Wilkinson

HIGH PERFORMANCE COMPUTING: PROGRAMMING AND APPLICATIONS
John Levesque with Gene Wagenbreth

HIGH PERFORMANCE PARALLEL I/O
Prabhat and Quincey Koziol

HIGH PERFORMANCE VISUALIZATION:
ENABLING EXTREME-SCALE SCIENTIFIC INSIGHT
Edited by E. Wes Bethel, Hank Childs, and Charles Hansen

INTRODUCTION TO COMPUTATIONAL MODELING USING C AND
OPEN-SOURCE TOOLS
José M Garrido

INTRODUCTION TO CONCURRENCY IN PROGRAMMING LANGUAGES
Matthew J. Sottile, Timothy G. Mattson, and Craig E Rasmussen

PUBLISHED TITLES CONTINUED

INTRODUCTION TO ELEMENTARY COMPUTATIONAL MODELING: ESSENTIAL
CONCEPTS, PRINCIPLES, AND PROBLEM SOLVING
José M. Garrido

INTRODUCTION TO HIGH PERFORMANCE COMPUTING FOR SCIENTISTS
AND ENGINEERS
Georg Hager and Gerhard Wellein

INTRODUCTION TO REVERSIBLE COMPUTING
Kalyan S. Perumalla

INTRODUCTION TO SCHEDULING
Yves Robert and Frédéric Vivien

INTRODUCTION TO THE SIMULATION OF DYNAMICS USING SIMULINK®
Michael A. Gray

PEER-TO-PEER COMPUTING: APPLICATIONS, ARCHITECTURE, PROTOCOLS,
AND CHALLENGES
Yu-Kwong Ricky Kwok

PERFORMANCE TUNING OF SCIENTIFIC APPLICATIONS
Edited by David Bailey, Robert Lucas, and Samuel Williams

PROCESS ALGEBRA FOR PARALLEL AND DISTRIBUTED PROCESSING
Edited by Michael Alexander and William Gardner

SCIENTIFIC DATA MANAGEMENT: CHALLENGES, TECHNOLOGY, AND DEPLOYMENT
Edited by Arie Shoshani and Doron Rotem

HIGH PERFORMANCE PARALLEL I/O

EDITED BY

PRABHAT

Lawrence Berkeley National Laboratory
California, USA

QUINCEY KOZIOL

The HDF Group, Urbana-Champaign
Illinois, USA

CRC Press
Taylor & Francis Group
Boca Raton London New York

CRC Press is an imprint of the
Taylor & Francis Group, an **informa** business

A CHAPMAN & HALL BOOK

CRC Press
Taylor & Francis Group
6000 Broken Sound Parkway NW, Suite 300
Boca Raton, FL 33487-2742

First issued in paperback 2019

© 2015 by Taylor & Francis Group, LLC
CRC Press is an imprint of Taylor & Francis Group, an Informa business

No claim to original U.S. Government works

ISBN-13: 978-1-4665-8234-7 (hbk)
ISBN-13: 978-0-367-37823-3 (pbk)

Visit the Taylor & Francis Web site at
http://www.taylorandfrancis.com

and the CRC Press Web site at
http://www.crcpress.com

Contents

List of Figures   xix

List of Tables   xxv

Foreword   xxvii

Preface   xxix

Acknowledgments   xxxi

Contributors   xxxix

I   Parallel I/O in Practice   **1**

1   Parallel I/O at HPC Facilities   **3**
Galen Shipman

2   National Energy Research Scientific Computing Center   **5**
Jason Hick
2.1   HPC at NERSC   5
2.2   I/O Hardware   6
    2.2.1   Local Scratch File Systems   7
    2.2.2   Storage Network   9
    2.2.3   The NERSC Global File Systems   10
    2.2.4   Archival Storage   11
2.3   Workflows, Workloads, and Applications   12
2.4   Conclusion   14

3   National Center for Supercomputing Applications   **17**
William Kramer, Michelle Butler, Gregory Bauer, Kalyana
Chadalavada, and Celso Mendes
3.1   The Blue Waters Computational and Analysis Subsystems .   18
3.2   Blue Waters On-line Storage Subsystem   19
    3.2.1   On-line Storage Performance   22
3.3   Blue Waters Near-line Storage Subsystem and External Server
    Subsystem   24
3.4   Blue Waters Applications   28

    3.4.1   Science and Engineering Team Application I/O
           Requirements 29
  3.5 Conclusion 31

4 Argonne Leadership Computing Facility   33
  William E. Allcock and Kevin Harms
  4.1 HPC at ALCF 34
    4.1.1 Intrepid 34
    4.1.2 Mira 35
  4.2 Overview of I/O at ALCF 35
  4.3 I/O Hardware 36
    4.3.1 Intrepid: ALCF Blue Gene/P System 37
    4.3.2 Mira: ALCF Blue Gene/Q System 39
  4.4 I/O Software 41
    4.4.1 GPFS 41
          4.4.1.1   Configuration 41
          4.4.1.2   Tuning 42
          4.4.1.3   Reliability 42
    4.4.2 PVFS 43
    4.4.3 Libraries 43
  4.5 Workloads/Applications 44
    4.5.1 Case Studies 46
  4.6 Future I/O Plans at ALCF 47

5 Livermore Computing Center   51
  Richard Hedges and Blaise Barney
  5.1 Introduction 51
  5.2 The Lustre® Parallel File System: Early Developments . . . 53
  5.3 Sequoia, Lustre® 2.0, and ZFS 54
  5.4 IBM Blue Gene Systems 55
  5.5 Sequoia File System Hardware 57
  5.6 Experience with ZFS-Based Lustre® and Sequoia in
      Production 59
  5.7 Sequoia I/O in Practice 60
    5.7.1 General Remarks 60
    5.7.2 Recommendations to Application Developers 61
    5.7.3 SILO: LLNL's I/O Library 62
    5.7.4 Scalable Checkpoint/Restart 62
  5.8 Conclusion 63

6 Los Alamos National Laboratory   65
  Gary Grider
  6.1 HPC at LANL 65
    6.1.1 Facilities and Environments 66
  6.2 I/O Hardware 66

6.2.1   Storage Environment   67

6.2.2   Storage Area Networks   67

6.2.3   Global Parallel Scratch File Systems   68

6.2.4   The Curse of the Burst: Economic Thinking behind
Burst Buffers   70

6.3   Workloads and Applications   72

6.3.1   Applications and Their Use of Storage   72

6.3.2   I/O Patterns and the Quest for Performance without
Giving Up   73

6.3.3   Defeating N-to-1 Strided   73

6.4   Conclusion   75

7   Texas Advanced Computing Center   79

Karl W. Schulz

7.1   HPC at TACC   79

7.2   I/O Hardware   80

7.2.1   Performance   82

7.2.2   Parallel File Systems—A Shared Resource   84

7.3   Conclusion   86

II   File Systems   89

8   Lustre®   91

Eric Barton and Andreas Dilger

8.1   Motivation   91

8.2   Design and Architecture   92

8.2.1   Overview   92

8.2.2   Networking   93

8.2.2.1   LNet   93

8.2.2.2   RPC   94

8.2.3   Distributed Lock Manager   96

8.2.4   Back-end Storage   97

8.2.5   Metadata Server   98

8.2.6   Object Storage Server   99

8.2.7   Management Server   100

8.2.8   Client   100

8.2.9   Recovery   102

8.3   Deployment and Usage   103

8.4   Conclusion   104

9   GPFS   107

Dean Hildebrand and Frank Schmuck

9.1   Motivation   107

9.2   Design and Architecture   108

9.2.1   Shared Storage Model   108

          9.2.2   Design Overview   110
          9.2.3   Distributed Locking and Metadata Management . . .   111
                  9.2.3.1   The Distributed Lock Manager   111
                  9.2.3.2   Metadata Management   112
                  9.2.3.3   Concurrent Directory Updates   113
          9.2.4   Advanced Data Management   114
                  9.2.4.1   GPFS Native RAID   114
                  9.2.4.2   Information Lifecycle Management   114
                  9.2.4.3   Wide-Area Caching and Replication   115
     9.3 Deployment and Usage   116
          9.3.1   Usage Examples   117
     9.4 Conclusion   117

10 OrangeFS   119
     Walt Ligon and Boyd Wilson
     10.1 Motivation   120
          10.1.1 PVFS1   120
          10.1.2 PVFS2   121
          10.1.3 OrangeFS   121
     10.2 Design and Architecture   121
          10.2.1 Overview   121
          10.2.2 OrangeFS Request Protocol   122
          10.2.3 File Structure Representation   122
                  10.2.3.1 Trove   123
          10.2.4 Bulk Messaging Interface   123
          10.2.5 Flows   124
          10.2.6 Job Layer   124
          10.2.7 Request State Machines   124
          10.2.8 Distributed File Metadata   125
          10.2.9 Distributed Directory Entry Metadata   125
          10.2.10 Capability-Based Security   126
          10.2.11 Clients and Interfaces   126
          10.2.12 Features under Development   130
     10.3 Deployment   131
          10.3.1 Cluster Shared Scratch   132
          10.3.2 Cluster Node Scratch   132
          10.3.3 Amazon Web Services   133
     10.4 Conclusion   133

11 OneFS   135
     Nick Kirsch
     11.1 Motivation   135
     11.2 Design/Architecture   136
          11.2.1 Isilon Node   137
     11.3 Network   138

11.3.1 Back-End Network 138
11.3.2 Front-End Network 138
11.3.3 Complete Cluster View 139
11.4 OneFS Software Overview 139
11.4.1 Operating System 139
11.4.2 File System Structure 139
11.4.3 Data Layout 141
11.5 Data Protection 142
11.5.1 Power Loss 142
11.5.2 Scalable Rebuild 142
11.5.3 Virtual Hot Spare 143
11.5.4 $N + M$ Data Protection 143
11.6 Dynamic Scale/Scale on Demand 145
11.6.1 Performance and Capacity 145
11.7 Conclusion 147

III I/O Libraries   **149**

12 I/O Libraries: Past, Present and Future   **151**
Mike Folk
12.1 Motivation 151
12.2 A Recent History of I/O Libraries, by Example 152
12.3 What Is the Future of I/O Libraries? 153

13 MPI-IO   **155**
Wei-keng Liao and Rajeev Thakur
13.1 Introduction 155
13.1.1 MPI-IO Background 156
13.1.2 Parallel I/O in Practice 156
13.2 Using MPI for Simple I/O 157
13.2.1 Three Ways of File Access 158
13.2.2 Blocking and Nonblocking I/O 159
13.3 File Access with User Intent 159
13.3.1 Independent I/O 160
13.3.2 MPI File View 161
13.3.3 Collective I/O 163
13.4 MPI-IO Hints 165
13.5 Conclusions 165

14 PLFS: Software-Defined Storage for HPC   **169**
John Bent
14.1 Motivation 169
14.2 Design/Architecture 170
14.2.1 PLFS Shared File Mode 170
14.2.2 PLFS Flat File Mode 172

14.2.3 PLFS Small File Mode 172
14.3 Deployment, Usage, and Applications 173
        14.3.1 Burst Buffers 174
        14.3.2 Cloud File Systems for HPC 174
14.4 Conclusion   175

15 Parallel-NetCDF   177
Rob Latham
15.1 Motivation 177
15.2 History and Background   179
15.3 Design and Architecture 179
15.4 Deployment and Usage 180
15.5 Additional Features 181
15.6 Conclusion 182
15.7 Additional Resources 183

16 HDF5   185
Quincey Koziol, Russ Rew, Mark Howison, Prabhat, and Marc Poinot
16.1 Motivation 186
16.2 History and Background 186
16.3 Design and Architecture 187
        16.3.1 The HDF5 Data Model 188
        16.3.2 The HDF5 Library 191
        16.3.3 The HDF5 File Format 192
16.4 Usage and Applications 192
        16.4.1 netCDF-4 193
                16.4.1.1 Design 193
                16.4.1.2 Applications 193
        16.4.2 H5hut 194
                16.4.2.1 Design 194
                16.4.2.2 Applications 194
        16.4.3 CGNS 195
                16.4.3.1 Design 195
                16.4.3.2 Applications 197
16.5 Conclusion 199
16.6 Additional Resources 199

17 ADIOS   203
*Norbert Podhorszki, Scott Klasky, Qing Liu, Yuan Tian, Manish
Parashar, Karsten Schwan, Matthew Wolf, and Sriram
Lakshminarasimhan*
17.1 Motivation 203
17.2 Design and Architecture 204
17.3 Deployment, Usage, and Applications 205
        17.3.1 Checkpoint/Restart 205

17.3.2 Analysis 206
17.3.3 Code Coupling 207
17.3.4 Visualization 208
17.3.5 Data Reduction 210
17.3.6 Deployment 210
17.4 Conclusion 211

18 GLEAN 215

Venkatram Vishwanath, Huy Bui, Mark Hereld, and Michael E. Papka

18.1 Motivation 215
18.2 Design and Architecture 216
18.2.1 Exploiting Network Topology and Reduced
Synchronization for I/O 217
18.2.2 Leveraging Application Data Semantics 218
18.2.3 Asynchronous Data Staging 219
18.2.4 Compression and Subfiling 219
18.3 Deployment, Usage, and Applications 220
18.3.1 Checkpoint, Restart, and Analysis I/O for HACC
Cosmology 220
18.3.2 Data Staging for FLASH Astrophysics 221
18.3.3 Co-Visualization for PHASTA CFD Simulation 222
18.4 Conclusion 223

IV   I/O Case Studies 225

19 Parallel I/O for a Trillion-Particle Plasma Physics Simulation 227

Surendra Byna, Prabhat, Homa Karimabadi, and William Daughton

19.1 Abstract 227
19.2 Science Use Case 228
19.3 I/O Challenges 229
19.4 Software and Hardware 229
19.4.1 Hardware Platform 229
19.4.2 Software Setup 230
19.5 Parallel I/O in VPIC 230
19.6 Performance 232
19.6.1 Tuning Write Performance 232
19.6.2 HDF5 Tuning 233
19.6.3 Tuning Lustre File System and MPI-I/O Parameters . 233
19.7 Conclusion 236
19.8 Acknowledgments 236

20 Stochastic Simulation Data Management   **239**

Dimitris Servis

20.1 Background 239
20.2 Science Use Case 240
20.3 The I/O Challenge 241
20.4 Using HDF5 in Industrial Stochastic Simulations 243
    20.4.1 Data Model and Versioning 244
    20.4.2 VFL and Filters 244
    20.4.3 Encryption 244
    20.4.4 Robustness 244
    20.4.5 Fragmentation 245
    20.4.6 Process and Thread Synchronization 245
20.5 A (Near) Efficient Architecture Using HDF5 245
20.6 Performance 247
20.7 Conclusion 248

21 Silo: A General-Purpose API and Scientific Database   **249**

Mark Miller

21.1 Canonical Use Case: ALE3D Restart and VisIt Visualization
    Workflow 250
21.2 Software, Hardware, and Performance 251
21.3 MIF and SSF Scalable I/O Paradigms 252
21.4 Successes with HDF5 as Middleware 256
21.5 Conclusion 257

22 Scaling Up Parallel I/O in S3D to 100-K Cores with ADIOS   **259**

Scott Klasky, Gary Liu, Hasan Abbasi, Norbert Podhorszki,
Jackie Chen, and Hemanth Kolla

22.1 Science Use Case 259
22.2 Software and Hardware 260
    22.2.1 ADIOS-BP 261
    22.2.2 Staged Write Method 262
    22.2.3 Group-Based Hierarchical I/O Control 262
    22.2.4 Aggregation and Subfiling 263
    22.2.5 Index Generation 266
    22.2.6 Staged Read Method 266
    22.2.7 Staged Opens 266
    22.2.8 Chunking 267
    22.2.9 Limitations 268
22.3 Conclusion 269

23 In-Transit Processing: Data Analysis Using Burst Buffers   **271**

Christopher Mitchell, David Bonnie, and Jonathan Woodring

23.1 Motivation 271
23.2 Design/Architecture 273

23.3 Systems Prototypes Related to Burst Buffers 274
23.4 Conclusion 275

V   I/O Profiling Tools   277

24 Overview of I/O Benchmarking   279
Katie Antypas and Yushu Yao
24.1 Introduction 279
24.2 I/O Benchmarking 280
24.3 Why Profile I/O in Scientific Applications? 283
24.4 Brief Introduction to I/O Profilers 283
24.5 I/O Profiling at NERSC 284
        24.5.1 Application Profiling Case Studies 284
                24.5.1.1 Checkpointing Too Frequently 285
                24.5.1.2 Reading Small Input Files from Every Rank 286
                24.5.1.3 Using the Wrong File System 286
24.6 Conclusion 287

25 TAU   289
Sameer Shende and Allen D. Malony
25.1 Abstract 289
25.2 Features 290
        25.2.1 MPI-IO Instrumentation 291
        25.2.2 Runtime Preloading of Instrumented Library 291
        25.2.3 Linker-Based Instrumentation 291
        25.2.4 Instrumented External I/O Libraries 292
25.3 Success Stories 292
25.4 Conclusion 294

26 Integrated Performance Monitoring   297
David Skinner
26.1 Design and Features 297
26.2 Success Stories 301
        26.2.1 Chombo's ftruncate 301
        26.2.2 MADBENCH and File System Health 302
        26.2.3 Buffer Size 303
        26.2.4 HPC Workload Studies 304
26.3 Conclusion 305

27 Darshan   309
Philip Carns
27.1 Features 309
27.2 Success Stories 311
27.3 Conclusion 313

28 Iota   **317**
Mark Howison, Prabhat, and Surendra Byna
28.1 Features 317
28.2 Success Stories 318
28.3 Conclusion 321

VI   Future Trends   **323**

29 Parallel Computing Trends for the Coming Decade   **325**
John Shalf
29.1 Technology Scaling 326
   29.1.1 Classical Scaling Period (1965–2004) 326
   29.1.2 End of Classical Scaling (2004) 326
   29.1.3 Toward Data-Centric Computing (2014–2022) 328
29.2 Implications for the Future of Storage Systems 329
29.3 Conclusion 331

30 Storage Models: Past, Present, and Future   **333**
Dries Kimpe and Robert Ross
30.1 The POSIX Era 334
30.2 The Current HPC Storage Model 335
   30.2.1 The POSIX HPC I/O Extensions 335
   30.2.2 MPI-IO 337
   30.2.3 Object Storage Model 337
30.3 Post POSIX 338
   30.3.1 Prior Work 338
   30.3.2 Object Abstractions in HPC 339
   30.3.3 Namespaces 341
30.4 Conclusion 341

31 Resilience   **345**
Gary Grider and Nathan DeBardeleben
31.1 Present 346
   31.1.1 Getting the Correct Answer 347
31.2 Future 348
31.3 Conclusion 350

32 Multi/Many Core   **353**
Ramon Nou, Toni Cortes, Stelios Mavridis, Yannis Sfakianakis,
and Angelos Bilas
32.1 Introduction 353
32.2 Storage I/O at Present 354
32.3 Storage I/O in the Near Future 355
32.4 Challenges and Solutions 356
   32.4.1 NUMA Effects 356

32.4.2 Improving I/O Caching Efficiency 357
32.4.3 Dynamic I/O Scheduler Selection 359
32.5 Conclusion 360

33 Storage Networks and Interconnects **363**
Parks Fields and Benjamin McClelland
33.1 Current State of Technology 363
33.2 Future Directions 365
33.3 Challenges and Solutions 366
33.4 Conclusion 367

34 Power Consumption **369**
Matthew L. Curry, H. Lee Ward, David Martinez, Jill Gemmill,
Jay Harris, Gary Grider, and Anna Maria Bailey
34.1 Introduction 370
34.2 Power Use in Recent and Current Supercomputers 370
34.2.1 Red Sky 371
34.2.2 Cielo 371
34.2.3 Palmetto 373
34.2.4 Dawn 374
34.2.5 Overall Survey Results 374
34.2.6 Extrapolation to Exascale 377
34.3 How I/O Changes at Exascale 377
34.3.1 Introducing More Asynchrony in the File System . . . 378
34.3.1.1 The Burst Buffer 378
34.3.1.2 Sirocco: A File System for Heterogeneous
Media 378
34.3.2 Guarding against Single-Node Failures and Soft Errors 379
34.4 Conclusion 380

Index **385**

List of Figures

2.1   NERSC compute and storage systems.   7

2.2   Edison local scratch diagram.   9

2.3   NERSC global file system architecture.   11

2.4   NERSC application codes.   13

3.1   The Blue Waters computational analysis subsystem.   20

3.2   The Blue Waters network subsystem.   21

3.3   The total Blue Waters I/O bandwidth is greater than 1.18 TB/s.   23

3.4   Blue Waters I/O performance tests scaled with the number of client nodes   24

3.5   The Blue Waters external server subsystem.   25

3.6   Snap-shot of jobs running on Blue Waters.   29

4.1   ALCF1 HPC center.   37

4.2   ALCF2 HPC system.   40

4.3   I/O interfaces by job size on Intrepid.   44

4.4   The amount of data transferred on `/intrepid-fs0` from 2010 to 2013.   45

4.5   File size CDF of project file systems.   46

4.6   Diagram of file system changes underway at ALCF.   48

5.1   Hardware packaging hierarchy of the BG/Q scaling architecture.   56

5.2   Hardware configuration of an OSS pair.   58

5.3   ZFS-based Lustre file system for LLN's Sequoia system. . .   59

6.1   LANL Parallel Scalable Backbone, as invented a decade ago.   69

6.2   Machine efficiency JMMTI over time for checkpoint.   70

6.3   Purchasing economics for disk, Flash, and hybrid storage for checkpoints.   71

6.4   PLFS internal data flow diagram.   74

6.5   PLFS N-to-1 application I/O speed-ups.   75

7.1   Lustre file system quotas and target usage on TACC's *Stampede* system.   81

7.2   Average software RAID performance for Lustre OST devices
      measured during disk burn-in procedure.   81
7.3   Lustre scaling across multiple Object Storage Servers (OSS)
      measured using Lustre (version 2.1.3).   82
7.4   Raw write performance characteristics of a large, parallel Lus-
      tre file system.   83
7.5   Daily file system performance measurements during normal
      production operations.   85
7.6   File system usage growth after starting production operations
      in January 2013.   86

8.1   Lustre architecture.   93
8.2   Lustre RPC.   95

9.1   GPFS configuration examples.   109

10.1 OrangeFS architecture.   122
10.2 OrangeFS: Certificate-based security.   127
10.3 OrangeFS: Clients and interfaces.   128
10.4 OrangeFS Direct interface.   129
10.5 Average job runtime vs. file system.   130
10.6 Average job runtime vs. number of remote clients.   131

11.1 OneFS distributed system.   137
11.2 All components of OneFS at work.   139
11.3 Single OneFS file system starting at the root inode /ifs. . .   140
11.4 OneFS: Data and parity in $N + M$ protect.   144
11.5 OneFS hybrid parity protection schemes $(N + M : x)$. . . .   146

13.1 MPI-IO in the I/O software stack.   156
13.2 Simple example of a parallel file access pattern and sample
      MPI-IO code.   158
13.3 A 2D array partitioned among 4 MPI processes in a block–
      block pattern.   160
13.4 MPI program fragments to write the 2D array in parallel. .   161
13.5 Example of individual process's file views for 2D array. . . .   162

14.1 The architecture of PLFS shared file mode.   171
14.2 The architecture of PLFS small file mode.   173
14.3 PLFS enabled burst buffers.   175

15.1 The parallel I/O software stack.   178
15.2 The NetCDF file layout.   180
15.3 A code fragment demonstrating the two modes of the Parallel-
      NetCDF API.   181

15.4   A Parallel-NetCDF code fragment demonstrating the use of
       the non-blocking routines.   182

16.1   HDF5 data model.   189
16.2   HDF5 dataset.   189
16.3   HDF5 datatypes.   190
16.4   HDF5 program.   191
16.5   CGNS/SIDS data model.   196
16.6   CGNS file layout and parallel computation.   198
16.7   A graphical view of CGNS/HDF5 file.   198

17.1   ADIOS coupling workflow. 209
17.2   In-transit visualization using ADIOS. 209

18.1   Relationships between GLEAN and principal components of
       an HPC application.   217
18.2   Aggregation groups formed within a set of nodes by GLEAN.   218
18.3   Efficacy of topology-aware aggregation, subfiling, and com-
       pression on HACC I/O performance   221

19.1   VPIC simulation configured using MPI and OpenMP.   231
19.2   Parallel I/O stack and tunable parameters. 232
19.3   Performance improvement with patching HDF5 truncate. . .   234
19.4   VPIC-IOBench weak scaling study.   235
19.5   Performance of writing a single HDF5 file to Lustre. 235

20.1   An architecture for efficient stochastic simulation data man-
       agement using HDF5. 246

21.1   Example of an ALE3D mesh decomposed into domains. . .   251
21.2   Example Silo-based MIF-IO. 253
21.3   Variation in ALE3D I/O performance as the number of file
       parts is varied. 254
21.4   Comparison of MIF-IO write and read performance on 3 ASC
       systems (Purple, Dawn and Graph) and improvement in I/O
       performance with block-based VFD. 257

22.1   Group-based hierarchical I/O control for ADIOS. 263
22.2   S3D write performance scaling with application size. 265
22.3   Metadata operation cost scaling with increasing number of
       writers. 267
22.4   S3D read performance scaling. 268

23.1   Potential system diagram for a supercomputer with burst
       buffers. 273

24.1 Application access patterns for moving data between memory and file. 281
24.2 Franklin XT-4 file system activity during an IOR run. . . . 282
24.3 Darshan statistics of a job that is checkpointing too frequently. 285
24.4 Hopper XE-6 file system activity during a user run. The user is frequently checkpointing, causing the I/O activity to be high. 285
24.5 Profile of a job spending its time in reading small input files. 286
24.6 Impact of using the wrong file system on job performance. . 286

25.1 I/O Profile for GCRM. 293
25.2 I/O profile for GCRM showing bytes for each file and read operation. 293

26.1 IPM's core framework. 298
26.2 IPM's double-open address hashing scheme. 299
26.3 Text output from an application run with IPM. 299
26.4 The POSIX and MPI-IO calls profiled by IPM's I/O module. 300
26.5 Steps required to improve performance of writes in HDF-based MPI codes. 302
26.6 Histograms of MADBENCH parallel reads before and after tuning the parallel file system. 303
26.7 Large numbers of jobs in a workload may be difficult to identify by name or other job metadata. 304

27.1 Excerpts from the `darshan-job-summary` utility included with Darshan. 311
27.2 Number of core hours consumed by Darshan-instrumented jobs in each partition size on Intrepid. 312
27.3 Total amount of data read and written by Darshan-instrumented jobs in each partition size category on Intrepid. 313
27.4 Prevalence of key I/O characteristics in each partition size category on Intrepid. 313

28.1 Overhead of the Iota library, tested with three I/O benchmarks. 319
28.2 Spatio-temporal pattern write patterns for the 12,000 core VPIC run. 320
28.3 Box and whisper plots show the distribution of write bandwidths to each OST in the 1,728 core VORPAL run. 320

29.1 The effect of the end of Dennard Scaling on microprocessor performance, power consumption, and architecture. 327
29.2 The Power and Clock Inflection point in 2004. 328
29.3 The energy consumed by data movement is starting to exceed the energy consumed by computation. 329

30.1 Domain decomposition resulting in highly non-contiguous access pattern. 336
30.2 Mapping of PnetCDF dataset to POSIX file, or EOF objects. 340

31.1 Estimates of the relative increase in error rates as a function of process technology. 349
31.2 Relationship between soft errors and voltage scaling through several process technology generations. 349

32.1 FIO read IOPS of native (XFS file system). 356
32.2 FIO read and write in a 64-core machine. 357
32.3 IOR read and write in a 64-core machine. 357
32.4 On-memory deduplication in fileservers. 358
32.5 Dynamic partition on multicores. 359
32.6 IOAnalyzer system architecture. 360

33.1 IBTA InfiniBand roadmap. 364
33.2 Wavelength division multiplexing. 366

34.1 Predicted power use for Red Sky UC. 372
34.2 Power use for Palmetto and its storage infrastructure. . . . 374
34.3 Absolute power use of Dawn over a one-month time period. 375
34.4 The percent of power used for disks and associated systems, by machine. 375
34.5 The number of disks installed in each system per teraFLOP of compute power, by machine. 376

List of Tables

2.1   NERSC storage systems noting storage type, bandwidth capabilities, and storage capacity.   8

2.2   Amount of archived data at NERSC in 2013 for major systems.   12

3.1   Blue Waters data payload bi-directional bandwidth in X, Y, Z dimensions.   20

3.2   Key Blue Waters performance information.   21

3.3   IOR-write performance on Blue Waters file systems.   23

3.4   IOR performance for writing 1-GB files on Blue Waters /scratch   24

3.5   PPM I/O performance.   31

4.1   Common I/O libraries at ALCF.   43

5.1   Performance characteristics of Blue Gene systems.   57

6.1   Detailed summary of LANL's 2013 computing environment.   67

6.2   Summary of the LANL storage environment.   67

23.1 Comparison of *In situ*, In Transit and conventional Post Processing methods.   272

34.1 Types of compute nodes used in Palmetto cluster.   373

Foreword

In the age of ever increasing emphasis on "big data" the topic of high performance parallel I/O should be amply covered in the literature. After all, what is the point of all the discussion of the ever increasing deluge of data without an understanding of how all the data are read and written quickly and efficiently? Yet, curiously a search on books on parallel I/O reveals that more than a decade has passed since any attempt has been made to summarize the state of our knowledge about high performance parallel I/O in the form of book for the High Performance Computing (HPC) community.

Prabhat and Quincey Koziol have made a significant accomplishment by editing this book on "High Performance Parallel I/O". This book is indeed remarkable since there has been so much progress in technology, software, and tools for parallel I/O in the last decade, but documenting this progress has been notably absent. I/O is often the bottleneck to achieving the best possible performance in HPC, but its treatment and discussion are quite frequently secondary to the discussion of CPU performance. The authors have set out to address this deficiency, and succeeded admirably. Their text provides a useful overview of an area of rapid development that is currently not represented in any book.

An important distinction of the current book is that is has been edited by practitioners in the field. Both editors and most of the chapter authors have been involved hands-on in developing software for parallel I/O as well as porting and optimizing scientific applications on large scale parallel I/O system. This practical experience has led the editors to direct their selection of topics for the book towards a highly usable set of themes for the individual book sections: an overview of parallel I/O system as currently implemented in leading HPC centers, a survey of file systems and I/O libraries currently in use, and a selection of case studies, augmented by a description of tools for parallel I/O. The individual chapters are contributed by the leading experts in the field. Thus the book will be a handy reference for applications developer as well as for computer center managers, who want to know about the state-of-the-art in parallel I/O.

In the last twenty years high performance computing has seen many dramatic developments. In the early 1990s computing technology made a dramatic transition to MPPs using commodity hardware and the MPI programming model. This transition and the new parallel model for HPC solidified in the early 2000s. Essentially this model has remained the same until now, while at the same time increasing performance by a factor of one million from the Gigaflops to the Petaflops level. Today were are close to yet another transformation of the HPC field as GPUs and accelerators become integrated, while the amount of parallelism seems to be ever increasing and the field is moving towards Exaflops level performance.

In this context of a potential rapid transformation of the high performance computing field, the book by Prabhat and Koziol arrives at exactly the right time. It succeeds perfectly and for the first time provides a survey of the significant accomplishments in file systems, libraries, and tools that have been developed for about a decade. These developments have now reached a state of relative maturity, and are ripe for a treatment in book format. Simultaneously the editors combine their technology and software survey with significant application development examples in a single volume. In the last set of chapters the book previews the I/O challenges in the Exaflops era. Thus the book will provide a solid foundation for anyone who is considering using the most recent tools for developing parallel I/O intensive applications today, and be also prepared for future Exascale platforms. I highly recommend this timely book for computational scientists and engineers.

Horst D. Simon
Lawrence Berkeley National Laboratory
Berkeley, September 2014

Preface

Parallel I/O is an integral component of modern high performance computing (HPC). Petascale-class simulations routinely produce terabyte to petabyte-sized datasets, which need to be stored efficiently. Data-centric analysis and visualization tools rely on efficient reads to ingest and process large datasets. Both write and read operations are critical for facilitating scientific discovery and insight.

This book captures the state of the art in the field of high performance parallel I/O in the 2013–2014 timeframe. We have drawn upon insights from leading practitioners, researchers, software architects, developers, and scientists. This rich tapestry of contributions from experts sheds light on the parallel I/O ecosystem.

The book is organized in six parts. Part I is intended to give readers a window into how large-scale HPC facilities scope, configure, and operate systems, with a specific emphasis on choices of I/O hardware, middleware, and applications. Readers will find leading storage experts from the National Energy Research Scientific Computing Center (NERSC), National Center for Supercomputing Applications (NCSA), Argonne Leadership Computing Facility (ALCF), Livermore Computing Center, and Texas Advanced Computing Center (TACC) sharing their perspectives in this part of the book.

Following this, the book traverses up the I/O software stack. In Part II, we deal with the file system layer. Leading designers and architects share their insights on the design, architecture, and application of the most prominent file systems in practice today: Lustre, GPFS, OrangeFS, and OneFS. Moving further up the I/O stack in part III, we review middleware (such as MPI-IO and PLFS), and user-facing libraries (such as Parallel-NetCDF, HDF5, ADIOS and GLEAN). These chapters give insight into design decisions made by library developers, library features, and applications.

Part IV of the book delves into real-world scientific applications that utilize the parallel I/O infrastructure. Application and library developers present case studies from particle-in-cell, stochastic, finite volume, and direct numerical simulations. Careful profiling and optimization are essential for obtaining peak (and sustained) parallel I/O performance. Part V of the book presents an overview of a number of profiling and benchmarking tools used by practitioners in the field. Finally, the world of HPC is forever in flux. Part VI of the book discusses implications of current trends in HPC on parallel I/O in the exascale world.

Acknowledgments

We would like to thank Mary Hester for an outstanding job in proofreading and editing the text. Her exemplary patience and diligence has vastly improved the quality of the book. Wes Bethel and Mike Folk encouraged us to take on this project. Randi Cohen from Taylor and Francis was very supportive of our endeavor and patient with our questions. Both of us have had a wonderful supportive environment in the Computational Research Division at Berkeley Lab, and the HDF Group, and we would like to acknowledge our colleagues. Finally, we would like to acknowledge the support and love offered by our families.

Prabhat, Quincey Koziol

April 15, 2014

Acknowledgments

The editors acknowledge the support rendered to them by the Lawrence Berkeley National Laboratory, and the HDF Group. This work was supported by the Director, Office of Science, Office and Advanced Scientific Computing Research, of the U.S. Department of Energy under Contract No. DE-AC02-05CH11231.

Chapter 1—Parallel I/O at HPC Facilities

This work is sponsored by the U.S. Department of Energy, Office of Science, Advanced Scientific Computing Research program, and was performed at Oak Ridge National Laboratory (ORNL), which is managed by UT-Battelle, LLC, for the Department of Energy, under Contract No. DEAC0500OR22725.

Chapter 2—National Energy Research Scientific Computing Center

This work is supported by the Director, Office of Science, Office of Advanced Scientific Computing Research, of the U.S. Department of Energy under Contract No. DE-AC02-05CH11231. This research used resources of the National Energy Research Scientific Computing Center (NERSC).

Chapter 3—National Center for Supercomputing Applications

This research is part of the Blue Waters sustained-petascale computing project, which is supported by the National Science Foundation (award number OCI 07-25070) and the state of Illinois. Blue Waters is a joint effort of the University of Illinois at Urbana-Champaign and its National Center for Supercomputing Applications.

Chapter 4—Argonne Leadership Computing Facility

This research used resources of the Argonne Leadership Computing Facility at Argonne National Laboratory, which is supported by the Office of Science of the U.S. Department of Energy under contract DE-AC02-06CH11357.

Chapter 5—Livermore Computing Center

The authors would like to acknowledge the entire Livermore Computing organization, which has supported the subject work for at least the last decade. Further, we acknowledge the efforts of the Lustre teams headed by Mark Gary, Chris Morrone, and Marc Stearman and the assistance of those three individuals in preparing and reviewing this manuscript.

This work was performed under the auspices of the U.S. Department of Energy by Lawrence Livermore National Laboratory under Contract DE-AC52-07NA27344. This chapter is an LLNL document: LLNL-BOOK-641234.

Chapter 6—Los Alamos National Laboratory

The author would like to acknowledge the entire Los Alamos High Performance Computing Division, which has supported the subject work for multiple decades. Los Alamos National Laboratory (LANL) is operated by Los Alamos National Security under its U. S. Department of Energy Contract No. DE-AC52-06NA25396.

Chapter 7—Texas Advanced Computing Center

This work was supported in part by the U.S. National Science Foundation under Award No. 1134872 from the Division of Cyberinfrastructure.

Chapter 8—Lustre

The authors' thanks go out to the US DOE for their initial funding and ongoing support for Lustre, along with Peter Braam, Mark Seager, and Gary Grider who started it all off.

Chapter 9—GPFS

GPFS is the result of the effort of a large number of very talented and dedicated people at IBM, all of whom have contributed to the design and implementation of GPFS over the last two decades. The authors would like to acknowledge the contributions of all of the members of the worldwide GPFS team to the work described here.

Chapter 11—OneFS

About Isilon: As the global leader in scale-out storage, Isilon delivers powerful yet simple solutions for enterprises that want to manage their data, not their storage. Isilon's products are simple to install, manage, and scale, at any size. And, unlike traditional enterprise storage, Isilon stays simple no matter how much storage is added, how much performance is required, or how business needs change in the future. Information about Isilon can be found at `http://www.isilon.com`. ©2011 Isilon Systems LLC. All rights reserved. Isilon, Isilon Systems, OneFS, and SyncIQ are registered trademarks of Isilon Systems LLC. Isilon IQ, SmartConnect, SnapshotIQ, TrueScale, Autobalance, FlexProtect, SmartCache, SmartPools, InsightIQ, "SIMPLE IS SMART," and the Isilon logo are trademarks of Isilon. Other product and company names mentioned are the trademarks of their respective owners. U.S. Patent Numbers 7,146,524; 7,346,720; 7,386,675. Other patents pending.

Chapter 13—MPI-IO

This work was supported in part by the U.S. Department of Energy under contracts DE-AC02-06CH11307 and DE-SC0005309 and in part by the U.S. National Science Foundation under Award No. CCF-0938000.

Chapter 14—PLFS: Software-Defined Storage for HPC

The author would like to acknowledge the many collaborators on PLFS: Garth Gibson, Milo Polte, and Chuck Cranor from CMU, Gary Grider, Meghan McClelland, Ben McClelland, Adam Manzanares, Aaron Torres, Brett Kettering, David Shrader, and Alfred Torrez from Los Alamos National Lab, and Sorin Faibish, Jingwang Zhang, Xuezhao Liu, Zhenhua Zhang, Percy Tzelnic, and Uday Gupta from EMC.

Chapter 15—Parallel-NetCDF

This research was supported by the Office of Science of the U.S. Department of Energy under Contract Nos. DE-AC02-05CH11231 and DE-AC02-06CH11357 including through the Scientific Discovery through Advanced Computing (SciDAC) Institute for Scalable Data Management, Analysis, and Visualization.

Chapter 16—HDF5

The authors would like to gratefully acknowledge the HDF5 development team at the HDF Group and others who have contributed to the HDF5 project.

Chapter 17—ADIOS

The authors would like to acknowledge the entire Oak Ridge Leadership Facility for their support for ADIOS. Oak Ridge National Laboratory (ORNL) is operated by UT-Battelle LLC under its U.S. Department of Energy Contract No. DE-AC05-00OR22725.

Chapter 18—GLEAN

We gratefully acknowledge the use of the resources of the Argonne Leadership Computing Facility at Argonne National Laboratory. This work was supported by the Office of Advanced Scientific Computing Research, Office of Science, U.S. Department of Energy, under Contract DE-AC02-06CH11357 including through the Scientific Discovery through Advanced Computing (SciDAC) Institute for Scalable Data Management, Analysis, and Visualization.

Chapter 19—Parallel I/O for a Trillion Particle Plasma Physics Simulation

This work is supported by the Director, Office of Science, Office of Advanced Scientific Computing Research, of the U.S. Department of Energy under Contract No. DE-AC02-05CH11231. This research used resources of the National Energy Research Scientific Computing Center (NERSC).

Chapter 20—Stochastic Simulation Data Management

The author would like to thank Autoform for giving me the opportunity to experiment with HDF5 and The HDF Group for supporting my efforts.

Chapter 21—Silo

This work was performed under the auspices of the U.S. Department of Energy by Lawrence Livermore National Laboratory in part under Contract W-7405-Eng-48 and in part under Contract DE-AC52-07NA27344.

Chapter 22—Scaling up Parallel I/O in S3D to 100K Cores with ADIOS

The authors would like to acknowledge the entire Oak Ridge Leadership Facility for their support for ADIOS. Oak Ridge National Laboratory (ORNL) is operated by UT-Battelle LLC under its U.S. Department of Energy Contract No. DE-AC05-00OR22725 including the Scientific Discovery through Advanced Computing (SciDAC) Institute for Scalable Data Management, Analysis, and Visualization.

Chapter 23—In-Transit Processing: Data Analysis Using Burst Buffers

The authors would like to thank the Los Alamos National Laboratory's Laboratory Directed Research and Development (LDRD) program for its support of this research under project 20130457ER: Co-Design of Burst Buffer Hardware and Data Analysis/Visualization Software for Large-Scale Simulations. Los Alamos National Laboratory (LANL) is operated by Los Alamos National Security under its U.S. Department of Energy Contract No. DE-AC52-06NA25396 This chapter was reviewed for release under Los Alamos National Laboratory LA-UR-13-27966.

Chapter 24—Overview of I/O Benchmarking

This work used resources of the National Energy Research Scientific Computing Center, which is supported by the Office of Science of the U.S. Department of Energy under Contract No. DE-AC02-05CH11231.

Chapter 25—TAU

The research at the University of Oregon was supported by grants ER26057, ER26167, ER26098, and ER26005 from the U.S. Department of Energy, Office of Science.

Chapter 26—Integrated Performance Monitoring

Integrated Performance Monitoring (IPM) extends earlier work by David Skinner and the ACTC group at IBM's TJ Watson Research Center. IPM is supported by the National Science Foundation (NSF0721397) and the Department of Energy Office of Science (DE-AC02-05CH11231). The authors thank Bill Kramer for his input on IPM's design goals.

Chapter 27—Darshan

This research was supported by the Office of Science of the U.S. Department of Energy under Contract Nos. DE-AC02-05CH11231 and DE-AC02-06CH11357 including through the Scientific Discovery through Advanced Computing (SciDAC) Institute for Scalable Data Management, Analysis, and Visualization.

Chapter 28—Iota

Iota is an extension of earlier work by Noel Keen and Karl Fuerlinger to incorporate I/O tracing into the Integrated Performance Monitoring (IPM) tool.

This research was conducted using computational resources and services at the Center for Computation and Visualization, Brown University. This work was supported by the Director, Office of Science, Office of Advanced Scientific Computing Research, of the U.S. Department of Energy under Contract No. DE-AC02-05CH11231. This research used resources of the National Energy Research Scientific Computing Center.

Chapter 29—Parallel Computing Trends for the Coming Decade

This work was supported by the ASCR Office in the DOE Office of Science under contract number DE-AC02-05CH11231. This work also has benefitted greatly from collaborator Peter Kogge whose long-term data collection on emerging trends in CMOS silicon technology have been the underpinning for the DARPA and DOE programs in exascale computing.

Chapter 30—Storage Models: Past, Present, and Future

The EOF work and the writing of this chapter were supported by the U.S. Department of Energy, under Contract DE-AC02-06CH11357.

Chapter 32—Multi/Many Core

We thankfully acknowledge the support of the European Commission under the 7th Framework Programs through the IOLANES (FP7-ICT-248615) and HiPEAC3 (FP7-ICT-287759) projects, the Spanish Ministry of Economy and Competitiveness under the TIN2012-34557 grant, and by the Catalan Government under the 2009-SGR-980 grant.

Chapter 33—Storage Networks and Interconnects

The authors would like to acknowledge the Department of Energy, the National Nuclear Security Administration, and our employer Los Alamos National Laboratory.

Chapter 34—Power Consumption

Sandia National Laboratories is a multi-program laboratory managed and operated by Sandia Corporation, a wholly owned subsidiary of Lockheed

Martin Corporation, for the U.S. Department of Energy's National Nuclear Security Administration under contract DE-AC04-94AL85000.

Disclaimer

This document was prepared as an account of work sponsored by the United States government. While this document is believed to contain correct information, neither the United States government nor any agency thereof, nor the Regents of the University of California, nor any of their employees, makes any warranty, express or implied, or assumes any legal responsibility for the accuracy, completeness, or usefulness of any information, apparatus, product, or process disclosed, or represents that its use would not infringe privately owned rights. Reference herein to any specific commercial product, process, or service by its trade name, trademark, manufacturer, or otherwise, does not necessarily constitute or imply its endorsement, recommendation, or favoring by the United States government or any agency thereof, or the Regents of the University of California. The views and opinions of authors expressed herein do not necessarily state or reflect those of the United States government or any agency thereof or the Regents of the University of California.

Contributors

Hasan Abbasi
Oak Ridge National Laboratory
Oak Ridge, TN, USA

William E. Allcock
Argonne National Laboratory
Argonne, IL, USA

Katie Antypas
National Energy Research Scientific
    Computing Center
Oakland, CA, USA

Anna Maria Bailey
Lawrence Livermore National
    Laboratory
Livermore, CA, USA

Blaise Barney
Lawrence Livermore National
    Laboratory
Livermore, CA, USA

Eric Barton
Intel Corporation
Bristol, UK

Gregory Bauer
National Center for Supercomputing
    Applications
Urbana, IL, USA

John Bent
EMC Corporation
USA

Angelos Bilas
Foundation for Research and
    Technology–Hellas
Heraklion, Greece

David Bonnie
Los Alamos National Laboratory
Los Alamos, NM, USA

Huy Bui
Argonne National Laboratory
Argonne, IL, USA

Michelle Butler
National Center for Supercomputing
    Applications
Urbana, IL, USA

Surendra Byna
Lawrence Berkeley National
    Laboratory
Berkeley, CA, USA

Philip Carns
Argonne National Laboratory
Argonne, IL, USA

Kalyana Chadalavada
National Center for Supercomputing
    Applications
Urbana, IL, USA

Jackie Chen
Sandia National Laboratory
Livermore, CA, USA

Toni Cortes
Barcelona Supercomputing Center
Barcelona, Spain

Matthew L. Curry
Sandia National Laboratories
Albuquerque, NM, USA

William Daughton
Los Alamos National Laboratory
Los Alamos, NM, USA

Nathan DeBardeleben
Los Alamos National Laboratory
Los Alamos, NM, USA

Andreas Dilger
Intel Corporation
Calgary, Canada

Parks Fields
Los Alamos National Laboratory
Los Alamos, NM, USA

Mike Folk
The HDF Group
Champaign, IL, USA

Jill Gemmill
Clemson University
Clemson, SC, USA

Garth Gibson
Carnegie Mellon University
Pittsburgh, PA, USA

Gary Grider
Los Alamos National Laboratory
Los Alamos, NM, USA

Kevin Harms
Argonne National Laboratory
Argonne, IL, USA

Jay Harris
Clemson University
Clemson, SC, USA

Richard Hedges
Lawrence Livermore National
    Laboratory
Livermore, CA, USA

Mark Hereld
Argonne National Laboratory
Argonne, IL, USA

Jason Hick
National Energy Research Scientific
    Computing Center
Oakland, CA, USA

Dean Hildebrand
IBM Almaden Research Center
San Jose, CA, USA

Mark Howison
Brown University
Providence, RI, USA

Homa Karimabadi
University of California
San Diego, CA, USA

Dries Kimpe
Argonne National Laboratory
Argonne, IL, USA

Nick Kirsch
Isilon
Seattle, WA, USA

Scott Klasky
Oak Ridge National Laboratory
Oak Ridge, TN, USA

Hemanth Kolla
Sandia National Laboratory
Livermore, CA, USA

Quincey Koziol
The HDF Group
Champaign, IL, USA

Bill Kramer
National Center for Supercomputing
  Applications
Urbana, IL, USA

Sriram Lakshminarasimhan
North Carolina State University
Raleigh, NC, USA

Rob Latham
Argonne National Laboratory
Argonne, IL, USA

Wei-keng Liao
Northwestern University
Evanston, IL, USA

Walt Ligon
Clemson University
Clemson, SC, USA

Qing Liu
Oak Ridge National Laboratory
Oak Ridge, TN, USA

Allen Maloney
University of Oregon
Eugene, OR, USA

David Martinez
Sandia National Laboratories
Albuquerque, NM, USA

Stelios Mavridis
Foundation for Research and
  Technology–Hellas
Heraklion, Greece

Benjamin McClelland
Los Alamos National Laboratory
Los Alamos, NM, USA

Celso Mendes
National Center for Supercomputing
  Applications
Urbana, IL, USA

Mark Miller
Lawrence Livermore National
  Laboratory
Livermore, CA, USA

Christopher Mitchell
Los Alamos National Laboratory
Los Alamos, NM, USA

Ramon Nou
Barcelona Supercomputing Center
Barcelona, Spain

Michael E. Papka
Argonne National Laboratory
Argonne, IL, USA

Manish Parashar
Rutgers University
Piscataway, NJ, USA

Norbert Podhorszki
Oak Ridge National Laboratory
Oak Ridge, TN, USA

Marc Poinot
ONERA: French Aerospace Lab
Châtillon, France

Prabhat
Lawrence Berkeley National
  Laboratory
Berkeley, CA, USA

Russ Rew
University Corporation for
  Atmospheric Research
Boulder, CO, USA

Rob Ross
Argonne National Laboratory
Argonne, IL, USA

Frank Schmuck
IBM Almaden Research Center
San Jose, CA, USA

Karl W. Schulz
Texas Advanced Computing Center
Austin, TX, USA

Karsten Schwan
Georgia Institute of Technology
Atlanta, GA, USA

Dimitris Servis
AutoForm Development GmbH
Zurich, Switzerland

Yannis Sfakianakis
Foundation for Research and
   Technology–Hellas
Heraklion, Greece

John Shalf
Lawrence Berkeley National
   Laboratory
Berkeley, CA, USA

Sameer Shende
University of Oregon
Eugene, OR, USA

Galen Shipman
Oak Ridge National Laboratory
Oak Ridge, TN, USA

David Skinner
National Energy Research Scientific
   Computing Center
Oakland, CA, USA

Rajeev Thakur
Argonne National Laboratory
Argonne, IL, USA

Yuan Tian
Oak Ridge National Laboratory
Oak Ridge, TN, USA

Venkat Vishwanath
Argonne National Laboratory
Argonne, IL, USA

H. Lee Ward
Sandia National Laboratories
Albuquerque, NM, USA

Boyd Wilson
Omnibond Systems LLC
Pendleton, SC, USA

Matthew Wolf
Georgia Institute of Technology
Atlanta, GA, USA

Jonathan Woodring
Los Alamos National Laboratory
Los Alamos, NM, USA

Yushu Yao
National Energy Research Scientific
   Computing Center
Oakland, CA, USA

Part I

Parallel I/O in Practice

Chapter 1

Parallel I/O at HPC Facilities

Galen Shipman

Oak Ridge National Laboratory

Modern high performance computing facilities deliver computational and data resources to an ever broadening set of scientific and engineering domains. What was once a cottage industry just two decades ago, HPC is now integral to studies ranging from biology to materials science and everything in between. These domains are using simulation at ever increasing scales driven by increasingly higher resolution models with more accurate representation of physical processes. This confluence has resulted in the build-out of extreme-scale HPC facilities with compute platforms composed of hundreds of thousands of compute cores, high performance networking infrastructures, and parallel I/O environments capable of scaling to terabytes/second of I/O bandwidth while providing tens of petabytes of capacity.

To meet the required performance and capacity levels of modern HPC facilities, these large-scale parallel I/O environments may comprise thousands or tens of thousands of hard disk drives, thousands of networking ports, and several hundred storage servers. These components are then integrated into usable systems through complex software stacks beginning with parallel file system technologies such as IBM's General Parallel File System (GPFS) , Lustre, Panasas, and the Parallel Virtual File System (PVFS). These parallel file systems have come to be relied upon as both a reliable and high performance persistent storage infrastructure. To maintain compatibility with the broadest base of applications while enabling high performance, each of these systems provides a POSIX interface while supporting concurrent access to one or more files within the namespace from one or more compute nodes in the HPC environment. This ability to provide parallel access while retaining POSIX semantics has fueled the adoption of parallel file systems across HPC.

While POSIX provides a ubiquitous interface for applications, the application developer is burdened with the increasingly complex task of mapping complex data structures that may span hundreds or even thousands of distributed memory compute nodes into one or more files. Many applications therefore make use of higher-level I/O libraries such as the Hierarchical Data Form (HDF), the Network Common Data Format (NetCDF), or the

Adaptable I/O System (ADIOS) to bridge this gap between complex distributed in-memory data structures to the underlying parallel file system. These libraries provide both a higher-level semantic than a simple byte stream while also optimizing parallel I/O operations to the underlying parallel file system environment.

Complementing these high performance parallel I/O environments are large-scale archival storage systems such the High Performance Storage System (HPSS). These systems provide HPC facilities with the ability to manage hundreds of petabytes of tape and/or disk storage for long-term data storage. These systems balance performance and capacity by supporting automated tiering of data between tape and disk while providing high performance reading and writing to and from the archive via parallel data movement nodes. In some cases, these large-scale archives are closely integrated within the parallel I/O environment through hierarchical storage management capabilities of the parallel file system and the archival storage system allowing datasets to automatically transition between these two distinct storage environments.

Part I of this book details the parallel I/O environments of a number of representative high performance computing facilities. While the specific technologies employed may differ from facility to facility, a great degree of commonality exists across these environments. In Chapter 2 the National Energy Research Scientific Computing Center (NERSC) facility is detailed including their use of multiple parallel file system environments for large-scale compute platforms and a more general-purpose center-wide storage environment. Chapter 3 provides an overview of the National Center for Supercomputing Applications (NCSA), the first site in the United States to achieve over 1 Terabyte/sec of sustained parallel I/O bandwidth. The Argonne Leadership Computing Facility (ALCF) is detailed in Chapter 4, unique in its use of PVFS at such a significant scale. Chapter 5 provides an overview of the Livermore Computing Center notable for their work to integrate the ZFS file system with the Lustre parallel file system. The Los Alamos National Laboratory HPC facility is highlighted in Chapter 6, an early proponent of center-wide accessible parallel file systems and the incorporation of burst buffers within the parallel I/O environment. Finally, we conclude Part I on HPC facilities with an overview the Texas Advanced Computing Center, an early adopter of commodity storage systems and software-based RAID within the parallel I/O environment.

Chapter 2

National Energy Research Scientific Computing Center

Jason Hick

National Energy Research Scientific Computing Center, Lawrence Berkeley National Laboratory

2.1	HPC at NERSC	5
2.2	I/O Hardware	6
	2.2.1 Local Scratch File Systems	7
	2.2.2 Storage Network	9
	2.2.3 The NERSC Global File Systems	10
	2.2.4 Archival Storage	11
2.3	Workflows, Workloads, and Applications	12
2.4	Conclusion	14
	Bibliography	14

2.1 HPC at NERSC

The National Energy Research Scientific Computing (NERSC) Center is the high-end scientific production computing facility for the Department of Energy (DOE) Office of Science (SC). It is located at the Lawrence Berkeley National Laboratory in the San Francisco Bay Area and serves over 4,500 users organized into about 700 projects. Scientists using the facility conduct a broad range of scientific experiments and simulations using NERSC's computing and storage resources.

NERSC's primary focus is maximizing user productivity for scientific gain using the Center's computing and storage systems. User feedback guides decisions on the particular systems and services that NERSC supports.[1] This has proven extremely successful because, since 2008, NERSC users have co-authored 1,500 journal publications per year on average and have contributed recently to two Nobel Prizes [5]. In order to achieve high productivity, NERSC

---

[1]NERSC was founded in 1974 at Lawrence Livermore National Laboratory and moved to Berkeley in 1996. For the past decade, NERSC has focused on a user-driven systems and services model.

ensures that compute, storage, and networking are balanced across the Center. Achieving balance means they are continuously augmenting both capacity and capability of the centralized storage systems based on improvements to computational and network capabilities.

NERSC is able to provide both external and internal users and collaborators with high-bandwidth access to data because of their security stance. In general, NERSC's network infrastructure eliminates up-front barriers when users or collaborators want to gain access to NERSC data and computational systems that are guided by each science team's desires. Instead of using firewalls as their main security policy, which impedes all data transfer performance, NERSC sponsors a unique network analysis-based security program called Bro [1] that actively monitors and enables or disables real-time access to systems and information at the facility.

The Center's computing resources are currently deployed at a multi-petaflop scale. The two largest systems, Hopper and Edison, together have over 250,000 cores, 550 TB of memory, and 3.5 PFLOPS of peak computational capability. These systems offer users the highest concurrency and are used at full scale.

NERSC has several data-centric or mid-range computing systems that continue to serve user's needs. The primary data-centric systems are PDSF and Genepool. They serve the high-energy and nuclear physics community, and the Joint Genome Institute,[2] respectively. The primary mid-range system is Carver which serves the broader NERSC user community. Figure 2.1 (JGI) shows all the computing and storage resources available at NERSC.

The compute systems are regularly utilized at 98% of their capability with a variety of jobs from all areas of science executing simultaneously on a node or on a system of nodes, depending on the particular compute system queue configuration. In conclusion, there is no particular workload that the compute or storage systems predominantly serve.

2.2   I/O Hardware

NERSC has focused on providing storage systems and services to cover a variety of I/O needs, from requirements of aggressive I/O to sharing data with collaborators around the world. Local scratch file systems are deployed as part of a particular computational system, and thus have about a five-year lifespan. The global or centerwide file systems that are part of what we call the NERSC Global Filesystems (NGF) are managed by an evergreen strategy where existing hardware is augmented and refreshed on a regular basis, so as

---

[2]JGI is a DOE facility focused on advanced genetic research operated by the University of California.

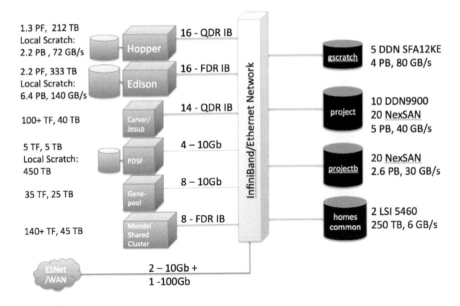

FIGURE 2.1: NERSC systems chart that shows how NERSC compute and storage systems are interconnected with each system's attributes. Table 2.1 enumerates these values in further detail. [Image courtesy of Shane Canon (NERSC).]

to replace portions of the file system (network, storage, and servers) as they age to about the five-year point. This benefits users by continuing to provide bandwidth and capacity regardless of computational system modification and work. Table 2.1 summarizes the parallel I/O systems at the facility that will be discussed. Though the names and characteristics (capacities and bandwidth) will change over the years, the categories of storage systems will remain the same for the foreseeable future.

2.2.1 Local Scratch File Systems

Currently, all computational systems, except the mid-range system called Carver, have dedicated local scratch file systems. This is to minimize contention of I/O bandwidth, thereby improving the utilization of the system. The strategy works very well for keeping stable or consistent performance on each local scratch file system. The other main aim of providing local scratch independently for each computational system is that bandwidth may be provisioned based on the amount of main memory available on each computational system. On systems where file system bandwidth approaches 1 GB/s for each 1 TB of main system memory, user satisfaction with the file system is high. In general, all local scratch file systems are purged of files older than about

TABLE 2.1: NERSC storage systems noting storage type, bandwidth capabilities, and storage capacity.

Storage System Name	Purpose	Type	Total Bandwidth	Total Capacity
Edison scratch 1-3	Local bandwidth	Lustre	140 GB/s	6.4 PB
Hopper scratch 1-2	Local bandwidth	Lustre	72 GB/s	2.2 PB
Global scratch	Global bandwidth	GPFS	80 GB/s	4 PB
Global project	Global capacity	GPFS	40 GB/s	5 PB
Global projectb	Global bandwidth	GPFS	30 GB/s	2.6 PB
Global dna	Global capacity	GPFS	12 GB/s	1.1 PB
Global common	Global throughput	GPFS	NA	6 TB
Global homes	Global throughput	GPFS	NA	250 TB
Archive	Long-term capacity	HPSS	12 GB/s	240 PB

12 weeks. These file systems provide the highest bandwidth at NERSC to a single computational system and are primarily used for output of all jobs on the computational system. For example, details of the Edison system's local scratch file system design are provided in Figure 2.2. The Edison scratch file systems are Lustre file systems and achieve over 140-GB/s bandwidth in aggregate. To maximize metadata performance in the scratch file system, Edison deploys three separate scratch file systems. Two of the scratch file systems have a bandwidth of 35 GB/s and a storage capacity of 1.6 PB with users evenly divided on each, therefore a user either uses /scratch1 or /scratch2. The third scratch file system, /scratch3, has a 70-GB/s bandwidth and 3.2 PB of storage capacity. The /scratch3 file system is a schedulable resource available to all users of the Edison system.

In order to externalize each local scratch file system from the computational system so that storage may remain operational to login nodes and other assets at the facility during computational system downtime, the LNET routers' purpose is to route storage traffic between the Edison Aries interconnect [3] and the file system fourteen data rate (FDR) InfiniBand (IB) network. The IB connections are provisioned to drive each file system at its maximum 35-GB/s bandwidth, and connect each LNET router to top-of-rack switches in each file system cabinet. The file system hardware makes use of embedded storage such that the object storage targets (OSTs) are run on embedded servers inside the storage enclosures.

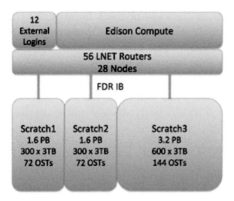

FIGURE 2.2: A diagram showing three different scratch file systems and connections via IB to the Edison compute nodes. [Image courtesy of Jason Hick (NERSC).]

Users are generally pleased with the performance and stability of the Center's local scratch file systems, with two typical points of improvement: metadata operation responsiveness and increasing bandwidth.

2.2.2 Storage Network

Starting more than a decade ago, NERSC established one of the largest HPC fiber channels (FCs)-based storage area networks (SANs). Although fiber channel technology was highly priced, it was the only truly lossless and full-bandwidth transport medium offered for storage systems. The FC SAN provided near full bandwidth access to storage in the NGF file systems from every computational system at the facility. However, the FC capacity increase from 8 Gigabits (Gb) to 16 Gb took a long time to be generally available. In the meantime, 40 Gb IB became stable and more cost effective. Though IB technology still lacks significant features that would make it an obvious choice for next-generation storage area networks, many HPC facilities, NERSC included, are building next-generation storage networks using IB technology.

Many facilities selected Ethernet as their storage protocol for providing bandwidth, but spent a significant effort tuning it to approach streaming performance over a lossy network technology. Storage systems require lossless network technology for achieving their full bandwidth capability. The NGF file systems have a secondary, failover, 10 Gigabit Ethernet (GigE) network interface. Having the capability to use distinct failover networks is a significant feature of the General Parallel File System (GPFS), discussed in Chapter 9.

For the centerwide file systems, many of the computational systems at the facility have I/O nodes that help route traffic between the computational system interconnect (a mix of proprietary and IB connections) and the SAN, which is a mix between FC and IB. The centerwide file system is redundantly served over 10 GigE in the case of SAN failures. NERSC is moving toward a purely IB-based SAN where only the systems with proprietary interconnects will have I/O nodes. The intent is for the IB-based compute systems to utilize hardware routers to bridge the computational IB and storage IB networks. This simplifies and centralizes the centerwide parallel file systems enabling maximum scalability and isolation of problems to either the storage or compute systems, but not both storage and compute at the same time.

2.2.3   The NERSC Global File Systems

NERSC pioneered the concept of providing a long-term centerwide file system with its /project file system in the early 2000s. By 2006, the main goals of the /project file system were realized when users could access the file system from all computational systems at the facility. Users accepted contended aggregate bandwidth in favor of having a storage resource accessible to all computational systems at the facility. The centerwide file system enabled users to focus more on their computational capabilities across several systems and less on moving data between various storage or compute systems. NERSC also saw a direct result of having less data move across its internal network between systems.[3] Today, the /project file system is a primary storage resource for enabling science projects to share data between multiple users or systems. This file system is used for data transfers on the center's data transfer nodes (DTNs), sharing with collaborators through portals on the Science Gateway Nodes (SGNs), and for data analysis on the mid-range systems. The file system is a global parallel file system and has a high-bandwidth capacity oriented with regular increases planned to sustain demand and growth.

Most recently the centerwide file systems demonstrated that they are also positioned to scale out in support of individual science team needs nearly on demand. An evident example was enabling the work of the Daya Bay project that had an unexpected deluge of data in their efforts to determine the mixing angle in their neutrino-oscillation experiment [2]. They had recently migrated from a model of local storage that was struggling at scale, to the centerwide file system. The move provided for easy scale-out (doubling their allocation) within less than a week's response and ultimately enabled rapid scientific results directly leading to a scientific discovery.

The centerwide file systems are also well suited for meeting the evolving needs of data-intensive science communities. NERSC initiated a Data Intensive Computing Pilot [8] with a number of science teams providing 1 PB of high-bandwidth storage capacity and a compute allocation to enable analysis of large datasets.

NERSC provides two other main centerwide file systems: global scratch and global homes. Global scratch provides high bandwidth simultaneously

---

[3]Bulk data movement represents about 50% of the NERSC network traffic, so reducing bulk data movement on the network has a significant effect on responsiveness of systems.

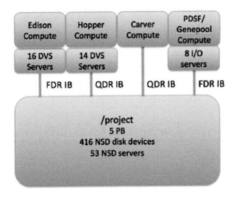

FIGURE 2.3: A diagram showing the basic connectivity and components of the NGF `/project` file system to major compute systems at NERSC. [Image courtesy of Jason Hick (NERSC).]

across multiple systems, currently at a rate of 80 GB/s in aggregate. Global homes gives users a common login environment across systems at NERSC. See Figure 2.3 for an example architecture for one of the centerwide file systems. The global scratch and global homes file systems are GPFS and primarily served over the Center's IB storage network. Global scratch uses storage controllers that embed the file system software on the controller and take advantage of knowledge of the underlying storage to optimize I/O through GPFS. This not only simplifies the architecture of the file system, but reduces the number of components that can fail.

2.2.4 Archival Storage

For long-term storage covering all the above file systems, the Center provides two High Performance Storage Systems (HPSS) [4]. These are hierarchical storage management (HSM) systems that provide high-bandwidth user access through a disk cache. The HPSS system then migrates data to enterprise tape devices—the best storage medium for long-term storage. The Center has compared costs of operating disk and tape, and found that tape is an order of magnitude cheaper for capacity storage. It is also highly reliable, as it does not require power to retain user data, and provides protection against undesired data destruction because it is independent of other systems and nearline storage. Designing the archive systems to 10% of the file system's bandwidth works well for retaining the data that requires long-term retention. HPSS enables parallel I/O by striping a single file across multiple disk and tape devices. This is key to HPSS's ability to scale both capacity and bandwidth over the years to handle file system demand.

One unique aspect of NERSC is its ability to back up such a high volume of data in its NGF file systems for restoration on user demand. The user restores are requested once every other week on average.

TABLE 2.2: Amount of archived data at NERSC in 2013 for major systems or categories of systems.

Client System Name	Total PB Moved
Hopper	6.67 PB
Genepool, Mendel	2.75 PB
DTN	2.48 PB
External to NERSC	0.57 PB
Carver	0.48 PB
PDSF	0.20 PB
NGF	0.03 PB

2.3 Workflows, Workloads, and Applications

At the highest workflow levels, users tend to utilize the local scratch file system for job input and output. The local scratch file systems have the least contention for bandwidth and latency. However, if they are utilizing more than one computational system at the Center, they may make a trade-off for the higher capacity or cross-system availability generally offered by the NGF systems to improve overall time to completion. Generally, the parallel file systems at NERSC complete hundreds of terabytes of I/O throughout an average day at the facility. The active archive handles between 50–100 TB of parallel I/O on a typical day, 30% of which are read operations from a combination of local scratch and NGF file systems. See Table 2.2 for information on the source and amount of data moving to and from the HPSS archive at NERSC.

Data at NERSC falls into two main categories: simulation and experimental. For the past decade, simulation data proved to be the most demanding on compute and storage system resources at the Center. Recently, experimental data from high-powered instruments such as the Large Hadron Collider or genomic sequencers present new challenges to NERSC's data systems and services. Simulation data can be regenerated by rerunning the simulation, but most experimental data cannot be regenerated due to cost or instrument changes. JGI, a partner of NERSC since 2010, has been sequencing and analyzing over 50 terabases[4] worth of experimental data a year. The scale of their demands calls for a parallel file system, but their workloads are a mix of parallel and serial I/O. The light sources and other experimental facilities are presenting significant challenges for storage as well. Instrument data rates are high and increasing rapidly, demanding very capable data acquisition systems that need to be local to the instrument to achieve success. NERSC provides

---

[4]Terabase is a unit of measure involving the amount of data needed to represent a given amount of genetic material; specifically, it is the genetic sequence data equivalent to 10^{12} base genetic pairs.

computing, data analysis, and other post data acquisition services to support the experimental facilities.

Recently, formal user requirement reviews [6] have identified a broad range of storage needs from a ratio of N compute notes to one file (or shared file) I/O demanding a multi-terabyte-sized file to a ratio of N compute node to N files (or file-per-process) I/O demanding millions of files per computational job. Users are interested in checkpointing to improve application resiliency for a more complex and high-scale computing and storage environment, and to enable running what would be a very long job in many small jobs using checkpoints to continue from a previous job.

In preparation for helping science projects ready their applications for Exascale environments, NERSC user services compiled a chart of the type and quantity of codes running on NERSC systems (see Figure 2.4. The chart shows the broad range of codes that have diverse I/O workload needs as well.

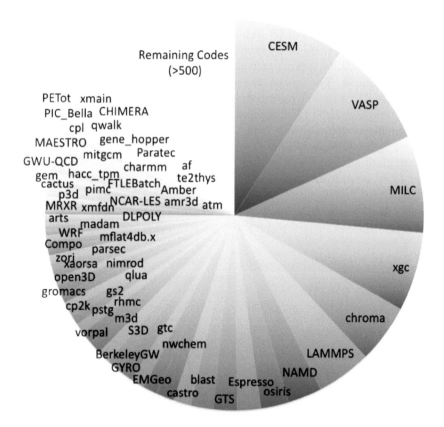

FIGURE 2.4: A pie chart of science applications for 2012 that were run at NERSC. [Image courtesy of Katie Antypas (NERSC).]

2.4 Conclusion

NERSC has a strong impact on the design and development of state-of-the-art parallel storage systems that are valued by a broad set of users. The Center pioneered the idea of global storage in building the NGF to enable users to spend more time on science and less time moving and managing copies of their data. They championed several features, most notably the ability to do multi-clustering, which are currently in the GPFS software. NERSC continues to actively participate in the HPSS collaboration and develop new features as part of the collaboration to support high performance archiving. In all monitoring usage, developing a user-centric approach to storage systems and services works well.

In recent years, NERSC reached a practical limit in its ability to use large-scale FC networks to support their global file system. Their current focus is in building an IB storage network and advancing the routing and monitoring features and capabilities of IB technology.

Trends show that users are demanding more of storage systems than they can easily provide, be it non-optimal I/O workloads, or extreme bandwidth, or capacity demands. The largest challenge NERSC sees is that this gap between user need and storage system capability is widening. Flash is emerging as a new tier of storage at HPC facilities and may eliminate the previously mentioned gap, but file system software will need to make some fundamental changes since all of the software was designed around disk systems. As a result, NERSC is participating in the Fast Forward research and development project [7] with other DOE laboratories, which aims to develop next-generation file systems and advanced burst buffer technologies. Also, parallel storage systems are growing in scale and complexity and, in order to remain user-centric, NERSC is strongly working toward state-of-the-art I/O quality-of-service features that do not exist today.

Bibliography

[1] The Bro Network Security Monitor. http://www.bro.org.

[2] F. P. An, J. Z. Bai, A. B. Balantekin, H. R. Band, D. Beavis, W. Beriguete, M. Bishai, S. Blyth, K. Boddy, R. L. Brown, et al. Observation of Electron-Antineutrino Disappearance at Daya Bay. *Phys. Rev. Lett.*, 108:171803, March 2012.

[3] Austin, Cordery, Wasserman, and Wright. Performance Measurements of a Cray Cascade System. 2013. https://cug.org/proceedings/cug2013_proceedings/includes/files/pap156.pdf.

[4] The HPSS Collaboration. The High Performance Storage System. IBM Corporation. http://www.hpss-collaboration.org, 2014.

[5] Sudip Dosanjh. NERSC Strategic Plan for FY2014–2023. Technical report, NERSC, 2013. https://www.nersc.gov/assets/pubs_presos/NERSCplan-FY2014-2023.pdf.

[6] Richard Gerber and Harvey Wasserman. Large Scale Computing and Storage Requirements: Requirements Workshop. Technical report, NERSC, 2009–2013. https://www.nersc.gov/science/hpc-requirements-reviews/reports.

[7] Various. Fast Forward R&D Draft Statement of Work. Technical report, National Nuclear Security Administration and US Department of Energy Office of Science, 2012. https://asc.llnl.gov/fastforward/rfp/04_FastForward_SOW_FinalDraftv3.docx.

[8] Linda Vu. What are the Computational Keys to Future Scientific Discoveries? NERSC Develops a Data Intensive Pilot Program to Help Scientists Find Out, August, 2012. http://cs.lbl.gov/news-media/news/2012/what-are-the-computational-keys-to-future-scientific-discoveries/

Chapter 3

National Center for Supercomputing Applications

William Kramer, Michelle Butler, Gregory Bauer, Kalyana Chadalavada, and Celso Mendes

University of Illinois Urbana-Champaign, National Center for Supercomputing Applications

3.1	The Blue Waters Computational and Analysis Subsystems	18
3.2	Blue Waters On-line Storage Subsystem	19
	3.2.1 On-line Storage Performance	22
3.3	Blue Waters Near-line Storage Subsystem and External Server Subsystem	24
3.4	Blue Waters Applications	28
	3.4.1 Science and Engineering Team Application I/O Requirements	29
3.5	Conclusion	31
	Bibliography	31

Blue Waters, a joint project funded by the National Science Foundation Advanced CyberInfrastructure Division, the State of Illinois, and the University of Illinois, is an exceptionally well balanced, sustained petascale system dedicated to solving a diverse range of unique science and engineering challenges that require huge amounts of sustained computational and data analysis performance. The Blue Waters system was the highest performing and largest storage system at the time of its installation and will likely be for some time after. Blue Waters has 1.66 PB of aggregate memory, which is more than any other known system to date. The challenging investigations for Blue Waters require not just billions of core hours of computational time but extreme amounts of storage and I/O performance as well. Approximately 70 science and engineering teams (SETs) are using Blue Waters at the time of this writing with about 30 "major teams" that have allocations ranging from 30 million to almost 5 billion AMD integer core hours. The SETs cross many disciplines including astrophysics, chemistry, climate, computational bio-medicine, computational biology, cosmology, engineering optimization of very large systems, fluid dynamics, molecular dynamics, physics, solar storms, seismology and

17

earthquakes, social networking, and weather.[1] The Blue Waters system consists of six primary subsystems the Cray XE6/XK7 computation and analysis subsystem, external server complex, the Cray Sonexion™ on-line storage, the HPSS near-line storage, wide-area networking, and cyber-protection subsystems. Four of the six subsystems are discussed below.

3.1   The Blue Waters Computational and Analysis Subsystems

The key feature of Blue Waters is the very balanced strategy for the system beginning with the 22,640 XE6 compute node, 4,224 XK7 compute nodes, 582 Lustre Network (or Lnet) I/O router nodes, and 202 other service nodes [2]. Each XE6 node has two AMD Interlagos processor modules,[2] fast access to 4 GB of memory per processor core, and the high-speed 3D Torus interconnect. The configuration is based upon the tightly coupled Cray XE6/XK7 system[3,4] system complete with powerful parallel storage and file system capabilities. The Cray XE6/XK7 is a hybrid system featuring AMD socket G34 Interlagos™ processors for x86 compute performance and NVIDIA Kepler K20X GPUs with powerful acceleration capabilities. The Cray XE6/XK7 balance was determined by the mission of Blue Waters in consultation with the major science teams and an in-depth analysis of the known SETs assessing their current and planned experimental and production use of accelerated computing.[5] Of the nodes, 84% are XE6 all-CPU AMD Interlagos processor nodes, and 16% are the XK7 nodes with one AMD Interlagos processor module and one NVIDIA Kepler GPU in a single node using the Cray-designed Gemini router.

The Cray XE6/XK7 system uses the latest AMD Opteron Series 6000 model 6276 "Interlagos" in both the Cray XE6 compute node and the Cray XK7 accelerator nodes. The Interlagos socket is a dual-die multi-chip module. The Interlagos processor has a peak performance of 156.8 GFLOPS per socket at 2.45 GHz. The Interlagos processor can be used as two 4-core modules with each core supporting two threads giving a total of eight results per clock per fused multiply-add. Each processor socket has four HyperTransport™ links,

---

[1]See the Blue Waters portal (http://bluewaters.ncsa.illinois.edu) for complete descriptions of the projects.

[2]http://support.amd.com/us/Processor_TechDocs/47414_15h_sw_opt_guide.pdf

[3]http://www.cray.com/Products/XE/Specifications.aspx

[4]http://www.cray.com/Products/XK6/Specifications.aspx

[5]If the Blue Waters funding was invested to target the highest possible peak performance by populating as many compute racks as possible with the NVIDIA GPUs, the peak performance of Blue Waters would approach 50 PFLOPS, but with only half the memory, which would have made many of the SET goals unfeasible.

up to 5.2 GB/s. The core module has shared fetch/decode units, shared instruction cache for each floating-point unit. Each Interlagos socket features eight "bulldozer" core modules, each capable of eight floating point operations per clock.

In addition the processor core is capable of running in a mode that shares the floating point unit between two integer units, which we call integer cores. In this mode, the AMD processors include an L1 cache for each integer unit and an L2 cache for each bulldozer core as well as two 6 MB L3 caches shared by all the cores of each of the two dies. The processors also share the DDR3 internal memory controllers, and an HT3 HyperTransport interface that increases the injection bandwidth between the interconnect network and the compute processor. The XE6 compute nodes consist of two sockets each with associated memory and HyperTransport^{TM} interconnection.

The XK7 compute nodes have an Interlagos socket with the associated memory and one NVIDIA Kepler K20X GPU. The Cray XK7 accelerator blade is similar to the Cray XE6 compute blade in form factor and placement of the Gemini network cards. It differs in that each of the four compute nodes on the blade consists of an AMD processor socket and a connection for a Kepler GPU (NVIDIA K20X) card. These GPU cards each contain the accelerator chip and 6 GB of GDDR5 memory and connect to the motherboard with a high-reliability connector. These cards sit up off the motherboard to allow the necessary cooling on both sides of the card. The blade will be managed, monitored, powered, and cooled within the Cray XE6/XK7 infrastructure. The Blue Waters system consists of 288 computational cabinets arranged in 12 rows, each with 24 cabinets.

The Cray Gemini High Speed Network is based on a custom Gemini router that connects to two XE or XK nodes with the rest of the system. The HSN interconnect topology is a 3D torus of dimension $X = 24$, $Y = 24$, and $Z = 24$ with a total injection bandwidth of over 276 TB/s. All torus links run at a minimum bit toggle rate of 3.125 GHz. Figure 3.1 shows the configuration of the XE6 and XK7 nodes. The resulting peak bi-directional bandwidth in each dimension is listed in the Table 3.1. The peak global bandwidth value is twice as large due to the fact that in all-to-all communication patterns, only half of the total traffic crosses the bi-section in a 3D torus topology. All I/O requests and traffic go across the interconnect from the compute nodes to the Lnet nodes. Key system performance and configuration information is provided in Table 3.2.

3.2   Blue Waters On-line Storage Subsystem

Blue Waters provides one of the most intense storage systems in the world using a combination of on-line and near-line storage devices and media. The

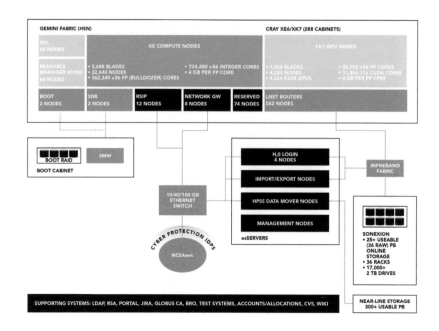

FIGURE 3.1 (See color insert): The Blue Waters computational analysis subsystem. [Image courtesy of Paula Popowski, NCSA.]

TABLE 3.1: Data payload bi-directional bandwidth in X, Y, Z dimensions.

$X = 23,\ Y = 24,$ and $Z = 24$	X dimension	Y dimension	Z dimension
Dimension size	24	24	24
Bits per direction per link	24	12	24
Bi-directional Bandwidth per link @ 3.125 Ghz	18.75 GB/s	9.375 GB/s	18.75 GB/s
Number of links per dimension (includes torus wrap-around links)	1152	1152	1152
Total Peak Bi-section Bandwidth per dimension	21.6 TB/s	10.35 TB/s	20.7 TB/s
Average Bi-section Bandwidth	17.55 TB/s		
Minimum Bi-section Bandwidth	10.32 TB/s (Y direction)		

TABLE 3.2: Key Blue Waters performance information.

Peak Floating Point Performance	13.1 PFLOPS
Aggregate Memory	1.66 PB
Sustained Floating Point Performance per Sustained Petascale Performance (SPP) benchmarks	1.31 PFLOPS
Sustained I/O Bandwidth performance	1.18 TB/s

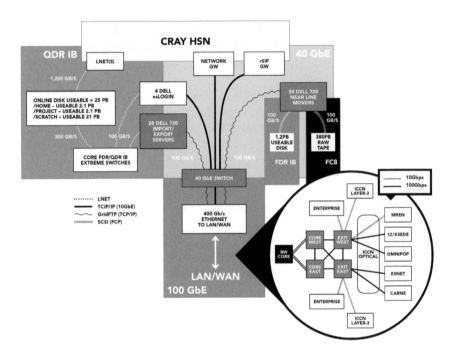

FIGURE 3.2: The Blue Waters network subsystem. [Image courtesy of Paula Popowski, NCSA.]

storage subsystem is connected with an integrated Infiniband fabric and a 40 GigE local-area network as shown in Figure 3.2.

The building block of the on-line storage subsystem is the Cray Sonexion CS-1600™.[6] The Sonexion 1600 is a high performance storage unit designed and built to uniquely address Lustre scalability and performance requirements. The Sonexion is based on Xyratex ClusterStore™ technology and has multiple high-level components (storage hardware, operating system, management user interface, and file system) bonded into a tightly integrated unit to create a reliable, performant, and manageable HPC storage service. The Blue Waters

---

[6]http://www.cray.com/Products/Storage/Sonexion/Specifications.aspx

storage subsystem integrates Scalable Storage Units (SSU) that each has two industry-standard x86 Embedded Server Modules (ESMs) based on the Intel Sandybridge^{TM} processors. The ESMs connect directly through a common mid-plane to all drives in the SSU and share a redundant high-speed interconnect across the midplane for failover services. The ESMs run an industry-standard Linux distribution and each module has its own dedicated CPU, memory, network, and storage connectivity.

Each SSU contains eighty-two, 2-TB, 7200-RPM NL-SAS disk drives housed in two trays. Eighty data drives are configured in eight RAID 6 (8+2) arrays resulting in 64 usable data drives. The other two drives in the SSU are global hot spares. Each SSU has two 100-GB SSDs for OSS metadata and two OSS servers. Together, the metadata and object storage servers present file systems to clients.

The Sonexion CS-1600 Management Server (MGS) stores configuration information for all Lustre file systems in Blue Waters. Each Lustre server and each Lustre client rely on the MGS to provide information. Metadata Servers (MDS) make metadata available to Lustre clients from the Metadata Target (MDT). The MDT stores file system metadata (filenames, directories, permissions, and file layouts) on disk and manages the namespace. The MDS provides network request handling for the file system. The OSSs enable file I/O service and network request handling for one or more local OSTs. The OST stores data (files or chunks of files) on a single LUN (disk drive or an array of disk drives). Cray XE6/XK7 Lustre clients, called LNETs, interface user applications to the Lustre file system. The client presents a POSIX file system interface to user-level applications running on compute/analysis nodes and is responsible for routing I/O requests, data, and metadata through the Cray XE6/XK7 system to the Lustre servers in the CS-1600 storage cluster. Cray's XE6/XK7 LNETs implement the Lustre networking protocol between the Lustre client and the Lustre server. The LNET layer allows clients and servers to be executed on the same system (i.e., direct attached Lustre) or for compute clients to communicate with external Lustre servers or Lustre appliances.

3.2.1 On-line Storage Performance

The on-line storage subsystem provides over 25 usable (36 raw) petabytes of storage to the science and engineering teams. The overall bandwidth exceeds 1.18 TB/s as measured by a range of tests [1]. Similarly, the measured metadata performance is over 25,000 mean creates per second of a single file from each node; 30,000 concurrent deletes per second and 40,000 `stat()` calls per second as aggregate rates using up to all XE6 client nodes in either a single directory or in separate directories.

To demonstrate Blue Waters' I/O capability, Table 3.3 lists observed results from executions of the IOR benchmark doing a "write" operation on each of its three file systems. Each value in the table corresponds to the mean of

TABLE 3.3: IOR-write performance on Blue Waters file systems.

File system	Performance
/home	104.3 GB/s
/project	100.0 GB/s
/scratch	980.7 GB/s

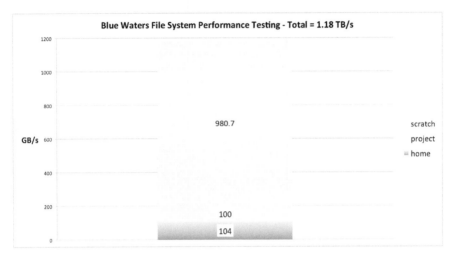

FIGURE 3.3: The total I/O bandwidth, tested at Blue Waters acceptance and then periodically after, is greater than 1.18 TB/s. [Image courtesy of Celso Mendes and Michelle Butler.]

ten independent IOR executions. As expected, the /scratch file system, which is ten times bigger than the other file systems, has nearly ten times more delivered bandwidth than /home and /project. Figure 3.3 shows the same data in graph form.

Another remarkable aspect of the Blue Waters file system is its scalable architecture. This feature ensures that the file system both maintains its performance characteristics as more clients access it, and delivers increasing performance as more servers are configured. The first property was verified by running IOR tests on an increasing number of clients; each client was running on a different node, writing a file with a size of 1 GB to the /scratch file system. Table 3.4 presents the results of these executions, and shows that the delivered file system performance does not vary significantly, regardless of the number of clients in use.

To confirm the file system scalability with the number of servers, Figure 3.4 displays the results of IOR executions, for both "read" and "write" operations, when the number of accessed file system racks (i.e., servers) in the /scratch file system is varied. Each IOR job had an number of clients proportional to the number of servers. As the figure shows, observed performance is nearly linear

TABLE 3.4: IOR performance for writing 1-GB files on /scratch

Number of Clients	Performance (GB/s)
5,000	679.9 GB/s
10,000	774.3 GB/s
15,000	767.2 GB/s
20,000	710.0 GB/s
22,500	708.5 GB/s

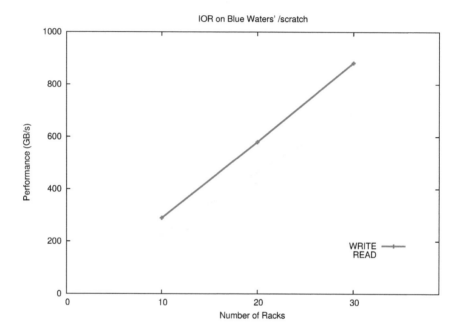

FIGURE 3.4: Blue Waters I/O performance tests scaled with the number of client nodes. Image courtesy of Celso Mendes, NCSA.

with the number of servers used. Similar behavior was observed in tests with the other two file systems, indicating that an addition of servers results in a proportional increase in obtained performance in the Blue Waters architecture.

3.3   Blue Waters Near-line Storage Subsystem and External Server Subsystem

Blue Waters Near-line Storage Subsystem and External Server Subsystem complements the on-line storage subsystem with a near-line automated storage

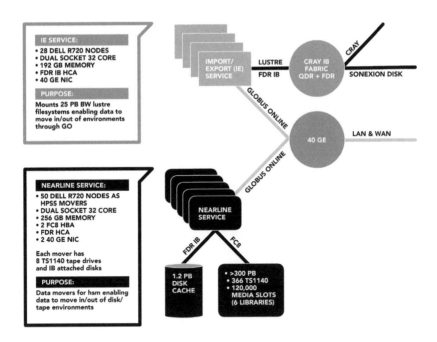

FIGURE 3.5: The Blue Waters external server subsystem. [Image courtesy of Paula Popowski.]

system composed of automated tape robots and caching disk under the control of.[7] The near-line subsystem provides traditional archive functions as well a new, closely integrated hierarchical storage manager (HSM) between the on-line and near-line storage that is under development, is the largest HPSS system in the open science community.

Blue Waters initially deployed fifty (50) Dell R720 servers for data movement, two IBM large 64 processor servers with a database environment for HPSS metadata, an extensive fourteen data rate IB fabric, a usable 1.2-PB (raw 1.8-PB) disk cache subsystem dedicated to HPSS, four SpectraLogic 19-frame T-Finity tape libraries with approximately 20,000 slots each, and 244 TS1140 tape drives. The near-line system provides a capacity of raw 380 PB and approximately 100 GB/s in performance. In 2014, a planned expansion will add two more libraries with an additional 122 tape drives for a total of 366 tapes drives at 240 MB/s each. The upgrade will complete NCSA's near-line storage with approximately 120,000 media cartridges. If media density increases in the future, the total capacity of the near-line storage subsystem will increase proportionally.

---

[7]www.hpss-collaboration.org

The HPSS data movers are dedicated Dell R720 servers with dual socket Intel Sandybridge^{TM} processors and 256 GB of memory. Each processor has 16 cores per socket. The data movers manage the movement of the data from one storage level to another between network, disk, and tape. Each mover is connected to eight tape drives, the disk cache fabric, and has two 40 GigE network cards. The Dell 2U R720 system was chosen based on the number of PCIe2 cards that could be placed within the system while maintaining full performance to all attached devices and networks. The useable 1.2-PB caching disk is used for the traditional archive data movement and data transfers. The environment has two large core servers to manage the DB2^{TM} database with all the metadata.

The near-line storage subsystem provides over 300 usable petabytes of storage to science and engineering teams with an aggregate bandwidth of about 100 GB/s. The physical robotic units have a capacity of over 500 PB if needed. The Blue Waters Project has an operating budget at current costs to provide 380 raw petabytes of tape cartridges over the course of full service operations. The implementation of will use about 22% of the raw capacity to provide protection from single points of tape failure.

RAIT technology, developed by NCSA and the HPSS consortium as part of the Blue Waters Project, is a new feature in that provides data integrity and protection through striped data parity technologies. RAIT avoids the traditional method of protection from tape errors that duplicates all user data on two or more tapes (also known as RAID-1). With media costs in the $16M range for 500 PB of data, an additional $16M cost for protection was not feasible for most of the scientific data. RAIT provides a variety of data and parity combinations from two data blocks plus one parity block written to three tapes, up to eight data plus eight parity written 16 tapes wide, depending on the data size and desired degree of redundancy for multiple failure. Data is written in a RAID-5-like form with data and parity blocks rotated across all tapes ensuring that the tapes are generally the same length and amount of data written to them.

NCSA utilizes two data service classes utilizing RAIT. Large files are written in a 4+1 RAIT configuration and the x-large storage class for files greater than 8 TB are written directly to tape in a 7+2 RAIT configuration. The 7+2 utilizes the media cartridge holder capacity of the SpectraLogic library which holds nine TS1140 tapes. A single mount request brings all nine tapes to the tape drives in one robotic motion, which provides less latency for mounting nine tapes before a write can begin.

Blue Waters intends to integrate the on-line and near-line storage subsystems into a transparent hierarchy using new features in Lustre 2.5. This will enable users to see a single storage repository namespace that transparently moves the data they need between on-line and near-line subsystems so the data is "in the right place at the right time." These features will enable more efficient use of the storage resources and more science productivity.

Acceptance testing of the Blue Waters near-line system stressed data sizes, volumes, and rates projected to occur during the third and fifth year of the project to verify the system would meet its fifth year requirements and goals. The NCSA HPSS near-line system achieved on average 3,538 creates per second (212,280 transactions per minute), which exceeds Blue Waters projected year 6 workload. Blue Waters' final test was to put the system under a 24-hour system load test. During normal operations of media repacks and other normal operations tasks, the near-line system wrote 9.8 million files and read 3.9 million files, and recalled more than 191,000 files from tape using all five storage classes from extremely small files to extremely large files. This scale and performance is well beyond any other system as of 2014.

Dedicated server systems, called Import/Export (IE) servers in Blue Waters (others label similar systems data transfer nodes or DTNs), move data into and out of the on-line disk subsystem, between the on-line disk environment and the near-line and onto the local-area and wide-area networks to other resources. The 28 Import/Export servers (IE servers) are the same Dell 720 configuration as the data movers, but have 192 GB of memory and different PCIe cards. With the 40 GigE LAN environment, data can be transferred to the near-line system described above or to the local-area or wide-area network environment to be stored elsewhere. Acceptance and periodic regression testing show sustained performance of 4 GB/s for each IE server for an aggregate sustained I/O bandwidth of 112 GB/s.

Blue Waters uses the.[8] Globus software suite for data transfers between the on-line storage subsystem and either the near-line subsystem or other sites across the wide-area network connections. The main advantages of the Globus environment are the "drag and drop" user interface, a *flight control* interface enabling users to see transfers as they happen, and the retry feature that automatically restarts interrupted transfers. NCSA encourages users to checksum their transfers. Checksums are performed at both ends of the data transfer to ensure data integrity. Checksumming adds to the transfer time and processing capacity at both ends, but ensures that the user transaction has completed properly.

The combination of the dedicated Lustre IE servers and the separate, but also dedicated near-line data movers, provide a balanced and stable data management strategy to data movement. The ability to tune IE servers for striped data transfers into and out of Lustre has proven to perform better depending on the size of the data being transferred. Tuning not only the GridFTP client on the IE servers, but the Lustre client version and all its interdependencies including the IB fabric driver separate from other services, has made the administration of the data movement environment much simpler by combining services into the same servers. NCSA is working to bring in a striped Globus server in 2014 for the on-line and near-line data transfer environment. This development work will enhance the single data transfer rates. Along with

---

[8]https://www.globus.org/

the automated data movement in Lustre 2.5, the striped transfer mode will provide significant performance improvement.

3.4 Blue Waters Applications

The allocation of resources on the Blue Waters system is handled by several allocation bodies; the National Science Foundation (NSF) allocates 80% of available resources with the remaining 20% allocated by the University of Illinois at Urbana–Champaign (UIUC), the Great Lakes Consortium for Petascale Computation (GLCPC), and by the Blue Waters Project for Industrial, Educational and Innovation opportunities. During the first year of operation or production, there were 30 NSF projects, 29 UIUC projects, 10 GLCPC projects, and a handful of Industry and Education projects. Collectively, the projects are called SETs. An up-to-date list of allocated projects is available from the Blue Waters portal.[9] The 70 SET projects from the first year of production utilized a wide variety of applications with a comparable wide range of I/O requirements.

The SETs typically have more than one primary application. A partial list of applications used by the SETs contains over 42 applications in use during the first year of operations. The areas of research range from astrophysics (ENZO, pGADGET, PPM, MAESTRO, CASTRO), biochemistry (AMBER, Gromacs, NAMD), and climate science (CCCM, CESM), to geophysics (CyberShake, AWP-ODC), heliophysics (H3D, VPIC, OSIRIS), lattice quantum chromodynamics (MILC, Chroma), and turbulence (PSDNS, DISTUF).

The NSF SETs account for the largest portion of the time available on Blue Waters; many of which were involved with Blue Waters project during the co-design deployment phase. An understanding of the SETs I/O methodologies and requirements came from analysis of their proposals, responses to questionnaires, and from interviews with project team members. The information provided by the teams was used to evaluate the effectiveness of the Blue Waters file system design, its configuration, and policies and practices used to manage the file system.

Blue Waters' focus is to enable investigations not possible elsewhere and to turn petascale computation and analysis at very large scales from a heroic event to an everyday event. Figure 3.6 shows a typical job mix for Blue Waters. This figure shows the job layout across the torus for the 10 largest running jobs as displayed on the Blue Waters portal. Each circle represents one Gemini (two nodes) in the torus. As shown in the figure, 99.8% of nodes were in use, which is a good day, but is not far from typical. One can see the special attention to topology-aware scheduling to reduce torus contention. The largest job displayed uses 13,851 nodes (443,232 integer cores) and ran for 8 hours and 27 minutes.

---

[9]bluewaters.ncsa.illinois.edu

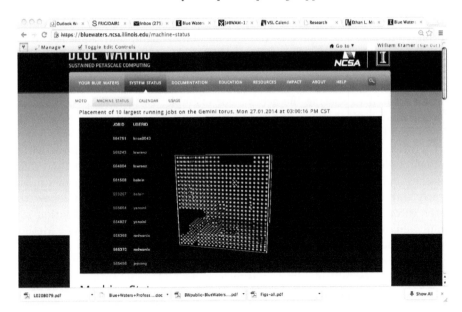

FIGURE 3.6: Snap-shot of the 10 largest running jobs on Blue Waters at February 11, 2014. At this time 99.8% of the nodes were in use by scientific jobs. [Image courtesy of Dave Semenaro.]

3.4.1 Science and Engineering Team Application I/O Requirements

For a majority of applications, I/O performance was identified as crucial for computational performance for scalable programs. Quantified estimates of application input (initial condition or restart), checkpoint and output (visualization, final state) file sizes, and counts were gathered from many of the SETs. Input volumes ranged from a single 100-GB file for molecular dynamics problems to 10 TB (across tens of thousands of files) for turbulence applications to 75 TB (across hundreds of thousands of files) for geophysical applications. Checkpoint and output sizes had comparable ranges. Defensive checkpoint intervals will vary according to the observed mean time to interruptions and node counts used for the jobs.

Estimates for total storage requirements for SETs' campaigns ranged from 10 TB to over 10 PB. The survey also highlighted the variety of application I/O schemes in use ranging from "file-per-process" to dedicated I/O writer tasks embedded in the applications, to "many-to-one" implementations for storage. Nine SETs utilize high-level I/O libraries such as HDF5; three SETs use NetCDF; and other SETs, such as Lattice QCD, which use USQCD's parallel QIO package and BoxLib from LBNL. For the remaining teams, POSIX I/O remains a popular choice.

In practice on Blue Waters, all the methodologies are working really well. None of the teams have reported insufficient I/O because Blue Waters is configured to have sustained I/O performance. Thus applications encounter other challenges like scaling before I/O becomes a significant challenge. Many applications are using the one-file-per-MPI process[10] model that works well in general because the metadata performance discussed above is sufficient for the large number of creates. Also, the single-file-per-MPI process reduces overheads related to sharing file access. For example, Enzo is using one file per process using serial HDF5 and the team reports good performance.

The PRAC team led by Paul Woodward studies flash events in early-generation stars, which result in expulsion into the early interstellar medium of heavy elements formed in the so-called s-process. To fully understand these flashes and to estimate reliably, the enrichment of the heavy elements in the early interstellar medium that they cause, the researchers must follow the star through the entire two-year duration of a flash. Their application is a multi-fluidics, hydrodynamics code based on the Piecewise-Parabolic Method (PPM) and has been used to simulate inertial confinement fusion (ICF) with numerical grids of 4160^3 and 10560^3 cells.

PPM successfully employs an asynchronous I/O model with dedicated I/O processes called "team leaders." The ratio of team leaders to compute workers can be configured as needed. The number of team leaders is matched with the parallelism in the file system. On Blue Waters, the team attempts to match the number of team leaders to the number of available OSTs, 1440. A typical run might use approximately 14,000 XE compute nodes with 1,000 or more nodes dedicated to I/O while full system runs have used 21,962 XE nodes with 1,331 nodes for I/O. Compute processes send dataset ready to be written to disk to the I/O processes using standard MPI calls. The compute processes continue processing their workload without waiting for the I/O to complete. This concurrency ensures that the code is not I/O bound and maintains the overall job performance at optimal levels. A compute process blocks only when it is ready to send the next dataset to the I/O process but the I/O process has not yet completed writing the previous dataset. Hence it is imperative for the I/O processes to complete writing the dataset before the compute process is ready with the next dataset. This minimum write throughput, which is required to be maintained to guarantee that compute processes never wait on a write operation, is referred to as "Required I/O." If the Required I/O cannot be maintained, the performance of the code measured in GFLOPS drops from its optimal value and the code becomes I/O bound. Any decrease in GFLOPS measured indicates a possible I/O problem encountered during the job's runtime.

The Required I/O varies based on the job size. A couple of examples of this variation are provided in Table 3.5. For the case of 1331 team leaders the aggregate, sustained I/O was observed to be 110 GB/s with restart files written in only 17 minutes, on the order of once an hour.[11] Currently, the job

---

[10]About 30 to 40% of Blue Waters applications use some form of hybrid parallelism.

[11]Scaling the Multifluid PPM Code on Blue Waters and Intel MIC https://www.xsede.org/documents/271087/586927/Woodward.pdf

TABLE 3.5: PPM I/O performance.

Domain Size	10560^3	1536^3
Restart Dump	4.687 PB	151 TB
Data Dump	587 TB	85 TB
Total Data Written	5.264 PB	236 TB
Data Saved	1.02TB	88 TB
Required I/O	17.56 GB/s	687 MB/s
Total Nodes	21,962	13,851
Total AMD integer cores	702,784	110,808

placement does not take into account the location of Lnet routers on the Blue Waters High Speed Network (HSN). Efforts are underway to provide a more intelligent topology-aware I/O worker placement to minimize data movement on the HSN.

3.5 Conclusion

Blue Waters is one of the largest and highest performing computational and analysis systems in the world. It is exceptionally well balanced for I/O intensive and data-focused use. It is actively supporting 70 intense science investigations, some of which produce and consume tens of petabytes of data for a single investigation. Working with science teams to prepare their applications to run at unprecedented scale, the Blue Waters team often identified I/O performance and implementations as major factors inhibiting scalable performance. For the current teams, these limitations have been overcome. Future teams will represent additional challenges.

Bibliography

[1] Celso L. Mendes, Brett Bode, Gregory H. Bauer, Joseph R. Muggli, Cristina Beldica, and William Kramer. Blue Waters Acceptance: Challenges and Accomplishments. In *Proceedings of the Annual Meeting of the Cray Users Group: CUG-2013*, Napa, California, May 2013.

[2] Jeffrey S. Vetter, editor. *The Blue Waters Super System for Super Science*. Chapman and Hall/CRC, 2013.

Chapter 4

Argonne Leadership Computing Facility

William E. Allcock and Kevin Harms

Argonne Leadership Computing Facility, Argonne National Laboratory

4.1	HPC at ALCF	34
	4.1.1 Intrepid	34
	4.1.2 Mira	35
4.2	Overview of I/O at ALCF	35
4.3	I/O Hardware	36
	4.3.1 Intrepid: ALCF Blue Gene/P System	37
	4.3.2 Mira: ALCF Blue Gene/Q System	39
4.4	I/O Software	41
	4.4.1 GPFS	41
	4.4.1.1 Configuration	41
	4.4.1.2 Tuning	42
	4.4.1.3 Reliability	42
	4.4.2 PVFS	43
	4.4.3 Libraries	43
4.5	Workloads/Applications	44
	4.5.1 Case Studies	46
4.6	Future I/O Plans at ALCF	47
	Bibliography	49

The Argonne Leadership Computing Facility (ALCF) is located at Argonne National Laboratory (ANL), 35 miles southwest of Chicago. ALCF is one of the two leadership computing facilities operated by DOE. The mission of ALCF is to accelerate major scientific discoveries and engineering breakthroughs for humanity by designing and providing world-leading computing facilities in partnership with the computational science community [1].

4.1 HPC at ALCF

In 2004, in response to Presidential and Congressional guidance that leadership in computing and computational science was a national priority, DOE released a call for proposals for "Leadership Computing Facilities" which would field systems capable of solving the largest, most complex, and most detailed problems. Access to these facilities would be allocated via the Innovative and Novel Computational Impact on Theory and Experiment (INCITE) program [3]. A joint proposal between ANL, Oak Ridge National Laboratory (ORNL), and Pacific Northwest National Laboratory (PNNL) was selected by DOE. The proposal called for ANL and ORNL to field systems of differing architectures, while PNNL would provide portions of the software stack. The differing architectures were proposed not only because some problems are more suited to one architecture than another, but also for risk mitigation should one of the new systems have significant start-up problems.

In 2004 ANL formed the Blue Gene Consortium in cooperation with IBM. In 2005, a 5 TFLOP, one rack Blue Gene/L system was fielded for evaluation, and then in 2006 began supporting six INCITE projects. In 2007, eight racks of Blue Gene/P were brought online, and in 2008 the machine was expanded to 40 racks (the current 557 TFLOP Intrepid system), and increased to 20 INCITE projects. In 2009 a 10 PFLOP machine was approved, which was installed in 2012—the current Mira system [1].

4.1.1 Intrepid

Intrepid consists of 40 racks, each containing 1024 "system on a chip" 850 MHz quad core nodes, which are based on the Power PC 450 core with dual floating point units per core and 2GB of RAM. This yields a total of 40,960 nodes, 163,840 cores, and 80 TB of RAM. The Blue Gene/P has five different networks: a 3D torus for internode point-to-point communications that have 5.1 GB/s per node, a $0.5\mu s$ per hop latency, and a $5\mu s$ farthest hop latency; a tree or collective network for doing MPI collective operations and I/O with 6.8 GB/s per link per direction and $1.3\mu s$ latency per tree traversal; a global barrier and interrupt network with $0.65\mu s$ hardware latency; 10 Gbps Ethernet from the I/O nodes for I/O to storage; and a 1 Gbps Reliability, Serviceability, and Availability (RAS) network, see Morozov [6]. For comparison, typical store and forward Ethernet switches have single hop hardware latencies in the range of tens of microseconds and Infiniband is around $1.7\mu s$, as noted by the HPC Advisory Council [5].

4.1.2 Mira

The Blue Gene/Q system is an evolution of Blue Gene/P and is similar in architecture. Mira, a 10 PFLOP Blue Gene/Q system, consists of 48 racks, each containing 1024 system on chip 1.6 GHz 18 core nodes. The "A2" cores are based on the 64-bit Power ISA v2.06 specification [2], with quad floating point units per core and 16 GB of RAM for a total of 49,152 nodes, 786,432 cores, and 768 TB of RAM. There are several unique features on the processor. Sixteen of the 18 cores are available for computation, one is used for operating system services, and the eighteenth core is a spare core in case one of the other cores fails in production, but it is shut down during normal operations. This core also supports transactional memory and speculative execution in hardware. In the Blue Gene/Q, IBM collapsed the collective and barrier network functionality into the torus network. It has a 5D torus network, which is $4\times4\times4\times4\times2$ in a 512 node half rack (midplane) that has 4 GB/s bi-directional bandwidth in each torus dimension with $80ns$ nearest-neighbor latency and $1.5\mu s$ maximum latency. There is an eleventh 4 GB/s link for doing I/O communication, which is covered in more detail in the Section 4.2, Parker [7].

Additionally, ALCF runs two 100 node visualization clusters, Eureka and Tukey. Eureka supports users on Intrepid and uses older single precision NVidia GPUs. Tukey supports users on Mira, which uses newer double precision NVidia GPUs.

4.2 Overview of I/O at ALCF

There are many classes of I/O in HPC. The one that is most common and the one most systems are designed around, is defensive I/O, usually called a checkpoint. The primary purpose of defensive I/O is to write sufficient information to the disk so that the application can restart from that point in the event the program fails before it completes. Sometimes restart is the only use for this file, and once the next checkpoint is written, or the program completes, this file can be deleted, but sometimes the file provides useful output. However, there are many other types of I/O that occur in the typical scientific workflow. These include post processing or analysis, file transfers in and out of the facility, file transfers from the scratch file system to a more permanent location, and transfer to tape.

The common storage system design for HPC systems has a scratch file system where checkpoint files are written. This file system is fast in order to minimize the I/O time. However, because these systems are designed to be fast and therefor expensive, the file systems are generally too small to hold all the data, so facilities implement purge policies. A typical purge policy states that if a file has not been accessed after a small number of weeks, say six or less, the data will be deleted. Purges may also occur based on the file system free space being below a given threshold. This forces the users of the system to transfer their data off of the scratch file system to some other longer term storage location. This could be another file system (typically larger, but slower, and therefore less expensive), tape, or transferred out to another institution. While this tends to be cost effective, it is very inconvenient to the users, to move data around. This time spent moving data is also overhead that does not directly contribute to the solution of the problem.

When designing the I/O system at ALCF, the typical HPC I/O system criteria were considered: integrity (the data read back is the data that was written), bandwidth (how fast can the data be written to the storage system), stability (how often do things break), and resiliency (how does the system respond when things do break). ALCF also added the user's experience to their list of requirements. Their goal is to create better, user-friendly storage systems by not having the typical scratch design, and not requiring users to move data as much. As noted, each supercomputer (Intrepid and Mira) has its own complete ecosystem of storage, network, analysis cluster, support infrastructure, etc. In order to meet the goal of avoiding unnecessary data movement, each supercomputer complex has a single storage system that is mounted on all user-facing nodes. This results in peak bandwidths that tend to be lower than other comparable sites, but the storage system is large enough that users can generally keep all their data in a single place on disk until they are finished with it. Then users can transfer the data to tape, or out of the facility for long-term archival storage.

4.3 I/O Hardware

The ALCF essentially runs two independent facilities centered around the two Blue Gene supercomputers. The systems are on two different networks, each running independent instances of all the required services such as authentication, domain name servers, etc.

At a high level, the I/O system design is the same on each of the machines. As is common on the largest supercomputers, the Blue Gene family uses dedicated I/O nodes each of which services the I/O needs of a subset of the compute nodes. It is simply not practical to build a storage fabric with tens of thousands of endpoints on it. User's computational jobs make file system calls on the compute nodes. These file systems calls are intercepted and forwarded by the operating system to the I/O nodes. The I/O nodes optionally do aggregation and optimization of the calls coming in and then replay the system calls on behalf of the compute nodes. The configuration of each system is covered in detail below.

4.3.1 Intrepid: ALCF Blue Gene/P System

ALCF's first-generation HPC data center, ALCF1, is shown in Figure 4.1. ALCF1 contains Intrepid, which has 40,960 compute nodes and 640 I/O nodes, so each I/O node services 64 compute nodes. The I/O nodes are identical to the compute nodes. When the compute node is inserted into a slot with 10 GigE ports, the node becomes an I/O node.

The project space storage system is formed from 16 Data Direct Networks (DDN) Silicon Storage Appliance (S2A) 9900 storage arrays. This system is a single shared file system referenced as /intrepid-fs0 in Figure 4.1, which is used for large parallel writes from the applications on the Blue Gene. As implied by the name silicon storage appliance, the controllers are based on custom ASICs. The ALCF configuration has two redundant controllers, referred to as a couplet, and 10 drawers, each capable of holding 60 disk drives. These systems were installed in 2007 and were initially configured with forty-eight 1-TB SATA drives, which was considered sufficient to saturate the controller bandwidth. The raw capacity of this system is given by

$$1\frac{\text{TB}}{\text{drive}} \times 48\frac{\text{drivers}}{\text{drawer}} \times 10\frac{\text{drawers}}{\text{couplet}} \times 16 \text{ couplets} = 7,680 \text{ GB}, \qquad (4.1)$$

which after overheads and a small partition kept unallocated for testing, resulted in a usable capacity of 5 PB. In 2010 a capacity upgrade was performed and an additional three 3-TB hard drives were added to each drawer, providing an additional usable capacity of 1 PB.

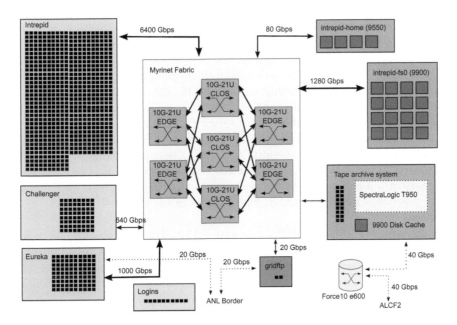

FIGURE 4.1: The ALCF1 HPC system.

The interconnect between the controllers and the drive drawers is a pair of redundant 3-Gbps Serial Attached SCSI (SAS) links. ALCF uses DDNs 8+2P data protection scheme which implements RAID 3 (byte striping) with 2 parity bytes.[1] The parity groups are distributed vertically through the drawers. If you consider the array to be a 3D matrix of hard drives, with the x and y dimensions the rows and columns inside the drawer, and the z dimension going vertically up and down the drawers, then the 10 hard drives that are in the same x and y coordinates in each drawer form a parity group. This arrangement means that two entire drawers can be lost without the loss of data. Another useful data protection feature of these arrays is parity verification on read, which DDN refers to as "SATAsure." Since the ASIC can generate the parity at line rates on reads, the parity is read from the parity drives, but it is also recalculated in the controller and compared. If the reads do not match, the data will be either corrected if possible or flagged if not, preventing what is referred to as "silent data corruption." In the ALCF configuration, each controller is the primary for half of the LUNs (a group of drives treated as a single storage resource), but it can see all the LUNs and can serve data from the non-primary LUNs (with a small performance penalty) should the other controller fail. Each controller also has four external facing Double Data Rate (DDR or 20 Gbps) Infiniband ports for connection to the file servers. These ports are directly connected to the servers (not via a switch). Any traffic between servers is handled over the converged Myrinet and Ethernet network.

The initial Intrepid design called for four 2U IBM x3650s, each with dual quad core processors and 12 GB of RAM, per couplet, with each server driving two Infiniband ports. However, a review of motherboard block diagrams along with speeds and feeds led to question if the servers would not be able to sustain the required I/O throughput. For this reason, the design was modified to use eight 1U IBM x3550s, each with a single quad core processor and 8 GB of RAM, driving a single Infiniband port. This change doubled the effective motherboard I/O bandwidth and had the additional advantage of increasing the aggregate RAM available for file server cache, without changing the rack space required, though it did double the number of hosts to manage and the number of Gigabit Ethernet ports required. Physically, the system was designed in three rack storage cells. Each cell consisted of two DDN storage arrays, with a server rack in between holding the 16 file servers, gigabit Ethernet switches for management, and in most cases, a large 512-port Myrinet switch.

Because the Blue Gene/P came with 10 GigE built on-board, there was a requirement for at least 640 ports of 10 GigE. Given that requirement, a converged solution was chosen. However, 10G Ethernet was relatively new in 2007 and the port cost was extremely high. Therefore, a hybrid solution

---

[1]This is typically referred to as RAID 6 because people have taken to using that term generically for any data protection scheme that can survive two drive failures.

from Myricom, Inc. was chosen. Myricom had two characteristics that made them attractive for this application. First, the relatively high port density, with 512 10 GigE ports in a 21U enclosure. The second was a brand-new technology, referred to as their "2Z" technology, which translated between 10 GigE frames and 10-Gb Myrinet frames at line rate. Because Myrinet is source routed, meaning that the sender (or the 2Z chip when the source is Ethernet) determines the route through the network and prepends the path on the header, the switches can be relatively simple, fast, and inexpensive relative to 10 GigE because the switches strip off the addresses, look at the next hop toward the destination address, and forward data packets accordingly. This is often referred to as cut-through routing.

Two different parallel file systems are used on Intrepid and they share the same disk and file servers. The primary file system, used for home and the larger of the two project file systems, is IBM's GPFS. The second file system is the Parallel Virtual File System (PVFS). Each file server runs both a GPFS server daemon and a PVFS server daemon, and the storage arrays are partitioned, such that each disk has one or more GPFS partitions and one or more PVFS partitions. While this arrangement does force the hard drive to move the heads back and forth between the GPFS and PVFS partitions when simultaneous writes are occurring, PVFS is not heavily used and HPC workloads tend to be bursty, so the impact was considered acceptable. PVFS is primarily used by file systems researchers for performance comparisons since it is uncommon and beneficial to have two parallel file systems running on identical hardware.

There are 16 arrays and each array has 2 couplets, with 4 IB ports and 1 server directly attached to each IB port for a total of 128 file servers. The file system setup is grouped together in what GPFS calls an NSD (network shared disk) cluster. Each group of 8 file servers is a redundancy group. In theory, as long as one of those 8 servers was up on each storage array and at least 5 of them were quorum managers, the file system could still operate, though in practice, the performance would be so bad that it would not be useful, and would more likely lack resources, particularly RAM, resulting in the Linux Out of Memory (OOM)—killing a critical process and causing the file system to go down completely. This of course is an extreme case, but it is not uncommon to have one or two of the eight servers down without problems. The 128 file servers that run GPFS also run the PVFS servers.

4.3.2   Mira: ALCF Blue Gene/Q System

The design of the Mira storage system is very similar to the Intrepid storage system. For comparison purposes, specific numbers, speeds, and feeds will be provided where different. Figure 4.2 shows a system diagram of ALCF's second-generation HPC center, ALCF2.

Like all members of the Blue Gene family, Mira has dedicated I/O nodes. Mira has 49,152 nodes, and 384 I/O nodes, for a ratio of 128:1—twice that

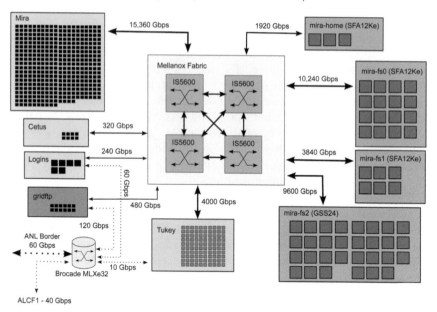

FIGURE 4.2: The ALCF2 HPC system.

of Intrepid. The I/O nodes on Mira are again the same processor. However, the processes are in separate dedicated drawers and are air cooled rather than liquid cooled. Further, rather than having the I/O on chip, there is a PCIe v2.0 × 8 slots available. Each slot was equipped with a Mellanox ConnectX 2 QDR (40 Gb/s) Infiniband card. The storage fabric consists of four large Mellanox IS5600 648-port switch chassis. The four core switches each have 324 ports of inter-switch links, with 108 ports going to each of the other three switches. The remaining edge ports connect to BG/Q I/O nodes, storage arrays, Tukey compute nodes, and any other user nodes.

The storage system consists of 16 DDN Storage Fusion Architecture (SFA) 12Ke storage arrays. Like Intrepid, these are dual controllers with 10 drawers per array, and each drawer is able to hold 60 drives. However, the controllers are server based, rather than ASIC based. There are no external file servers. The file servers run as virtual machines (VMs) embedded inside the storage controller. Each controller has four VMs. Each VM has two IB ports, bonded together as a single logical port. Capacity-wise, 56 slots in each drawer are filled with 3 TB SATA drives, for a raw aggregate capacity of 28.8 PB. After overheads and a small amount of space reserved for testing, the usable storage capacity is 20 PB. Each array also contains 32 SSD units in sixteen RAID 0 LUNs. Connectivity between the controllers and drawers is via 6-Gbps SAS.

File system-wise, there is a single GPFS file system across the entire storage space, which is 20 PB. From lessons learned with Intrepid, ALCF kept the eight-server resiliency groups on each DDN array, and they started out with dedicated nodes to be GPFS managers. ALCF also decided to improve metadata performance by allocating SSD LUNs to metadata only and SATA LUNs to data only.

4.4 I/O Software

4.4.1 GPFS

ALCF deployed similar configurations for GPFS on their main systems, Intrepid and Mira. On Intrepid, they ran the GPFS versions 3.2 and 3.3 for the lifetime of the system. On Mira, they are running GPFS version 3.5. On Intrepid, they only upgraded GPFS when they needed to fix a problem rather than updating software proactively. This became a problem when issuing a file system check and upgrading GPFS multiple times because there were several fixes for the fsk feature. On Mira, ALCF plans to track GPFS software updates more closely and always vet new updates on their test and development system.

4.4.1.1 Configuration

For both Intrepid and Mira, ALCF configured the storage system into an NSD cluster, which contains only file server and dedicated manager nodes; and then several remote clusters, which are client clusters only. The core configuration parameters of the file systems are the block size: 4 MiB on Intrepid and 8 MiB on Mira. Both file systems use scatter block allocation. On Intrepid, there is no replication for data or metadata, thereby making data protection completely reliant on RAID hardware. On Mira, metadata is replicated. From experiences on Intrepid, it was extremely disruptive for the file system to be offline for any reason. Even if a single LUN was down (1 out of a possible 1152) and there was no metadata replication, there is the risk that key top-level directories will become unavailable and the majority of the file system can no longer be navigated.

Another key lesson learned on Intrepid was poor performance related to the compiler linking of executables. Intrepid mixed both data and metadata on the same SATA storage. Later, the GPFS home file system was upgraded on Intrepid to use FusionIO Flash storage PCIe cards for metadata, and this greatly improved the user experience. On Mira, ALCF expanded on this performance improvement and designed all DDN SFA systems to have SSD LUNs, which are dedicated to metadata. This generally improves the user experience for operations like `ls` and directory navigation.

4.4.1.2 Tuning

The initial configuration and tuning of these systems took a significant effort to achieve good performance levels. Once the basic hardware was validated to achieve its performance, then the system was tested as a whole with GPFS. One of the common complications was the differing needs of the hardware for best performance. For example, the Myrinet or Infiniband networks achieve maximum throughput more easily using smaller message sizes, such as 64–256 KiB; however the storage arrays deliver much better performance using larger request sizes such as 4096 or 8192 KiB. On the Blue Gene systems specifically, the I/O forwarder must also transfer messages in certain sizes, which needs to be tuned as well since the larger the maximum transfer size, the more memory the I/O forwarder process needs to reserve for data transfer. On both systems the message size is based on the request size to optimize the disk storage performance. The time spent to tune the component pieces as well as GPFS was around six months for each system. One of the major difficulties is that GPFS (and PVFS) have many tunable parameters to dial in performance. These parameters often have internal dependencies, so setting one may affect how another behaves. Testing and changing these parameters is the most tedious task facing the deployer of a parallel file system.

4.4.1.3 Reliability

GPFS has proven to be quite reliable in day-to-day operations. If a file server or controller goes offline, the system will continue to operate normally without applications noticing the failure with the exception of reduced performance. However, the complexity of GPFS does introduce its own set of problems. GPFS has several manager functions (quorum, token, file system) that are critical to operations. Originally on Intrepid, all 128 servers operated as both quorum nodes and manager nodes. This means that all nodes were able to contribute to decision making and possibly assume a particular management function. This caused unusual failure modes and, in consultation with IBM, the number of quorum and managers was reduced to 16: one for each array. This resolved the issue of certain failover operations taking much longer than expected.

For an extended period of time, GPFS was ALCF's number one source of job failures on Intrepid by a large margin. The primary mode of failure was that a job would fail to boot because the I/O node could not join the GPFS cluster. This problem boiled down to a lack of resources for token management on the client cluster. The client cluster of the Blue Gene /P I/O node consisted of only one manager node, the service node, to handle all management functions. At the time, this node was quite powerful but it also had to run the entire Blue Gene control system. The I/O nodes could not be manager nodes because they were not persistent. The I/O nodes rebooted with every job. ALCF deployed two additional servers, with 24 GB of RAM, which became dedicated token managers in an active/passive redundancy configuration.

Once completed, this change reduced the failures attributed to GPFS back to levels similar to other sources of failure. This same strategy was used on Mira for allocating the number of quorum and manager nodes. ALCF saw a much more stable and predictable system upon initial testing.

4.4.2 PVFS

On Intrepid, ALCF also deployed PVFS version 2.6 and eventually ended up at version 2.8.2. PVFS was set up in high-availability mode using Linux-ha. The same storage hardware that GPFS was using was also being used by PVFS. The PVFS file system was deployed about six months after the primary GPFS file system was made available. This initial delay hampered user adoption of this file system since all of the initial users already had terabytes of data on GPFS.

The most important finding to ALCF was that both GPFS and PVFS took considerable amounts of time and effort to tune. Though both parallel file systems are quite different, the same basic principles were present when tuning performance or resiliency characteristics.

Although PVFS was not widely used, it was important for the ALCF because it allowed them to take GPFS offline, allowing Intrepid to run with users switching over to PVFS. This critical success led ALCF to design multiple distinct file systems for Mira, although both are GPFS.

4.4.3 Libraries

ALCF supports a number of compute and I/O libraries for user codes. They selected these libraries based on what was most popular with respect to their users. ALCF builds and supports this small set of libraries, and tries to make the libraries as effective on the Blue Gene architecture as possible. Table 4.1 gives a listing of the I/O libraries ALCF has available for both Mira and Intrepid.

Although ALCF provided several I/O libraries, POSIX was still the dominant API of choice for I/O. Figure 4.3 shows the break down on interface

TABLE 4.1: Common I/O libraries at ALCF.

Library	Version	Library	Version
ADIOS	1.6.0	HDF5	1.6.6
HDF5	1.8.0	HDF5	1.8.10
Parallel netCDF	1.0.2	Parallel netCDF	1.0.3
Parallel netCDF	1.3.1	Parallel netCDF	1.4.0
netCDF	3.6.2	netCDF	4.0
MOAB	4.1	MOAB	4.5
MOAB	4.6	SILO	4.8

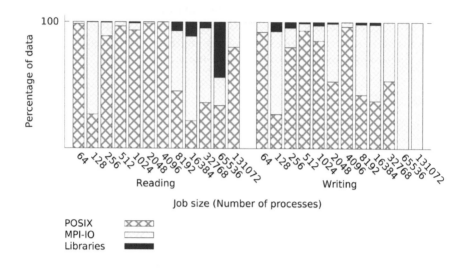

FIGURE 4.3: The choice of I/O interface by job size breakdown as captured by Darshan on Intrepid.

choices by job size based on data captured by Darshan during the period of January through March 2010. As job size tends to increase in number of MPI ranks though, users start to adopt MPI-IO. MPI-IO and other I/O libraries, which use it significantly, help scale up the efficiency of I/O on Intrepid and Mira by "automating" some of the key performance rules for GPFS which is to organize data into file system block-sized aligned chunks so that there is minimal lock contention and 4-MiB request sizes.

4.5   Workloads/Applications

Given that ALCF is an open science computing facility, users are drawn from many areas of science. The wide variety of applications results in a varied I/O workload for the systems. The users and applications may be internal or external to ANL, so it is difficult to obtain detailed information about the I/O any particular application does. Consider Figure 4.4, which clearly shows that the ALCF workload varies over the course of the year. This relates to various projects running heavily in a campaign mode and then once the campaign is finished or much of their CPU allocation is exhausted, other projects become the primary consumers of resources and the overall system I/O workload changes. Intrepid's I/O profile shows two major concepts; (1)

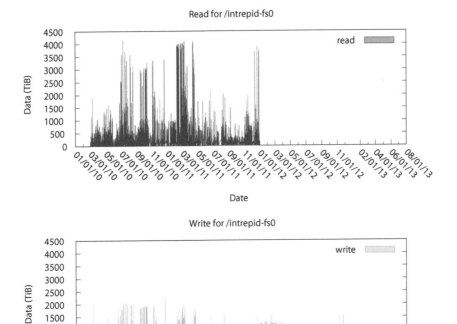

FIGURE 4.4: The amount of data transferred on `/intrepid-fs0` in 1-minute intervals from March 2010 through July 2013.

that I/O is bursty, which is a long-held belief of HPC I/O and which this data supports; and (2) read is quite important. Many people view HPC I/O as mainly a write-intensive workload and read being secondary, but this data indicates that read performance is equally as important to ALCF users as write performance.

Another aspect of file system utilization is how applications store files, which is based on how many and what size. Figure 4.5 shows the cumulative distribution of file sizes on `/intrepid-fs0`. The ALCF discovered that users create large numbers of files. The number of files on `/intrepid-fs0` is 402,687,835 for July 2012. The typical workload responsible for generating such a large number of files is using a file-per-process technique. Using a file-per-process also results in generally smaller files, where small is relative to the size of the file system. The design of the file system is primarily designed

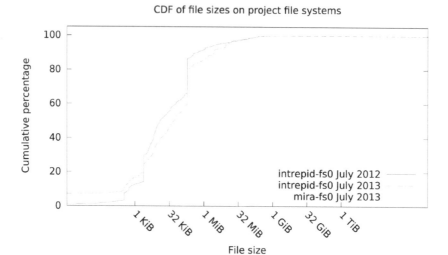

FIGURE 4.5: The cumulative distribution of file sizes on ALCF project file systems.

to support large files well, although a workload of a lot of simultaneous file I/O will generally work because all LUNs will still be utilized.

4.5.1 Case Studies

In 2010, ALCF deployed an I/O profiling tool named Darshan (see Chapter 27), which is lightweight enough to be used in continuous operations. Applications compiled after ALCF deployed this tool would automatically pick up the Darshan intercept libraries and began generating log files with statistical information about the I/O of that application. They analyzed about three months of data collected to examine what type of I/O was being done at this time and published the findings in Carns et al. [4]. In this study, they instrumented about 30% of the total core hours that ran during those three months.

During that study, Carns et al. looked at common I/O profiles for various applications. They found that the file-per-rank model is the most popular method for I/O. This model will utilize all the I/O node resources but will only scale up well to about 8192 nodes. At this point, metadata overhead for creating files starts becoming significant. This can be partly mitigated by pre-creating unique directories for each file before the application run. This reduces the serialization at the directory level when creating files. Scaling beyond eight racks typically requires an application to start using shared files. Either a single shared file may be used or a number of shared files. Shared files are best handled using some form of aggregation and coordination like that provided by MPI-IO (or libraries derived on top of it). The MPI ranks which share a given I/O node will likely not be sequential and as such, writing a shared file can become problematic if I/O requests are smaller than a file system block size. If the same block is needed by more than one I/O node, then those updates will be serialized by GPFS.

The other common problem faced by new users is that of "rank zero" I/O. This I/O model either reads or writes the entire file from a single MPI rank. The rank zero model will work for small files, such as input configuration, but for simulation data, this model becomes bottlenecked because it will only utilize a single I/O node. That will limit the output rate to around 300 MB/s.

4.6   Future I/O Plans at ALCF

With the second generation of compute and storage systems at the ALCF, staff feel that their project-based file system strategy has been successful and useful to their users. They will continue to improve this process by adding quota enforcement to the file system and tools for users to better manage data usage.

While ALCF users have generally provided positive feedback on the single file system solution, it does have one glaring issue: it has a single point of failure. If the file system goes down, the entire facility is down. In order to address this issue on Mira, ALCF is working with IBM to use the Active File Management (AFM) feature of GPFS to achieve the desired benefits, like a single namespace with no additional file management for the users, while eliminating the single point of failure. To accomplish this, ALCF purchased an additional six DDN SFA12Ke storage arrays, which are identical to the ones already in place. These were brought up as a separate 7-PB file system and achieved 90 GB/s with IOR. A total of 30 IBM GPFS Storage Server (GSS) Model 24 units (where 24 means 2 servers and 4 JBOD units) were also purchased and a third 13-PB file system was created across them. GSS takes IBM x3650 servers and NetApp Engenio JBOD drawers, and rather than use the NetApp RAID heads, uses the GPFS Native RAID (software RAID) implementation. The GSS file system achieved 400 GB/s with IOR. As shown in Figure 4.6, the design calls for all users to write to the GSS cache, and then have AFM transparently migrate the files out of the cache to their home directory. This configuration increases the peak performance available, maintains a single namespace, requires no effort on the part of the users, and removes the single point of failure.

In the near future, ALCF wishes to extend this concept to tape as well. They already employ HPSS for archival tape storage. There is a software tool called the GPFS/HPSS Interface (GHI), which allows HPSS to act as a hierarchical storage manager for GPFS. With this system in place, the file life cycle would follow as:

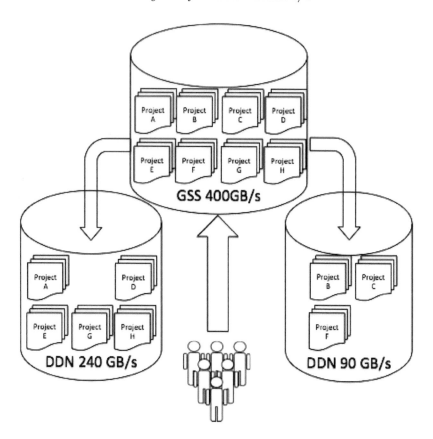

FIGURE 4.6: Diagram of file system changes underway at ALCF.

- A file is written to disk.

- After a period of time, a copy is written to tape—now two copies of the data exist: one on disk and one on tape (the delay is to avoid writing files to tape that may be deleted).

- After another period of time, if the file has not been accessed it is deleted from disk (with the only copy being on tape now).

- The metadata stays in GPFS and it will appear in a file listing.

- If the file is accessed, the system retrieves it from tape automatically.

The delays at each step are configurable and would need to be tuned based on usage patterns. However, the intent is that the removal from disk would be a long enough delay (months) that the odds of having to retrieve it are small. The potential advantages of this system are as follows:

- A backup of the scratch file system exists. Since a copy is written to tape shortly after creation, there is an alternative if a file is deleted or corrupted on disk. Usually none of the major government or academic computing centers have backup scratch file systems.

- It helps users manage their disk usage by automatically removing files that have not been accessed from disk.

- Zero effort is required to manage data of completed projects. The data will automatically migrate off the disk, and if users do request access to their files at a later date, it is a simple copy from the file system and the data will be automatically migrated back.

The primary possible disadvantage of this solution is being too aggressive with removing the data from disk and the users compute jobs are forced to idle while waiting for data to be staged back in from disk. The size of the inode pool will not be an issue because ALCF employs GPFS filesets for each project and the way they are configured, each fileset has its own inode pool.

Bibliography

[1] Argonne Leadership Computing Facility. http://www.alcf.anl.gov.

[2] PowerPC A2. http://en.wikipedia.org/wiki/PowerPC_A2\#Blue\ _Gene.2FQ.

[3] U.S. Department of Energy INCITE Leadership Computing. http://www. doeleadershipcomputing.org/incite-program/.

[4] P. Carns, K. Harms, W. Allcock, C. Bacon, S. Lang, R. Latham, and R. Ross. Understanding and Improving Computational Science Storage Access through Continuous Characterization. *ACM Transactions on Storage (TOS)*, 7(3):8, 2011.

[5] HPC Advisory Council. Interconnect Analysis: 10GigE and Infiniband in High Performance Computing. http://www.hpcadvisorycouncil.com/ pdf/IB_and_10GigE_in_HPC.pdf, 2009.

[6] Vitali Morozov. Blue Gene/P Architecture—Getting Started Workshop. http://press.mcs.anl.gov/gs11/files/2011/01/Vitali_WSS11. pdf, 2011.

[7] Scott Parker. BG/Q Architecture. http://www.bgconsortium.org/ sites/bgconsortium.drupalgardens.com/files/BGQ-arch.pdf.

Chapter 5

Livermore Computing Center

Richard Hedges and Blaise Barney

Livermore Computing Center, Lawrence Livermore National Laboratory

5.1	Introduction	51
5.2	The Lustre® Parallel File System: Early Developments	53
5.3	Sequoia, Lustre® 2.0, and ZFS	54
5.4	IBM Blue Gene Systems	55
5.5	Sequoia File System Hardware	57
5.6	Experience with ZFS-Based Lustre® and Sequoia in Production	59
5.7	Sequoia I/O in Practice	60
	5.7.1 General Remarks	60
	5.7.2 Recommendations to Application Developers	61
	5.7.3 SILO: LLNL's I/O Library	62
	5.7.4 Scalable Checkpoint/Restart	62
5.8	Conclusion	63
	Bibliography	63

This contribution is a snapshot of the IBM Blue Gene/Q system, which is presently the largest deployed system in the Livermore Computing Center (LC) at the Lawrence Livermore National Laboratory (LLNL). The primary focus of this chapter is to elaborate on the details of the file system component of this system.

5.1 Introduction

LLNL is one of the research and development facilities of the Department of Energy (DOE), founded in 1952, and is presently operated by Lawrence Livermore National Security. LLNL's general mission is to support the national interest in science through the application of wide-ranging and advanced science, engineering, and technology. One enduring critical mission is to ensure the safety, security, and reliability of the nation's nuclear weapons.

Since the 1992 moratorium on nuclear testing, computer simulation has had an increasingly important role in this stockpile stewardship. The goal of these simulation efforts is to provide scientists and engineers with the technical capabilities to maintain the nuclear weapon stockpile without the key tool that had been applied for 50 years: physical testing of nuclear devices.

The Advanced Simulation and Computing program (ASC, formerly known as the Accelerated Strategic Computing Initiative, ASCI) was established in 1995 to develop this simulation capability. ASC is creating these capabilities using advanced codes and high performance computing that incorporates more complete scientific models based on experimental results, past tests, and theory. To meet these needs, ASC is solving progressively more difficult problems. Applications must achieve higher resolution, higher fidelity, three-dimensional physics, and full-system modeling to reduce reliance on empirical evidence. This level of simulation requires computing resources at ever-increasing scales and levels of performance. To accomplish this, ASC collaborates with industry to accelerate development of more powerful computing systems and invests in creating the necessary software environment.

LC is home to a first-class computational infrastructure that supports the computing requirements of LLNL's research scientists and collaborating scientists from around the world. A particular focus of LC is to develop solutions (in collaboration with the "Tri-Lab" partners at Los Alamos and Sandia National Laboratories) that will create a functional problem-solving environment for high performance computers under the ASC program [1]. Another goal is to provide leveraged, cost-effective high performance computing to multiple programs and independent researchers under the Multiprogrammatic and Institutional Computing (M&IC) program [9].

LC has been involved with bringing high performance parallel file systems into production since the inception of the ASCI Initiative. LC's first experiences with IBM's General Parallel File System [6] were with the initial ASCI systems. They had increasingly large instances of GPFS through the progression of the ASC machines: Blue-Pacific (2.1 TFLOPS), then White (7.3 TFLOPS), and finally Purple (76 TFLOPS). The GPFS file system on ASC Purple was the largest installed parallel file system at the time with 2 PB of deployed storage and a bandwidth capability of 100 GB/s (which could be delivered to a single application program).

In order to achieve the I/O requirements and the related components of the Livermore usage model for the ASC and M&IC program, LC collaborated with other sister DOE National Laboratories at Los Alamos and Sandia. The Tri-Labs began work in 1999 with industrial partners Cluster File Systems, Inc. (founded by Peter Braam), Hewlett–Packard, and Intel to develop the Lustre® file system with the 1.0 release in 2003.

As a part of the procurement that brought ASCI Purple to LC, LLNL also began work with the Blue Gene series of computers from IBM. The Blue Gene series of systems is distinguished from previous ASC systems not only by utilizing low-power consumption processor technology, but by using this technology at a greater scale to achieve higher levels of performance.

LC has used the Lustre file system on all three generations of Blue Gene systems. Sequoia is the third-generation BG/Q system [2], and went into production at Livermore in 2013.

5.2 The Lustre® Parallel File System: Early Developments

Lustre [7, 8, 12] is a file system architecture and implementation suitable for very large clusters, such as those at LC. Lustre was initially designed, developed, and maintained by Cluster File Systems, Inc. (CFS) within an ASCI Path Forward project funded by the DOE. The initial collaboration with CFS included Hewlett–Packard and Intel and the three NNSA research laboratories: Livermore, Los Alamos, and Sandia.

Sun Microsystems acquired CFS in 2007 to fortify their storage business. After their acquisition of Sun in 2010, Oracle mapped out their exit from Lustre involvement. WhamCloud, Inc. was formed in 2012 as an entity to provide support and development independently from Oracle, only later to be acquired by Intel. Oracle eventually sold their remaining rights interests to Xyratex, Ltd. in 2013.

Lustre runs on commodity hardware, using object-based storage and separate metadata servers to isolate these functions and improve scalability. A key advantage of OSDs in a high performance environment is the ability to delegate low-level allocation and synchronization for a given segment of data to the device on which it is stored, leaving the file system to decide only on which OSD a given segment should be placed. Since this decision is quite simple and allows massive parallelism of bulk data transfer, each OSD need only manage concurrency locally, allowing a file system built from thousands of OSDs to achieve massively parallel data transfers. Lustre is a POSIX-compliant file system presenting a unified client interface such as `open()`, `read()`, `write()`, etc. to the application. This is the portion of the file system that is running on (or close in the case of the Blue Gene systems) to the node doing the computation. At LLNL, Lustre uses the InfiniBand network switch in the more recent instances. Network independence is another Lustre design strength, facilitated originally by its use of the Portals protocol stack, an abstract approach to networking originally developed at Sandia National Laboratory (now available as open source software). This functionality, now called LNet, is implemented as part of Lustre at LLNL.

5.3   Sequoia, Lustre® 2.0, and ZFS

Historically, Lustre supported `ext4/ldiskfs` servers, but as early as 2007, the Livermore Lustre team began to question its viability for the Sequoia era (and beyond) due to a variety of scalability and performance issues. ZFS was identified as technically the best solution and work proceeded with much of the effort of the initial port of ZFS from Solaris to Linux being done at Livermore [15, 14].

Some of the logic for porting ZFS is as follows: previous Lustre servers used ext4 (ldiskfs), where the performance of the random writes were bounded by disk IOPS rate, not by disk bandwidth; OST sizes were limited; fsck time was unacceptable; expensive hardware was required to make disks reliable, but with the new technology, expensive RAID controllers were unnecessary. In late 2011, new systems were being deployed that required 50 PB of high performance storage capacity. LC had new requirements for economical throughput: 512 GB/s to 1 TB/s. LC also needed to implement copy-on-write to serialize random writes so that performance would no longer be bound by drive IOPS. In addition, the center needed single volume size limit of 16 EB, and zero fsck time including online data integrity and error handling.

Extending Lustre to use a next-generation file system like ZFS allows the file system to achieve greater levels of scalability and introduces new functionality. Some of the new ZFS Lustre server features include data integrity, pooled storage, capacity, snapshots, compression, and copy-on-write. With the data integrity features in ZFS, data is always checksummed and self-repairing to avoid silent corruption. Pooled storage allows easy aggregation of multiple devices into a single OST. (The capacity features gave a 256 ZB—2^{78} bytes—OST size limit enabling larger servers.) Snapshots of the Lustre file system are stored prior to maintenance and updates. In addition, transparent compression increases the total usable capacity. Finally, copy-on-write improves write performance by transforming random I/O into sequential I/O.

Using ZFS with Lustre was a major undertaking. Native kernel support for ZFS on Linux was not available, so LLNL undertook the significant effort required to make that a reality. The Lustre code itself had grown tightly coupled to `ldiskfs`, and another significant programming effort was funded by LLNL to create an abstracted OSD in Lustre. This allowed Lustre to interact with any file system for which an OSD layer is created, and allowed Lustre to initially support both `ldiskfs` and ZFS. Lustre support for ZFS first appeared in Lustre version 2.4.0, released in May of 2013 [5].

5.4 IBM Blue Gene Systems

The IBM Blue Gene [3, 4] Supercomputer system design began in a research and development effort at IBM with the combined objectives of studying protein folding and investigating novel ideas in massively parallel machine architecture and software. The BG/L system that followed was designed as a more general-purpose supercomputer that combined those ideas with a network where messages could be routed from any node to any other and a parallel I/O subsystem.

Some of the unique aspects of the BG/L system were: processor speed reduced for lower power consumption; scaling architecture leading to a large range of system configurations; toroidal interconnect plus auxiliary networks for global communication, I/O and system management; lightweight operating system on compute nodes for minimal system overhead and minimal operating system "noise"; I/O functions shipped to I/O nodes, which run a more comprehensive operating system; and 64 compute nodes per I/O network for the installation.

One of the unique and interesting aspects of the Blue Gene computer systems is the particular packaging of the hardware components (here called the "Blue Gene Scaling Architecture") into a hierarchy, allowing the configuration of systems over a great range of scale. All of the generations of Blue Gene systems have followed this design concept. To give a bit more detail, let's look at each level of the hierarchy while traversing a BG/Q system upward from the CPU chip to a full Sequoia system [13]. In terms of the hardware components, there is (ascending the hierarchy) (1) the chip with 16 cores, 16 quad-FPUs, memory controllers, networks, etc. on a single chip; (2) a single compute (or I/O) card, which has one chip with some memory available; (3) a drawer with 32 compute cards comprising a "drawer-like" node card, and eight I/O cards that comprise an I/O drawer; (4) a midplane with 16 node cards; (5) a rack which consists of two midplanes and an I/O drawer; and finally, (6) a system composed of multiple racks that connect to complete the system (i.e., in Sequoia's case there are 96 racks in the system). This hierarchy is represented pictorially in Figure 5.1.

For the purposes of discussing I/O on BG/Q systems, there are many similarities and some differences between the compute node and I/O node. Note that both are at the same level of the hardware packaging hierarchy in Figure 5.1. Some similarities include that the compute nodes and I/O nodes are physically set up to be virtually identical; and both are composed of the same components (one BG/Q compute chip; 72 SDRAM chips; and connectors to the power, JTAG, and 5D Torus network).

However, the main differences are due to how the nodes are used, or what their function is meant to be. Compute nodes run a light-weight, Linux-based kernel, called the compute node kernel (CNK), whereas the I/O nodes run

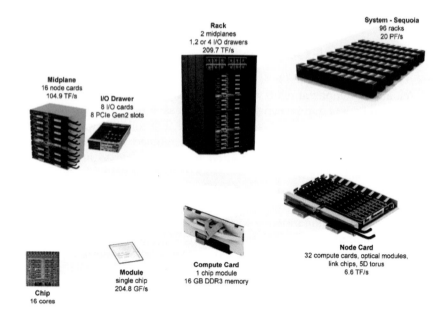

FIGURE 5.1 (See color insert): A pictorial representation of the hardware packaging hierarchy of the BG/Q scaling architecture. The smallest configuration could be a portion of a midplane and a single I/O card. The Sequoia system is composed of 96 racks each with one I/O drawer containing eight I/O cards (768 I/O nodes total).

a full Red Hat Enterprise Linux-based kernel (the Lustre client software is run at this level). Compute nodes are connected to other compute nodes by the 5D torus network; but I/O nodes perform all I/O requests on behalf of compute nodes. These compute nodes "function ship" I/O requests to their designated I/O node. I/O nodes are the only connection to the "outside world" (at LLNL, this is by means of a PCIe IB adapter card to a QDR Infiniband network). Further, I/O nodes number only a fraction of the compute nodes (1:32, 1:64, 1:128). For example, on Sequoia, one I/O node is paired to 128 compute nodes. Compute nodes are located inside the rack, and I/O nodes are housed in drawers external to the main rack (usually). And finally, compute nodes are water-cooled, and I/O nodes are air-cooled.

When LC's initial BG/L system arrived at LLNL, LC was already committed to Lustre. This was the first system from IBM where they ran the Lustre file system instead of GPFS, and also the first IBM system to run Lustre. The first great challenge was to port the Lustre client to the BG/L I/O node. The second great challenge was to deal with the performance ramifications of the BG/L design: (1) at a greater scale where an application would likely be accessing more files (likely many more); (2) though the BG/L I/O node was

TABLE 5.1: Comparison of some relevant performance-related characteristics of the generations of Blue Gene systems that LC sited.

Feature	Blue Gene/L	Blue Gene/P	Blue Gene/Q
Cores per node	2	4	16+1+1
Clock speed	700 MHz	850 MHz	1.6 GHz
Memory per node	512 MB–1 GB	2-4 GB	16 GB
Memory bandwidth	5.6 GB/s	13.6 GB/s	43 GB/s
Peak performance per node	5.6 GFLOPS	13.6 GFLOPS	204.8 GFLOPS per node
Network bandwidth	2.1 GB/s	5.1 GB/s	40 GB/s
Peak performance	410 TFLOPS	1 PFLOPS	20 PFLOPS
GFLOPS per watt	.23	.37	2.1
Cores/ION	128	256	2048

weak relative to the nodes on the commodity Linux systems, they would be handling the I/O for all of the 64 compute nodes serviced by it.

The BG/P systems continued down the path forged by the BG/L design. There were more cores per compute node, but now some symmetric multi-processing (SMP) operations were possible and there were more compute nodes per I/O node.

Sequoia is a BG/Q system, following the BG/P systems. Again there are faster processors with even more cores. There are relatively more compute nodes per I/O node, leading to the situation that 2048 cores are now being serviced by a single I/O node. The I/O node runs a full Linux operating system, now based on a Red Hat Enterprise Linux release.

As with the initial BG/L system at LC, the first major challenge for the local team of Lustre developers was to get the Lustre client working on the BG/Q system. The Lustre client underwent a complete rewrite for version 2.0, and there was new software (now Red Hat Enterprise Linux-based) for the I/O node. The implication of these changes was that getting client software working on BG/Q put LC behind the desired schedule.

5.5 Sequoia File System Hardware

The file system hardware configuration for the Lustre file system for Sequoia is based on NetApp E5400 RAID devices with a Mellanox-based InfiniBand SAN infrastructure. The OSS nodes were leveraged from the TLCC2 [11] node design from the cost-effective computing platforms designed to support

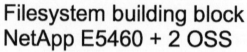

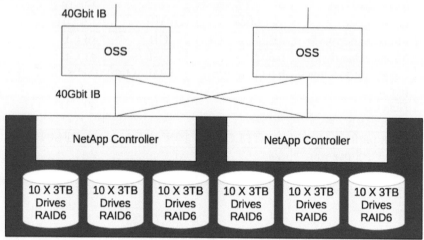

FIGURE 5.2: Block diagram representing the hardware configuration of an OSS pair in the instantiation of the ZFS-based Lustre file system for Sequoia at LLNL.

the ASC and M&IC programs in the facility. The OSS design consists of: Appro GreenBlade dual socket board, Intel Xeon 8 core processors, 64 GB of RAM, QDR Mellanox ConnectX-3 IB (LNET to Lustre), and DualPort QDR ConnectX-2 (to disks).

This hardware is configured into a file system building block consisting of a NetApp E5460 and two OSS nodes. The file system building block incorporates two OSS nodes, two NetApp controllers, and six RAID 6 sets consisting of ten 3-TB drives (Figure 5.2).

Eight of these are integrated into a rack, RSSU (rack scalable storage unit), and then 48 of them make up the resulting Lustre file system with 55-PB storage, 850 GB/s sustained write throughput, and 768 OSSs and OSTs (each OST is 72 TB). Recall the Sequoia Blue Gene system hardware has 96 racks with 768 I/O nodes, and 98304 compute nodes; and a total of 1572864 cores. The comprehensive Sequoia Lustre Architecture is represented in Figure 5.3.

Tracing an I/O request through the system: the I/O request originates from an application running on a compute node, which is running a lightweight kernel (CNK). Then the I/O request is "function shipped" from the compute node to the I/O node, where the torus network includes an eleventh link specifically for shipping I/O from the compute nodes to the I/O nodes. A

LLNL Sequoia Lustre Architecture

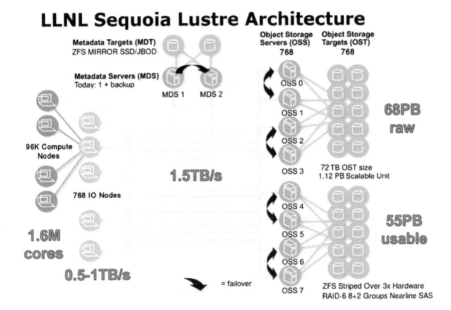

FIGURE 5.3 (See color insert): Block diagram of the ZFS-based Lustre file system for LLNL's Sequoia system. The 96,000 compute node system with 768 I/O nodes is served by a 55-PB ZFS-based Lustre file system composed of 768 OSTs and a metadata server with single failover.

given compute node is always serviced by the same I/O node (by default, i.e., in the absence of a hardware/software failure which can be covered by a failover). Also, a 128-compute-node partition is serviced exclusively by an I/O node (by default, again); and the I/O node is running a full Linux operating system, based on Red Hat Enterprise Linux. The Lustre client software is a part of the I/O node operating system; and the I/O node talks to the file system through an InfiniBand network, ZFS-based Lustre, TLCC2 OSS nodes, and NetApp RAID controllers and disks.

5.6 Experience with ZFS-Based Lustre® and Sequoia in Production

To call the file system component of the Sequoia BG/Q installation in LC a major effort would be a profound understatement. The need for a new back-end file system was anticipated well in advance of the Sequoia installation date and development efforts were committed early on. Multiple transitions of the ownership of Lustre interests and support organizations were navigated.

New and unique performance issues were anticipated in a general sense, in as much as: (1) the BG/Q system was different enough from previous Blue Gene generations, due to the new system software, if nothing else; (2) the Lustre client was all new code; (3) ZFS as a back-end file system for storage and the metadata server would have an entirely unknown performance profile; and (4) LC changed storage hardware vendors.

LC's benchmarks, which included data throughput and metadata measures, appeared that they would be good enough, but turned out to miss some factors relevant to performance requirements in production. LC users had a greater initial level of complaints regarding interactive responsiveness. There were initial ZFS metadata server performance issues that were addressed, and while absolute performance is not entirely on par with `ldiskfs` at this time, the work is still in its infancy and is expected to improve rapidly.

The version of ZFS initially employed write throttling behavior to ensure that reads were not starved by a write workload. However, this write throttling proved overzealous and prevented certain key write workloads from running at acceptable rates. LC worked around the issue by disabling the throttling option, but the ZFS community is addressing the underlying problem. This will no longer be an issue in upcoming releases of ZFS.

There were pluses anticipated as well. Indeed, these motivated the ZFS decision in the first place, as discussed in Section 5.3. The reliability of the new storage hardware has been a big plus for the new generation of Lustre file systems at LLNL.

5.7 Sequoia I/O in Practice

5.7.1 General Remarks

The Blue Gene series of systems from IBM is a departure from previous systems and from the cost-effective Linux systems (peloton, TLCC1, TLCC2) in that I/O calls are shipped from the large set of compute nodes to a smaller set of I/O nodes supporting I/O and other system services. This organization leads to an I/O subsystem which is relatively low powered in comparison to the TLCC2 systems where every compute node can perform I/O operations. This is a likely view of future HPC systems, including possible future generations of TLCC systems, for example. For those systems, configuring I/O nodes which are more capable in terms of memory, processors, and even connectivity, rather than sticking so closely to the IBM scaling architecture, might be more worthwhile.

On Sequoia, overall balance between Lustre client capability, network, and disk system performance is good. Generally, the Lustre client software is LC's largest problem, and the network probably constrains only the top speed (which no applications achieve in practice). For the case where an application is running on a partition smaller than the entire system, and the applicaiton will not be able to saturate bandwidth capability (as is possible with tens of client nodes on a TLCC2 system), there will be file system bandwidth left for each partition in the system.

Present application designers are adopting an $N - M$ strategy where files are shared over a subset of the N compute processes, resulting in a set of M files smaller than the number of compute processes. This gives some latitude to adapt to metadata performance constraints. Future applications will have to move away from the POSIX model to achieve greater performance. For the BG/L generation of system, the practical sweet spot was that for N processes, M was the number of I/O nodes in the compute partition running N processes. This seemed to hold for the BG/P generation. For the BG/Q generation, a good starting point seems to be having M be the number of compute nodes (about 1/16 of the total process count).

5.7.2 Recommendations to Application Developers

At LLNL, LC is often called upon to advise application developers and users of various application codes how to efficiently interact with the Lustre file systems. Before discussing a couple of specific efforts along these lines, here is a high-level outline of the major points:

- *Minimize I/O.* Although this may seem obvious, there is a temptation to save all data that might be of use. This is an issue for the overall performance of the code.

- *Minimize opens and closes.* Opens and closes are expensive operations which hit the metadata server. It is best to open a file once during the execution of a code, and to close it once.

- *Aggregate data.* Lustre is designed around efficient transfers of larger blocks of data, around 1 MB in the case of Sequoia and the Lustre file system attached to it. Aggregating transfers of data into larger blocks of contiguous data is a good practice. For example, a subset of tasks can collect the data over the network, and then write fewer, larger, aggregate chunks rather than having each MPI task writing its own smaller chunk of data.

- *Align data.* I/O transfers that are aligned on 1-MB boundaries is another good practice.

Now consider two examples of application efforts at LLNL that use the Lustre file systems more efficiently: SILO and scalable checkpoint/restart.

5.7.3   SILO: LLNL's I/O Library

At LLNL, SILO [10] is the local I/O middleware most heavily used for application checkpointing (also known as "restart dumps") and plot dumps. Performance of SILO in these scenarios tends to be dominated by the size and mix of I/O requests. Performance is best when I/O requests are few in number and as large as practical. Unfortunately, the SILO library itself as well as other libraries, manage tiny bits of metadata "in band" with the application's raw (or bulk) data. This has a profoundly negative impact when run on file systems that operate on large page sizes and/or buffer pages in multiple hardware resources between the application and the file system.

Preliminary analyses of I/O requests that are sent out the bottom of the SILO-HDF5 I/O stack to the file system indicated that tiny bits of library metadata requests (less than 1 KB in size) accounted for more than 90% of all requests but less than 5% of all data. Once this picture came into focus, the solution also became obvious. The approach was to split metadata and raw data streams of the applications and buffer both streams in large, file-system-friendly blocks. A new HDF5 called the "SILO Block-Based VFD" was developed for this purpose.

The VFD breaks a file into blocks of an application-specified size (with a default megabit) and then keeps some maximum number of blocks cached in memory at any one time (with a default of 32). In addition, I/O requests are tagged as being composed primarily of the application's raw (or bulk) data, or primarily of library metadata, and then targeted for different metadata or raw data blocks accordingly. A least recently used (LRU) policy is employed to determine which cache blocks to pre-empt when the maximum cached block count is reached, and which metadata blocks are favored to keep in the cache over raw data blocks.

The result was that the application's interface to SILO and its interface to HDF5 could be left unchanged but I/O request patterns sent out the bottom of the I/O stack were made significantly more file-system-friendly. Performance for some applications was improved by 50× or more.

5.7.4   Scalable Checkpoint/Restart

Another Exascale-focused effort to improve application I/O performance is the Scalable Checkpoint/Restart library (SCR) [16], which may be described as distributed caching in the application layer. The SCR multilevel system can store checkpoints to a compute node's local memory, to its random access or flash memory, or even its disk, in addition to the parallel file system. Regular checkpoints can be saved quickly to local memory and duplicated on other nodes. If one node fails, its data can be restored from a duplicate node. With this technique, the parallel file system is accessed much less frequently.

SCR stores, or caches, only the most recent checkpoints, discarding an older one as each new checkpoint is saved. It can also apply a redundancy scheme to the cache and recover checkpoints after a failure disables a small portion of the system.

The SCR team uses a technique called remote direct memory access (RDMA), which pulls data off the node without involving the processor in data movement. Different nodes can be coordinated to schedule their writing to the file system.

5.8   Conclusion

The scientific mission of LLNL requires unique and cutting-edge computer systems. Deliverables require balanced I/O capability and an equally cutting-edge combination of file system hardware and software. Meeting such requirements for BG/Q was a significant undertaking requiring a refactoring of file system internals for scalability. The undertaking was successful, but not without challenge. In particular, applications can make work easier by leveraging the strengths of the underlying system and avoiding known system weaknesses.

The move from the present systems to Exascale systems will be even more daunting. Continued scaling of the file system will be difficult in part due to the progressing disparity between the aggregate CPU performance vs. bandwidth advances on spinning storage devices. Particular attention will need to be paid to the use of burst buffer (NVRAM) technologies to address bandwidth challenges. Also fundamental APIs will need to be reconsidered/refactored (POSIX).

Bibliography

[1] Advanced Simulation and Computing. http://asc.llnl.gov/.

[2] Advanced Simulation and Computing :Sequoia. http://asc.llnl.gov/computing_resources/sequoia/.

[3] Blue Gene. http://en.wikipedia.org/wiki/Blue_Gene.

[4] Blue Gene. http://www-03.ibm.com/ibm/history/ibm100/us/en/icons/bluegene/.

[5] Community Lustre Roadmap. http://lustre.opensfs.org/community-lustre-roadmap.

[6] General Parallel File System. http://www.ibm.com/systems/software/gpfs.

[7] Lustre. http://www.lustre.org.

[8] Lustre. http://en.wikipedia.org/wiki/Lustre_%28file_system%29.

[9] Multiprogrammatic and Institutional Computing. http://computing.llnl.gov/mic/.

[10] SILO. https://wci.llnl.gov/codes/silo/.

[11] The Tri-Lab Linux Capacity Cluster (TLCC)Unifying Computing across the NNSA Defense Complex. https://asc.llnl.gov/computing_resources/tlcc/.

[12] Understanding Lustre Filesystem Internals. http://wiki.lustre.org/lid/ulfi/complete/ulfi_complete.html.

[13] Using the Sequoia and Vulcan BG/Q Systems. http://computing.llnl.gov/tutorials/bgq/.

[14] ZFS and Lustre. http://wiki.lustre.org/index.php/ZFS_and_Lustre.

[15] ZFS on Linux. http://zfsonlinux.org/lustre.html.

[16] A. T. Moody, G. Bronevetsky, K. M. Mohror, and B. R. de Supinski. Detailed Modeling, Design, and Evaluation of a Scalable Multi-Level Checkpointing System. Technical report, Lawrence Livermore National Laboratory LLNL-TR-440491, 2010.

Chapter 6

Los Alamos National Laboratory

Gary Grider

Los Alamos National Laboratory

6.1	HPC at LANL		65
	6.1.1	Facilities and Environments	66
6.2	I/O Hardware		66
	6.2.1	Storage Environment	67
	6.2.2	Storage Area Networks	67
	6.2.3	Global Parallel Scratch File Systems	68
	6.2.4	The Curse of the Burst: Economic Thinking behind Burst Buffers	70
6.3	Workloads and Applications		72
	6.3.1	Applications and Their Use of Storage	72
	6.3.2	I/O Patterns and the Quest for Performance without Giving Up	73
	6.3.3	Defeating N-to-1 Strided	73
6.4	Conclusion		75
	Bibliography		76

6.1 HPC at LANL

Los Alamos National Laboratory (LANL) has been using HPC capabilities to enable science and decision support for the US nuclear weapons complex for 61 years. From the use of ENIAC (Electronic Numerical Integrator and Computer) and building MANIAC-1 (Mathematical Analyzer, Numerical Integrator, and Computer or Mathematical Analyzer, Numerator, Integrator, and Computer) designed by Nicholas Metropolis and John von Neumann, to petaflop-class machines installed in 2009, to the present, LANL has been an avid HPC site. LANL has fielded over 120 supercomputers in 61 years. Throughout the eras of computing—with wires and tubes, transistors, serial, vector, data parallel, process parallel, and heterogeneous—LANL continuously strives to provide users with a state-of-the-art I/O and storage infrastructure, which has historically been challenging.

6.1.1 Facilities and Environments

The current computing environment at LANL consists of three computing facilities with a total of 104,000 ft^2 of raised computing floor and over 100,000 ft^2 of indoor mechanical space. The site currently has 28 megawatts (MW) available for the HPC computing environment with active plans for about 50 MW total. The computational capability is split into three environments: secure, open, and compartmented at 85%, 13%, and 2%, respectively.

The computing environment at LANL contains three primary types of machines: capacity, capability, and advanced architecture machines. Capacity machines are commercial, off-the-shelf Linux clusters ranging from 10,000 to 30,000 standard AMD or Intel cores with a subset of machines with accelerators attached and typically 2 GB of dynamic random-access memory (DRAM) per core interconnected by IB. Capacity machines are used for jobs in the 100–10,000 core range. Typical applications include 1D and 2D physics problems, and validation of codes and runs. Capability machines are 100,000–200,0000 standard AMD or Intel cores with typically 2 GB of DRAM per core interconnected by a proprietary interconnect. These machines are reserved for jobs that use nearly the entire machine for long periods of time (weeks to months) doing 3D physics calculations. Advanced architecture machines have some advanced features, like Roadrunner, the first machine to reach petaflop-class computing, made up of about 14,000 AMD cores and 14,000 cell cores, each with eight special processing cores interconnected by IB. All supercomputers contain compute nodes and I/O nodes with a ratio of compute to I/O nodes from 20:1 to 100:1. The I/O nodes serve as routers between the machine interconnect and SAN.

In addition to the capacity, capability, and advanced architecture machines, LANL also has visualization clusters that are a few thousand cores with GPUs that are used for parallel hardware rendering and compositing to drive the many large power wall theaters, immersive cave environments, and end-user 3D workstations.

6.2 I/O Hardware

The following sections discuss details of the LANL storage environment. Many of these sections discuss early adopter methods and deployments including large-scale use of I/O nodes for data storage routing, and first use of a scalable SAN to share a globally visible parallel file system between multiple large Linux supercomputers. This section will also discuss how struggles with unaligned data patterns created issues and opportunities for more innovative implementations.

TABLE 6.1: Detailed summary of LANL's 2013 computing environment.

Total machines	20
Nodes	18321
Cores/cell units	354232
Memory	637472 GB

Largest machine	107,000 cores
Memory	212 TB
Size of largest machine	1.37 PFLOP/s
Installation	2010
Size of future largest machine	50–100 PFLOP/s
Memory	2–4 PB
Installation	2015–2016

6.2.1 Storage Environment

The SANs at LANL use 10 GigE and IB-based interconnects. The file systems are Panasas- and Lustre-based. The parallel archives in use are the HPSS and IBM GPFS with Tivoli storage managers (TSM). Both archive systems are hierarchical storage management systems with parallel tape as the bulk storage method.

6.2.2 Storage Area Networks

LANL utilizes the typical HPC topology of compute nodes connected to I/O nodes via the cluster interconnect. The I/O nodes are connected to the parallel scratch file system via a scalable SAN. Additionally, non-scalable services like NFS for home and project spaces, and parallel archives are connected to the scalable SAN.

From 2001 to 2002, LANL deployed its first large Linux cluster, which contains more than 1,000 nodes. One of the main requirements in deploying

TABLE 6.2: Summary of the LANL storage environment categorized by attributes, largest environment, largest machine, and the total available site-wide.

Attribute	Largest Env	Largest Mach	Total
SAN Bandwidth TiBits/s	34	6	40
SAN Ports GigE/IB QDR	2688/192	0/192	2920/192
I/O Nodes	666	192	772
Scratch Storage PB	20	10	23
Scratch Storage GB/s	346	160	409
Home and Project Space TB	800	Shared	1000
File Systems	8	3	11

this system was to implement the use of compute and I/O nodes for check-point/restart purposes. Storage network traffic is routed to/from the storage systems that are connected to the cluster's internal network and the facility local-area network. This large Linux cluster was deployed with routing though I/O nodes using TCP/IP via Myrinet to Gigabit Ethernet and onto disk storage. That I/O node routing mechanism was designed in 2001 to support massive parallelism to enable any number of I/O nodes and Ethernet switches to be used with extensibility. Further, the ability to route around bad I/O nodes and bad Ethernet switches or links was also contemplated (though this capability was not added until later).

In 2003 LANL began planning its second large Linux cluster. By using the same SAN design which eventually became known as the Parallel Scalable Backbone (PaScalBB) [4], they implemented the first large-scale sharing of a global parallel file system between two supercomputers (see Figure 6.1.) This was done using Ethernet technology because in 2002, Ethernet was the only technology available that was stable and scalable enough to be used for storage access. At this time, Myrinet was not yet usable for storage networking and FC was not scalable enough. It is important to note that this PaScalBB was utilized before IB had been invented, which is commonly used for large-scale SANs. The routing, dead I/O node detection, load balancing, and failover characteristics of PaScalBB have not been surpassed by any design to date. And although IB is not as robust as Ethernet SAN interconnects, IB is more cost effective and has therefore become the default media connection for SANs.

6.2.3   Global Parallel Scratch File Systems

In the early 2000s, LANL planned for a very large Linux Myrinet cluster. At this time, there were not many choices for parallel file systems that would work on a large Linux cluster. IBM's GPFS [10] was only supported then on IBM clusters. Lustre [11] was being developed via the DOE Advanced Strategic Computing Initiative (ASCI) Path Forward program, which was being guided by the Sandia, Lawrence Livermore, and Los Alamos National Laboratories. There was work to bring forth Lustre Lite, which was an early version of Lustre with only partial functionality, but Lustre Lite was not quite ready when LANL needed the file system. The ability to use a single instance of Lustre as a site-wide global parallel file system would not come along until much later. Instead, Panasas [9], a new company that worked with LANL and DOE on their parallel file systems (starting in the 2000s), was the most mature project. In 2002, Panasas won an open request for proposal for a site-wide shared global parallel file system, and Panasas has been in use at LANL as a site-wide global parallel file system for a decade.

There were several Panasas features that helped LANL immensely in the early days. One such advantage was the ability to connect Panasas to PaScalBB in such a way that not every I/O node needed to talk directly to every

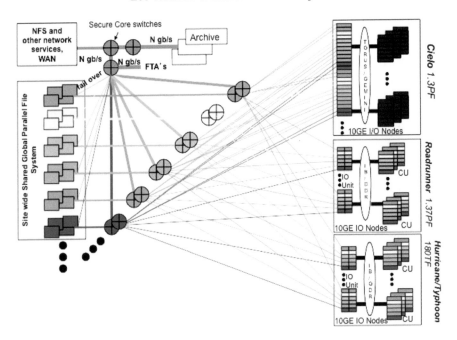

FIGURE 6.1: LANL Parallel Scalable Backbone, as invented a decade ago. The compute nodes route data via their cluster interconnect fabric to an appropriate I/O node which then routes via a Lane Ethernet switch to a set of parallel GPFSs. IP round-robin routing with failover is used in the I/O node to route around bad I/O nodes. Dead gateway detection is used on the I/O nodes to find and kill bad I/O nodes or switches, and Equal Cost Multi-Path (ECMP) routing is used to balance the work across I/O nodes and Ethernet paths. [Image courtesy of Gary Grider (LANL).]

storage server, which enabled site-wide sharing—a great asset that was reasonably low cost. The multiple metadata servers for one file system was also very useful to isolate important users on their own metadata servers. The declustered RAID [7] and scalable rebuild was one of the most important features that kept LANL's systems available for years. Declustered RAID reads from many disks and writes the rebuilt parts to many other disks, which means the rebuild process can go as fast as many disks (therefore scaling by the number of disks one has). Also, it maintained the ability to run a reconstruction on portions of a huge file system while keeping the file system available. Panasas's management interface was ahead of its time as well. Many of its features are just now showing up in other parallel file systems. More recently, for LANL's largest capability machine, they have a Lustre parallel file system which is working well. The hardware includes NetApp/LSI RAID disk systems with the availability of 10 PB and 160 GB/s.

6.2.4   The Curse of the Burst: Economic Thinking behind Burst Buffers

HPC I/O currently is dominated by extreme bursts of data, not only in the checkpoint workload but also in analysis workloads. Since I/O time is non-productive time in general, the goal is to make I/O time minimal. As machine memory sizes get bigger, from 1 PB of memory to exascale-class machines with 50–100 PB of memory, the size of bursts is becoming enormous. Further, given the shrinking *job mean time to interrupt* (JMTTI), for the checkpoint use case, the time for the I/O burst is shrinking. Figure 6.2 shows the effect of the ratio of JMMT over checkpoint time. As JMTTI goes down, checkpoint time must also go down non-linearly in order to keep machine utilization high.

To add to this dilemma of JMTTI and checkpoint times, disk drives (which are used currently for checkpoint I/O) typically get denser, nearly to the square of increases in streaming bandwidth. This means that the number of

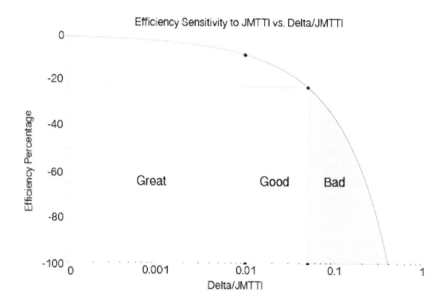

FIGURE 6.2: Machine efficiency JMMTI over time for checkpoint. As JMTTI goes down, checkpoint time must also go down non-linearly in order to keep machine utilization high. In the Great region, only a small percent (about 5%) of the supercomputer's time is spent on checkpoint/restart (defensive I/O). In the Good region, only about 15% or less of the time is being spent on defensive I/O, and in the Bad region greater than 15% of the time is being spent on defensive I/O. In conclusion, the efficiency of the supercomputer depends heavily on the defensive I/O mechanisms' abilities. [Image courtesy of Josip Loncaric (LANL).]

disk drives required to keep up with JMTTI is non-linear as well. Furthermore, this indicates that sites will be buying disks for bandwidth, not capacity, and disks are not priced economically for bandwidth.

As seen in Figure 6.3, buying disks for bandwidth is very expensive as is buying flash storage for capacity. A hybrid hierarchical approach is the most affordable method for providing a way to deal with the horrible burst of data associated with JMTTI and checkpoint time. The key to this strategy is to place flash storage, or other storage, priced well for bandwidth near the compute nodes. This approach minimizes the expense of moving the burst of data quickly and then migrating some portion of the data residing in this solid-state burst buffer. The genesis of this economic model came from work at LANL, which was related to the Defense Advanced Research Projects Agency (DARPA) Exascale Study [5] conducted in 2008.

A future concern for LANL is the need to deal with and differentiate between massive bursts of data from memory to file system vs. file system to

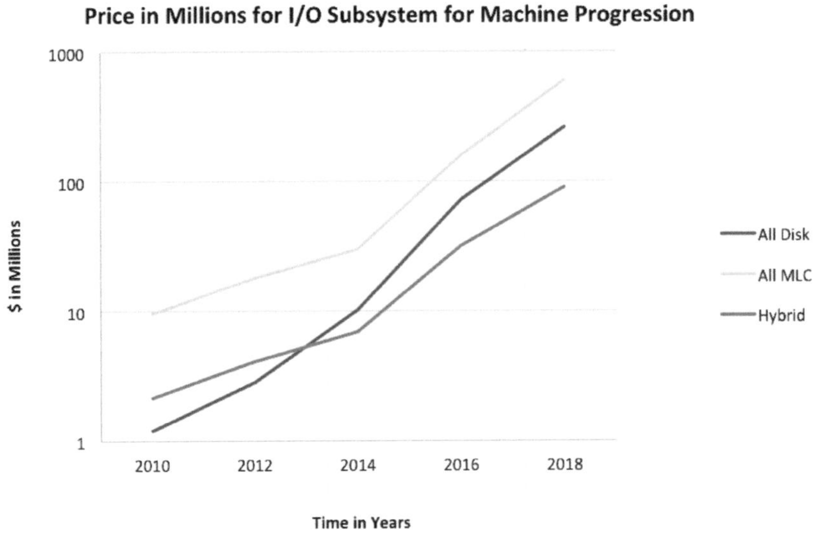
Price in Millions for I/O Subsystem for Machine Progression
1000
100
10
1
$ in Millions
2010
2012
2014
2016
2018
Time in Years
All Disk
All MLC
Hybrid

FIGURE 6.3: Purchasing economics for disk, Flash, and hybrid storage for checkpoints, circa 2009. This analysis is based on two requirements: a 900 PB storage capacity and a bandwidth of 100 TB/s. Note that in 2010, when purchasing disks for capacity, bandwidth was free. Purchasing Flash storage for bandwidth requirements is always too expensive. By 2017, buying disks to meet bandwidth capacities will be too expensive as well. However, looking forward, a hybrid system is projected to be the most reasonable solution for storage and network capacity requirements. [Image courtesy of Gary Grider (LANL).]

archive in order to understand bandwidth requirements. If parallel file systems built from disk technology alone are not economical due to the massive burst bandwidth needed, will parallel archives, which are based on tape, be economical? HPC sites depend on striping across tapes just like parallel file systems depend on striping across disks. Just as disks are not economically priced for bandwidth, neither are tape solutions. Since bandwidth in a tape environment does not come from the tape media or cartridges (it comes from the tape drives) and since tape drives are quite expensive compared to disks (30–100 times the price), there is a distinct possibility that total cost of ownership for parallel tape solutions may become more related to tape drive costs than tape media costs (with bandwidth vs. capacity).

6.3   Workloads and Applications

6.3.1   Applications and Their Use of Storage

Since one of the primary missions of LANL is science-based nuclear weapons stockpile stewardship, it is no surprise that the bulk of the computation done utilizing the HPC environments at LANL is in support of that mission. There are two basic categories of applications run at LANL. One category is single physics science applications, like molecular dynamics and particle-in-cell materials or plasma-type codes, which are typically a few hundred thousand lines of code and run at all scales. The second category is multi-physics integrated weapons applications, which are complicated multi-physics and multi-package applications that are often many million lines of code— again run at all scales. The bulk of the cycles at LANL are used by the large multi-physics codes providing science-based decision support for important nuclear weapon stockpile issues. Because of the dominance of the integrated weapons codes, LANL is perhaps more of a production-computing site and less of a computational science experimental site. Further, LANL is heavily engaged in validation and verification runs to quantify potential errors in calculations to assist the decision support nature of the science work being done. Many of the capacity runs, ranging from 100 to 10,000 cores, are parameter sweeps to gain statistical validity for an ensemble of calculations to understand a weapon phenomenon. Typical large runs can be on $1/3$ to $2/3$ of the largest capability machines, lasting for weeks to many months. Typical runs on capacity systems can last for hours or days, but there can be thousands of these runs in a logical set of decision support calculations. Because of the nature of its mission, LANL sees users from Los Alamos, Sandia, and Lawrence Livermore National Laboratories running weapons stockpile stewardship calculations. The number of large-cycle users is small, about 20–30 people. Also the number of codes is small, around 10–20 codes, but the bulk of the cycles are used by 4–5 codes.

LANL applications use both the N processes writing to N files (N-to-N) and N processes writing to 1 (N-to-1) file modes of I/O. However, the bulk of the cycles used by LANL users utilize the N-to-1 file mode. The primary applications at LANL are able to use POSIX and MPI-IO as I/O methods and one code utilizes HDF5 heavily. The bulk of the I/O is used for checkpoint restart but some I/O is used for data analysis and visualization.

Users utilize the scratch file system as much as possible, but given that this scratch file system is not backed up or automatically archived, users must decide what data to save to the parallel archive system. Over the past 25 years, LANL has seen an increase in archive storage growth by about three memories/month; although recently, the size of the working sets users want to save to the parallel archive has been stretching the ability of the parallel-tape-based systems, such as HPSS and IBM GPFS/TSM.

6.3.2 I/O Patterns and the Quest for Performance without Giving Up

The applications that use the most resources at LANL utilize the N-to-1 file I/O pattern. In fact, it is N-to-1 strided, making a small unaligned I/O access pattern for the parallel file systems. The applications prefer this method of I/O because it allows them to easily manage restarting to a different number of processors, which is complicated as the code is an Automated Mesh Refinement [3] code. The users also find it easier to manage the one-file-per-run as well, for management and archive reasons.

One problem, however, is that all three top parallel file systems do not perform N-to-1 using a strided pattern well, even though N-to-1 is really an excellent way for the users to work. LANL staff worked hard to use various forms of collective buffering [13], persistent file domains [8], and other techniques to help maintain N-to-1 performance, as opposed to switching to N-to-N for I/O. Luckily, LANL's HPC center was able to keep the N-to-1 strided model for users, and today they see the pay off since N-to-N is not user friendly when hundreds of thousands of cores are each producing a file every few hours.

6.3.3 Defeating N-to-1 Strided

After trying to get collective buffering and other alignment techniques to work well for years, LANL and Carnegie Mellon University (CMU) decided to try parallel log structured storage. An MPI-IO ADIO (Abstract Device Interface for I/O) [12] implementation was contemplated, but LANL pursued a more ambitious parallel log-structured file system (PLFS) [2] layer because it would work with many I/O application performing interfaces (APIs).

The PLFS turns N-to-1 file traffic into N-to-N files as depicted in Figure 6.4, which yields good performance without the user having to deal with

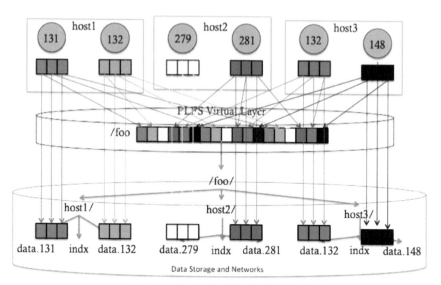

FIGURE 6.4: PLFS internal data flow diagram. The diagram shows that the user thinks data is being written into a single file, but the actual data is being striped across many files across many storage resources in parallel. [Image courtesy of John Bent (LANL).]

hundreds of thousands of small files. PLFS can map N-to-1 patterns to N-to-N or N-to-M files where M<N. Furthermore, because PLFS is creating lots of smaller files unbeknownst to the user, it has the ability to place the small container files into different directories or even different file systems, giving PLFS the ability to scale namespace operations and data operations across multiple metadata servers, as well as across multiple file systems. PLFS has a mode that allows user-initiated N-to-N traffic to be spread across multiple metadata servers or file systems, and a mode that allows multiple small files to be put into a single container as well. This remapping of traffic and breaking the dependence between processes allows the N-to-1 dominant code to get good performance on Panasas and Lustre.

The PLFS speed-up chart in Figure 6.5 depicts speed-ups for various N-to-1 applications using PLFS. This ability to remap I/O patterns is a useful mechanism—so useful that PLFS technology is being used in the DOE Exascale Storage Fast Forward Effort, which started in 2012. This effort is prototyping a next-generation I/O stack for exascale-class computing later this decade.

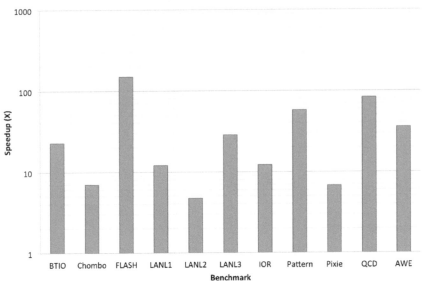

FIGURE 6.5: PLFS N-to-1 application I/O speed-ups. [Image courtesy of John Bent (LANL).]

6.4 Conclusion

LANL is innovative in its implementation of an HPC infrastructure, as they are early adopters of parallel file systems, globally shared parallel file systems, and burst buffers; but this also may lead to future challenges. They pushed users to use N-to-1 with a lot of self-describing information in their I/O, and the users have suffered poor performance, but middleware is now available that makes N-to-1 perform well.

One important part of LANL's I/O strategy is to be involved in the national community. Some examples include:

- Helping to actively coordinate the Path Forward activity to bring products, like Lustre and Panasas, to fruition;

- Helping to coordinate the High End Computing Inter-Agency Working Group File Systems [1] and I/O effort that helped to form a large community around HPC I/O and storage issues;

- Helping to coordinate the DOE Fast Forward Storage project [5], which targets prototypes for future I/O and storage solutions toward exascale-class computing.

Further, LANL supports university efforts that have helped develop pNFS [6], a parallel NFS protocol, and Ceph [14], a parallel file system invented to try out various scalability concepts (i.e., parallel file system metadata and parallel file system security). Additionally, LANL has tried to be inclusive of other agencies, like the Department of Defense (DOD), in the coordination of efforts in the I/O and storage area. Finally, LANL continues to explore various solutions in all areas of SAN, parallel file systems, middleware, and parallel archives.

The I/O and storage strategy success at LANL varies with time, but in general the principles that underlie the strategy are sound.

Bibliography

[1] M. Bancroft, J. Bent, E. Felix, G. Grider, J. Nunez, S. Poole, R. Ross, E. Salmon, and L. Ward. HEC FSIO 2008 Workshop Report. High End Computing Interagency Working Group (HECIWG) Sponsored File Systems and I. In *O Workshop HEC FSIO*, 2009.

[2] John Bent, Garth Gibson, Gary Grider, Ben McClelland, Paul Nowoczynski, James Nunez, Milo Polte, and Meghan Wingate. PLFS: A Checkpoint File System for Parallel Applications. In *Proceedings of the International Conference for High Performance Computing, Networking, Storage and Analysis. SC09*, page 21. ACM, 2009.

[3] Graham F. Carey. A Mesh-Refinement Scheme for Finite Element Computations. *Computer Methods in Applied Mechanics and Engineering*, 7(1):93–105, 1976.

[4] HB Chen, Parks Fields, and Alfred Torrez. An Intelligent Parallel and Scalable Server I/O Networking Environment for High Performance Cluster Computing Systems. In *Proceedings of the International Conference on Parallel and Distributed Processing Techniques and Applications (PDPTA)*, 2008.

[5] DARPA Exascale Computing Study, http://www.cse.nd.edu/Reports/2008/TR-2008-13.pdf

[6] Garth Gibson and Peter Corbett. pNFS Problem Statement. Technical report, Internet Draft, 2004.

[7] Mark Holland and Garth A. Gibson. *Parity Declustering for Continuous Operation in Redundant Disk Arrays*, volume 27. ACM, 1992.

[8] Wei-keng Liao and Alok Choudhary. Dynamically Adapting FIle Domain Partitioning Methods for Collective I/O Based on Underlying Parallel File System Locking Protocols. In *Proceedings of the International Conference for High Performance Computing, Networking, Storage and Analysis. SC08*, pages 1–12. IEEE, 2008.

[9] David Nagle, Denis Serenyi, and Abbie Matthews. The Panasas ActiveScale Storage Cluster: Delivering Scalable High Bandwidth Storage. In *Proceedings of the International Conference for High Performance Computing, Networking, Storage and Analysis. SC04*, page 53. IEEE Computer Society, 2004.

[10] Frank Schmuck and Roger Haskin. GPFS: A Shared-Disk File System for Large Computing Clusters. In *Proceedings of the First USENIX Conference on File and Storage Technologies*, pages 231–244, 2002.

[11] Philip Schwan. Lustre: Building a FIle System for 1000-Node Clusters. In *Proceedings of the 2003 Linux Symposium*, volume 2003, 2003.

[12] Rajeev Thakur, William Gropp, and Ewing Lusk. On Implementing MPI-IO Portably and with High Performance. In *Proceedings of the Sixth Workshop on I/O in Parallel and Distributed Systems*, pages 23–32. ACM, 1999.

[13] Rajeev Thakur, William Gropp, and Ewing Lusk. Optimizing Noncontiguous Accesses in MPI-IO. *Parallel Computing*, 28(1):83–105, 2002.

[14] Sage A. Weil, Scott A. Brandt, Ethan L. Miller, Darrell D. E. Long, and Carlos Maltzahn. Ceph: A Scalable, High Performance Distributed File System. In *Proceedings of the 7th Symposium on Operating Systems Design and Implementation*, pages 307–320. USENIX Association, 2006.

Chapter 7

Texas Advanced Computing Center

Karl W. Schulz

The Texas Advanced Computing Center, University of Texas at Austin

7.1	HPC at TACC	79
7.2	I/O Hardware	80
	7.2.1 Performance	82
	7.2.2 Parallel File Systems—A Shared Resource	84
7.3	Conclusion	86
	Bibliography	87

The Texas Advanced Computing Center (TACC) at the University of Texas at Austin (UT Austin) develops and deploys an integrated infrastructure of advanced computing resources to enhance the research and education activities of the faculty, staff, and students at UT Austin, and in Texas and across the United States through its involvement in various state and national programs. This infrastructure includes HPC systems, advanced scientific visualization (SciVis) systems, data servers and storage/archival systems, grid and cloud computing servers, IT systems, high-bandwidth networks, and a comprehensive software environment comprising applications, tools, libraries, databases, and grid software. TACC services include technical documentation, consulting, and training in HPC, SciVis, and distributed computing.

7.1   HPC at TACC

TACC operates several large-scale HPC computing systems, the largest and most recent of which is the *Stampede* supercomputer. Stampede entered production operations in January 2013 and is a high performance Linux cluster consisting of 6,400 computes nodes, each with dual, eight-core processors for a total of 102,400 available CPU cores. The dual CPUs in each host are Intel Xeon E5 (Sandy Bridge) processors running at 2.7 GHz with 2 GB/-core of memory and a three-level cache. The compute nodes also include one Intel Xeon Phi co-processor in each of the 6,400 hosts (plus 480 hosts configured with two co-processors) yielding a total peak system performance of over 9.5 PFLOPS. Stampede has a 56-Gb/s FDR Mellanox InfiniBand network connected in a fat tree configuration, which carries all high-speed traffic (including both MPI and parallel file system data). System management traffic is accommodated via a separate TCP/IP network.

7.2   I/O Hardware

The parallel file system components on Stampede are built from 76 individual Dell DCS8200 commodity storage servers, each with sixty-four 3-TB drives configured across six individual RAID devices. The RAID sets are set up in an $(8 + 2)$ RAID 6 configuration using standard Linux software RAID tools with two wandering spares defined. Note that although standard software RAID is used to manage the underlying devices, the ext4 journals are purposefully separated from the raw storage target, and the journals are allocated on mirrored RAID 1 partitions. This is a common approach using this type of storage architecture and helps to increase file system performance.

To aggregate the storage hardware, the Lustre file system [1] is used to provide three parallel file systems that are available system-wide (HOME, WORK, and SCRATCH). The largest and most capable of these three file systems is SCRATCH, which is supported by 58 of the 76 servers. With six RAID devices defined per server, this equates to a total of 348 OSTs defined within Lustre for SCRATCH, resulting in a total of 7.4 PB of user-addressable storage. The adoption of multiple parallel file systems is common across TACC HPC system deployments and is designed to provide users with tiered storage alternatives that vary in size, performance, and file longevity. As a general-purpose compute platform for the national academic community, Stampede must support thousands of users during its operational lifespan; indeed, more than 2,400 individual users ran jobs during the first seven months of operation. Consequently, fairly modest quotas are implemented for the HOME and WORK file systems. The user quota limits and associated target usage modes for each file system are presented in Figure 7.1.

An important step in the deployment of a production file system is the completion of a burn-in process for all of the hard drives, which support the file system. In Stampede's case, there are over 4,800 drives installed in the OSSs and the peak global file system performance is contingent on ensuring consistent performance across all of these drives. The file system burn-in process on Stampede was carried out over the course of one month (in tandem with the compute-hardware deployment) and was performed in a two-step process. First, low-level I/O tests were performed to every disk sector on each drive in the OSSs. These low-level disk tests ran for multiple 24-hour periods and were used to identify and replace slow performers along with drives

File System	User Quotas	Life Time	Target Usage
$HOME	5 GB 150K inodes	Project	Permanent user storage; automatically backed up.
$WORK	400 GB 3M inodes	Project	Large allocated storage; not backed up.
$SCRATCH	none	14 Days	Large temporary storage; not backed up, purged periodically.

FIGURE 7.1: Lustre file system quotas and target usage on TACC's Stampede system.

containing abnormally high bad-sector counts. After completing the individual disk burn-in tests, the second step of the process was to build and test the production RAID sets that would ultimately be formatted to support Lustre. These multiple device (MD) RAID-level tests performed large block I/O to each of the six RAID devices per OSS in parallel in eight-hour intervals. For this particular hardware and RAID 6 software RAID configuration, the performance for a satisfactory MD device was 595 MB/s. Any RAID set which did not meet this performance threshold was re-examined to identify slow drives inhibiting performance. Note that this approach follows similar deployment strategies on previous large-scale systems which have proved useful in isolating outliers and detecting infant mortality [4]. The entire process was repeated until the RAID set performance was consistent across all OSSs. To demonstrate the resulting performance consistency, Figure 7.2 presents the measured MD write speeds obtained for the OSSs serving HOME and WORK. Based on

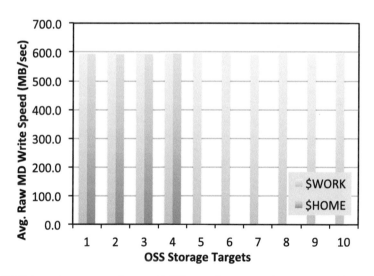

FIGURE 7.2: Average software RAID performance for Lustre OST devices measured during disk burn-in procedure.

the burn-in process, approximately 50 drives were placed prior to production formatting to ensure maximum performance characteristics for the hardware.

7.2.1   Performance

After completing a thorough burn-in procedure, the final step in a large file system deployment is to format the file systems and benchmark for end-user performance and scalability. One of the architectural designs of Lustre is to provide good scaling characteristics across multiple OSSs. To quantify this scaling with Lustre 2.x, Figure 7.3 presents measured performance data starting with only a single OSS active (6 OSTs) up to a maximum of 58 servers active (348 OSTs), which corresponds to the entirety of Stampede's SCRATCH file system. In these tests, 48 write clients were used to test an active OSS, and a single OSS delivered an aggregate bandwidth of over 2.5 GB/s. As additional OSSs were activated, controlled weak scaling tests were repeated maintaining the 48 client–server ratio, and near-linear scaling was observed across the file system. Comparing the performance between 1 and 58 OSSs, a 95% scaling efficiency of over was observed.

The results in Figure 7.3 present performance as a function of the number of active OSSs. In contrast, the results shown in Figure 7.4 present performance for Stampede's SCRATCH file system as a function of the number of participating clients. These results were obtained by measuring the total time required for each client to write a fixed payload size of 2 GB per host (using one MPI task per host) to individual files. The tests compare results for a single host participating at the small scale, to more than 6,000 hosts writing simultaneously at the large scale. Note that these tests were carried out on

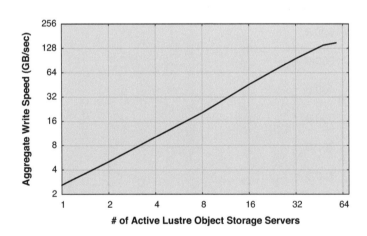

FIGURE 7.3: Lustre scaling across multiple Object Storage Servers (OSS) measured using Lustre (version 2.1.3).

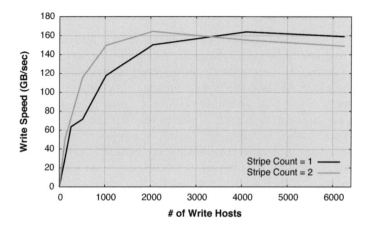

FIGURE 7.4: Raw write performance characteristics of a large, parallel Lustre file system. Results measured using one I/O task per host on TACC's Stampede SCRATCH file system which contains 348 OSTs (aggregate rates measured using a fixed payload size of 2 GB per host writing to individual files).

a quiescent system shortly after the file system was formatted such that it had very little capacity utilized. Consequently, these tests represent best-case file system performance as there is no competing I/O traffic or significant impact from fragmentation. Two sets of results are shown in Figure 7.4, which are varied by the underlying Lustre stripe count for the files written. In both cases, the peak file system write speed was seen to be over 160 GB/s (the corresponding peak read rate, which is generally lower than write in Lustre, was measured to be 127 GB/s). However, the peak value was obtained at smaller client counts with the stripe count equivalent to 2 at the expense of having a slightly lower aggregate rate when using 4,000 clients or more. Based on these performance signatures, and the fact that a stripe count value of 2 essentially doubles single-client performance, the default stripe count on SCRATCH was set to a value of 2. System users are required to increase this striping default to larger values when using an N-to-one approach where many clients are performing I/O to a single file.

The results in Figure 7.4 also highlight another attractive Lustre feature in that significant fractions of the overall file system performance can be maintained with large client counts. At the largest scale, the number of simultaneous write clients is 18× the number of available Lustre OSTs. However, the performance at these large client counts is within 94% of the peak measured performance and this is a primary motivating reason for deploying these types of parallel file systems for a large, general-purpose compute system in which many users will likely be performing I/O simultaneously.

7.2.2   Parallel File Systems—A Shared Resource

Often, ideal measurements, taken under ideal conditions, are the type that are used to quote file system performance for a given system. However, from a user perspective, it is important to understand that these peak numbers may not be indicative of the level of performance they can expect to achieve in a multi-user, production system environment. Indeed, on most modern HPC systems, the file system is truly a *shared* resource; one in which the instantaneous performance is influenced by how many users are accessing the file system and what type of workloads they are performing. Consequently, when estimating application runtime requirements, users are recommended to pad the I/O portion of their code to account for runtime variability introduced by using a shared I/O resource. To quantify the level of variability on a system with thousands of users, daily performance rates were sampled across two different intervals during the first 8 months of Stampede's production. The first sampling interval corresponds to measurements taken immediately after the system went into production in January 2013 (and includes approximately two months' worth of data). These tests were submitted daily as normal user jobs into the Simple Linux Utility for Resource Management (SLURM) queuing system [3]. Although they were submitted at the same time each day, they ran at different times depending on the availability of sufficient resources to schedule the job. Each job wrote 4 TB of data from 512 hosts to individual files, and two types of runtime performance were monitored: aggregate and throughput. The *aggregate* performance number corresponds to the total time required to complete writing all 4 TB of data. Since it is aggregated across all writes, the value can be reduced in the case where one or more OSTs are slower than others due to usage by the other system users. In contrast, the *throughput* performance number is based on the time required for each client to write only its portion of the 4-TB total. This value is generally higher than the aggregate performance number as the measured timings are not synchronized across all writes.

Figure 7.5(a) presents a time history of the daily I/O results beginning in January 2013 and extending through mid-March. From these results, the level of variability possible on a shared I/O resource can be seen, particularly in the aggregate performance results where the difference can vary by more than a factor of two. The average aggregate performance over the 65 measurements during this period was 110 GB/s, but a general decline is observed over this initial period after the system entered production. Although system utilization was ramping up during this time frame, which explains some of the decline as more users accessed the shared I/O resource, another contributing factor was the fragmentation associated with the file system filling up. Figure 7.6 shows the corresponding growth in usage on both the WORK and SCRATCH file systems during the first three months of operation and illustrates a rapid increase in usage to over 1 PB in approximately two months for SCRATCH. This fragmentation is another common contributor to the difference a typical

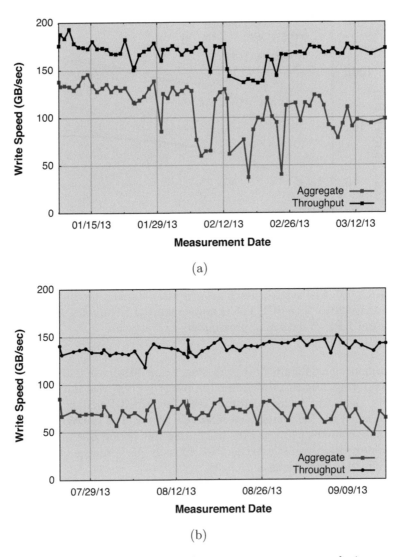

FIGURE 7.5: Daily file system performance measurements during normal production operations. Each job writes 4 TB of new data to Stampede's SCRATCH file system.

system user can expect to see once a file system has been in production for a while versus the quoted performance results often reported on a nearly empty file system. As the file system continued to fill up on SCRATCH, it was necessary to begin purging older files on the system; this process began in June 2013 and is a common policy on large HPC resources to avoid filling up the file system. At this point, the file system mostly reached a steady-state level of

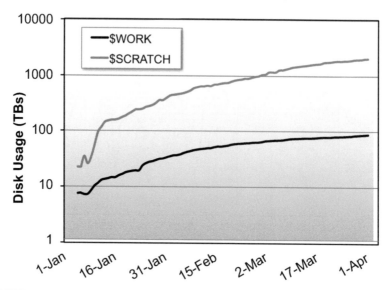

FIGURE 7.6: File system usage growth after starting production operations in January 2013. The SCRATCH system started from being nearly empty to amassing 1 PB of data in approximately two months.

performance and Figure 7.5(b) presents a time history of daily I/O measurements during August 2013 (after the purge process was initiated). In these results, there was a fairly constant response, albeit lower than the measured values when the file system was relatively empty. The average aggregate performance over the 52 measurements during this period was 71 GB/s and this value provides a realistic expectation of daily performance using 512 clients in production operations.

7.3   Conclusion

Like many HPC sites across the world, parallel I/O performance and stability remains a key component in the overall design of large-scale systems at TACC. Indeed, significant burn-in time and performance evaluation is devoted to the I/O subsystem during the deployment phase. Fortunately, much of the low-level disk and RAID testing can be performed in parallel with the compute system and interconnect installation and validation.

While peak system IO rates remain useful for overall system characterization, it is important for users to understand that these peak numbers may not be indicative of the level of performance they can expect to achieve in a multi-user, production system environment. Results presented here in documented daily performance samples from a Lustre file system on Stampede as it transitioned from an empty file system at the beginning of production to a fully utilized file system with periodic purging enforced and the natural fragmentation that results.

As a fundamentally shared and interactive resource, the I/O subsystem is often the primary avenue where users notice interrupts (whether they are caused by the file system or not). It is also the source of the majority of system interrupts by users who (often unknowingly) inject high-transaction workloads over long periods of time that may impact performance or stability across the resource. Consequently, TACC devotes significant effort toward monitoring I/O usage at the application level. This monitoring process combines low-level monitoring on each of the production I/O servers coupled with queries into the underlying resource manager in order to delineate client I/O requests on an individual job basis [2]. This allows TACC staff to identify applications which may not be utilizing the I/O system effectively.

Finally, in order to improve application efficiency and portability, TACC staff continue to push community and individual research group applications to adopt tuned I/O libraries that include parallel I/O semantics. In support of this effort, TACC pro-actively promotes the use of libraries like HDF5 in its scientific computing curriculum as a must-have component for researchers to include in their application development toolbox.

Bibliography

[1] Peter J. Braam. The Lustre Storage Architecture. Technical report, Cluster File Systems, Inc., 2003.

[2] John Hammond. Log Analysis and lltop. In *Lustre User Group (LUG)*, Orlando, FL, April 2011.

[3] Morris A. Jette, Andy B. Yoo, and Mark Grondona. SLURM: Simple Linux Utility for Resource Management. In *Lecture Notes in Computer Science: Proceedings of Job Scheduling Strategies for Parallel Processing (JSSPP) 2003*, pages 44–60. Springer-Verlag, 2002.

[4] T. Minyard, K. Schulz, J. Boisseau, B. Barth, K. Milfeld, J. Cazes, J. Foster, S. Johnson, G. Jost, B.-D. Kimand L. Koesterke, and L. Wilson. Experiences and Achievements in Deploying *Ranger*, the First NSF Path to Petascale System. In *Proceedings of the 2008 TeraGrid Conference*, Las Vegas, NV, June 2008.

Part II

File Systems

Chapter 8

Lustre®

Eric Barton and Andreas Dilger

Intel

8.1	Motivation	....	91
8.2	Design and Architecture	....	92
	8.2.1	Overview	92
	8.2.2	Networking	93
		8.2.2.1 LNet	93
		8.2.2.2 RPC	94
	8.2.3	Distributed Lock Manager	96
	8.2.4	Back-end Storage	97
	8.2.5	Metadata Server	98
	8.2.6	Object Storage Server	99
	8.2.7	Management Server	100
	8.2.8	Client	100
	8.2.9	Recovery	102
8.3	Deployment and Usage		103
8.4	Conclusion		104
	Bibliography		105

8.1 Motivation

The Lustre[1] file system is an Open Source (GPLv2) high performance parallel file system widely used in the HPC community to provide a global POSIX namespace and horizontally scalable I/O to the computing resources of an entire datacenter. It was originally designed for scalability and is capable of handling extremely large volumes of data and huge numbers of files with high availability and strong coherence of both data and metadata. This makes it the premier choice for the most demanding HPC applications spanning the world's largest HPC clusters.

The Lustre file system originated in 1999 at Carnegie Mellon University with a project led by Dr. Peter Braam to develop an object-based disk file

---

[1]Other names and brands may be claimed as the property of others.

91

system named *obdfs*. Over the next three years, and with early funding from the ASCI Path Forward project, obdfs evolved into the first versions of Lustre [4] with a debut at number 5 in the Top500 on the 1000-node MCR cluster at Lawrence Livermore National Laboratory (LLNL) [12]. Continued development over the next ten years saw increasing adoption of Lustre on a wide range of HPC systems in academia and industry. By 2013, Lustre was deployed on 7 out of the top 10 and around 60% of the top 100 supercomputers in the world as listed by the Top500. Several of these support tens of thousands of clients, 10s of Petabytes of capacity, and I/O performance of over 1TB/s [16, 6].

8.2 Design and Architecture

8.2.1 Overview

Lustre is a Linux file system implemented entirely in the kernel. Its architecture is founded upon distributed object-based storage. This delegates block storage management to its back-end servers and eliminates significant scaling and performance issues associated with the consistent management of distributed block storage metadata.

Lustre objects come in two varieties—data objects, which are simple byte arrays typically used to store the data of POSIX files, and index objects, which are key-value stores typically used to implement POSIX directories. These objects are implemented by the Lustre Object Storage Device (OSD), an abstraction that enables the use of different back-end file systems, including ext4 and ZFS. A single OSD instance corresponds to a single back-end storage volume and is termed a storage *target*. The storage target depends on the underlying file system for resilience to storage device failure, but may be instantiated on any server that can attach to this storage to provide high availability in the event of server or controller failure.

Storage targets are exported either as metadata targets (MDTs), used for file system namespace operations, or object targets (OSTs), used to store file data. These are usually exported by servers configured specifically for their respective metadata or data workloads—e.g., RAID 10 storage hardware and high core counts for metadata servers (MDSs) and high capacity RAID6 storage hardware and lower core counts for object storage servers (OSSs). Historically, Lustre clusters have consisted of a pair of MDS nodes configured for active-passive failover and multiple OSSs configured for active-active failover. More recent Lustre releases support multiple MDTs in the same file system and therefore multiple MDS nodes with active-active failover are expected to become more common.

Lustre clients and servers communicate with each other using a layered communications stack. The underlying physical and/or logical networks such

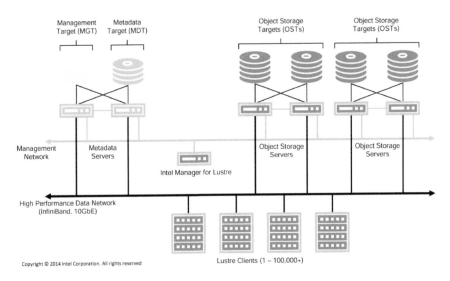

Management   Metadata   Object Storage   Object Storage
Target (MGT)   Target (MDT)   Targets (OSTs)   Targets (OSTs)

Management   Metadata   Object Storage   Object Storage
Network   Servers   Servers   Servers

Intel Manager for Lustre

High Performance Data Network
(InfiniBand, 10GbE)

Lustre Clients (1 – 100,000+)

FIGURE 8.1 (See color insert): Lustre architecture. [Image courtesy of Intel Corporation.]

as Infiniband or TCP/IP are abstracted by the Lustre Networking layer, LNet. LNet provides both message passing and remote memory access (RMA) for efficient zero-copy bulk data movement. The Lustre RPC layer (Ptlrpc) is built on top of this to provide robust client–server communications in the face of message loss and server failures.

The Lustre Distributed Lock Manager (LDLM) is a service provided by storage targets in addition to object storage services. LDLM locks are used to serialize conflicting file system operations on objects managed by that target, and are the mechanism used to ensure distributed cache coherency. The combination of coherent locking and recovery protocols exercised on server startup ensure that caches remain consistent through server restart or failover. This boosts server throughput for file system modifying operations by allowing the use of write-back rather than write-through caches for file system-modifying operations since uncommitted operations are recovered from the clients in case of server failure.

8.2.2 Networking

8.2.2.1 LNet

Lustre networking (LNet) was originally based on a port of Sandia Portals [5] to the Linux kernel. Portals has a very clean and simple API which supports non-blocking network operations and both dual-sided (message passing) and single-sided (RMA) styles of communication. Together these made Portals ideal for the implementation of Lustre RPC since non-blocking operation greatly simplifies coding of algorithms designed to keep large deep pipes full, message passing is ideal for RPC request processing and RMA not only enables zero-copy for bulk data movement but also limits congestion by giving control of this movement to the server.

Lustre has to operate in a heterogeneous networking environment where communications span different network types. Consider a compute cluster with its own HPC fabric connected via gateway nodes to a site-wide storage facility. Most efficient use of available network resources occurs when native protocols can be used on both the HPC fabric and the site-wide storage network. LNet diverged from Sandia Portals to accommodate this usage model by dividing the Portals network ID (NID) into a two-level network address including a network number and an address within that network. LNet therefore includes a routing subsystem that enables communications to span multiple networks connected by multiple routers for resilience and scalable throughput.

LNet is implemented in two layers. The upper layer implements all generic communications while the lower layer abstracts physical networks and network-specific protocols through the Lustre Network Driver (LND). LNet therefore supports a wide range of networks including TCP/IP, all fabrics such as Infiniband supported by OFED, and HPC fabrics with non-standard APIs such as the Cray Seastar and Gemini networks.

When the underlying network supports only two-sided communications, the LND will typically support zero-copy on sends but is forced to copy from pre-posted network buffers into MBs posted by the upper levels. However, when the underlying network supports RDMA, the LND implements small message queues both for small LNet communications and to negotiate RDMA for large MBs to support zero-copy for both incoming and outgoing bulk data. These message queues use a system of credits for peer-to-peer communications to avoid congestion problems associated with having to handle unsolicited messages.

LNDs may also be tuned to support "long fat pipes" efficiently by increasing message queue depth and RDMA concurrency, and by optionally mapping RDMA buffers on demand to reduce RDMA fragmentation on the wire. These optimizations enable Lustre to operate efficiently over wide-area networks.

8.2.2.2 RPC

Lustre's PtlRPC layer is designed to support efficient communications between clients and servers and, most significantly, to maximize server-side control over network utilization to minimize the problem of congestion. This is achieved by ensuring that the only unsolicited message a client may send is the initial RPC request. All subsequent communication, including bulk data transfer and the final RPC reply is initiated by the server.

A Lustre RPC progresses in phases. First the client must create MBs for the request and reply buffers and any bulk data buffers. MEs for the bulk and reply MBs are then attached for access only by the server targeted by

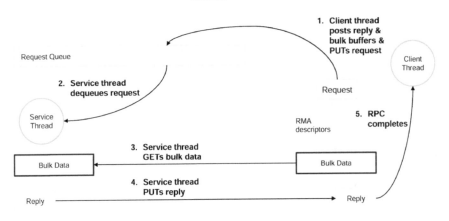

FIGURE 8.2: Lustre RPC. [Image courtesy of Intel Corporation.]

the request using unique matchbits, usually the sender's RPC XID. These matchbits are passed in the RPC request and used by the server effectively as RDMA descriptors. The client then PUTs the RPC request MB which sends the request to the server, and waits for all completion events on all MBs. If successful, all bulk data will now have been transferred under server control and the reply buffer will contain the RPC reply status.

On startup, Lustre servers attach an initial working set of MEs and associated MBs to well-known portals corresponding to the services they export. MEs are set to match incoming PUTs from any Lustre client. They are matched in the order in which they are attached and each MB is capable of buffering many incoming RPC requests. A completion event is posted on each incoming PUT, which is handled by queuing the request on an appropriate service request queue. This event also signals whether the ME has been detached because its MB is now full. If the number of attached MEs falls below a low water threshold, additional ME/MBs are allocated and attached to handle the increased buffering requirement.

Each server maintains a pool of service threads which consume the service request queues. At first, only urgent processing is performed—e.g., to determine whether the client's RPC timeout is inconsistent with current expected service latency—and requests are queued for processing later. When request processing proper starts, the service thread handling the request initiates any required bulk data movement using the RMA descriptors in the request and then finally PUTs the RPC reply to complete the request.

The number of threads in the service queue determines the number of RPCs that are processed concurrently. This in turn determines both the number of concurrent bulk data movements between client and server and the number of concurrent I/O requests to back-end storage.

Any requests that modify back-end file system data or metadata must be made idempotent to ensure that retry attempts due to lost RPC replies are harmless and that clients receive the correct replies. Clients therefore include a unique XID in each request to allow repeated requests to be identified and the server retains a copy of the RPC reply buffer until it has positive confirmation that the reply was received by the client.

The server also includes both the OSD transaction number in which the request was executed and the OSD's *last_committed* transaction number in RPC replies. Clients retain the RPC request and reply buffers until the OSD transaction associated with the request has been committed to persistent storage so that the request can be replayed in the event of server failure.

8.2.3   Distributed Lock Manager

The Lustre Distributed Lock Manager (LDLM) enables Lustre clients and servers to serialize conflicting file system operations and ensure client caches remain coherent. Every Lustre storage target provides this service so that locks are co-located with the objects they protect and total locking concurrency scales with the number of storage targets. Lustre clients hold locks on behalf of the entire kernel—effectively aggregating lock requests by all client processes which are serialized in the client VFS.

The design of the LDLM was based on the VAX/VMS Distributed Lock Manager [14] in which named abstract *resources* can be locked in a variety of *modes* to control how corresponding physical resources may be accessed. For example, *protected read* locks are mutually compatible and are used to permit read-only access to a shared resource, while *protected write* locks are used by clients to cache dirty data, and *exclusive* locks are incompatible with all lock modes other than *null* and are therefore used by servers wishing to modify a resource and invalidate the caches of all other lock holders.

The VAX/VMS DLM also provided so-called Asynchronous System Traps (ASTs) to provide notification when locks are granted if the lock could not be granted immediately upon request or when granted locks block other lock requests. The LDLM implements these using a callback service on the client. They enable a lazy locking scheme that minimizes unnecessary communication by allowing Lustre clients to continue to hold locks protecting their caches until a conflict actually occurs.

Each lock may also have a Lock Value Block (LVB) that contains information about the resource being locked (e.g., size, blocks, and timestamps) that is passed along with the granted lock to avoid an extra RPC to fetch commonly used state.

The LDLM added some new features to the original VAX/VMS functionality to further increase efficiency. *Extent* locks were added to enable Lustre clients to lock byte ranges within OST objects to support shared file I/O by allowing different clients to cache different extents of the same object. In the case of an uncontended or lightly contended resource, the extent locking policy will grow the granted lock to cover the largest non-conflicting extent that covers the requested extent. This minimizes the number of DLM requests needed in common use cases.

Intent lock requests were added to avoid lock ping-pong on highly contended resources. The initial lock request for a resource will also contain sufficient information (i.e., the client's reason for enqueing the lock) to execute the request on the server if the lock is contended. If the server chooses to execute the client's intent on its behalf, it may return a completion status without any lock, or a lock on a different resource than was originally requested.

Glimpse (trylock) requests and associated lock callbacks were added to provide a means of taking a transient snapshot of the object state (i.e., fetching the LVB) if it is currently locked by another client without forcing lock revocation. If the lock has not recently been used by the holder it will be scheduled for cancellation, and if the resource has no users, the lock is granted and its LVB is returned immediately.

Inode Bit (*IBITs*) locks were added to allow a single resource to have multiple attributes for the same lock. This allows finer-grained locking without increasing DLM RPC traffic. The attribute bits may be enqueued together or separately, though typically they are granted in a single lock for efficiency. Only in the face of contention are the lock bits granted separately.

The DLM is also used for locking the file system configuration data, block and inode quotas, as well as POSIX flock locking of files by applications.

8.2.4 Back-end Storage

The Lustre OSD is a Lustre-specific abstraction that provides object storage services using different types of persistent storage. The OSD has exclusive control over its underlying storage and handles all allocation and block metadata for it. This aids scalability by containing and distributing this overhead across the Lustre servers and also provides a layer of security against malicious or badly behaving clients compared to a shared-disk file system. Current Lustre OSDs are based on *ldiskfs*, a modified version of ext4 [10, 11] and ZFS [3].

The OSD implements a transactional data store for two types of objects. Data objects store byte-range extents, and index objects allow efficient access to key-value pairs. Objects are accessed by a file system–unique 128-bit File IDentifier (FID) that is composed of a 64-bit sequence number to locate the storage target, a 32-bit Object ID within the sequence, and a 32-bit version.

Both types of objects also have efficient storage for typical file attributes such as timestamps, ownership, size, and blocks, as well as named extended attributes for storage of more complex fields, though management of most of these attributes is done by layers above the OSD. Only block usage is managed directly by the OSD, since it allocates the space to store object data and attributes.

The OSD is responsible for the transactional consistency of its local storage, but it is free to cache object updates and aggregate these as they are committed asynchronously to disk with minimal dependency on the network protocol. Servers may therefore avoid all unnecessary synchronous disk operations since clients retain uncommitted transactions for replay in the event of server failure. The main requirement is that object transactions are committed in total order. This enables clients to track committed transactions using a single *last committed* transaction counter. The last committed transaction number is piggy-backed on all RPC replies so that clients can prune their replay buffers when transactions are eventually committed.

8.2.5 Metadata Server

Metadata Server (MDS) nodes export one or more Metadata Targets, each of which is stored on a single underlying OSD. The MDTs are typically stored on RAID 1+0 storage arrays that provide good random I/O performance, such as high-RPM disks or solid-state storage. The MDTs contains the application-visible file system namespace (filenames, directories), as well as file access (ownership, permissions, ACLs), file layout, and other attributes.

The MDS controls OST object selection and assignment to files for load balancing, unless specified directly by the client/application. In order to reduce latency at file open/create time, the MDS pre-allocates objects on each of the available OSTs and chooses objects from this pool when a new file is first opened. This also ensures that the file's layout can be created in a single local atomic transaction, which avoids a complex distributed operation for each file.

To allow tuning of a file layout optimally for application I/O patterns, it is possible to specify a different file layout (number of OST stripes, stripe size, OST storage pool) independently for each file. However, for simplicity it is possible to specify a default file layout for parent directories that is inherited by new files created therein.

After a file is opened, the MDS does not participate in client I/O operations until the file is closed again. To avoid repeatedly modifying the OST objects during read operations, a file's access time is cached in memory on the client inodes and OST objects. It is only written to disk on the MDS inode at close time.

When a file is unlinked from the MDT namespace, its inode and OST objects are may be destroyed only after the last process holding the file open exits or closes it. Lustre therefore keeps a persistent reference on the MDT inode until the last close in case the MDS restarts with open unlinked files. The object destroy RPCs are logged in the same transaction that removes the MDT inode, but only sent when that transaction commits to ensure that a rollback of the pending MDT unlink does not resurrect references to now-destroyed OST objects.

As with the OSS, the MDS has its own LDLM servers, one for each MDT that it services. Each inode can have one or more *IBITS* DLM locks associated with its resource. The lock bits are used to protect different aspects of the inode, such as its namespace lookup visibility (name, permission, owner, group,

ACLs), modification state (size, links, timestamps), open read/write/execute state, object layout, and extended attributes. For directories, it is also possible to lock individual entries in a directory using the hash of the filename as part of the DLM resource name, to allow concurrent lookup, insertion, and removal of entries in a directory.

The MDT lock server will typically grant all of the IBITS for a resource upon any enqueue request to reduce locking traffic, but will not grant bits for contended attributes unless explicitly requested. This allows clients to cache the lookup bit to do directory traversal, but the MDS can hold the update bit to allow file creation or deletion within the directory without contention on the lock bits.

The MDS makes heavy use of LDLM *intent* locking in order to reduce contention when many threads are creating files in a single directory. In the initial lock enqueue to open and create a file, the client will include the filename, FID, mode, permission, and other attributes with the initial lock request. The lock server on the MDS can then execute the create request on behalf of the client and return a lock on the FID associated with that filename (whether old or new) instead of a lock on the parent directory. This avoids two extra network round trips for enqueuing and canceling the parent directory lock, in favor of a short MDS-local locking of the parent directory.

8.2.6 Object Storage Server

OSSs export one or more OSTs, each of which is stored on a single underlying OSD. Each OSS typically attaches to a high-capacity RAID 6 storage array that normally provides between two and eight (or more) OSTs with tens of TB of capacity and hundreds of MB/s of bandwidth.

Each OST operates completely independent of other OSTs, and the OSTs are in fact totally unaware of other OSTs—there is no inter-OST communication. Since the OST object namespace is not hierarchical, there are no dependencies of any kind between objects. This ensures that bandwidth continues to scale linearly as OSTs are added.

OST objects are identified by a FID which remains constant for each object's lifetime. Zero-length OST objects are normally pre-created in batches on demand by the MDS to avoid latency during create to reduce MDS-OSS traffic and to simplify transactional consistency of OST object assignment. Upon first modification, the objects are labeled with their assigned parent MDT inode FID (for recovery and verification) and have their user and group ID set (for quota tracking).

Multiple clients may read and write the same object concurrently and each OST serves an LDLM namespace to resolve object access conflicts. Data and cache coherency for OST objects is managed by byte-range DLM *extent* locks for each object using the object FID as the lock resource. There may be multiple non-overlapping write extent locks for a single object, and multiple possibly overlapping read extent locks, or a combination of both read and write locks.

Object I/O is specified by a triple of FID, start offset, length both by clients and within the OST. The mapping from file extents to disk blocks is managed entirely in the OSD. The underlying blocksize used for a given object is therefore only relevant for I/O efficiency and accounting purposes. As data is written to an OST object, it grows in size like a regular data file and OST objects may be sparse for some or all of their lifetime depending on the I/O pattern of the application.

8.2.7   Management Server

The Management Server (MGS) stores and manages one or more file system-wide configurations for both the client and server nodes. Clients specify the MGS hostname (for TCP networks) or NID (for any network) as part of the mount device name in order to locate the MGS node, and the file system name (fsname) is used to locate the configuration log for that file system. The MGS typically stores its configuration logs and other state in a separate OSD device, but it may also share the MDT storage if required. The MGS also notifies clients of configuration changes and server restarts.

8.2.8   Client

The Lustre client is responsible for combining the data and index objects exported by the data and metadata storage targets that make up a cluster of Lustre servers into a single coherent POSIX-compliant file system. Since this aggregation is done at the client, and since extent metadata is handled locally by storage targets, non-contending data access at the POSIX level can be mapped to non-contending data access at the object level, leading to near-linear scaling of I/O performance.

The file system root FID is retrieved from MDT0 during mount. When looking up any filename, the client sends the MDS an RPC to get a lock on the parent directory. This request will either be a read lock with a lookup *intent*, or a write lock with a *create* intent, and includes the filename to be resolved. For create intents, the request will also contain a client-generated FID for the new file. Resolving the intent on the MDS allows it to avoid contention on the directory lock.

The MDS will resolve the lock intent locally, and instead return a DLM lock on the new or existing child object FID to the client, along with all of the metadata attributes and object layout (if a regular file). If the file was newly created, the MDS will allocate OST objects for the file layout at open time so that no further communication is needed with the MDS during I/O.

The file layout contains a data access pattern and the OST object FID(s), which allows the client to access the file data directly from the OSTs. Each file has a unique layout, and may be set by the user or application. The client is responsible to map the logical file offset for each I/O request to a specific OST object and its object-local offset. In the RAID 0 pattern, files with multiple objects are mapped in a round-robin fashion, and the size of each object is approximately the total file size modulo the number of objects.

Typically the file layout does not change during the file's lifetime. If this is necessary (e.g., to change the number of stripes or migrate it to different OSTs) the MDS can revoke the layout lock, which drops it from the clients' cache. The client will refetch the new layout from the MDS with a DLM lock request upon its next access.

In order to avoid a single point of contention during writes to a file with multiple OST objects, the object size and client-generated timestamps are stored with each write only on the OST object being modified. The aggregate file size and timestamp is only computed from the objects and layout as needed, such as stat or append operations. The MDT inode object stores the other attributes such as owner, group, permissions, ACLs, xattrs, etc. When combining the OST and MDT object attributes of a file for stat(), the object with the newest change time provides the access and data modification time.

Clients keep data and metadata DLM locks referenced only for the duration of a single system call. They cache unreferenced DLM locks in a variable- sized LRU list per target, that is managed in conjunction with hints from the lock servers. For as long as the locks are held by the client, it can cache data, attributes, ACLs, and directory contents. In the common use case of a single client performing uncontended reads or writes of a file, only a single-lock RPC is needed for all data access, since the server will return a full-object lock on the first enqueue. Similarly, when a client holds a directory-update lock, it can cache all of the directory entries locally for lookup, as well as cache negative entries for names that do *not* exist, until the directory lock is revoked.

Clients aggregate I/O in their local caches to ensure bulk data is streamed to or from the servers efficiently. On read, the client can detect strided read patterns and use this to guide readahead. Similarly on write, dirty pages are aggregated whenever possible. In both cases, many aggregated bulk data RPCs may be kept "on the wire" to hide latency and ensure full bandwidth utilization of the underlying networking and storage hardware and both the number of size of outstanding RPCs can be tuned e.g., to support remote mount over wide-area networks. The Lustre client also takes care to align these aggregated bulk RPCs at regular offsets and sizes to help servers maximize consistency between allocating writes and subsequent reads and reduce disk seeks, and also to align the disk I/O operations with the underlying RAID storage chunks.

In order to manage unwritten data in the clients' write-back cache, each client is given a *grant* of space from each OST. The grant space is consumed with each write request, and refilled with each write reply subject to availability of space on the OST. This ensures that the cached client writes cannot exceed the available space in the file system.

8.2.9   Recovery

Lustre exploits caches on both client and server to hide disk and network latency for performance-critical operations. Since failures can prevent these caches from being flushed, Lustre clients and storage targets retain stateful connections to ensure transactions that are completed but not yet committed at the storage target are replayed transparently in the event of server failure and subsequent restart or failover.

The client-side state contains a list of complete but uncommitted RPCs, ordered by the server's transaction sequence number, incomplete RPCs ordered by the client execution ID (XID), and locks held by the client at each storage target. When clients reconnect to the storage target after a service interruption, these RPCs and locks are replayed to complete recovery and allow the storage target to continue service. Storage targets also retain a list of currently connected clients in the `last_rcvd` file, and ensure this is persistent for newly connected clients before their first RPC that modifies data or metadata completes to ensure the target knows which clients may later need to participate in recovery.

When a storage target starts up, it notifies the MGS, which in turn notifies all clients that were connected to the last running instance of the storage target. In the event that the MGS is not present or unresponsive, clients discover this for themselves, albeit with substantially increased latency, by attempting to connect to all previously configured target NIDs in turn until successful.

The storage target then waits for all clients that were connected at the time of failure to reconnect, replay all uncommitted RPCs, and re-acquire in-use locks. Locks that are not currently protecting any cached state are dropped to reduce the time needed for lock recovery. Recovery time is bounded to ensure that unresponsive clients cannot hold up recovery indefinitely. A tighter bound is used when the MGS is able to assist with restart notification.

Executed but uncommitted RPC *replay* is then conducted in strict transaction order to ensure that transaction dependencies within and between clients are respected. Replayed RPCs may also include the versions (previous transaction numbers) of the objects they updated to allow consistent replay of isolated operations even if unrelated operations were lost due to concurrent client failure (causing a gap in the transaction sequence numbers).

Next, clients replay their held locks, which also recovers the state of open files on the MDS. Finally, clients *resend* incomplete RPCs in XID order. Since these RPCs may or may not have been committed by the server before the failure, the server guarantees idempotence by comparing the RPC XID against that stored for the client in the `last_rcvd` file to determine if this operation was previously committed. If so, the server does not execute the update and reconstructs the RPC reply message from data saved in the `last_rcvd` file.

Clients that do not participate in recovery in a timely manner are *evicted* from the server and their uncommitted operations are lost. Dependent operations executed by other clients (e.g., create within a directory created by the failing client) are also lost. This can be eliminated by enabling Commit-on-Share (COS), which flushes relevant uncommitted state at the server before a change of DLM lock ownership completes.

8.3 Deployment and Usage

Since Lustre is an open-source file system, it can run on a huge variety of different platforms. There is no vendor lock-in and storage purchases can be made to best suit the buyer's requirements and budget. Lustre therefore provides the foundation for a healthy ecosystem of key storage vendors including among others, DataDirect Networks, EMC, Hitachi Data Systems, NetApp and Xyratex. Such variety makes it hard to collect precise data about the number of deployments in production, but a conservative estimate would be in the thousands worldwide.

Many sites use Lustre as global storage, shared site-wide across multiple computing resources from supercomputers through visualization and analysis clusters down to individual workstations. Lustre routers provide the bridge between the HPC fabrics used internally within supercomputing clusters and the storage network—often Infiniband or high performance Ethernet—used site-wide. This eliminates the "islands of data" associated with previous HPC file systems and enables workflows to span all the computing resources at a site without having to copy data unnecessarily [2].

Lustre's origins from research funded by US government labs has meant that widespread use was first established in the research and academic sectors. They used Lustre primarily for checkpointing and to store simulation and modeling datasets. However, as the product has matured, a growing number of organizations in the private sector have adopted Lustre, particularly in genomics and in the oil and gas industry.

The oil and gas industry relies heavily on seismic data for the exploration and appraisal of new oil and gas reserves. Single datasets can stretch to hundreds of terabytes in size and require dedicated high performance computing resources for processing and interpretation. Lustre is attractive in this field since it is significantly speeding up the processing times, it presents a single global file system namespace, and additional storage can be added without needing to take the system out of service.

Large volumes of data are also a factor in geonomics. New improvements in laboratory technologies and processes continue to increase the demand at an astonishing rate. For example, the Sanger Institute reports that they produce ten thousand times the amount of sequencing data compared to five years ago, therefore the ability provided by Lustre to expand seamlessly, both in performance and capacity, to meet evolving capacity demands is crucial.

The majority of Lustre deployments are single-site, however a number of prominent Lustre users have deployed Lustre over wide-area networks (WAN) in order to share data between geographically distant locations. The Naval Research Laboratory [8] pioneered the deployment of Lustre using RDMA over WAN networks to create a globally accessible storage and compute cloud. Indiana University, funded by the National Science Foundation, created the "Data Capacitor"—a 535-TB Lustre file system connected to wide-area networks, first across 10 Gigabit connections [13], and most recently across 100 Gigabit connections [7]. The latest Data Capacitor (DC II) is 10 times larger and roughly 3 times faster than its predecessor and continues to run Lustre because of its speed and scalability.

8.4   Conclusion

The Lustre file system has grown from a DOE research initiative to become the extreme-scale HPC file system of choice. Large Lustre deployments have reported tens of thousands of clients, tens of petabytes of capacity, and sustained write/read speeds measured in terabytes per second. For example, the "Spider" file system deployed at ORNL has 26,000 clients [2]; the Sequoia system at LLNL has 55 PB of storage capacity [15]; and the Fujitsu K System has reported 1.2 TB/s sustained write and over 2.0 TB/s sustained read performance [16].

In response to the increasing momentum behind "big data" and especially a growing interest in MapReduce as a tool for analysis in the HPC community, a corresponding interest has developed in providing Hadoop runtime that can exploit Lustre storage effectively. In recent developments, a storage abstraction that allows Hadoop to use Lustre in place of HDFS has been shown to double I/O performance [9] while retaining the benefits of full POSIX access so that datasets can be analyzed in-site.

Lustre is also being used in the DOE Fast Forward Storage and I/O project to leverage research in Exascale storage systems [1]. These systems will push I/O scaling limits to the absolute extreme and require a drastic re-think of POSIX storage semantics. From a surface appearance, therefore, they will have very little in common with Lustre. However, distributed shared-nothing object storage will continue, as it is in Lustre today, to be a foundational system component. As the Fast Forward prototype evolves into tomorrow's production Exascale storage systems, this underlying architecture, including some of the actual source code, will be able to trace its roots back to Lustre.

Bibliography

[1] Fast Forward Storage and IO Program Documents. `https://wiki.hpdd.intel.com/display/PUB/Fast+Forward+Storage+and+IO+Program+Documents`.

[2] Spider Lustre File System a Trailblazer at OLCF. `http://computing.ornl.gov/SC10/documents/SC10\_Spider.pdf`, November 2010.

[3] Jeff Bonwick, Matt Ahrens, Val Henson, Mark Maybee, and Mark Shellenbaum. The Zettabyte File System. Technical report, Sun Microsystems, 2003.

[4] Peter J. Braam. The Lustre Storage Architecture. Technical report, Cluster File Systems, Inc., 2003.

[5] Ron Brightwell, Trammel Hudson, Rolf Riesen, and Arthur B. Maccabe. The Portals 3.0 Message Passing Interface Revision 1.1. Technical report, December 1999.

[6] Mike Feuerstein. Petascale Storage Solutions. `http://storageconference.org/2013/Presentations/Feuerstein1.pdf`, May 2013. 29th IEEE (MSST 2013) Conference on Massive Data Storage.

[7] Robert Henschel, Stephen Simms, David Hancock, Scott Michael, Tom Johnson, Nathan Heald, Donald Berry, Matt Allen, Richard Knepper, Matthew Davy, Matthew Link, Craig A Stewart, and Thomas William. Demonstrating Lustre over a 100-Gbps Wide Area Network of 3,500 km. *SC '12 Proceeding of the International Conference on High Performance Computing, Networking, Storage and Analysis*, November 2012.

[8] James B Hofmann and David McMillen. Use of Lustre in a WAN Environment. `http://wiki.lustre.org/images/3/3a/JamesHoffman.pdf`, April 2009. Lustre User Group 20009.

[9] Omkar Kulkarni. Hadoop MapReduce over Lustre. `http://www.opensfs.org/wp-content/uploads/2013/04/LUG2013_Hadoop-Lustre_OmkarKulkarni.pdf`, April 2013. Lustre User Group 2013.

[10] Avantika Mathur, Ming-Ming Cao, and Andreas Dilger. Ext4: The Next Generation of the ext3 File System. *login*, June 2007.

[11] Avantika Mathur, Mingming Cao, Suparna Bhattacharya, Andreas Dilger, Alex Tomas, and Laurent Vivier. The New ext4 Filesystem: Current Status and Future Plans. *Proceedings of the 2007 Ottawa Linux Symposium*, 2007.

[12] Philip Schwan. Lustre: Building a File System for 1,000-Node Clusters. *Proceedings of the 2003 Linux Symposium*, July 2003.

[13] Stephen C Simms, S. Teige, Bret Hammond, Yu Ma, Larry L. Simms, Gregory G. Pike, C. Westneat, and Douglas A. Balog. Empowering Distributed Workflow with the Data Capacitor: Maximizing Lustre Performance across the Wide Area Network. *Proceedings of the 2007 Workshop on Service-Oriented Computing Performance: Aspects, Issues and Approaches*, 2007.

[14] W. Snaman and D. Thiel. The VAX/VMS Distributed Lock Manager. *Digital Technical Journal*, September 1987.

[15] Marc Stearman. Installation of LLNL's Sequoia File System. `http://www.opensfs.org/wp-content/uploads/2011/11/Installation-of-LLNL\%E2\%80\%99s-Sequoia-File-System-Marc-Stearman-Lawrence-Livermore-National-Laboratory.pdf`, April 2012. Lustre User Group 2012.

[16] Shinji Sumimoto. FEFS* Performance Evaluation on K Computer and Fujitsu's Roadmap towards Lustre 2.x. `http://www.opensfs.org/wp-content/uploads/2013/04/LUG2013-FJ-20130410-final-1.pdf`, April 2013. Lustre User Group 2013.

Chapter 9

GPFS

Dean Hildebrand and Frank Schmuck

IBM Research

9.1   Motivation 107
9.2   Design and Architecture 108
    9.2.1   Shared Storage Model 108
    9.2.2   Design Overview 110
    9.2.3   Distributed Locking and Metadata Management 111
        9.2.3.1   The Distributed Lock Manager 111
        9.2.3.2   Metadata Management 112
        9.2.3.3   Concurrent Directory Updates 113
    9.2.4   Advanced Data Management 114
        9.2.4.1   GPFS Native RAID 114
        9.2.4.2   Information Lifecycle Management 114
        9.2.4.3   Wide-Area Caching and Replication 115
9.3   Deployment and Usage 116
    9.3.1   Usage Examples 117
9.4   Conclusion 117
    Bibliography 118

9.1   Motivation

The GPFS is IBM's parallel file system for high performance computing and data-intensive applications [7, 10]. GPFS is designed to enable seamless and efficient data sharing between nodes within and across small-to-large clusters using standard file system APIs and standard POSIX [1] semantics. At the same time, GPFS exploits the parallelism and redundancy available in a cluster to provide the large capacity, high performance, and high availability required by the most demanding scientific and commercial applications.

GPFS originates from an IBM research project in the early 1990s called TigerShark, which focused on high performance lossless streaming of multimedia video files [6]. It was subsequently extended to serve as a general-purpose file system for high performance computing applications on IBM's Scalable

POWERparallel Systems. In May 1998, IBM's Systems and Technology Group (STG) introduced the IBM GPFS software product.

Since then, GPFS has evolved to support heterogeneous clusters including AIX, Linux, and Windows systems, and serves an expanding and diverse range of applications. Over the years, GPFS has added advanced features and data management functions, such as snapshots and scalable backup, information lifecycle management, and data sharing across wide-area networks [7, 8]. GPFS continues to push the boundaries of reliable, efficient, and scalable parallel I/O performance.

9.2   Design and Architecture

9.2.1   Shared Storage Model

GPFS is a parallel file system based on a shared storage model. GPFS automatically distributes and manages files while providing a single consistent view of the file system to every node in the cluster. Processes running on different nodes in the cluster see the same directory structure and share access to the same set of files with the same semantics as if the processes were running on a single node.

A GPFS cluster consists of a set of file system nodes, on which applications run, connected to a shared storage system. All data, metadata, and recovery log information is therefore accessible by every node in the cluster. By convention, each device in the shared storage system is referred to as a "disk." In reality, while a "disk" may refer to a conventional magnetic disk, more commonly it is a storage controller volume, such as a small computer system interface logical unit number (SCSI LUN), SSD, or even a leading-edge non-volatile random-access memory (NVRAM) device. The same GPFS code is installed on all nodes in the cluster, consisting of an administrative system, to manage the cluster, a kernel module that implements the operating system–specific file system interface and handles most file system operations, and a daemon process that communicates with other nodes within the cluster to coordinate access to shared data and metadata and implements advanced data management functions.

A GPFS cluster can be configured in one of three typical models as illustrated in Figure 9.1.

The *Storage Area Network (SAN) model* uses two networks: a SCSI-based storage network for access to the shared storage system and a TCP/IP-based network for communication between nodes.

The *Network Shared Disk (NSD) server model* is more common in large clusters since it avoids the cost and administrative overhead of maintaining two separate networks. In this configuration, GPFS application nodes use the

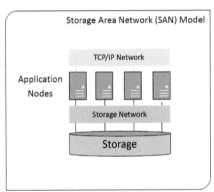
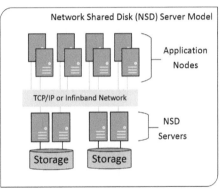
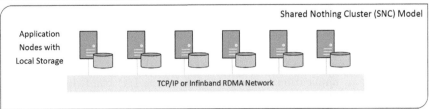

FIGURE 9.1: Three basic GPFS configuration examples: SAN, NSD, and SNC. It is also common to see a combination of these models deployed within a cluster.

GPFS NSD protocol, a block-I/O protocol that is built into GPFS and runs over the same network that is used for general inter-node communication, to access disks attached to a set of NSD servers. To avoid the loss of data access upon NSD server failure, each disk attaches to multiple NSD servers to provide redundant paths to the data.

The *Shared-Nothing Cluster (SNC) model* employs internal disks in each cluster application node. Data or metadata that are not available on the local GPFS node are accessed over the network using the GPFS NSD protocol. Unlike the NSD server model, data and metadata are replicated across local disks on multiple nodes to guarantee availability in case of node failures.

It is common to combine these different models within or across clusters. For example, an SNC configuration can use internal disks to store data and then use a set of dedicated NSD servers that include low latency storage devices such as SSDs for faster and more reliable metadata access. As another example, a SAN may be used for data access within a cluster, while sharing the data with other clusters (within or across data centers) over the NSD protocol via GPFS cross-cluster mounts [7, 8].

Nodes that are not part of a GPFS cluster can use the Network File System (NFS) protocol to access GPFS. In this configuration, some GPFS nodes are designated as Cluster NFS (CNFS) server nodes that export a file system to NFS clients. GPFS monitors NFS daemons and networking components on each CNFS node, and implements IP address takeover and NFS lock recovery to handle component failures by automatically redirecting NFS clients to another CNFS node. In all, these functions provide a scalable, highly available NFS solution.

9.2.2   Design Overview

This section provides a high-level overview of the methods GPFS uses to achieve highly scalable performance and high availability while supporting standard POSIX file system APIs.

The GPFS approach to scalability is to distribute everything—data and metadata—as evenly as possible across all available resources. This is called *wide striping*. Large files are divided into large, equal-sized blocks, and consecutive blocks are placed on different disks in a round-robin fashion. The block size is configurable and can be as large as 16 MB in order to take advantage of higher sequential data rates of individual disks or storage controller LUNs. Different nodes may read and write different parts of a large file concurrently. This allows an application to make full use of the I/O bandwidth of the underlying disk subsystem and interconnect, even when accessing only a single large file. Aggregating large numbers of physical disks into a single file system allows file system capacity and I/O bandwidth to scale with the cluster size.

GPFS optimizes the organization of data within and across blocks. For space efficiency, GPFS stores small files, as well as the data at the end of a large file, as fragments; which are allocated by dividing a full block into several smaller subblocks. With the GPFS file placement optimizer (FPO), the blocks are laid out to take advantage of storage and network topology [8]. For example, when FPO is deployed using the SNC model, data blocks of a file can be grouped into larger chunks, and each chunk is stored on disks attached to the same node. Analytic applications can then distribute their computation across the cluster so most data is read from local disks, thereby minimizing data transfer over the network [2].

GPFS uses *distributed locking* to synchronize access to data and metadata on a shared disk. This protects the consistency of file system structures in the presence of concurrent updates from multiple nodes and provides single system image semantics without a centralized server handling all metadata updates. It also allows each node to cache the data and metadata being accessed on that node while maintaining cache consistency between nodes. That means non-shared workloads can run with near-local file system performance because each node can independently read data and metadata of the files it accesses, cache data locally, and write updates directly back to disk. For shared workloads, GPFS optimizes locking granularity and metadata update algorithms to minimize interactions between nodes, so shared data can be read and written at maximum I/O bandwidth speeds.

For *high availability*, GPFS must allow uninterrupted file system access in the presence of node failures, disk failures, and system maintenance operations. Similar to other journaling file systems, GPFS records all metadata updates that affect file system consistency in a recovery log. There is a separate log for each node stored on the shared disks. When GPFS detects a node failure, using its internal heartbeat mechanism, a different cluster node reads and re-applies updates recorded in the failed node's log before locks that were held by the failed node are released. This guarantees that any metadata updated by the failed node is quickly restored to a consistent state and can then be accessed again by other nodes.

To protect against data loss or the unavailability of data due to failures in the disk subsystem, GPFS provides two options: use of RAID-based storage controllers together with redundant paths to disk, or replication at the file system level. As an alternative to traditional RAID controllers, GPFS also offers an advanced software RAID implementation integrated into the NSD server called *GPFS Native RAID* (GNR) [7, 8]. If file system replication is chosen, GPFS allocates and writes two or more copies of each data block and/or metadata object.

To avoid data being unavailable due to maintenance, GPFS supports on-line system management. This includes the ability to grow or shrink a file system by adding or removing disks and optionally rebalancing data and metadata in response to disk configuration changes while the file system is mounted. System software, including GPFS, can also be upgraded one node at a time without ever taking down the whole cluster.

9.2.3 Distributed Locking and Metadata Management

9.2.3.1 The Distributed Lock Manager

The GPFS distributed lock manager uses a collection of global lock managers running on a designated subset of nodes in the cluster, in conjunction with local lock managers in each file system node. For each file, directory, or other file system object, a hash of the object ID is used to select one of the global lock manager nodes to coordinate distributed locks for that object by handing out *lock tokens*. Once a node has obtained a token from the global lock manager responsible for the object, subsequent operations accessing the object on that node can lock the object locally, without requiring additional network communication. Additional network communication is only necessary when an operation on another node requires a conflicting lock on the same object.

Lock tokens also serve as the mechanism for maintaining cache consistency between nodes. A "read-only" token may be shared among nodes and allows each token holder to cache objects it has read from disk. An "exclusive-write" token may only be held by one node at a time and allows the node to modify the object in its cache. When a write token is revoked or downgraded to read-only mode, GPFS first waits for local locks to be released and commits local changes to disk before allowing the token to be granted to another node. This serializes reads and writes to support the POSIX semantic that ensures that readers always see the most recent updates. Furthermore, it provides proper failure semantics because it prevents updates seen on other nodes from suddenly disappearing if the node that last updated an object fails.

GPFS uses *byte-range locks* rather than whole-file locks to synchronize reads and writes to file data. These locks allow concurrent access to the same file from multiple nodes. The underlying byte-range tokens are negotiated dynamically based on the access pattern, as explained in greater detail by Schmuck et al. [10]. In the absence of concurrent write sharing, a byte-range token covering the whole file can be obtained in a single interaction with the token server for that file, and is therefore just as efficient as whole-file locking. Under concurrent write sharing, additional messages are required, but in a common case, where multiple nodes are writing sequentially to non-overlapping sections of the same file, all nodes can acquire the necessary tokens in a single round of token revokes during their first write to the file. Subsequent writes proceed without additional overhead for distributed locking.

For finer-grained sharing, such as small interleaved strided writes from multiple nodes, token traffic becomes more significant; and if sharing granularity drops below the disk sector size, lock conflicts due to false sharing are unavoidable. Therefore, applications that require fine-grain sharing typically use MPI-IO, or a similar application-level I/O library, to divide a file into a collection of large ranges, collect small updates to the same range on a single node, and then write those large ranges to the file system.

For database applications that do their own locking and buffering, GPFS supports direct-I/O mode, where read and write operations bypass distributed locking and caching in the file system. This allows database workloads to run at near raw disk speeds.

9.2.3.2 Metadata Management

Like other file systems, GPFS uses inodes and indirect blocks to record file attributes and data block addresses. Multiple nodes writing to the same file result in concurrent indirect block updates to store the addresses of newly allocated data blocks and concurrent inode updates to record changes to file size and modification time (mtime). Synchronizing these updates via exclusive write locks would result in a lock conflict on every write operation. Instead, one of the nodes accessing the file is designated as the *metanode* for the file, which is responsible for collecting indirect block updates and merging inode updates from other nodes and periodically writing them to disk.

To guarantee POSIX semantics in the presence of read/write sharing, write operations in GPFS use a shared-write lock on the inode, which allows concurrent file size and timestamp updates, but conflicts with operations that require exact file size and/or mtime. A stat() system call or a read operation that attempts to read past end-of-file, for example, revokes inode tokens from writers, prompting them to send their inode updates to the metanode. This guarantees that the reader is able to obtain accurate file size and mtime from the metanode. On the other hand, the common cases of reader-only readers, writer-only writers, or reads and updates within an existing file with no file size changes, can run concurrently without any inode lock conflicts. For applications that do not require accurate mtime, GPFS offers a "stat-lite" option that propagates mtime changes asynchronously and handles stat() calls without revoking inode tokens. This option is the default for access time (atime). Furthermore, in the common case of a single writer, the node writing to the file becomes the metanode for the file, and therefore incurs no additional overhead for sending metadata updates over the network.

When writing a new file or extending an existing file, each node independently allocates disk space for the data blocks it writes. For this purpose, byte-range tokens are rounded up to block boundaries, so only one node allocates storage for any particular data block. The block allocation map, which records the allocation status (free or in-use) of all disk blocks in the file system, is divided into a large, fixed number of separately lockable regions; and each region contains the allocation status of a fraction of the disk blocks on every disk in the file system. Hence, access to a single region with enough free space is sufficient for a node to properly stripe the files it writes across all disks. One of the nodes in the cluster acts as the *allocation manager*, which collects free space statistics about all allocation regions and provides hints about which region to try whenever a node runs out of disk space in the region it is currently using. To the extent possible, the allocation manager prevents lock conflicts between nodes by directing different nodes to different regions.

9.2.3.3 Concurrent Directory Updates

To support efficient lookups in very large directories, GPFS uses *extendible hashing* [5] to organize entries within a directory. The directory block that contains the entry for a particular file name can be found by hashing the name and using the n low-order bits of the hash value as the block number, where n depends on the size of the directory.

Handling directory updates in a cluster efficiently poses a challenge, because write sharing for directories is more common and much finer grained than for regular files. Each file create or delete operation updates a single entry in a directory block that can hold thousands of entries, and there is little locality because hashing randomizes the placement of directory entries. Hence, when concurrent directory updates are detected, GPFS switches to a finer-grained locking mode, where a directory operation locks the hash value of the file name being inserted or deleted instead of the directory block being updated. This allows creates and deletes of different files to proceed concurrently, even if the associated directory entries fall in the same directory block, while still properly synchronizing concurrent operations on the same file name. The metanode then collects the directory updates from multiple nodes and writes the modified directory blocks to disk.

The global lock manager handling the lock tokens for a directory monitors access patterns through the token requests it receives and dynamically adjusts the locking strategy accordingly. For directories that are only accessed by a single node, it grants a token that covers the whole directory, so subsequent operations within that directory incur no additional overhead for distributed locking.

9.2.4 Advanced Data Management

GPFS supports a wide range of standard and advanced file system features; three of these are described in more detail below. Other notable features include access control lists; extended attributes; immutability and append-only restrictions; quotas; snapshots of all or part of a file system, including individual files (clones); defragmentation; rebalancing; and online reconfiguration.

9.2.4.1 GPFS Native RAID

In addition to support for traditional RAID controllers, GPFS offers an advanced software RAID implementation integrated into the NSD server called *GPFS Native RAID (GNR)* [7, 8]). Using a conventional, dual-ported disk enclosure filled with disks in a JBOD (or "just a bunch of disks") configuration, GNR implements sophisticated data placement and error correction algorithms to deliver high levels of storage reliability, availability, and performance. GNR offers a variety of data protection techniques ranging from simple replication up to three fault-tolerant Reed–Solomon codes. It *declusters* data, parity and spare space across large numbers of disks to speed up rebuild times and minimize impact on the foreground workload during rebuild. Write version number tracking and end-to-end checksums allow it to detect and recover from silent disk errors, such as dropped writes or off-track writes, as well as network transport errors. A background scrubbing process verifies data/parity consistency and data checksums to detect and fix silent disk corruption or latent sector errors before additional errors might render them uncorrectable. GNR can also exploit NVRAM and twin-tailed SSD as a multi-level fast write cache for its own internal metadata updates and to speed up small writes.

9.2.4.2 Information Lifecycle Management

Applications have diverse reliability and performance demands of the datasets they access, and the storage requirements for a particular piece of data frequently changes over the lifetime of the data. To accommodate such applications efficiently and economically, GPFS supports powerful policy-driven automated storage management through *storage pools*, *filesets* and *user-defined policies* that match data to its most appropriate and cost-effective type of storage [8].

Storage pools allow partitioning a file system into collections of storage devices with similar properties that are managed together as a group. In addition to the *system pool*, which contains all metadata and possibly some of its data, a file system may have one or more *data pools*, which store file data as specified by user-defined policy rules. *External pools* allow the policy-driven migration of rarely accessed data to archival storage.

Filesets provide a way to partition the file system namespace to allow administrative operations at a finer granularity than that of the entire file system. For example, GPFS allows defining user and group quotas separately for each fileset: it allows creating snapshots of individual filesets instead of a whole file system, and it allows placing limits on the amount of disk space occupied by files in each fileset. Filesets also provide a convenient way to refer to a collection of files in policy rules.

The Information Lifecycle Management (ILM) policy language supports an SQL-like syntax for selecting files based on file attributes, such as its name, owner, file size, and time stamps, as well as custom extended attributes set by the user. GPFS distinguishes between *placement policies*, which are evaluated at file creation time and determine initial file placement and replication attributes of a file; and *management policies*, which are evaluated periodically or at a user's request and allow managing files during their lifecycle. A policy rule may change file replication; move files to another storage pool; delete files; or invoke an arbitrary, user-specified command on the selected list of files. Data migrated to external storage either via policy or a traditional external storage manager is recalled on demand using the standard Data Management API (DMAPI) [9].

9.2.4.3 Wide-Area Caching and Replication

Although it is possible to configure a GPFS cluster to span data center boundaries or use cross-cluster mounts to share data between clusters in different data centers, GPFS configurations work best over dedicated, high-bandwidth, low-latency connections, typically within a data center. Active file management (AFM) is a scalable, high performance caching layer integrated into GPFS that makes it possible to share data effectively across geographically distributed sites using networks with fluctuating latencies and even occasional outages [8, 4].

Data that reside in one cluster are cached on disk in one or more other local or remote clusters. Once cached, data from a remote cluster can be accessed with the same parallel I/O performance as local data and remain available during network outages (disconnected operation). Changes are written to local disk first then propagated asynchronously between clusters. Customizable propagation delays and rules for resolving conflicting updates originating in different clusters provide an *eventual consistency* model across clusters. Thus, AFM trades strict POSIX consistency across clusters for high performance access to remote data over unreliable networks.

To make optimum use of available network bandwidth, data may be transferred in parallel between multiple nodes and over multiple connections between clusters. For its data transport protocol, AFM can use the NSD and NFS protocols, allowing access to data that resides in both GPFS and non-GPFS file systems.

AFM has several data management features, such as pre-population of cache datasets prior to application execution. Further, consistency points across clusters can be taken through a feature called peer snapshots, which makes it possible to use AFM as an asynchronous replication engine for disaster recovery purposes.

9.3　Deployment and Usage

GPFS is deployed in thousands of data centers on hundreds of thousands of nodes. The largest installations contain thousands of nodes in up to sixty GPFS clusters and store petabytes of data, with many connected to an online tape system with an even greater capacity. Some of these systems transfer data at more than 400 GB/s and contain close to a billion files. Further, GPFS is the key storage technology in several IBM products, including IBM Scale Out Network Attached Storage (SONAS), DB2 Purescale, and IBM Linear Tape File System Enterprise Edition (LTFS-EE).

A typical HPC GPFS installation uses the NSD server model, which allows GPFS to scale beyond shared SCSI storage limitations and offers greater flexibility in the storage architecture. Existing clusters typically use 1 or 10 GigE networks between GPFS clients and NSD servers, but most newer clusters are deploying InfiniBand for reduced latency and higher throughput. With InfiniBand, GPFS clients utilize remote direct memory access (RDMA) to communicate with the NSD servers and use the native InfiniBand protocol for inter-client communication. In large deployments, which typically have many more GPFS clients than NSD servers, it is common to create a separate storage cluster of the NSD servers and one or more GPFS client clusters that use cross-cluster mounts to access data in the storage cluster. This configuration simplifies cluster management by allowing for the separate administration of storage and compute clusters and fine-grained access control across datasets.

GPFS configurations based on the SNC model are currently being deployed at several sites, either as a general cluster file system or as a scale-out data analytics solution.

While GPFS AFM was originally designed to facilitate wide-area caching, users have found new and unexpected use cases. These include scale-out application access to legacy NAS devices, asynchronous replication of data to allow for business continuity in case of a site failure, and construction of a global namespace among GPFS clusters in one or more data centers, providing global access to data at local network speeds.

GNR was first deployed on the IBM Power 775 server. Increasingly, more GNR deployments are appearing with IBM System x GPFS Storage Server (GSS), which is the first storage appliance that is designed specifically for GPFS [3].

9.3.1 Usage Examples

Two iconic examples of the many scientific and commercial application domains in which GPFS is used include weather modeling and digital media.

GPFS has a long history of working with the weather forecasting community around the world. Currently their performance requirements are typically not as extreme as some other HPC workloads, but their availability requirements are much higher—some systems are designed to not miss a forecast for several decades. To ensure applications can always retrieve and store their data, this requirement demands not just a stable file system code base, but the ability to seamlessly recover from failures and the ability to incrementally add compute power and storage capacity over time.

Media workloads have a lot in common with HPC workloads. High bandwidth requirements are combined with a rich, real-time, and heterogeneous workflow. A single project, such as commercial or film post-processing, consists of numerous teams, each working on different platforms and with different data requirements, to generate and share data. Furthermore, digital media is pushing the boundaries of modern data management as frame resolution, bit depth, and frame rate continue to increase.

In many GPFS media deployments, a single file system is accessed by applications running on Linux, Windows, and Mac OSX platforms from both Fibre Channel and Ethernet networks. Linux and Windows clients use the native GPFS client for high-bandwidth applications, and NFS/SMB for lower bandwidth applications. OSX clients use NFS to access file data through GPFS CNFS servers. Users make extensive use of filesets and ILM policies to scope projects and dynamically manage data placement in a tiered storage system.

9.4 Conclusion

For 15 years, GPFS has continued to grow and adapt to new application domains and cluster architectures. For most applications, the scale-out and distributed design allows GPFS to offer POSIX semantics with minimal, if any overhead. Further, GPFS has proven its ability to adapt to emerging application domains while innovating new features such as policy-based management, disaster recovery support, data tiering, global data caching, and much more.

There are still many ongoing challenges—adapting to new workloads, meeting ever-increasing performance requirements, and keeping up with emerging network and storage technologies remains a continuous challenge with every new GPFS release. Simplifying the management complexity of GPFS's rich set of features, many of which are targeted at a specific application domain, represents an opportunity for improvement. One goal is for GPFS to become a more dynamic, self-configuring, and self-tuning system that automatically adapts to the application workload and cluster architecture. Finally, some additional items that are under investigation include improved cloud and multi-tenancy support, seamless integration of SSDs and NVRAM in the storage hierarchy, file-level encryption and compression, and quality of service management for user applications as well as background file system processes.

Bibliography

[1] POSIX. http://standards.ieee.org/regauth/posix/.

[2] IBM Wins Supercomputing Storage Challenge with GPFS-SNC. http://www.networkcomputing.com/servers-storage/ibm-wins-supercomputing-storage-challeng/229500841, November 2010.

[3] IBM System x GPFS Storage Server. http://www.ibm.com/systems/x/hardware/highdensity/gpfsstorage/, April 2013.

[4] M. Eshel, R. Haskin, D. Hildebrand, M. Naik, F. Schmuck, and R. Tewari. Panache: A Parallel File System Cache for Global File Access. In *Proceedings of the 8th USENIX Conference on File and Storage Technologies*, 2010.

[5] R. Fagin, J. Nievergelt, N. Pippenger, and H. R. Strong. Extendible Hashing: Fast Access Method for Dynamic Files. *ACM Trans. Database Syst.*, 4(3):315–344, September 1979.

[6] R. L. Haskin and F. B. Schmuck. The TigerShark File System. In *Proceedings of the 41st IEEE International Computer Conference*, 1996.

[7] IBM. *General Parallel File System Version 3 Release 5.0.7 Administration and Programming Reference (SA23-2221-07)*, December 2012. http://publib.boulder.ibm.com/epubs/pdf/a2322217.pdf.

[8] IBM. *General Parallel File System Version 3 Release 5.0.7 Advanced Administration Guide, (SC23-5182-07)*, December 2012. http://publib.boulder.ibm.com/epubs/pdf/c2351827.pdf.

[9] IBM. *General Parallel File System Version 3 Release 5.0.7 Data Management API Guide (GA76-0414-07)*, December 2012. http://publib.boulder.ibm.com/epubs/pdf/a7604147.pdf.

[10] F. Schmuck and R. Haskin. GPFS: A Shared-Disk File System for Large Computing Clusters. In *Proceedings of the 1st USENIX Conference on File and Storage Technologies*, 2002.

Chapter 10

OrangeFS

Walt Ligon

Clemson University

Boyd Wilson

Omnibond, LLC

10.1	Motivation	120
	10.1.1 PVFS1	120
	10.1.2 PVFS2	121
	10.1.3 OrangeFS	121
10.2	Design and Architecture	121
	10.2.1 Overview	121
	10.2.2 OrangeFS Request Protocol	122
	10.2.3 File Structure Representation	122
	10.2.3.1 Trove	123
	10.2.4 Bulk Messaging Interface	123
	10.2.5 Flows	124
	10.2.6 Job Layer	124
	10.2.7 Request State Machines	124
	10.2.8 Distributed File Metadata	125
	10.2.9 Distributed Directory Entry Metadata	125
	10.2.10 Capability-Based Security	126
	10.2.11 Clients and Interfaces	126
	10.2.12 Features under Development	130
10.3	Deployment	131
	10.3.1 Cluster Shared Scratch	132
	10.3.2 Cluster Node Scratch	132
	10.3.3 Amazon Web Services	133
10.4	Conclusion	133
	Bibliography	133

10.1 Motivation

OrangeFS is the next evolution of the Parallel Virtual File System (PVFS), an open-source high performance cluster file system. OrangeFS delivers high performance parallel access for a wide array of applications ranging from engineering/scientific to advanced computing and emerging "big data" applications. The goals of OrangeFS are:

- Run at user level

- Allow parallel access to data and metadata

- Minimize bottlenecks that limit parallelism

- Provide a diverse set of client interfaces

OrangeFS can be run entirely at user level, or a small kernel module can be used to mount it like any other file system under Linux, Windows, and OSX for the use of standard programs and utilities. Data and metadata are transparently distributed across multiple servers and can be accessed in parallel by multiple clients. OrangeFS relaxes POSIX consistency semantics where necessary to eliminate bottlenecks while offering a global POSIX namespace. Client interfaces include mounting via the OS kernel, MPI-IO, Hadoop JNI Client, and WebDav support.

A large community contributes to ongoing OrangeFS development, including a staff of professional developers who support OrangeFS, improve stability and functionality for the base system, and develop new features and interfaces. Professional support, development, and documentation make OrangeFS a superior high performing open-source file system for a growing range of scientific, advanced computing, and "big data" applications.

10.1.1 PVFS1

PVFS1 was developed in 1993 for Parallel Virtual Machine (PVM) as part of a NASA grant. In 1994, the software was rewritten to use TCP/IP, targeted for a cluster of Digital Equipment Corp. Alpha workstations networked using switched FDDI, PVFS1 striped data across multiple servers and allowed I/O requests based on a file view that described a strided access pattern. Striping and file view were independent of common record size.

PVFS1 [4] was ported to Linux and featured on the first Beowulf computer at Goddard Space Flight Center [3]. In 1997 at a cluster meeting in Pasadena, California, the developing group agreed that PVFS should be released as an open-source package [5].

10.1.2   PVFS2

Development of PVFS2 began in 1999 and was completed by a team from Clemson University, ANL, and Ohio Supercomputer Center in 2003. The new design featured object servers, distributed metadata, views based on MPI, support for multiple network types, and a software architecture designed for easy experimentation and extensibility.

10.1.3   OrangeFS

OrangeFS builds on the solid PVFS2 modular foundation and includes advanced features like distributed directories and encryption-based security. Enhancements such as self-healing, fault acceptance, and redundancy capabilities will be part of v3. In 2011, Omnibond began offering commercial-grade support for OrangeFS and collaborates continuously with the community on work toward v3.

10.2   Design and Architecture

10.2.1   Overview

OrangeFS is designed around an object-based server. The server responds to requests that operate on objects known as "data-spaces." Collections of these objects are used to implement files, directories, and other file system structures by storing the data and metadata and provide access to these components. A client interface library works with the server to translate file system operations into the corresponding object manipulations. User interfaces further map these file system operations into familiar program APIs. A central design principle of OrangeFS is its management of asynchronous operations. The major internal interfaces are all non-blocking. For example, network interaction, rather than blocking `send` and `receive` operations, has non-blocking `post_send` and `post_receive` operations and `test` or `wait` to complete the posted operations. This structure is reflected throughout the code, particularly in the servers low-level I/O layers (BMI and Trove). OrangeFS servers do not share any state with each other or with clients. If a server crashes, another can be easily restarted in its place. Updates are performed without using locks. The common interface for all file system access is the system interface, which is designed around the Linux virtual file system (VFS) and other Unix-based operating systems and resembles the request protocol of NFS. Figure 10.1 shows the architecture of the OrangeFS server and client library (libpvfs2), mapping the system interface to the low-level storage calls (Trove layer). The various layers, their function, responsibility, and interaction are described below.

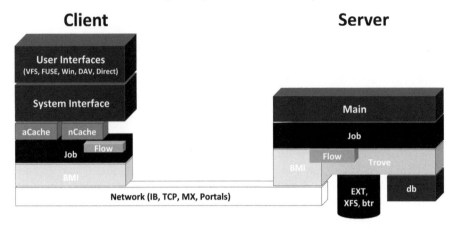

FIGURE 10.1: OrangeFS architecture. The client on the left translates user I/O calls into requests sent on the network to the server, which carries out the requests using Trove and sends a response back to the client.

10.2.2 OrangeFS Request Protocol

Everything in OrangeFS is based on a set of requests and responses between the OrangeFS client and server. These are grouped into strict request-response pairs, and the servers do not maintain state from one request to another. The requests are based on the system interface. Example requests include:

- create and remove

- lookup

- getattr and setattr

- io and smallio

These calls allow the client to manage and access objects on the server to implement file structures. Much of the code in the implementation is organized around the requests and responses for these operations.

10.2.3 File Structure Representation

Files in OrangeFS are represented by two or more objects stored on the servers. One object is known as the *metafile*, where most of the file's metadata is stored. (Although this sounds like a distinct file, it is just a type of object.) This includes traditional metadata such as owner, permissions, and user attributes, as well as OrangeFS specific metadata, such as the distribution method and list of data objects. In addition, one or more *datafile* objects contain the actual file contents. For small files, this may be a single datafile, and for larger files this may be as many as desired, up to the number of file servers in the system. The metafile contains a list of the datafiles for the file and a distribution method used to map logical file data to the datafiles. Directories have a similar structure with one *dirmetafile*, and one or more *dirdatafiles*. Dirdatafiles contain directory entries (*dirents*) with references to the metafile of each file in the directory. An extensible hashing scheme is used to locate dirents among the dirdatafiles. OrangeFS uses a database to hold attributes, leaving the management of *bytestreams* (the storage component of a datafile) to each node's local file system. After accessing the metadata server once for a file's location, an OrangeFS client can thereafter interface directly with the data servers, eliminating a major bottleneck.

10.2.3.1   Trove

Servers in the file system operate on objects through *Trove*. Trove is a software abstraction layer that implements dataspaces (or objects), provides a non-blocking interface to those objects, and serves as a means to manage multiple implementations of itself (optimized for different environments). Each Trove object has its own unique handle, a bytestream, and a set of key-value pairs. Every object within a given file system can be located using its handle. Bytestreams are sequences of bytes with an arbitrary length that generally store file data. Key-value pairs allow data to be stored and retrieved using a "key" and generally store attributes and other file metadata. Objects serve different purposes in the file system and may utilize the bytestream, the key/-value pairs, or both, as needed. Trove has a range of methods for accessing the different parts of an object. There are several implementations of the Trove methods, but currently, all of them implement bytestreams in a local file system (ext3 [9], xfs [10], zfs [8], etc.) and key-value pairs in a key value store (i.e., Berkeley DB [2]). Different implementations vary in how they manage concurrency and how they interact with storage. For example, the DirectIO method is optimized for use with servers that have large commercial RAID back-ends.

10.2.4   Bulk Messaging Interface

Both client and server communicate with each other over a local-area network. OrangeFS provides a bulk messaging interface (BMI) as a layer that provides a common interface for many different network fabrics and uses the post/test non-blocking model to allow the server to manage concurrency. Much like Trove, BMI defines a common interface and an internal set of methods that can be implemented by many different network substrates. To date there are BMI methods for TCP/IP, MX (Myrinet), IB (Infiniband), portals, and others. For those networks that provide a zero-copy interface, BMI allows OrangeFS to bypass kernel interaction where possible.

10.2.5 Flows

Flow is an important I/O mechanism that combines Trove and BMI for transporting large amounts of data from disk (via Trove) across the network (via BMI) to the client's memory (via BMI on the client) or vice versa. Flow works like software Direct Memory Access (DMA), so client and server can start a complex transfer and then simply allow it to complete. The alternative is to repeatedly interact with higher-layer code to start and complete each part of the transfer, which involves considerably more latency. Flows also utilize a protocol based on MPI's datatypes to implement non-contiguous data access on the server without constructing a distinct request for each part of the transfer. This involves using the file's distribution as well as the request description to manage data flows from each server to the client efficiently.

10.2.6 Job Layer

Each invocation of BMI, Trove, or the flow subsystem is considered a job. The job layer manages concurrent tasks and interfaces to the high-level code implemented in the state machines. The basic workflow involves a state machine running until it issues a job (asynchronously), at which point other state machines can run until the job completes and restarts the state machine. The code that implements and facilitates this interaction is the job layer.

10.2.7 Request State Machines

Both the server and the client library utilize state machines to implement the complex set of steps needed to start, complete, and finish a request/response between the client and server. On the server, whenever a request is received, its opcode is used to map the receiving state machine to the correct state machine for that request. Thus there is generally one state machine per request on the server. On the client, when an application calls a system interface function, it creates a state machine, which in its course will create one or more requests and then wait for the responses. Thus there is one state machine per system interface call. On each end there may be a few additional state machines for common operations and management function. A state machine is simply a collection of C-language functions, tied together by a set of data structures, that allows a program to execute one function at a time and then move on to the next depending on the return value of the function. A simple language is used to implement the state transition code. Multiple state machines can be executing concurrently, and the program can move back and forth between them in a manner similar to coroutines. Each state potentially issues an asynchronous operation via the job layer, and it will not execute until that task has returned. In this way, the code cleanly handles large amounts of concurrency without manual intervention by the programmer. This feature makes it very easy for users to modify the file system, even when adding new requests and developing new optimizations and interfaces, without needing to understand all of the operational details. Many features in the current code were developed for this level of usability. For example, large data transfers involve setting up a flow—a fairly complex process. Very small reads and writes could be performed without a flow—by simply including them in the request or response. Thus, a new request, SMALLIO, was developed to take advantage of this optimization. State machines are also important for maintenance and debugging. In many cases, problems can be found and fixed without debugging more than a small fraction of the code.

10.2.8 Distributed File Metadata

OrangeFS differs from many file systems in that it can distribute file metadata among multiple servers. Metadata for each file will be stored on a single server (often referred to as "the" metadata server, only with respect to a given file). The metadata for all files and directories is distributed among a designated set of servers using a random variable to select the metadata server each time a file is created. The configuration file allows as few as one server to be used for metadata, or as many as all of the servers. Metadata servers can also be data servers, or they can be used to store only metadata. The best configuration depends on the situation. When there are large numbers of users accessing a large number of smaller files, more metadata servers provide more parallelism. On the other hand, when servers are doing both data and metadata service, there is the potential for interference. In a situation where a few users are working with very large files, a single dedicated metadata server may be better. The cost of implementing the file server will also affect how they are configured. OrangeFS provides as many options as possible.

10.2.9 Distributed Directory Entry Metadata

One of the most recent additions released in OrangeFS v2.9 is distributed directories. In earlier versions, each directory is implemented as a single object that holds all directory entries on the same server as the directory metadata. Newer applications involve large numbers of processes that access an extremely large number of files. In this case, providing parallelism at the directory level allows more tasks to look up files at the same time. This is implemented by having multiple objects on different servers hold the directory entries. The various entries are assigned to one dirdatafile or another using a hash. This is further optimized by using extensible hashing based on Giga+ [6], which allows small directories to have just one dirdatafile and then add more dirdatafiles (and more parallelism) as the number of items in the directory grows.

10.2.10   Capability-Based Security

OrangeFS 2.9 and later provide three modes of system-wide security: default, key-based, and certificate-based. All modes use standard file ownership and permissions to control access to OrangeFS files and directories.

- *Default Security.* This was the sole security mode used in OrangeFS prior to v2.9. While it enforces standard file ownership and permissions, it was unable to prevent a number of simple attacks as it relied on the client library to provide the correct uid. It also was unable to prevent processes from snooping the network to acquire object handles which could be used to access data, circumventing the permission checks. The two following security modes were developed to provide much more robust protection.

- *Key-Based Security.* In key-based security mode, OrangeFS uses public key cryptography to authenticate client systems. Each OrangeFS server and client has a key pair (a public and a private key that are cryptographically related). A file used by the servers, known as the keystore, contains public keys for all servers and clients. Each server and client has its own private key which is kept secret. All keys and the keystore must be created together, and then copied to their appropriate locations. The keys and keystore are created in a temporary folder on the build system during the OrangeFS installation. When a client sends a request to the server, it submits a credential object signed by its private key. The server verifies the signature using the client's known public key.

- *Certificate-Based Security with LDAP.* In certificate-based security mode, all servers share a common CA (certificate authority) certificate with which all other certificates are associated. Figure 10.2 outlines the basic function of certificate-based security mode. Each OrangeFS user is assigned a unique certificate with an associated private key. The certificate is signed by the CA certificate and stored in the user's home directory. The subject of the user certificate is mapped to a Linux uid or gid by the server, using an LDAP (Lightweight Directory Access Protocol) directory. Each server knows where to reference the LDAP directory through an entry in the OrangeFS configuration file.

10.2.11   Clients and Interfaces

OrangeFS is architected to allow a variety of interfaces for client access. Figure 10.3 shows the seven interfaces currently supported. In some cases (such as the Direct Interface), there are actually several layers of user-level interface not shown in this diagram. There are experimental and under-development interfaces in addition to all of these.

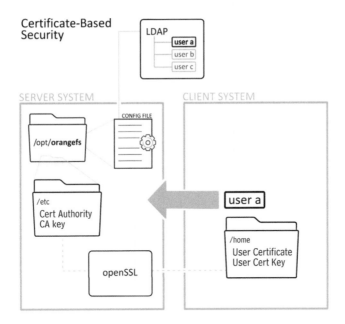

FIGURE 10.2: Certificate-based security. A client provides a user certificate to a server, which looks up the user via LDAP to obtain credentials.

- *Linux Kernel Module.* The most common OrangeFS interface, the Linux Kernel Module leverages the PVFS protocol to minimize metadata interactions and increase I/O throughput.

- *FUSE.* The OrangeFS client interface for FUSE enables access to an OrangeFS file system from a Mac.

- *MPI-IO.* The ROMIO implementation of MPI-IO includes support for OrangeFS, thus any MPI Library implementation that supports ROMIO (i.e., MPICH and Open MPI) also has support for OrangeFS via ROMIO. The MPI-IO interface bypasses the Linux kernel and provides access to MPI-IO features not supported by POSIX standard interfaces.

- *Direct Interface.* The Direct Interface allows user programs to directly call the OrangeFS client library. It bypasses the Linux kernel for a more efficient path to OrangeFS, providing high performance access for programs that are not written for MPI. This also allows access to file system features not supported by the kernel. The Direct Interface is actually three layered interfaces that can be used by programmers (see Figure 10.4). The top layer is the POSIX standard `stdio` interface including `fopen()`, `fread()`, etc. The next interface contains the POSIX standard system calls such as `open()`, and `write()`. The lower layer contains OrangeFS specific calls such as `pvfs_open()`, `pvfs_close()`.

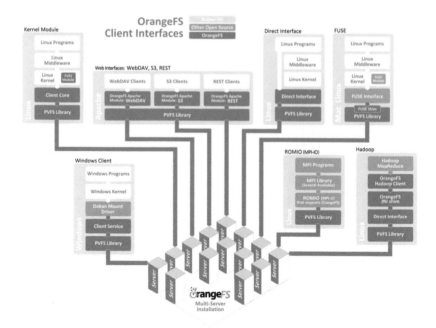

FIGURE 10.3: Clients and interfaces for various operating systems, operating environments, and development system.

There is an additional "iocommon" layer which can be used by system programmers to implement new interfaces using the facilities provided by the Direct Interface. This layer makes its calls directly to the OrangeFS system interface.

- *Windows.* The Windows client provides native parallel access to OrangeFS/PVFS2 file systems for desktops and servers using Microsoft Windows via standard parallel programming APIs. Options for authentication and user mapping include LDAP and X.509 certificates. The client, which runs as a standard Windows service, supports Windows Vista, Windows 7, Windows 8, and Windows Server 2008 R2 and 2012 (all editions); x86 and x64. The Windows client enables viewing files through Windows Explorer and the command prompt or accessing files programmatically through standard function calls, for example, `fopen()` in C programming. In testing, the Windows client performs nearly as fast as the Linux client.

- *WebDAV.* The OrangeFS Web Pack provides Direct WebDav support. It enables cross platform Web-based access to OrangeFS with more seamless upload and download operations on Mac and Windows clients. The

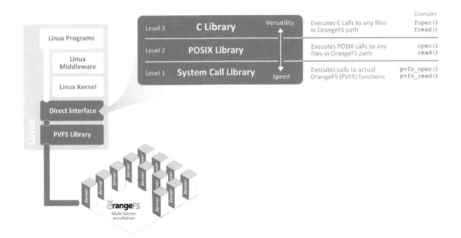

FIGURE 10.4: Direct interface showing the three user-level interface layers available to programmers. Upper layers provide compatibility with POSIX, lower layers provide non-standard features.

`libmod_dav_orangefs` module works with the Apache Web server and the standard WebDav module and the OrangeFS client.

- *Hadoop.* MapReduce can be run directly over OrangeFS using an extension of the MapReduce "FileSystem" class and a Java Native Interface (JNI) shim to the OrangeFS client. No modifications of Hadoop are required, and existing MapReduce jobs require no modification to utilize OrangeFS. With HDFS, clients and data servers are paired together, running on the same hardware. OrangeFS, as part of an HPC cluster, leverages an existing investment in HPC to run Hadoop MapReduce workloads. Tests running Hadoop MapReduce over OrangeFS have provided the following insights: MapReduce clients accessing a remote OrangeFS storage cluster yielded a 25% faster combined runtime than the traditional approach, where MapReduce clients access data locally for the three operations (`teragen`, `terasort`, and `teravalidate`). OrangeFS and HDFS, without replication enabled, performed similarly under identical local (traditional HDFS) configurations, (within 0.2%); however, OrangeFS adds the advantages of a general-purpose, scale-out file system. With a general-purpose file system, applications can read and write data to OrangeFS while it remains available for Hadoop MapReduce job input, improving runtime by eliminating time-consuming HDFS stage-in and stage-out operations.

Doubling the number of compute nodes accessing remote OrangeFS results in about a 300% improvement on terasort job runtime. OrangeFS provides good results when clients significantly overcommit storage servers.

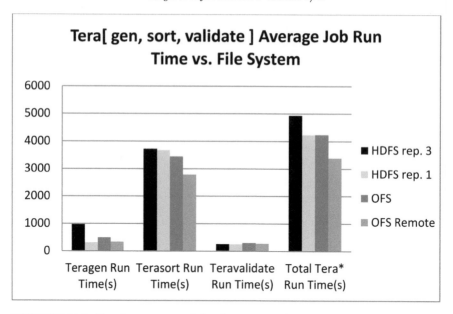

FIGURE 10.5: Tera[gen, sort, validate] average job runtime vs. file system. Using remote file servers, OrangeFS produces a clear performance improvement on the three terasort-related jobs.

10.2.12   Features under Development

Version 3 of OrangeFS is underway after a decade of development and support for v2. The primary goal for v3 is to support scaling to a much larger number of servers and clients, to support direct interaction of file systems at different locations, and to provide much richer management features for support personnel. Version 3 will support several key items:

- extensive and flexible replication of objects,

- hierarchical storage management,

- flexibility to add and remove servers as needed,

- using the metadata engine to reference remote objects, and

- a powerful asynchronous management tool framework.

These features all reflect the realization that the object handle model implemented in v2 is no longer adequate. Version 2 requires that each server and client is aware of every server in the file system, and exactly which objects are stored on each. This is accomplished by distributing a static configuration file to each client on start-up. Version 3 is changing this model. Each object no longer has a single copy. A specific server no longer has the object. Servers

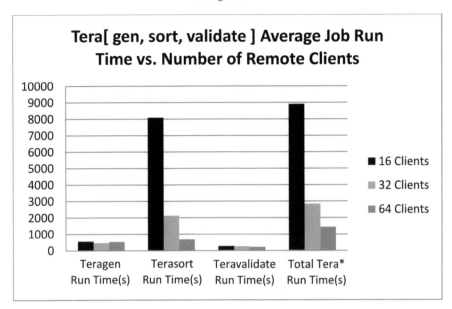

FIGURE 10.6: Tera[gen, sort, validate] average job runtime vs. number of remote clients. As the number of clients increases performance continues to scale even through the number of servers is fixed.

(and clients) need not contact other servers in order to create objects that will ultimately reside on another server. Servers (and clients) don't need to know about all of the servers, only the servers with which each interacts. The initial implementation of v3 uses universal unique identifiers (UUIDs [1]) as handles for objects. This way, whenever an object is created, its handle can be allocated without concern for its ultimate location. Later, a client or server can select one or more locations for the object and send copies to each one. The locations are recorded in metadata just as they are in v2. Servers also have a UUID, which is used to manage sets of known servers. Protocols are provided for locating nearby servers based on a variety of attributes. Still other protocols manage new servers and servers leaving service. Management routines perform scrubbing operations to maintain consistency, replication levels, and related operations.

10.3 Deployment

Easy to deploy and manage, OrangeFS builds out-of-the-box on a wide variety of Linux distributions and has only a few required dependencies.

OrangeFS builds and runs directly on a Linux installation and requires no kernel patches or specific kernel versions. It operates on a wide variety of systems, including IA32, IA64, Opteron, PowerPC, Alpha, and MIPS. It is easily integrated into local or shared storage configurations and provides support for high-end networking fabrics, such as Infiniband and Myrinet. OrangeFS is easily scalable, allowing the addition of storage servers as needed to provide both additional disk space and improved I/O performance [7]. Hardware failover provides invaluable services for large storage systems. Some installations want additional redundancy, and smaller installations want redundancy without the high cost of hardware solutions. OrangeFS is developing configurable redundancy and failover mechanisms as part of the file system. These allow different files to have different levels of redundancy as required by the application and also allow file system redundancy to be turned off for maximum performance. Currently, files marked immutable can be replicated.

10.3.1   Cluster Shared Scratch

OrangeFS is a highly efficient file system for scratch space, where it essentially provides a working directory for computations to read or write files that are too large for local storage. It is a temporary file system for actively running jobs. When used as shared scratch space, OrangeFS provides access to the same input files and a location to store intermediate and output files for all nodes involved in a computation job. Job workflow involves staging data into and out of the shared scratch file system to another location for permanent storage. For the many jobs that create a large amount of this temporary or intermediate data, a scratch file system can provide higher capacity than archived production file systems. OrangeFS supports Global Namespace, which provides a consistent file system view to all compute nodes, allowing multiple compute nodes to read and write to the same input and output files.

10.3.2   Cluster Node Scratch

Cross-node scratch space is similar to shared scratch space, only no permanent, system-wide OrangeFS file system is required. Instead, an OrangeFS file system is created only for the duration of a job. Part of the scripting for a cross-node scratch job includes setting up the file system. After nodes are allocated to the job, one or more is identified to run OrangeFS servers, where the server software is installed. Storage areas reside on local disks on the server nodes. Client software is installed on nodes used to access the file system. Typically, scripts perform cleanup functions at the end of a cross-node scratch space job. This would include steps to copy results from the temporary file system to permanent storage and tear down the temporary file system.

10.3.3 Amazon Web Services

OrangeFS now provides a scalable storage solution for cloud cluster computing on Amazon Web Services. Amazon Marketplace provides easy access to two options: OrangeFS High Performance Cloud Storage—Community and OrangeFS High Performance Cloud Storage—Advanced (provisioned IOPS). Both configurations come in 4-, 8- and 16-instance OrangeFS storage clusters that can be leveraged for various big data and HPC applications.

10.4 Conclusion

OrangeFS is an open-source high performance cluster file system. As the next evolution of PVFS, it continues the tradition of community development, user-level coding to make it easy to integrate and maintain, and high levels of parallelism in both data and metadata access. OrangeFS has worked to extend this to new application areas with a rich collection of user interfaces for different operating systems and development environments, improved security, professional documentation, better metadata parallelism, and the availability of commercial support. One of the most often cited features is how easy it is to obtain, build, and install OrangeFS. The design focuses on performance first, in some cases relaxing POSIX consistency semantics, but above all it is driven by users' needs. OrangeFS is maintained by a dedicated development team, and continues to be used extensively for research in universities due to its clean design and modular structure. The latest developments, Version 3, will extend OrangeFS into exascale with built-in replication, dynamic server management, support for remote sites, and policy-based distribution of data and metadata. OrangeFS remains one of the earliest community developed parallel file systems and a leader in bringing the latest technologies to bear.

Bibliography

[1] A Universally Unique Identifier (UUID) URN Namespace. RFC 4122, 2005.

[2] Michael A.Olson, Keith Bostic, and Margo I. Seltzer. Berkeley DB. In *USENIX Annual Technical Conference, FREENIX Track*, 1999.

[3] Donald Becker and Walter Ligon. Beowulf: Low-Cost Supercomputing Using Linux. *IEEE Software*, 16(1):79, 1999.

[4] III Ligon, W.B. and R.B. Ross. Implementation and Performance of a Parallel File System for High Performance Distributed Applications. In *Proceedings of 5th IEEE International Symposium on High Performance Distributed Computing*, pages 471–480, 1996.

[5] Walt Ligon and Rob Ross. Parallel I/O and the Parallel Virtual File System. In William Gropp, Ewing Lusk, and Thomas Sterling, editors, *Beowulf Cluster Computing with Linux, 2nd Edition*. MIT Press, Cambridge, 2003.

[6] Swapnil Patil and Garth A. Gibson. Scale and Concurrency of GIGA+: File System Directories with Millions of Files. In *Proceedings of FAST 2001*, volume 11, 2011.

[7] Scott Roberts. Next Generation Storage for the HLTCOE. Technical Report 9, Human Language Technology Center of Excellence, Johns Hopkins University, April 2013.

[8] Ohad Rodeh and Avi Teperman. ZFS: A Scalable Distributed File System Using Object Disks. In *Proceedings of the 20th IEEE/11th NASA Goddard Conference on Mass Storage Systems and Technologies (MSST 2003)*. IEEE, 2003.

[9] Stephen C. Tweedie. EXT3 Journaling File System. olstrans sourceforge net/release/OLS2000-ext3/OLS2000-ext3, 2000.

[10] Randolph Y. Wang and Thomas E. Anderson. xFS: A Wide Area Mass Storage File System. In *Proceedings of the Fourth IEEE Workshop on Workstation Operating Systems*, 1993.

Chapter 11

OneFS

Nick Kirsch

Isilon

11.1	Motivation	135
11.2	Design/Architecture	136
	11.2.1 Isilon Node	137
11.3	Network	138
	11.3.1 Back-End Network	138
	11.3.2 Front-End Network	138
	11.3.3 Complete Cluster View	139
11.4	OneFS Software Overview	139
	11.4.1 Operating System	139
	11.4.2 File System Structure	139
	11.4.3 Data Layout	141
11.5	Data Protection	142
	11.5.1 Power Loss	142
	11.5.2 Scalable Rebuild	142
	11.5.3 Virtual Hot Spare	143
	11.5.4 $N + M$ Data Protection	143
11.6	Dynamic Scale/Scale on Demand	145
	11.6.1 Performance and Capacity	145
11.7	Conclusion	147

11.1 Motivation

In 2000, seeing the challenges with traditional storage architectures, and the pace at which file-based data was increasing, the founders of Isilon began work on a revolutionary new storage architecture—the OneFS Operating System. The fundamental difference of EMC Isilon storage is that it uses intelligent software to scale data across vast quantities of commodity hardware, enabling explosive growth in performance and capacity. The three layers of the traditional storage model—file system, volume manager, and RAID—have evolved over time to suit the needs of small-scale storage architectures, but introduce significant complexity and are not well adapted to petabyte-scale systems. OneFS replaces all of these, providing a unifying clustered file system with built-in scalable data protection, and obviating the need for volume management. OneFS is a fundamental building block for scale-out infrastructures, allowing for massive scale and tremendous efficiency.

Crucially, OneFS is designed to scale not just in terms of machines, but also in manpower—allowing large-scale systems to be managed with a fraction of the personnel required for traditional storage systems. OneFS eliminates complexity and incorporates self-healing and self-managing functionality that dramatically reduces the burden of storage management. OneFS also incorporates parallelism at a very deep level of the operating system, such that virtually every key system service is distributed across multiple units of hardware. This allows OneFS to scale in virtually every dimension as the infrastructure is expanded, ensuring that what works today, will continue to work as the dataset grows.

OneFS is a fully symmetric file system with no single point of failure—taking advantage of clustering not just to scale performance and capacity, but also to allow for any-to-any failover and multiple levels of redundancy that go far beyond the capabilities of RAID. The trend for disk subsystems has been slowly increasing performance while rapidly increasing storage densities. OneFS responds to this reality by scaling the amount of redundancy as well as the speed of failure repair. This allows OneFS to grow to multi-petabyte scale while providing greater reliability than small, traditional storage systems.

Isilon scale-out network-attached storage (NAS) hardware provides the appliance on which OneFS executes. Hardware components are best-of-breed, but commodity-based—ensuring that Isilon hardware benefits from commodity hardware's ever-improving cost and efficiency curves. OneFS allows hardware to be incorporated or removed from the cluster at will and at any time, abstracting the data and applications away from the hardware. Data is given infinite longevity, protected from the vicissitudes of evolving hardware generations. The cost and pain of data migrations and hardware refreshes are eliminated.

OneFS is the ideal solution for "big data" and cloud applications, and is widely used in many industry solutions today, including energy, financial services, Internet and hosting services, HPC, business intelligence, engineering, manufacturing, media and entertainment, bioinformatics, and scientific research.

11.2   Design/Architecture

OneFS combines the three layers of traditional storage architectures—file system, volume manager, and RAID—into one unified software layer, creating a single intelligent distributed file system that runs on an Isilon storage cluster.

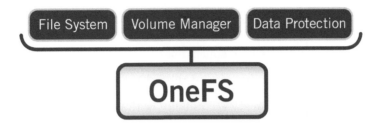

FIGURE 11.1: Notional diagram of OneFS distributed system. OneFS combines file system, volume manager, and RAID protection into one single intelligent, distributed system.

This is the core innovation that directly enables enterprises to successfully utilize the scale-out NAS in their environments today. It adheres to the key principles of scale-out; intelligent software, commodity hardware, and distributed architecture. OneFS is not only the operating system but also the underlying file system that drives and stores data in the Isilon scale-out NAS cluster.

11.2.1 Isilon Node

OneFS works exclusively with the Isilon scale-out NAS nodes, referred to as a "cluster." A single Isilon cluster consists of multiple "nodes," which are constructed as rack-mountable enterprise appliances containing: memory, CPU, networking, non-volatile random-access memory (NVRAM), low-latency Infiniband interconnects, disk controllers, and storage media. Each node in the distributed cluster thus has compute or processing capabilities, as well as storage or capacity capabilities.

An Isilon cluster starts with as few as three nodes and can scale to 144 nodes. There are many different types of nodes, all of which can be incorporated into a single cluster where different nodes provide different ratios of capacity to throughput or I/O operations per second (IOPS).

OneFS has no built-in limitation in terms of the number of nodes that can be included in a single system. Each node added to a cluster increases aggregate disk, cache, CPU, and network capacity. OneFS leverages each of the hardware building blocks, so that the whole becomes greater than the sum of the parts. The RAM is grouped together into a single coherent cache, allowing I/O on any part of the cluster to benefit from data cached anywhere. NVRAM is grouped together to allow for high-throughput writes that are safe across power failures. Spindles and CPU are combined to increase throughput, capacity, and IOPS as the cluster grows, for access to one file or for multiple files. A cluster's storage capacity can range from a minimum of 18 TB to a maximum of 20.7 PB. The maximum capacity will continue to increase as disk drives continue to get denser. The available nodes today are broken into several classes, according to their functionality:

- *S-Series*: IOPS-intensive applications,

- *X-Series*: high-concurrency and throughput-driven workflows,

- *NL-Series*: near-primary accessibility, with near-tape value,

- *Performance Accelerator*: independent scaling for ultimate performance,

- *Backup Accelerator*: high-speed and scalable backup and restore solution, and

- *EX Capacity Extension*: independent scaling of capacity.

11.3   Network

There are two types of networks associated with a cluster: internal and external.

11.3.1   Back-End Network

All intra-node communication in a cluster is performed using a propriety, unicast (node-to-node) protocol. Communication occurs using an extremely fast low-latency, Infiniband network. This back-end network, which is configured with redundant switches for high availability, acts as the backplane for the cluster, enabling each node to act as a contributor in the cluster and isolating node-to-node communication to a private, high-speed, low-latency network. This back-end network utilizes IP over Infiniband (also called IPoIB or IP over IB) for node-to-node communication.

11.3.2   Front-End Network

Clients connect to the cluster using Ethernet connections (1 GigE or 10 GigE) that are available on all nodes. Because each node provides its own Ethernet ports, the amount of network bandwidth available to the cluster scales linearly with performance and capacity. The Isilon cluster supports standard network communication protocols to a customer network, including NFS, CIFS, HTTP, iSCSI, and FTP.

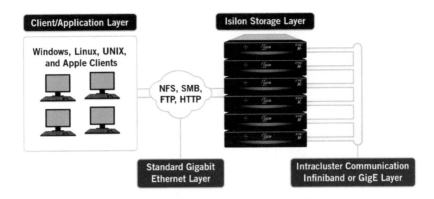

FIGURE 11.2: Depicts the complete architecture; software, hardware, and network all working together in the environment.

11.3.3 Complete Cluster View

The complete cluster is combined with hardware, software, networks, as shown in Figure 11.2. It depicts the complete architecture; software, hardware, and network all working together in the environment with servers to provide a completely distributed single file system that can scale dynamically as workloads and capacity needs or throughput needs change in a scale-out environment.

11.4 OneFS Software Overview

11.4.1 Operating System

OneFS is built on a BSD-based operating system foundation. It supports both UNIX and Windows semantics natively, including hard links, delete-on-close, atomic rename, access control lists (ACLs), and extended attributes. It uses BSD as its base operating system because it is a mature and proven operating system and the open-source community can be leveraged for innovation.

11.4.2 File System Structure

The OneFS file system is based on UFS and, hence, is a very fast, distributed file system. Each cluster creates a single namespace and file system. This means that the file system is distributed across all nodes in the cluster and is accessible by clients connecting to any node in the cluster. There is no

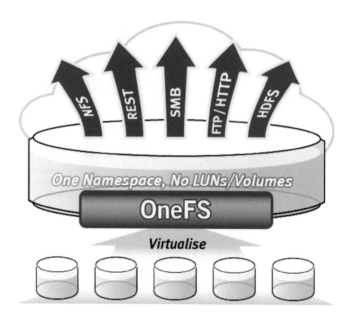

FIGURE 11.3: Single file system starting at the root inode `/ifs`.

partitioning, and no need for volume creation. Instead of limiting access to free space and to non-authorized files at the physical volume level, OneFS provides for the same functionality in software via share and file permissions, and via the SmartQuotas service, which provides directory-level quota management.

Because all information is shared among nodes across the internal network, data can be written to or read from any node, thus optimizing performance when multiple users are concurrently reading and writing to the same set of data.

Figure 11.3 illustrates that OneFS is truly a single file system with one namespace. Data and metadata are striped across the nodes for redundancy and availability. The storage has been completely virtualized for the users and administrator. The file tree can grow organically without requiring planning or oversight about how the tree grows or how users use it. No special thought has to be applied by the administrator about tiering files to the appropriate disk, because SmartPools will handle that automatically without disrupting the single tree. No special consideration needs to be given to how one might replicate such a large tree, because the SyncIQ service automatically parallelizes the transfer of the file tree to one or more alternate clusters, without regard to the shape or depth of the file tree.

This design should be compared with namespace aggregation, which is a commonly used technology to make traditional NAS "appear" to have a single namespace. With namespace aggregation, files still have to be managed in separate volumes, but a simple "vaneer" layer allows for individual directories in volumes to be "glued" to a "top-level" tree via symbolic links. In that model, LUNs and volumes, as well as volume limits, are still present. Files have to be manually moved from volume to volume in order to load-balance. The administrator has to be careful about how the tree is laid out. Tiering is far from seamless and requires significant and continual intervention. Failover requires mirroring files between volumes, driving down efficiency and ramping up purchase cost, power, and cooling. Overall, the administrator burden when using namespace aggregation is higher than it is for a simple traditional NAS device. This prevents such infrastructures from growing very large.

11.4.3   Data Layout

OneFS uses physical pointers and extents for metadata and stores file and directory metadata in inodes. B-trees are used extensively in the file system, allowing scalability to billions of objects and near-instant lookups of data or metadata. OneFS is a completely symmetric, and highly distributed file system. Data and metadata are always redundant across multiple hardware devices. Data is protected using erasure coding across the nodes in the cluster. This creates a cluster that has high efficiency, allowing up to 80% raw-to-usable data on clusters of five nodes or more. Metadata (which makes up generally less than 1% of the system) is mirrored in the cluster for performance and availability. As OneFS is not reliant on RAID, the amount of redundancy is selectable by the administrator, at the file or directory level beyond the defaults of the cluster. Metadata access and locking tasks are managed by all nodes collectively and equally in a peer-to-peer architecture. This symmetry is key to the simplicity and resiliency of the architecture. There is no single metadata server, lock manager, or gateway node.

Because OneFS must access blocks from several devices simultaneously, the addressing scheme used for data and metadata is indexed at the physical level by a tuple of {node, drive, offset}. For example, if 12345 was a block address for a block that lived on disk 2 of node 3, then it would read, 3,2,12345. All metadata within the cluster is multiply mirrored for data protection, at least to the level of redundancy of the associated file. For example, if a file were at an erasure-code protection of "$N + 2$," implying the file could withstand two simultaneous failures, then all metadata needed to access that file would be $3\times$ mirrored, so it too could withstand two failures. The file system inherently allows for any structure to use any and all blocks on any nodes in the cluster.

Other storage systems send data through RAID and volume management layers, introducing inefficiencies in data layout and providing non-optimized block access. Isilon's OneFS controls the placement of files directly, down to the sector level on any drive anywhere in the cluster. This allows for optimized data placement and I/O patterns and avoids unnecessary read-modify-write operations. By laying data on disks in a file-by-file manner, OneFS is able to flexibly control the type of striping as well as the redundancy level of the storage system at the system, directory, and even file levels. Traditional storage systems would require that an entire RAID volume be dedicated to a particular performance type and protection setting. For example, a set of disks might be arranged in a RAID 1+0 protection for a database. This makes it difficult to optimize spindle use over the entire storage estate (since idle spindles cannot be borrowed) and also leads to inflexible designs that do not adapt with the business requirement. OneFS allows for individual tuning and flexible changes at any time, fully online. In 2013, the most current version of OneFS was 6.5.4.

11.5 Data Protection

11.5.1 Power Loss

A file system journal, which stores information about changes to the file system, is designed to enable fast, consistent recoveries after system failures or crashes, such as power loss. The file system replays the journal entries after a node or cluster recovers from a power loss or other outage. Without a journal, a file system would need to examine and review every potential change individually after a failure (an `fsck` or `chkdsk` operation); in a large file system, this operation can take a long time.

OneFS is a journaled file system in which each node contains a battery-backed NVRAM card used for journaling. The NVRAM card battery charge lasts many days without requiring a recharge. When a node boots up, it checks its journal and selectively replays transactions to disk where the journaling system deems it necessary. OneFS will mount only if it can guarantee that all transactions not already in the system have been recorded. For example, if proper shutdown procedures were not followed, and the NVRAM battery discharged, transactions might have been lost; to prevent any potential problems, the node will not mount the file system.

11.5.2 Scalable Rebuild

OneFS does not rely on hardware RAID either for data allocation, or for reconstruction of data after failures. Instead OneFS manages protection of file data directly, and when a failure occurs, it rebuilds data in a parallelized fashion. OneFS is able to determine which files are affected by a failure in constant time, by reading inode data linearly, directly off disk. The set of affected files are assigned to a set of worker threads that are distributed among the cluster nodes by the job engine. The worker nodes repair the files in parallel. This implies that as cluster size increases, the time to rebuild from failures decreases. This has an enormous efficiency advantage in maintaining the resiliency of clusters as their size increases.

11.5.3   Virtual Hot Spare

Most traditional storage systems based on RAID require the provisioning of one or more "hot spare" drives to allow independent recovery of failed drives. The hot spare drive replaces the failed drive in a RAID set. If these hot spares are not themselves replaced before more failures appear, the system risks a catastrophic data loss. OneFS avoids the use of hot spare drives, and simply borrows from the available free space in the system in order to recover from failures; this technique is called virtual hot spare. In doing so, OneFS allows the cluster to be fully self-healing, without human intervention. The administrator can create a virtual hot spare reserve, allowing for a guarantee that the system can self-heal despite ongoing writes by users.

11.5.4 $N + M$ Data Protection

The Isilon cluster is designed to tolerate one or more simultaneous component failures without preventing the cluster from serving data. The Isilon system can use either a Reed–Solomon error correction ($N + M$ protection) system, or a mirroring system for files. Data protection is applied at the file level, and not the system level, enabling the system to focus on recovering only those files that are compromised by a failure rather than having to check and repair the entire file set. Metadata and inodes are protected at least at the same level of protection as the data they reference. Metadata and inodes are always protected by mirroring, rather than Reed–Solomon coding.

Because all data, metadata, and parity information are distributed across the nodes of the cluster, the Isilon cluster does not require a dedicated parity node or drive, or a dedicated device or set of devices to manage metadata. This ensures that no one node can become a single point of failure. All nodes share equally in the tasks to be performed, providing perfect symmetry and load balancing in a peer-to-peer architecture.

The Isilon system provides several levels of configurable data protection settings, which can be modified at any time without needing to take the cluster or file system offline.

For a file protected with erasure codes, each of its protection groups is protected at a level of $N + Mb$, where $N > M$ and $M \geq b$. The values N and M represent, respectively, the number of drives used for data and for erasure codes within the protection group. The value of b relates to the number of data stripes used to lay out that protection group, and is covered below. A common and easily understood case is where $b = 1$, implying that a protection group incorporates N drives worth of data; M drives worth of redundancy, stored in erasure codes; and that the protection group should be laid out over exactly one stripe across a set of nodes. This implies that M members of the protection

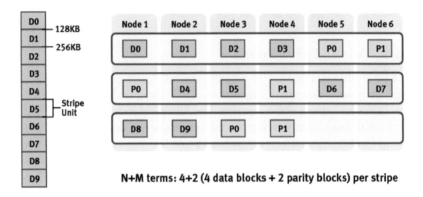

<figure>

N+M terms: 4+2 (4 data blocks + 2 parity blocks) per stripe

FIGURE 11.4: Data and parity in $N + M$ protect.
</figure>

group can fail simultaneously and still provide 100% data availability. The M erasure code members are computed from the N data members. Figure 11.4 shows the case for a regular $4 + 2$ protection group ($N = 4$, $M = 2$, $b = 1$).

Because OneFS stripes files across nodes, this implies that files striped at $N+M$ can withstand M simultaneous node failures without loss of availability. OneFS therefore provides resiliency across any type of failure, whether it be to a drive, a node, or a component within a node (say, a card). Furthermore, a node counts as a single failure, regardless of the number or type of components that fail within it. Therefore, if five drives fail in a node, that still only counts as a single failure for the purposes of $N + M$ protection.

OneFS can uniquely provide a variable level of M, up to four, providing for quadruple-failure protection. This goes far beyond the maximum level of RAID commonly in use today, which is the double-failure protection of RAID 6. Because the reliability of the storage increases geometrically with this amount of redundancy, $N + 4$ protection can be hundreds or thousands of times more reliable than traditional RAID 6. This added protection means that large Serial AT Attachment (SATA) drives, such as 3 and 4 TB, can be added with ease.

Smaller clusters can be protected with $N + 1$ protection, but this implies that while a single drive or node could be recovered, two drives to two different nodes could not. Drive failures are orders of magnitude more likely than node failures. For clusters with large drives, it is desirable to provide protection for multiple drive failures, though single-node recoverability is acceptable. Fortunately, this can be provided very efficiently on disk by using a value of $b > 1$.

To provide for a situation where double-disk redundancy and single-node redundancy is desired, one can set $M = b = 2$. Instead of creating protection groups of $N + M$ members, "double-length" protection groups are built up of size $N' + M$ where $N' = 2N + M$. These double-length protection groups will "wrap" once over the same set of nodes, as they are laid out. Clearly, since each protection group contains exactly two disks' worth of redundancy ($M = 2$), this mechanism will allow for the double-drive failure. When a node fails, it causes two erasures in the protection group, but again $M = 2$ will provide double-disk redundancy.

Most important for small clusters, this method of striping is highly efficient, with an on-disk efficiency of $1 - Mb(N + M)$. For example, on a cluster of five nodes with double-failure protection, were one to use $N = 3$, $M = 2$, and $b = 1$, one would obtain a 3+2 protection group with an efficiency of $1 - \frac{2}{5}$ or 60%. Using the same 5-node cluster but with each protection group laid out over $b = 2$ stripes, we could obtain $1 - 22(3+2)$ or 80% efficiency on disk, retaining the double-drive failure protection and sacrificing only double-node failure protection.

OneFS supports erasure code protection levels of $N + 1$, $N + 2$, $N + 3$, and $N + 4$ (all $b = 1$), as well as $N + 2 : 1$ (double-drive and single-node tolerant, $b = 2$) and $N + 3 : 1$ (triple-drive and single-node tolerant, $b = 3$), as well as mirroring levels between 2× (twice mirrored) and 8× (eight-times mirrored). Protection levels can be applied to individual files, directories, and their contents; or the entire system.

OneFS enables an administrator to modify the protection policy in real time, while clients are attached and are reading and writing data. Note that increasing a cluster's protection level may increase the amount of space consumed by the data on the cluster.

11.6 Dynamic Scale/Scale on Demand

11.6.1 Performance and Capacity

In contrast to traditional storage systems that must "scale up" when additional performance or capacity is needed, OneFS enables an Isilon storage system to "scale out," seamlessly increasing the existing file system or volume into petabytes of capacity while increasing performance in tandem in a linear fashion.

Adding capacity and performance capabilities to an Isilon cluster is significantly easier than with other storage systems—requiring only three simple steps for the storage administrator: adding another node into the rack, attaching the node to the Infiniband network, and instructing the cluster to add the additional node. The new node provides additional capacity and performance since each node includes CPU, memory, cache, network, NVRAM, and I/O control pathways.

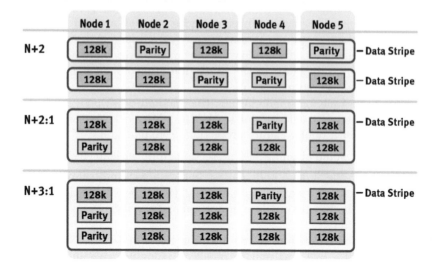

FIGURE 11.5 (See color insert): OneFS hybrid parity protection schemes $(N + M : x)$.

The Autobalance feature of OneFS will automatically move data across the Infiniband network in an automatic, coherent manner so existing data that resides on the cluster moves onto this new storage node. This automatic rebalancing ensures the new node will not become a hot spot for new data and that existing data is able to gain the benefits of a more powerful storage system. The Autobalance feature of OneFS is also completely transparent to the end user and can be adjusted to minimize impact on high performance workloads. This capability alone allows OneFS to scale transparently, on-the-fly, from 18 TB up to 20.7 PB with no added management time for the administrator, nor increased complexity within the storage system.

A large-scale storage system must provide the performance required for a variety of workflows, whether they are sequential, concurrent, or random. Different workflows will exist between applications and within individual applications. OneFS provides for all of these needs simultaneously with intelligent software. More importantly, with OneFS, throughput and IOPS scale linearly with the number of nodes present in a single system. Due to balanced data distribution, automatic rebalancing, and distributed processing, OneFS is able to leverage additional CPUs, network ports, and memory as the system scales.

11.7   Conclusion

With OneFS, organizations and administrators can scale from 18 TB to 20.7 PB within a single file system, single volume, with a single point of administration. OneFS delivers high performance, high throughput, or both, without adding management complexity.

Next-generation data centers must be built for sustainable scalability. They will harness the power of automation, leverage the commoditization of hardware, ensure the full consumption of the network fabric, and provide maximum flexibility for organizations intent on satisfying an ever-changing set of requirements. OneFS is the next-generation file system designed to meet these challenges. OneFS provides:

- fully distributed single file system,

- high performance, fully symmetric cluster,

- file striping across all nodes in a cluster,

- automated software to eliminate complexity,

- dynamic content balancing,

- flexible data protection,

- high availability, and

- web-based and command-line administration.

Part III

I/O Libraries

Chapter 12

I/O Libraries: Past, Present and Future

Mike Folk

The HDF Group

12.1   Motivation 151
12.2   A Recent History of I/O Libraries, by Example 152
12.3   What Is the Future of I/O Libraries? 153

12.1   Motivation

Why do we need an I/O stack? What is the importance of various layers in the stack? Why do we need I/O libraries?

There was a time when computers mostly exported data to magnetic tape or punch cards. I/O was pretty simple in those days, but there were still important principles a programmer needed to think about in order to read, write and store data efficiently. Instead of writing a byte of time, programs would *aggregate* data into fields, records, or collections of records. By exploiting redundance, programmers used *data compression* in order to write it more quickly and store it more efficiently.

Computer users also discovered that a little extra information, like an *index* or *tree structure*, could enable users to find things more quickly, and to add and delete items from a collection of records more quickly. They also found that a data file could itself be broken into *chunks*, *subfiles*, and other organizations to provide faster I/O, including easier search and retrieval of information, and partial access.

Because there were enormous differences between the time it took to move data within memory and to move data from memory to secondary storage, experts allocated space in memory to serve as *buffers*, allowing computation to continue at the same time that the slower I/O process completed.

Special commands and subroutines were added to programming languages that could *hide the details* of writing data and reading data, so that programmers didn't have to bother with those details. And when spinning disks arrived, those commands and subroutines were modified to take advantage of the new technology. Spinning disks also offered new opportunities for direct access, and *B-trees and other structures* were invented that made searching, sampling, and subsetting much easier and faster.

As systems evolved, people employed combinations of these techniques, mixing and matching particular methods in ways that worked best for the architecture on which a system resided, and for the applications most likely to run on the system. In many cases these combinations were provided as different software layers. One layer might aggregate a collection of data elements into a buffer, another might compress the data, and another might write it out in a certain format. The same package might use the same steps in reverse to read the data. Thus, perhaps, emerged the idea of the *I/O stack*.

Over time, software packages were created that included some of these combinations. As often as not, they were motivated by application developers who didn't want to be bothered with such details, but did want to get as good performance as they could on their systems. These solutions were made available in the form of *I/O libraries*.

12.2   A Recent History of I/O Libraries, by Example

What you will read in the next six chapters is a snapshot covering the last two decades in the history of I/O and high-end computing systems. These I/O libraries employ pretty much the same basic principles we have seen for more than half a century, but in new and clever ways that address today's architectures and applications, and do their best to anticipate the next generation of architectures and applications.

MPI-IO anticipated the rapid growth of highly parallel systems and parallel file systems. The MPI-IO library is a middle layer that provides options to support the different kinds of I/O applications perform, and hides the details from applications or their I/O libraries. Although the other I/O libraries in this section can read and write without using MPI-IO, most of them provide options that enable applications to take advantage of this powerful tool.

The Parallel Log-structured File System (PLFS) was designed for massively concurrent checkpointing, but ultimately became an effective way to adapt a variety of workloads and I/O patterns to a single storage system, hiding the details from applications. Moreover, PLFS is positioned to support high performance I/O in the future by showing it can accommodate GPU processing in the data pipeline, take advantage of burst buffers, and play well with cloud file systems.

Parallel-NetCDF is perhaps the most user-friendly of the parallel I/O libraries because it adapts an existing serial I/O library to parallel I/O without asking the user to adapt their data model or their format in any way. Because netCDF is one of the most popular of all scientific data formats, the availability of Parallel-NetCDF brings enormous computational resources to a huge population of scientists who would rather not be bothered with the details of MPI-IO or any other parallel I/O middleware. Furthermore, Parallel-NetCDF provides additional capabilities that users can grow into as they become comfortable with their parallel computing environments.

HDF5 is similar to Parallel-NetCDF in that it is a general-purpose technology for managing scientific and engineering data, and it provides a portable container for distributing data. Its biggest difference, in the context of this book, is that it was designed from the start to perform well on high-end systems. Most notable in this regard are the ability of the HDF5 format to store and access data objects of virtually any size efficiently, and the existence of a software layer in the HDF5 library that permits I/O drivers to be written for new I/O modalities. The generality of HDF5 also allows applications themselves to include special data structures, such indexes computed by FastQuery, that can greatly improve accessibility of data.

ADIOS has many of the same capabilities we've already seen, but emphasizes particularly matching the data and I/O requirements of an application on a given system with the underlying capabilities of any of a variety of file systems. The ADIOS API hides and exploits the capabilities of POSIX, MPI-IO, Lustre, DataSpaces, and others. ADIOS pays particular attention to scalability, for instance, supporting aggregation into a single file or several files if the single file approach fails to scale adequately. Similarly, ADIOS can improve scalability in the way that it minimizes communication among processes when handling I/O. ADIOS comes with its own format (BP), but provides file conversion to HDF5 and netCDF.

At first glance, *GLEAN* appears quite similar to ADIOS and PLFS, and the differences are definitely in the details. Like ADIOS, GLEAN adapts I/O strategies to the underlying network topology, and makes use of the data semantics of applications in order to improve data movement, but it has its own architecture and approach. GLEAN also performs asynchronous data staging, efficient compression, and subfiling. Unlike ADIOS and PLFS, GLEAN directly supports the HDF5 and netCDF I/O libraries.

12.3 What Is the Future of I/O Libraries?

Given their growing acceptance and institutional support, it seems likely that at least some of the I/O libraries we see here will grow and prosper. The success of ADIOS, PLFS, and GLEAN suggests that more packages will become available that enable applications to adapt their I/O to specific architectures and interconnect topologies, especially on high-end computing systems.

Their successes with specific applications will lead more and more application developers to design the I/O in their applications to take advantage of such packages. This in turn will motivate I/O library developers to make them as easy to use as compilers are today. Indeed, some of these capabilities will no doubt find their way into common language compilers.

Container-based I/O libraries like HDF5 and Parallel-NetCDF are also continuing to find widespread acceptance. The big data phenomenon has shone a light on these technologies, making them visible in application domains as varied as oil and gas exploration, healthcare, finance, and movie production. These successes, coupled with their continuing adoption in the HPC community, make it very likely they will continue to develop and find ways to incorporate more of the features we find in the other libraries.

Beyond merely improving how I/O libraries serve current needs, what new challenges will I/O libraries have to deal with? One of them will be to play well with the technologies that accompany the big data phenomenon. There is already pressure on many of these I/O libraries to support data analytics, including methods such as MapReduce. We have seen a few experiments in this direction, and PLFS does support Hadoop. Will this become a common capability for most I/O libraries?

As for the future, every I/O library aims for scalability, but how well will they respond to the many different forms of scalability that the future brings? Future systems are expected to deliver many terabytes of data per second. Millions of processes will be opening, reading, and writing files. File systems will contain trillions of files on millions of storage devices. How will our I/O libraries cope? It's going to be fun to watch.

Chapter 13

MPI-IO

Wei-keng Liao

Northwestern University

Rajeev Thakur

Argonne National Laboratory

13.1	Introduction	155
	13.1.1 MPI-IO Background	156
	13.1.2 Parallel I/O in Practice	156
13.2	Using MPI for Simple I/O	157
	13.2.1 Three Ways of File Access	158
	13.2.2 Blocking and Nonblocking I/O	159
13.3	File Access with User Intent	159
	13.3.1 Independent I/O	160
	13.3.2 MPI File View	161
	13.3.3 Collective I/O	163
13.4	MPI-IO Hints	165
13.5	Conclusions	165
	Bibliography	166

13.1 Introduction

MPI-IO is a standard, portable interface for parallel file I/O that was defined as part the MPI-2 (Message Passing Interface) Standard in 1997. It can be used either directly by application programmers or by writers of high-level libraries as an interface for portable, high performance I/O in parallel programs. It has many features specifically designed to efficiently support the I/O needs of parallel scientific applications. MPI-IO is an interface that sits above a parallel file system and below an application or a high-level I/O library, as illustrated in Figure 13.1. Hence it is often referred to as "middleware" for parallel I/O.

MPI-IO is intended as an interface for multiple processes of a parallel (MPI) program that is writing or reading parts of a single common file. For this purpose, an implementation of MPI-IO is typically layered on top of a parallel file system that supports the notion of a single, common file shared

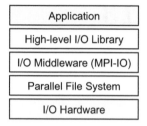

FIGURE 13.1: MPI-IO in the I/O software stack.

by multiple processes. Of course, MPI-IO can also be trivially used for the case where each process reads or writes a separate file.

13.1.1   MPI-IO Background

MPI-IO originated in an effort that began in 1994 at IBM Watson Research Center to investigate the impact of the then new MPI message-passing standard on parallel I/O. A group at IBM wrote an initial paper [7] that explored the analogy between MPI message passing and I/O. Roughly speaking, one can consider writing to file as sending a message, and reading from a file as receiving a message. This paper was the starting point of MPI-IO in that it was the first attempt to exploit this analogy by applying the (then relatively new) MPI concepts for message passing to the realm of parallel I/O.

The idea of using message-passing concepts in an I/O library appeared successful, and the effort was expanded into a collaboration with parallel I/O researchers from NASA Ames Research Center. The resulting specification appeared in an IBM technical report [1]. At this point, a large email discussion group was formed, with participation from a wide variety of institutions. This group, calling itself the MPI-IO Committee, pushed the idea further in a series of proposals, culminating in the version 0.5 release of the MPI Standard [13].

During this time, the MPI Forum had resumed meeting to address a number of topics that had been deliberately left out of the original MPI Standard, including parallel I/O. The MPI-IO Committee eventually merged with the MPI Forum and, from the summer of 1996, the MPI-IO design activities took place in the context of the MPI Forum meetings. The MPI Forum used the latest version of the existing MPI-IO specification (v 0.5) [13] as a starting point for the I/O chapter in MPI-2. The I/O chapter evolved over many meetings of the Forum and was released in its final form along with the rest of MPI-2 in July 1997 [6]. MPI-IO now refers to this I/O chapter in the MPI Standard.

13.1.2   Parallel I/O in Practice

There are three ways to do I/O from a parallel program perspective. In the first method, each process accesses a separate file, which is also known as the one-file-per-process I/O method. This method is easy to program and requires no MPI communication. However, it results in a large number of files that are hard to manage. Another drawback is that the same number of processes must be used to read the files as the parallel program that created the files. Otherwise, additional effort is required, such as determining the mapping of files to processes and the logical data layout from files to memory (most likely noncontiguous in file space). Due to these concerns, it is desirable to store data in a canonical order in files such that the mapping is independent of the number of processes. The second method of performing I/O addresses this limitation, and it involves funneling all I/O through one process of the program. All I/O requests are forwarded to that process and carried out there. Obviously, this approach can result in poor performance for large jobs due to communication congestion and limited memory space available in one process.

The third method, parallel I/O to a shared file, overcomes the limitations of both approaches. In this method, all processes open a common file and read or write different parts of the same file simultaneously. This approach maintains the logical view of a single file and can also result in high performance given sufficient I/O hardware, a parallel file system, and an efficient MPI-IO implementation. The following sections describe how MPI-IO can be used to perform this form of parallel I/O efficiently.

13.2   Using MPI for Simple I/O

Based on the third method described in Section 13.1.2, high performance parallel I/O can be achieved by enabling all processes to read or write to different parts of a single shared file. Figure 13.2 shows a simple example of such a program. Overall, this code is not much different from how one would do it using regular POSIX I/O. It simply uses the MPI-IO equivalents of POSIX open, lseek, read, and close functions.

MPI_File_open takes an MPI communicator as the first argument, which represents the group of processes that will access the file. The second argument is the file name. MPI does not specify the format of the file name; implementations are free to specify the format. For example, in some cases, the user may need to prefix the file name with an implementation-specified string (such as nfs:) to specify the type of file system on which the file is located. In many cases, implementations may be able to determine the type of file system automatically, without the prefix. The third argument indicates the mode of access, in this case read only. The fourth argument provides users with a way to pass "hints" to the file system that may improve performance. In this simple example, the default set of hints are used (MPI_INFO_NULL); Section 13.4 will describe how to pass hints. The file handle is returned as the last argument. It is used in all future accesses to the file. MPI_File_open

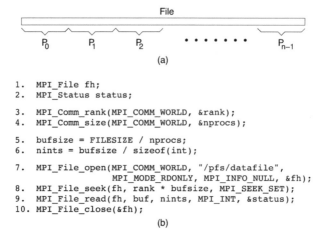

(a)

```
1.  MPI_File fh;
2.  MPI_Status status;

3.  MPI_Comm_rank(MPI_COMM_WORLD, &rank);
4.  MPI_Comm_size(MPI_COMM_WORLD, &nprocs);

5.  bufsize = FILESIZE / nprocs;
6.  nints = bufsize / sizeof(int);

7.  MPI_File_open(MPI_COMM_WORLD, "/pfs/datafile",
                  MPI_MODE_RDONLY, MPI_INFO_NULL, &fh);
8.  MPI_File_seek(fh, rank * bufsize, MPI_SEEK_SET);
9.  MPI_File_read(fh, buf, nints, MPI_INT, &status);
10. MPI_File_close(&fh);
```

(b)

FIGURE 13.2: (a) A simple example in which each process of a parallel program needs to access a separate portion of a common file. (b) Sample MPI-IO code used to perform the I/O.

is a *collective* function: all processes in the communicator passed as the first argument must call the function.

After the file is successfully opened, each process can independently access and read its portion of data from the file. For this purpose, each process seeks to the right offset in the file by calling MPI_File_seek. Then, each process reads the amount of data it needs by calling MPI_File_read. Each process reads the number of integers, **nints**, into the buffer, **buf**, in its local memory. The **status** object is the same as in an MPI_Recv function; it can be used to query the amount of data actually read. Finally, all processes call MPI_File_close to close the file.

13.2.1 Three Ways of File Access

MPI supports three ways of specifying the location from which data is accessed in a file. The first method is by using *individual file pointers*, as in the above example. In this case, each process maintains its own file pointer, independent of other processes. The file pointer can be moved to a specific offset in the file by calling MPI_File_seek. The following call to MPI_File_read or MPI_File_write will access data starting from the current location of the individual file pointer. The file pointer will be incremented by the amount of data read or written by the read/write call.

An alternate way is by using *explicit offsets*. No seek function is needed in this case. Instead, the user calls the functions MPI_File_read_at or MPI_File_write_at. These functions take the file offset as an argument. The individual file pointer is not affected by reads or writes using these functions.

Using explicit offsets is also a thread-safe way of accessing the file, since there are no separate seek and read/write functions.

MPI-IO also supports a third way that involves using a *shared file pointer*. The shared file pointer is a common file pointer shared by all processes in the communicator passed to the file open function. This file pointer can be moved by calling `MPI_File_seek_shared`. The corresponding read/write functions are `MPI_File_read_shared` and `MPI_File_write_shared`. This method is useful for writing log files, for example. However, maintaining a shared file pointer involves some overhead for the implementation. Hence, for performance reasons, the use of these functions is generally discouraged.

13.2.2 Blocking and Nonblocking I/O

MPI-IO supports both blocking and nonblocking I/O functions. The read-/write functions mentioned above are all blocking functions, which block until the specified operation is completed. Each of these functions also has non-blocking variants: `MPI_File_iread`, `MPI_File_iwrite`, `MPI_File_iread_at`, `MPI_File_iwrite_at`, `MPI_File_iread_shared`, and `MPI_File_iwrite_shared`. They return an `MPI_Request` object immediately after the call, similar to MPI nonblocking communication functions. The user must call `MPI_Test`, `MPI_Wait`, or their variants to test or wait for completion of these operations. The nonblocking I/O functions offer the potential for overlapping I/O and computation or communication in the program.

13.3 File Access with User Intent

Besides the POSIX-equivalent basic I/O functions, MPI-IO contains additional functions that can better convey the user's I/O intent. In our terminology, a user's I/O intent refers to the user's expectation on how the I/O operation should be carried out, and a user's I/O requirement refers to the end result. Consider an example that describes and distinguishes between a user's I/O intent and requirement. Figure 13.3 shows a 5×8 two-dimensional integer array that is partitioned among four processes in a block–block pattern. Each of process ranks 0 and 1 is assigned a subarray of size 3×4. Each of process ranks 2 and 3 is assigned a subarray of size 2×4. (The use of a small array and small number of processes here is only for explanation purposes. In practice, MPI-IO is used for large datasets and large system sizes.) The 2D array can be considered as a representation of the problem domain to a parallel application, and the subarrays represent the sub-domains distributed among the MPI processes. It is assumed that the user's intent is to write the entire 2D array to a file in parallel and the data layout in the file follows the array's canonical order. Such I/O operations often occur during an application's checkpoint.

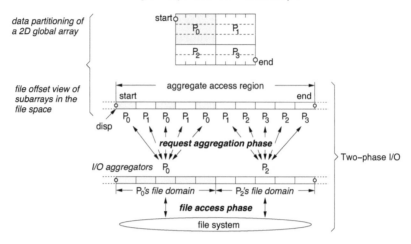

FIGURE 13.3: A 5×8 2D array partitioned among 4 MPI processes in a block–block pattern and its data layout in the file. The data layout in the file follows the array's canonical order. The bottom part describes the two-phase I/O operation carried out in MPI collective I/O.

At each checkpoint, the intention considers writing the 2D array as a single request. The outcome, and hence the user requirement, is that the 2D array is saved in the file starting from the given file offset, denoted as `disp`, and occupies a contiguous space of size equal to $5 \times 8 = 40$ integers. This section continues to describe three ways of using MPI-IO functions to carry out such I/O operations and discusses how they differ in their way of expressing the user intent.

13.3.1   Independent I/O

MPI-IO functions consist of two types: independent and collective. The MPI-IO read/write functions discussed so far belong to the independent I/O category, and their use is very similar to that of POSIX I/O functions. As for collective I/O functions, their appearance and syntax look the same as the independent ones, except that the collective functions have a suffix, `_all`, added to their names. The name "independent" implies the functions can be called by a process independently from another process. There is no restriction on the number of calls a process can make, and they need not match with calls on other processes. Collective functions, on the other hand, require the participation of all processes that collectively open the shared file. The participant processes are identified by the MPI communicator passed to `MPI_File_open`.

For example, Figure 13.4(a) shows an MPI code fragment that uses `MPI_File_write_at`, an independent I/O function, to write the 2D array in parallel. In this case, the loop at line 2 runs N iterations where N is equal to 3 for process ranks 0 and 1, and 2 for ranks 2 and 3. From this example,

```
1.   offset = disp + (rank / 2) * 3 * 8 + (rank % 2) * 4
2.   for (i=0; i<N; i++, offset+=8)
3.       MPI_File_write_at(fh, offset, buf, 4, MPI_INT, &status);
```

(a) Write the 2D array using MPI independent I/O with explicit offsets.

```
1.   int    gsizes[2] = {5, 8};   /* global array size */
2.   int subsizes[2] = {N, 4};   /*  local array size */
3.   int starts[2];              /* starting file offsets */
4.   starts[0] = (rank / 2) * (gsizes[0] / 2 + 1);
5.   starts[1] = (rank % 2) * (gsizes[1] / 2);
6.   MPI_Type_create_subarray(2, gsizes, subsizes, starts,
7.                            MPI_ORDER_C, MPI_INT, &ftype);
8.   MPI_Type_commit(&ftype);
```

(b) Create an MPI derived data type that maps local subarray to global array.

```
1.   MPI_File_set_view(fh, disp, MPI_INT, ftype, "native", info);
2.   MPI_File_write(fh, buf, N*4, MPI_INT, &status);
```

(c) Write the 2D array using MPI independent I/O with file view.

```
1.   MPI_File_set_view(fh, disp, MPI_INT, ftype, "native", info);
2.   MPI_File_write_all(fh, buf, N*4, MPI_INT, &status);
```

(d) Write the 2D array using MPI collective I/O.

FIGURE 13.4: MPI program fragments to write the 2D array in parallel as illustrated in Figure 13.3.

using independent functions allows MPI processes to make an unequal number of calls. Each call to MPI_File_write_at at line 3 is equivalent to a call to POSIX lseek with the given file offset, followed by a write with the same request amount. From an MPI-IO perspective, the program expresses the following I/O intent. At first, the loop at line 2 asks the MPI-IO library to handle the requests one after another, in that exact order. Secondly, the use of independent functions tells MPI-IO that requests from one process can arrive independently from other processes and expects MPI-IO to protect the data consistency for each individual request. Obviously, the above interpretation is not exactly the same as the user's intent, in which the order does not matter and the consistency is for the whole 2D array. In order to prevent such misunderstanding, MPI-IO provides a feature named *file view* to let users better convey their I/O intent.

13.3.2   MPI File View

An MPI file view defines the portion of a file that is "visible" to a process. A process can only read and write the data that is located in its file view. When a file is first opened, the entire file is visible to the process. A process's file view can be changed with the function MPI_File_set_view. When using individual file pointers, a process's file view can be different from others. When using the shared file pointer, all processes must define the same view. A file view can consist of multiple noncontiguous regions in the file. When this happens, the noncontiguous regions are logically stitched together into a contiguous region, which is read or written as if the view is a contiguous byte stream.

MPI datatypes, both basic and derived, are used to set file views. File views are specified by a triplet: *displacement, etype,* and *filetype*. The displacement is the number of bytes to be skipped from the beginning of the file. The etype (elementary datatype) is the smallest unit for file access and positioning, which can be an MPI basic or derived datatype. The file offset argument in all MPI-IO functions is specified in terms of the number of etypes. The filetype is an MPI basic or derived datatype that specifies the portions of the file that are "visible" to a process. The filetype must be either the same as the etype or a derived datatype constructed out of the etype. A process's file view starts at the displacement, followed by repeated copies of the filetype. When a call to MPI_File_open returns, the default file view sets the displacement to 0 and both etype and filetype to MPI_BYTE. The example programs shown in Figures 13.2 and 13.4(a) use the default file view.

The program fragment shown in Figure 13.4(b) constructs the derived datatype, ftype, through a call to MPI_Type_create_subarray to describe the file view for each of the four processes in the 2D array example. The arguments gsizes and subsizes are the sizes of global array and local subarray, respectively. The starting array offsets relative to the global array are set in the argument starts. Once the newly created filetype, ftype, is committed, it can be used in MPI_File_set_view to change a process's file view. This example uses disp for the file displacement, MPI_INT for etype, "native" for data representation, and info for MPI-IO hints (Section 13.4).

Figure 13.5 illustrates the file views of the four processes in this example. The file portions visible to individual processes are marked as shaded areas. Note that the filetype extents specified by ftype across four processes all

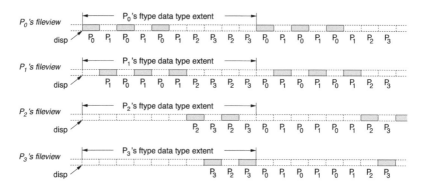

FIGURE 13.5: Individual process's file views for the 2D array example in Figure 13.3. The shaded area indicates the file portions visible to a process. A file view is constructed by repeatedly applying the filetype's extent, starting from the displacement argument, disp.

point to the same file location. The same filetype and its extent are applied recursively to the file space, and all visible portions together comprise a process's file view. The program shown in Figure 13.4(c) sets file views and calls an independent write function to write the 2D array in parallel. The write amount is of size ($N \times 4$) integers, equal to the entire subarray size in each process. Note that the amount requested in an MPI-IO function call need not be the same as the size of the filetype.

From this example, by defining a process's file view, writing the entire subarray can be accomplished by making just one MPI-IO function call. This program fragment also tells a different user I/O intent from the one expressed in Figure 13.4(a). MPI-IO interprets the user's intent as to write the whole subarray as a single request. The restriction of write order for the individual subarray rows as intended by Figure 13.4(a) is eliminated. Instead of protecting data consistency for each individual row, the MPI-IO library enforces the consistency for the entire subarray. Given such interpretation, an MPI-IO implementation has more freedom to adopt certain optimizations to improve performance. One of the well-known optimizations for such I/O requests is called "data sieving" [12]. Since most of the modern file systems do not perform well for a large number of small, noncontiguous requests, data sieving is an I/O strategy that makes large I/O requests to the file system and extracts, in memory, the data that is actually needed. Data sieving has been incorporated into ROMIO, a very popular MPI-IO implementation developed at Argonne National Laboratory [10]. When applied to the discussed example, data sieving will first read a contiguous file segment that is large enough to cover a process's entire file view, the whole subarray, into a temporary buffer and then copy the requested data to the user's buffer. As a result, this read-modify-write strategy reduces the number of I/O requests to the file system. Significant performance improvement has been observed on noncontiguous I/O requests when data sieving is enabled.

13.3.3 Collective I/O

The MPI file view feature gets us one step closer to meeting the user I/O intent for this example, which is to write a global 2D array in parallel from four processes as a single I/O operation. However, there are still four independent I/O requests, one from each process. Hence, the MPI-IO library must protect the data integrity for the four requests individually. When data sieving is enabled, the entire file region involved in a single read-modify-write operation must be protected from another. A common solution to provide such protection is to use an advisory file locking mechanism to guarantee the exclusive access for a file region from concurrent access. In this example, the region to be locked by process rank 0's request overlaps with rank 1's lock region. Similarly, process rank 1's lock region overlaps with the one requested by rank 2. As a result, only half of the four processes are actively writing their data to the file system while the other half are waiting for their lock requests to be granted. Thus, the achievable performance is significantly limited by the conflicted file locks.

To overcome such problems, MPI collective I/O functions can convey the exact user intent in this example that considers the parallel write of the whole global array as a single request. The program fragment using a collective write function is shown in Figure 13.4(d). It appears almost the same as the independent case, except the name of the write function. MPI collective I/O requires the participation of all processes that open the shared file. This requirement provides a collective I/O implementation an opportunity to exchange access information and reorganize I/O requests among the processes. Several process-collaboration strategies have been proposed, such as two-phase I/O [2], disk directed I/O [4], and server-directed I/O [8].

Two-phase I/O is a representative collaborative I/O technique that runs in the user space [11]. It exchanges data among processes, so that the rearranged requests can be processed by the underlying file system with the best performance. Two-phase I/O conceptually consists of a *request aggregation phase* (or referred as the communication phase) and a *file access phase* (or simply the I/O phase). In the request aggregation phase, a subset of MPI processes is picked as I/O aggregators that act as I/O proxies for the rest of the processes. The aggregate file access region requested by all processes is divided among the aggregators into non-overlapping sections, called *file domains*. For collective writes, the non-aggregator processes send their requests to the aggregators based on their file domains. In the file access phase, each aggregator commits the aggregated requests to the file system. ROMIO adopts the two-phase I/O strategy for implementing the collective MPI-IO functions.

The bottom part of Figure 13.3 depicts the two-phase I/O operation for the 2D array example. Assuming P_0 and P_2 are chosen as I/O aggregators, the aggregate access region of the collective write operation is evenly divided into two file domains, one for each aggregator. I/O data are redistributed from all four processes to the two aggregators during the request aggregation phase. Specifically, aggregator process rank 0 receives data from both rank 0 and 1, while aggregator rank 2 receives data from ranks 1, 2, and 3. In the file access phase, each aggregator aggregates the received data into a single, contiguous request and then makes a write call to the file system.

Recently, there were several optimizations that further improve the performance of collective I/O. Various file domain partitioning methods have been studied that can be adaptively determined based on the file locking policies of the underlying file systems in order to minimize lock conflicts for collective I/O [5]. In Sehrish et al.'s work [9], a pipelined strategy was developed to overlap the two phases in the two-phase I/O method. In this work, large requests are divided into smaller ones, each of size equal to the file stripe size, and redistributed to the I/O aggregators using MPI asynchronous communication in a pipeline fashion so that the asynchronous communication overlaps with the file access phase. In Venkatesan et al.'s study [14], I/O aggregator placement methods are proposed to minimize the communication cost in the request aggregation phase. Based on the file views, it calculates the non-aggregator-to-aggregator communication matrix, divides processes with high-volume communication into groups, and maps the process groups to the underlying network topology.

13.4 MPI-IO Hints

MPI-IO hints are a mechanism for users to pass information, such as access patterns, to the implementation so that it can help optimize file access. This is done by setting an MPI_Info object and passing it to the functions MPI_File_open, MPI_File_set_view, or MPI_File_set_info. An MPI-IO implementation may choose to ignore all hints, and the program would still be functionally correct. Some of MPI predefined I/O hints are cb_buffer_size (size of allowable buffer to be used by collective I/O), cb_nodes (maximum number of aggregators), striping_factor (number of file system stripes), and striping_unit (file stripe size). An implementation may define additional hints to make use of file system specific features. Readers are referred to the ROMIO user guide for the full list of available hints [10].

13.5 Conclusions

This chapter describes several important MPI-IO features to allow users to describe the data access patterns and the intent of their applications. The MPI-IO functions convey such information to the implementation so that better I/O strategies can be used to achieve high performance for parallel applications. MPI-IO has become a building block for several high-level I/O libraries, such as Parallel NetCDF (Chapter 15) and HDF5 (Chapter 16), which are widely used in various scientific communities. There are other MPI-IO features not covered in this chapter, including data consistency control, portable data representation, and split collective I/O. For their detailed information and learning materials, readers are referred to the MPI-2 Standard [6] and MPI tutorial books, such as *Using MPI-2* [3].

Bibliography

[1] Peter Corbett, Dror Feitelson, Yarsun Hsu, Jean-Pierre Prost, Marc Snir, Sam Fineberg, Bill Nitzberg, Bernard Traversat, and Parkson Wong. MPI-IO: A Parallel File I/O Interface for MPI. Technical Report IBM Research Report RC 19841(87784), IBM T.J. Watson Research Center, November 1994.

[2] J. del Rosario, R. Brodawekar, and A. Choudhary. Improved Parallel I/O via a Two-Phase Run-time Access Strategy. In the *Workshop on I/O in Parallel Computer Systems at IPPS*, 1993.

[3] William Gropp, Ewing Lusk, and Rajeev Thakur. *Using MPI-2: Advanved Features of the Message-Passing Interface.* MIT Press, Cambridge, MA, USA, 1999.

[4] D. Kotz. Disk-Directed I/O for MIMD Multiprocessors. *ACM Transactions on Computer Systems*, 15(1):41–74, February 1997.

[5] Wei-keng Liao. Design and Evaluation of MPI File Domain Partitioning Methods under Extent-Based File Locking Protocol. *IEEE Transactions on Parallel and Distributed Systems*, 22(2):260–272, February 2011.

[6] Message Passing Interface Forum. MPI-2: Extensions to the Message-Passing Interface, July 1997. http://www.mpi-forum.org/.

[7] Jean-Pierre Prost, Marc Snir, Peter Corbett, and Dror Feitelson. MPI-IO, a message-passing interface for concurrent I/O. Technical Report RC 19712 (87394), IBM T.J. Watson Research Center, August 1994.

[8] K. Seamons, Y. Chen, P. Jones, J. Jozwiak, and M. Winslett. Server-Directed Collective I/O in Panda. In *Supercomputing*, November 1995.

[9] Saba Sehrish, Seung Woo Son, Wei-keng Liao, Alok Choudhary, and Karen Schuchardt. Improving Collective I/O Performance by Pipelining Request Aggregation and File Access. In the *20th EuroMPI Conference*, September 2013.

[10] R. Thakur, W. Gropp, and E. Lusk. Users Guide for ROMIO: A High Performance, Portable MPI-IO Implementation. Technical Report ANL/MCS-TM-234, Mathematics and Computer Science Division, Argonne National Laboratory, October 1997.

[11] Rajeev Thakur, William Gropp, and Ewing Lusk. Data Sieving and Collective I/O in ROMIO. In *Proceedings of the 7th Symposium on the Frontiers of Massively Parallel Computation*, pages 182–189. IEEE Computer Society Press, February 1999.

[12] Rajeev Thakur, William Gropp, and Ewing Lusk. Optimizing Noncontiguous Accesses in MPI-IO. *Parallel Computing*, 28(1):83–105, January 2002.

[13] The MPI-IO Committee. MPI-IO: A Parallel File I/O Interface for MPI, version 0.5, April 1996.

[14] Vishwanath Venkatesan, Rakhi Anand, Jaspal Subhlok, and Edgar Gabriel. Optimized Process Placement for Collective I/O Operations. In *Proceedings of the 20th European MPI Users' Group Meeting*, EuroMPI '13, pages 31–36, New York, NY, USA, 2013. ACM.

Chapter 14

PLFS: Software-Defined Storage for HPC

John Bent

EMC

14.1   Motivation 169
14.2   Design/Architecture 170
     14.2.1   PLFS Shared File Mode 170
     14.2.2   PLFS Flat File Mode 172
     14.2.3   PLFS Small File Mode 172
14.3   Deployment, Usage, and Applications 173
     14.3.1   Burst Buffers 174
     14.3.2   Cloud File Systems for HPC 174
14.4   Conclusion 175
     Bibliography 176

14.1   Motivation

Just as virtualization has provided massive flexibility for computation across diverse processor hardware, software-defined storage provides that flexibility for I/O workloads across diverse storage hardware. The Parallel Log-structured File System (PLFS) is one such software-defined storage platform. Originally designed as middleware to solve massively concurrent checkpointing, PLFS has become a powerful reminder of how not all workloads are well suited to all storage systems. PLFS is also a compelling example of how a layer of software indirection can change the base abilities of existing storage systems. PLFS has since extended its functionality to address additional storage challenges, thereby growing from single-purpose middleware into a more general software-defined storage platform.

The main benefit of PLFS is that a system administrator can buy a single storage system, configure it just once, and then use PLFS to allow a variety of workloads to use that single storage system. The basic mechanism of PLFS is an interception and transformation of unstructured application I/O into well-structured I/O better suited to the underlying storage system. PLFS has three main modes of operation (shared, flat, and small) essentially comparable to mount time options and several interesting use cases for each mode.

14.2   Design/Architecture

PLFS is mainly designed to run as middleware on the compute nodes themselves. It can run in the user space of applications using MPI-IO and a patched MPI library, or in the user space of applications which are ported to link directly into the PLFS API. The PLFS API closely mirrors the standard POSIX API; thus porting several applications and synthetic benchmarks have been straightforward. PLFS is also available as a FUSE file system [1] for unmodified applications which do not use MPI-IO. Since the FUSE approach can incur high overhead, there is also an LD_PRELOAD interface which brings PLFS into the user space of unmodified applications [8].

There are three main modes of PLFS which are set in a PLFS configuration file and defined on a per-path basis. The options for each path define the path that the user will use (i.e., /mnt/plfs/shared_file), the mode of operation, and the underlying storage system(s) that PLFS will use for the actual storage of the user data as well as its own metadata. Typically, the underlying storage system is a globally visible storage system, and the PLFS configuration file is shared across a set of compute nodes such that each compute node can write to the same PLFS file(s) and each compute node can read PLFS files written from a different compute node.

The three main configurations of PLFS are *shared file, small file, and flat file*, each of which is intended for different application I/O workloads. Additionally, there is a *burst buffer* configuration (which currently works only in shared file mode) to transparently gain performance benefits from a smaller, faster storage tier such as flash memory. All three modes support the ability to use PLFS as an *umbrella* file system that can distribute workloads across multiple underlying storage systems to aggregate their bandwidth and utilize all available metadata servers. Finally, there is support in PLFS to run with all three modes on top of *cloud* file systems such as Hadoop.

14.2.1   PLFS Shared File Mode

Shared file mode is the original PLFS configuration [3] and is designed for highly concurrent writes to a shared file, such as a checkpoint file which is simultaneously written by all processes within a large parallel application. The architecture of PLFS shared file mode is shown in Figure 14.1. Note that the figure shows the PLFS layer as a separate layer; this is accurate from the perspective of the application but in fact the PLFS software runs on each compute node. This mode was motivated by the well-known observation that

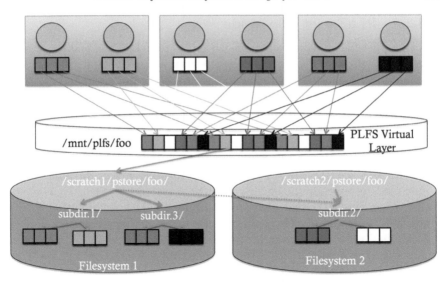

FIGURE 14.1 (See color insert): PLFS shared file mode transforms multiple writes to a shared file into streams of data sent to multiple subfiles on the underlying storage system(s). Not shown is the internal PLFS metadata used to reconstruct the file. [Image courtesy of John Bent (EMC).]

many applications naturally have partitions of a large distributed data structure which are poorly matched to the block alignment of many storage systems and therefore lose performance to various locks and serialization bottlenecks inherent in parallel file systems.

By decoupling the concurrent writes, PLFS sends data streams to the underlying storage systems, which avoids these locks and bottlenecks. The basic mechanism is that PLFS first creates a PLFS *container* and then stores all the individual subfiles in this container as well as the metadata necessary to re-create the logical file. Functionally, the container is very similar to how inodes are used in almost all file systems since the Berkeley Fast File System [7]. When the user requests data from the file, PLFS consults the metadata within the container to resolve which subfile(s) contain the requested data and then reads from the subfile(s) to return the data to the reading application.

Note that at no point is the application aware of this transformation: all operations on the shared file work functionally, exactly the same as if PLFS was not present. One concern in PLFS, however, is that the amount of PLFS metadata can grow to challenging sizes; this concern is addressed by discovering hidden structure within seemingly unstructured I/O [6].

14.2.2　PLFS Flat File Mode

PLFS flat file mode was subsequently added to reduce metadata contention when many processes concurrently create files within a single directory. The basic motivation is that when multiple processes modify a shared object concurrently, they often incur locks and serialization bottlenecks in many storage systems. In the PLFS shared file mode, the shared object is a file and the concurrent modifications are writes, whereas the PLFS flat file mode is for the case in which the shared object is a directory and the concurrent modifications are file creations. Just as PLFS shared file mode creates a virtual container to store the subfiles, the PLFS flat file mode creates a virtual directory from a set of subdirectories on the underlying storage system(s). When a user creates a file, PLFS hashes the filename to determine in which subdirectory to store that file. Reads and queries of files share the hash function so that they can quickly find requested files from the set of subdirectories. The PLFS flat file mode will achieve maximum performance improvements when it is configured to use multiple storage systems, and therefore multiple metadata servers to create its set of subdirectories.

In this way, when multiple files are concurrently created with a PLFS directory, PLFS spreads the create workload across multiple metadata servers. This is an important feature of the software-defined storage approach. It is easy for a system administrator to buy multiple storage systems but difficult to allow unmodified applications to spread their workload across them. With PLFS, it is a simple matter of modifying the PLFS configuration file to include all of the available storage systems. PLFS flat file mode is described in more detail in Bent et al. [4].

14.2.3　PLFS Small File Mode

The third mode of PLFS is the small file mode, the architecture of which is shown in Figure 14.2. This mode is designed for the workload in which individual processes want to create a large number of small files in a short period of time. This workload is challenging for storage systems, which must allocate some amount of resource for each file. For a stream of many small files, this resource allocation quickly becomes a bottleneck. PLFS small file mode, like the PLFS shared file mode, creates a PLFS container. However, PLFS small file mode creates a PLFS small file container for each PLFS directory, whereas the PLFS shared file mode creates a PLFS shared file container for each PLFS file.

When an application creates a set of small files, PLFS small file mode will aggregate all of the data for each small file into a single large file stored on the underlying storage system. It will also create a metadata file to store the necessary information to allow finding small files and their data within the single large aggregated file.

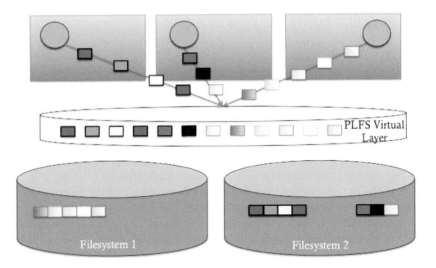

FIGURE 14.2: PLFS small file mode transforms a stream of small file creates from an individual process into two large streaming files sent to the underlying file system (one for user data and one for PLFS metadata). Note how PLFS can also aggregate the performance of multiple file systems; flat-file mode is the same except that PLFS stores each logical file as its own physical file instead of as a chunk within a single physical file as shown here. Flat-file mode therefore does not need another file for PLFS metadata since the mapping between logical and physical is purely algorithmic. [Image courtesy of John Bent (EMC).]

This mode transforms the performance extracted from the underlying file system to match its maximum bandwidth for streaming data instead of matching its maximum file creation rate. The amount of performance gained is dependent on the size of the individual files.

14.3   Deployment, Usage, and Applications

PLFS is currently installed on most of the classified and unclassified supercomputers at LANL. It has also been directly ported into several LANL applications. Additionally, the PLFS shared file mode has been used in two use-cases not originally envisioned when PLFS was first developed: for burst buffers and for enabling parallel I/O to file systems which do not natively support parallel I/O.

14.3.1   Burst Buffers

As HPC transitions from petascale to exascale, the economics of storage media dictate a new storage architecture. HPC users have two basic checkpointing requirements from their storage systems: they require a minimum bandwidth for checkpointing to enable a sufficient utilization of the supercomputer and they require a minimum capacity to store a sufficient amount of checkpoint data. In the petascale, disk-based storage systems provisioned for the capacity requirement met the bandwidth requirement as well. However, as the improvements in disk capacity have outpaced the improvements in disk bandwidth, disk-based storage systems for exascale HPC will need to be provisioned for bandwidth. Unfortunately, purchasing disks for bandwidth is extremely economically inefficient. Luckily, emerging media such as NVRAM and flash storage allow an economically efficient way to purchase bandwidth, but they are not a solution for capacity. Therefore, exascale will require a new storage architecture which has become known as a burst buffer storage architecture. This name reflects its intended usage for checkpointing in which checkpoint data can be quickly saved to a small, fast flash-based tier (i.e., the burst buffer); while the computation resumes, the checkpoint data can be more slowly transferred to the larger, slower disk-based storage system.

The PLFS containers used within the PLFS shared file mode have proven to be very effective in enabling burst buffer storage systems [2]. By storing the metadata in the container, PLFS can store (and retrieve) the data itself very quickly into subfiles in a burst buffer tier. Later, the data is transferred to the disk tier and the PLFS metadata is correspondingly modified. The advantage of this approach is that the user only sees a single namespace. PLFS transparently knows whether the data is available in the flash and/or disk tier and will retrieve it appropriately. This allows unmodified applications to benefit from the performance enhancements of the burst buffer architecture. The architecture of PLFS running in burst buffer mode is shown in Figure 14.3.

14.3.2   Cloud File Systems for HPC

PLFS can also be used to enable HPC parallel workloads using storage that wasn't designed for parallel I/O. For example, early versions of the Hadoop file system, HDFS, do not allow multiple writers to a single file nor do they allow appending data to a previously created file. By layering PLFS above these file systems, the user can use them for parallel I/O since PLFS transparently transforms the shared file writing into individual processes writing to individual subfiles within the PLFS container [5].

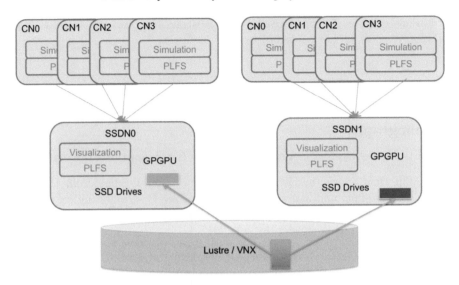

FIGURE 14.3: By using the PLFS middleware layer, the illusion of a single file is preserved in a manner completely transparent to the application and the user. Physically however, PLFS transforms the I/O to leverage both the global visibility of the parallel file system to store its metadata as well as the faster performance of the storage in the burst buffers to store user data. Later, the user data is migrated to the parallel file system. This figure shows an example burst buffer architecture where a simulation application sends simulation data from compute nodes to burst buffer nodes that have been augmented with GPUs to allow in-transit analysis by a visualization program (see Chapter 23). The data will be later migrated to a Lustre file system running on VNX storage. [Image courtesy of John Bent (EMC).]

14.4 Conclusion

Through a variety of configurations and use cases, PLFS is a dramatic example of the power of software-defined storage. An underlying storage system can be configured to work well with well-arranged streams of data. The PLFS software is then layered around that storage system and can be configured to export it for a variety of different workloads, such as shared file, small file, and flat file, for better metadata load balancing. Additionally, PLFS can enable parallel I/O using storage systems not defined for parallel I/O. Finally, PLFS can create a single virtual file system from a collection of multiple storage systems both for bandwidth aggregation as well as metadata distribution. PLFS development continues today to expand PLFS functionality for an exascale future in which POSIX is finally replaced with a more parallel-amenable interface using well-defined concurrency abstractions, and transactional consistency across sets of related objects.

Bibliography

[1] FUSE: File System in Userspace. http://fuse.sourceforge.net/.

[2] John Bent, Sorin Faibish, James Ahrens, Gary Grider, John Patchett, Percy Tzelnic, and Jon Woodring. Jitter-Free Co-Processing on a Prototype Exascale Storage Stack. In *28th IEEE Symposium on Massive Storage Systems and Technologies*, MSST, 2012.

[3] John Bent, Garth Gibson, Gary Grider, Ben McClelland, Paul Nowoczynski, James Nunez, Milo Polte, and Meghan Wingate. PLFS: A Checkpoint File System for Parallel Applications. In *Proceedings of the Conference on High Performance Computing Networking, Storage and Analysis*, SC '09, pages 21:1–21:12, New York, NY, USA, 2009. ACM.

[4] John Bent, Gary Grider, Brett Kettering, Adam Manzanares, Meghan McClelland, Aaron Torres, and Alfred Torrez. Storage Challenges at Los Alamos National Lab. In *28th IEEE Symposium on Massive Storage Systems and Technologies*, MSST, 2012.

[5] Chuck Cranor, Milo Polte, and Garth Gibson. HPC Computation on Hadoop Storage with PLFS. Technical Report CMU-PDL-12-115, Parallel Data Lab, Carnegie Mellon University, November 2012.

[6] Jun He, John Bent, Aaron Torres, Gary Grider, Garth Gibson, Carlos Maltzahn, and Xian-He Sun. I/O Acceleration with Pattern Detection. In *ACM Symposium on High Performance Parallel and Distributed Computing*, HPDC 13, New York, NY, June 2013.

[7] Marshall Kirk McKusick, William N. Joy, Samuel J. Leffler, and Robert S. Fabry. A Fast File System for UNIX. *ACM Transactions on Computer Systems*, 2:181–197, 1984.

[8] S. A. Wright, S.D. Hammond, S. J. Pennycook, I. Miller, J. A. Herdman, and S.A. Jarvis. LDPLFS: Improving I/O Performance without Application Modification. In *Parallel and Distributed Processing Symposium Workshops PhD Forum (IPDPSW), 2012 IEEE 26th International*, pages 1352–1359, 2012.

Chapter 15

Parallel-NetCDF

Rob Latham

Argonne National Laboratory

15.1   Motivation 177
15.2   History and Background 179
15.3   Design and Architecture 179
15.4   Deployment and Usage 180
15.5   Additional Features 181
15.6   Conclusion 182
15.7   Additional Resources 183
       Bibliography 184

15.1 Motivation

Parallel-NetCDF (often abbreviated as simply "pNetCDF"), is a high-level parallel I/O library providing a portable, self-describing file format for the storage of multi-dimensional arrays of typed data. Parallel-NetCDF provides an application-oriented interface on top of the more general, lower-level MPI-I/O interface, while maintaining the standard netCDF file format.

Computational scientists, in addition to mastering their scientific domain, also have the challenge of mastering the computer systems upon which their simulations run. To help hide the hardware details of these machines, scientists can use compilers, programming languages, and math kernel libraries. In order to manage the tens of thousands of nodes and millions of processing elements, scientists can rely on communication middleware such as MPI. In much the same way, scientists have at their disposal *high-level I/O libraries*. These I/O libraries sit atop an I/O middleware (such as MPI-IO, discussed in Chapter 13), packaging and presenting some of the complexity of the lower-level, general purpose middleware into a format more appropriate for a scientific programmer. Figure 15.1 depicts this I/O software stack, and Parallel-NetCDF's role in it.

The "data problem" facing computational scientists consists of three main challenges. First, the simulations of physical phenomena improve their fidelity with each new generation of hardware. As the gap between what computer

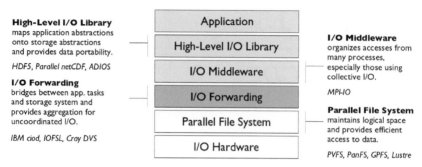

High-Level I/O Library
maps application abstractions
onto storage abstractions
and provides data portability.

HDF5, Parallel netCDF, ADIOS

I/O Forwarding
bridges between app. tasks
and storage system and
provides aggregation for
uncoordinated I/O.

IBM ciod, IOFSL, Cray DVS

I/O Middleware
organizes accesses from
many processes,
especially those using
collective I/O.

MPI-IO

Parallel File System
maintains logical space
and provides efficient
access to data.

PVFS, PanFS, GPFS, Lustre

Application

High-Level I/O Library

I/O Middleware

I/O Forwarding

Parallel File System

I/O Hardware

FIGURE 15.1: Parallel-NetCDF sits just below applications in the I/O software stack. It provides a more application-oriented interface to the more general and complex MPI-IO library. Applications can describe I/O needs in terms of multi-dimensional arrays. Parallel-NetCDF turns these requests into MPI-IO collective I/O operations.

simulations predict and reality bears out shrinks, the amount of data produced by these simulations grows. In 2012, DOE INCITE applications for time on high-end computing platforms routinely predicted needing terabytes of data. Second, hard drives double in capacity every 18 months, but the performance of a hard drive does not match that pace. In order to achieve high storage rates, many devices must be harnessed in parallel. The computational scientist looking to produce or analyze terabytes of data needs some way to manage parallelism in the I/O layer.

Parallelism in the I/O layer brings its own challenges. In order to provide high performance, storage systems deploy a large number of disks, servers, and storage links. Applications could operate directly upon these parallel storage systems. For the sake of developer productivity and I/O performance, however, I/O libraries exist to provide the abstractions and optimizations computational scientists need.

Stepping back from the topic of performance briefly and taking a broader view of the role of high-level I/O libraries in the life of a modern computational scientist, scientists operate in collaborations, exchanging datasets with other scientists conducting experiments on machines with different architectural characteristics. Raw binary files or custom file formats complicate the collaboration story. Instead, standard file formats mean every scientist can read data produced by any other scientists. Portability in file formats means no matter the byte-endianness or word size of a machine, the data will always look the same. One can also imagine "portability over time": these I/O libraries provide routines to annotate the stored data, or the entire file itself. These annotations help put the data in context, describing when the data was produced, by what application, or something as mundane yet important as what units the data are in.

15.2 History and Background

In 2002, when Argonne National Laboratory and Northwestern University started the Parallel-NetCDF project, the climate community had for nearly a decade prior been using the serial netCDF package [6] from UCAR. Serial netCDF provided climate scientists half of what they needed: the library and file format had at its foundation the kinds of multi-dimensional arrays of typed data that naturally fit with the kinds of simulations climate scientists carry out.

The missing half of serial netCDF was how to access these datasets in parallel. At the time, simulations faced two unappealing choices. Either they could do "file-per-process" I/O, producing one netCDF file for each parallel process, or they could send all data to a master process and have that process do all I/O. An "N-to-N" I/O model, where N processes operate on N (or more) files, quickly poses challenges to the underlying file system as it tries to deal with thousands of files. Writing N-to-N is far simpler than reading N files and re-assembling the simulation state. Sending a collection of N files to a collaborator also poses challenges. A far better solution would be to just operate on one file.

Sending all data to a master rank to manage one file poses two challenges. First, the master process needs enough memory to hold data from the other parallel processors. Second, the master process quickly becomes a critical resource, preventing all other processes from making progress. In an era where thousand-way parallelism is routine, an approach that serializes access to one processor may certainly be possible, but will result in unacceptable bottlenecks.

At the time, the only other application-oriented I/O library was HDF5. Like netCDF, HDF5 provided (and continues to provide) a data model and API well-suited to multi-dimensional arrays of typed data. (See Chapter 16 for more information about HDF5.) The HDF5 API and model differs significantly from netCDF's API and file format. Those HDF5 differences allow for many powerful features, but make some optimization more difficult. A parallel version of netCDF offered a chance to explore parallel I/O in a more constrained context.

15.3 Design and Architecture

The Parallel-NetCDF design should look familiar to anyone familiar with serial netCDF. Having existed a decade prior to Parallel-NetCDF, serial netCDF had already established data files and codes. Nothing about the

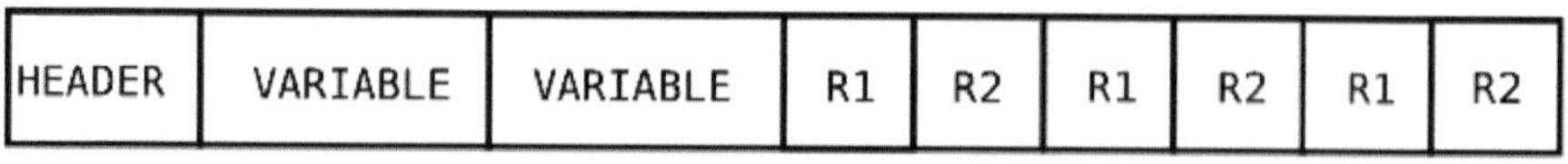

HEADER	VARIABLE	VARIABLE	R1	R2	R1	R2	R1	R2

FIGURE 15.2: The NetCDF file layout (used in both serial NetCDF and Parallel-NetCDF). A small header describes the contents of the file and any attributes on variables, dimensions, or the file itself. Variables follow in contiguous regions. The "non-record variables," those that can grow in one dimension, follow in an interleaved fashion.

established file format precluded parallel I/O, so Parallel-NetCDF used that file format as the foundation. By maintaining file format compatibility, scientists could introduce Parallel-NetCDF to their workflows with minimal disruption. Parallel-NetCDF could not implement some of its ideas for optimized parallel I/O without altering the programming API, but such alterations were done in the spirit of serial-NetCDF, and retain much of the same feel and semantics.

Both libraries support the "classic" netCDF file format, depicted in Figure 15.2. The first bytes of the file contain a header. This header describes the name and size of the dimensions used by the variables; the name, type, shape, and starting location in the file of variables; and annotations or "attributes" associated with dimensions, variables, or the entire dataset.

Serial netCDF introduced the idea of a bi-modal API: to write a dataset, a program enters "define mode." In define mode, the programmer defines the dimensions being used, associates those dimensions with variables, possibly annotates the components of the dataset, and then switches to "data mode." The program can only transfer data after it has described how the data will be stored. This pre-declaration of the file structure benefits parallel I/O greatly— a process can compute where every element of every array will go, and need not coordinate with any other process. The listing in Figure 15.3 provides a brief example of how define mode and data mode work together. Readers can find entire code samples in the on-line Parallel-Netcdf Quick Tutorial [1].

15.4   Deployment and Usage

In many situations, the choice of which I/O library to use depends on the domain in which one operates. Climate codes, for example, have a large repository of datasets in the classic netCDF file format. Analysis and visualization tools were written to read this file format, so when a climate simulation generates data, that data should be in netCDF format to simplify data management.

Parallel-NetCDF, despite a different API and its parallel I/O features, maintains compatibility with the serial netCDF file format. This compatibility

```
1    ret = ncmpi_create(MPI_COMM_WORLD, filename,
2                NC_CLOBBER|NC_64BIT_OFFSET, MPI_INFO_NULL, &ncfile);
3    /* after create, file is automatically in define mode */
4    ncmpi_def_dim(ncfile, "d1", DATA_PER_PROC, &(dimarray[1]));
5    ncmpi_def_dim(ncfile, "d2", nprocs, &(dimarray[0]));
6    /* note how this call associates a name, a datatype, and a shape
7       to the variable */
8    ncmpi_def_var(ncfile, "v2d", NC_INT, ndims, dimarray, &varid1);
9
10   ncmpi_def_var(ncfile, "v2d", NC_INT, ndims, dimarray, &varid1);
11
12   ncmpi_enddef(ncfile);
13
14   ncmpi_put_vara_int_all(ncfile, varid1, start, count, data);
15   ncmpi_close(ncfile);
```

FIGURE 15.3: A code fragment demonstrating the two modes of the Parallel-NetCDF API. By requiring a separate declaration step, the data transfer step can occur in parallel without additional coordination.

allowed Parallel-NetCDF to see rapid adoption in the climate community. Science groups could introduce parallelism piecewise, but still use serial tools. For example, the code writing history files in a climate simulation could be updated written in parallel, but the tools to visualize that data could remain serial for a bit longer.

With its long history of using netCDF-formatted files, naturally the climate communities use Parallel-NetCDF. Parallel-NetCDF has also seen adoption in weather, fluid dynamics [5], and astrophysics [3].

Parallel-NetCDF saw tremendous interest from its earliest days. The Leadership Computing Facilities at Argonne and Oak Ridge National Laboratories have installed Parallel-NetCDF for the past three generations of systems. Many other sites have installed Parallel-NetCDF, particularly if those sites host computational scientists from the climate domain. If a user should happen to find Parallel-NetCDF not already installed on a system, its minimal dependencies make building it straightforward.

15.5 Additional Features

Parallel-NetCDF's similarity to serial netCDF provides its strongest selling point. Maintaining that similarity means a new Parallel-NetCDF user need not spend much time learning about the distinction between define mode and data mode or how to view or analyze the generated file. However, Parallel-NetCDF provides several features not available in serial netCDF.

The *Flexible Interface* to Parallel-NetCDF allows a developer to describe arbitrary data in memory when writing to a multi-dimensional file. The various

```
1   /* post two non-blocking operations, writing data to
2   two variables (varid1, varid2) in the \dataset{} */
3   ncmpi_iput_vara(ncfile, varid1, &start, &count, &data, count,
4               MPI_INT, &requests[0]);
5   ncmpi_iput_vara(ncfile, varid2, &start, &count, &data, count,
6               MPI_INT, &requests[1]);
7
8   /* here in ncmpi_wait_all the library will inspect all non-blocking
9   operations, combine them, and service the new larger request collectively */
10  ncmpi_wait_all(ncfile, 2, requests, statuses);
11      if (ret != NC_NOERR) handle_error(ret, __LINE__);
```

FIGURE 15.4: A code fragment demonstrating the use of the non-blocking routines. The Parallel-NetCDF library will stitch these two requests into one single more efficient MPI-IO operation.

data transfer methods in serial netCDF (the var, vars, vara, varm routines) all take a contiguous memory buffer. Parallel-NetCDF's Flexible Interface allows the caller to specify the type and structure of memory with an MPI datatype. Jianwe Li's SC 2003 paper [4] goes into more detail.

Parallel-NetCDF also introduced non-blocking operations in its API. These nonblocking operations were not interesting at first: they would call the non-blocking MPI-IO routines, but most MPI-IO implementations provided little if any non-blocking support. The non-blocking interface, however, provided a good location to apply an operation-combining optimization.

Figure 15.4 lists a code fragment using this non-blocking interface. Parallel-NetCDF's non-blocking interface follows the same post-and-wait model used in MPI.

Both the Flexible Interface and the non-blocking interface re-enforce a common theme in high performance parallel I/O: providing as much information as possible to the storage system. In Latham et al.'s case study [3], using these extended features of Parallel-NetCDF improved checkpoint bandwidth at scale by a factor of 3.

15.6   Conclusion

The I/O library has seen much research in the decade since Parallel-NetCDF began. HDF5 continues development. ADIOS offers an alternative approach to data management. The serial netCDF project has incorporated parallel I/O features by implementing its API (with some extensions) on top of the HDF5 library. Despite these innovations, Parallel-NetCDF still provides a useful tool in the toolbox of parallel I/O libraries.

The first challenge a scientific application faces when managing data is how to drive the large storage systems in parallel. The developers must first devise a parallel data decomposition strategy, no matter which library will be used. Often, this decomposition strategy is the trickiest part. Once a strategy is in place, the I/O library used is secondary, and can often be hidden by an abstraction layer (climate codes, for example, use PIO [2] for just this purpose). The glib answer to "Which I/O library should I use?" is "It doesn't matter, as long as you use *something.*"

Parallel-NetCDF still provides the standard for a low-overhead I/O library. The classic netCDF file format imposes some restrictions, but these restrictions mean the file layout is known ahead of time. The library does not need additional coordination among processes to know where to place data.

Other I/O libraries can borrow ideas proven in Parallel-NetCDF. When serial netCDF introduced parallel I/O to its API, they could use Parallel-NetCDF's approach for incorporating parallel I/O parameters such as the MPI communicator and how to express collective I/O. An upcoming release from the HDF5 project will contain a "multi-dataset" family of routines following the Parallel-NetCDF approach.

In the flourishing ecosystem of parallel I/O libraries, Parallel-NetCDF still represents a compelling option for codes using regular arrays to describe their data, or are willing to transform their data into such arrays. As scientific data models increase in complexity, the relative simplicity of Parallel-NetCDF might one day no longer be appropriate. As we in the I/O library community develop successor libraries for more sophisticated application data models, Parallel-NetCDF will remain the standard for a lightweight abstraction layer.

15.7 Additional Resources

More Parallel-NetCDF information can be found at the following places:

www.mcs.anl.gov/parallel-netcdf The Parallel-NetCDF home page contains an overview of the package, instructions for joining the mailing list, tutorials, documentation, and bug tracker.

cucis.ece.northwestern.edu/projects/PnetCDF Northwestern University's Parallel-NetCDF page contains additional material and documentation.

Parallel-NetCDF requires only an MPI-IO implementation, and so is available on nearly every parallel computer. Users should consult local documentation for details of any site-specific quirks.

Bibliography

[1] The Parallel-NetCDF Quick Tutorial. `http://trac.mcs.anl.gov/projects/parallel-netcdf/wiki/QuickTutorial`. Accessed: 2014-03-20.

[2] John M. Dennis, Jim Edwards, Ray Loy, Robert Jacob, Arthur A. Mirin, Anthony P. Craig, and Mariana Vertenstein. An Application-Level Parallel I/O Library for Earth System Models. *International Journal of High Performance Computing Applications*, 26(1):43–53, 2012.

[3] Rob Latham, Chris Daley, Wei keng Liao, Kui Gao, Rob Ross, Anshu Dubey, and Alok Choudhary. A Case Study for Scientific I/O: Improving the FLASH Astrophysics Code. *Computational Science & Discovery*, 5(1):015001, 2012.

[4] Jianwei Li, Wei keng Liao, Alok Choudhary, Robert Ross, Rajeev Thakur, William Gropp, Rob Latham, Andrew Siegel, Brad Gallagher, and Michael Zingale. Parallel netCDF: A High Performance Scientific I/O Interface. In *Proceedings of Supercomputing: The International Conference for High Performance Computing, Networking, Storage and Analysis*, SC 03, page 39, Phoenix, AZ, November 2003. IEEE Computer Society Press.

[5] Andreas Lintermann, Matthias Meinke, and Wolfgang Schrder. Fluid Mechanics Based Classification of the Respiratory Efficiency of Several Nasal Cavities. *Computers in Biology and Medicine*, 43(11):1833–1852, 2013.

[6] Russ Rew and Glenn Davis. Data Management: NetCDF: An Interface for Scientific Data Access. *IEEE Comput. Graph. Appl.*, 10(4):76–82, 1990.

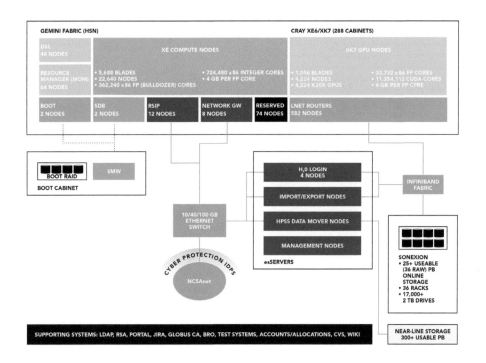

FIGURE 3.1: The Blue Waters computational analysis subsystem. [Image courtesy of Paula Popowski, NCSA.]

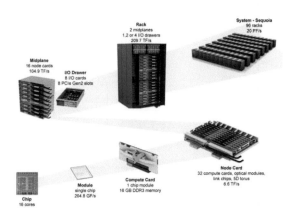

FIGURE 5.1: A pictorial representation of the hardware packaging hierarchy of the BG/Q scaling architecture. The smallest configuration could be a portion of a midplane and a single I/O card. The Sequoia system is composed of 96 racks each with one I/O drawer containing eight I/O cards (768 I/O nodes total).

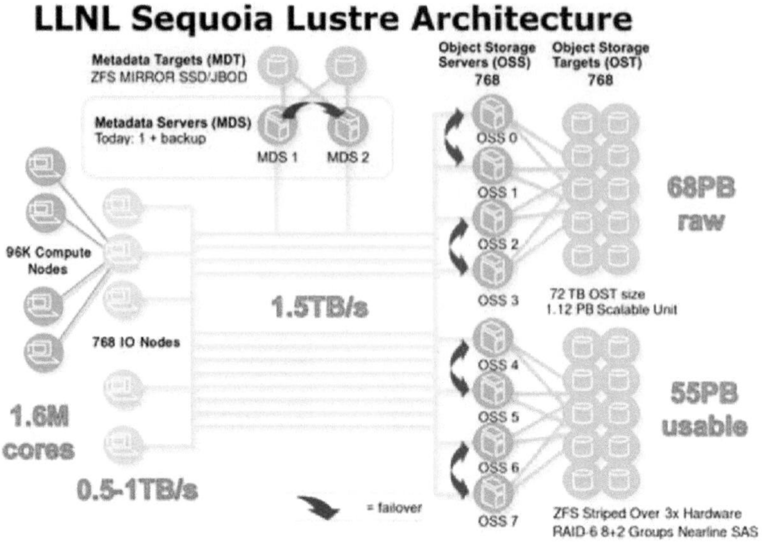

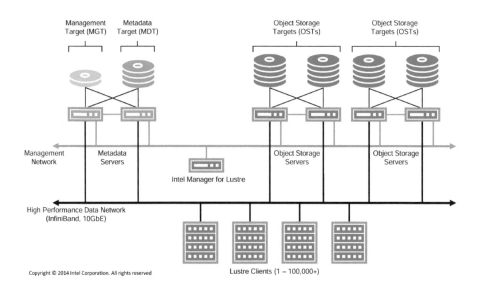

LLNL Sequoia Lustre Architecture

Metadata Targets (MDT)
ZFS MIRROR SSD/JBOD

Metadata Servers (MDS)
Today: 1 + backup

MDS 1   MDS 2

Object Storage   Object Storage
Servers (OSS)   Targets (OST)
768   768

OSS 0

OSS 1   **68PB**
                                raw
OSS 2

96K Compute
Nodes

OSS 3   72 TB OST size
             1.12 PB Scalable Unit

768 IO Nodes

1.5TB/s

OSS 4

OSS 5   **55PB**
                                usable
OSS 6

1.6M
cores

0.5-1TB/s

= failover   OSS 7   ZFS Striped Over 3x Hardware
                       RAID-6 8+2 Groups Nearline SAS

FIGURE 5.3: Block diagram of the ZFS-based Lustre file system for LLNL's Sequoia system. The 96,000 compute node system with 768 I/O nodes is served by a 55-PB ZFS-based Lustre file system composed of 768 OSTs and a metadata server with single failover.

Management   Metadata
Target (MGT)   Target (MDT)

Object Storage   Object Storage
Targets (OSTs)   Targets (OSTs)

Management   Metadata
Network   Servers

Object Storage   Object Storage
Servers   Servers

Intel Manager for Lustre

High Performance Data Network
(InfiniBand, 10GbE)

Lustre Clients (1 – 100,000+)

FIGURE 8.1: Lustre architecture. [Image courtesy of Intel Corporation.]

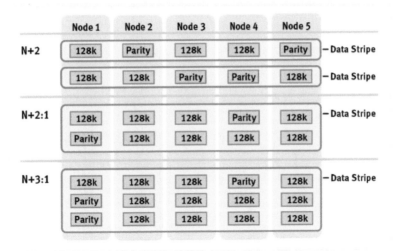

FIGURE 11.5: OneFS hybrid parity protection schemes $(N + M : x)$.

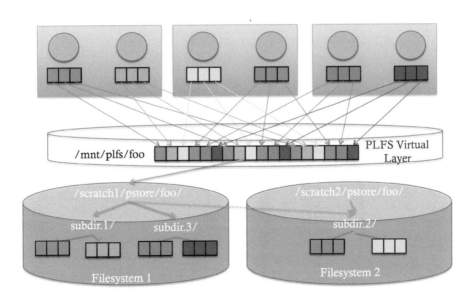

FIGURE 14.1: PLFS shared file mode transforms multiple writes to a shared file into streams of data sent to multiple subfiles on the underlying storage system(s). Not shown is the internal PLFS metadata used to reconstruct the file. [Image courtesy of John Bent (EMC).]

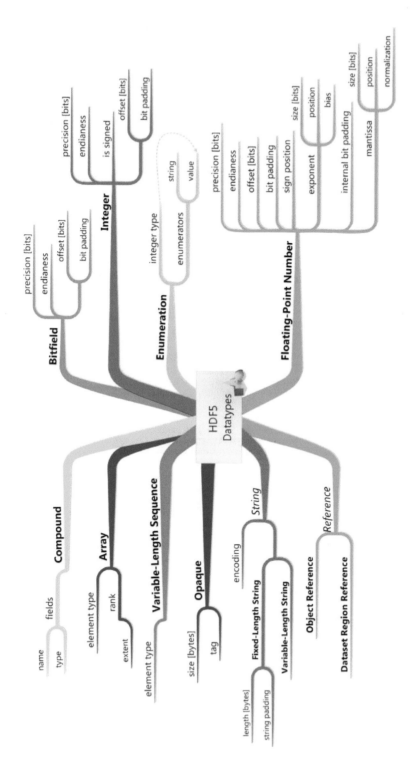

FIGURE 16.3: An overview of HDF5 datatypes. [Image courtesy of Gerd Heber, The HDF Group.]

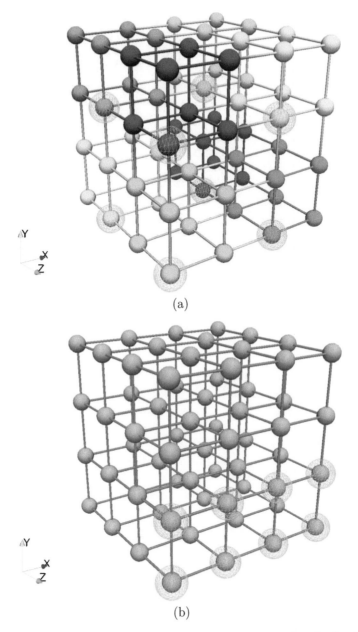

(a)

(b)

FIGURE 18.2: Aggregation groups formed within a set of nodes by GLEAN (a) with aggregator nodes highlighted, and (b) aggregator node configuration used by MPI I/O.

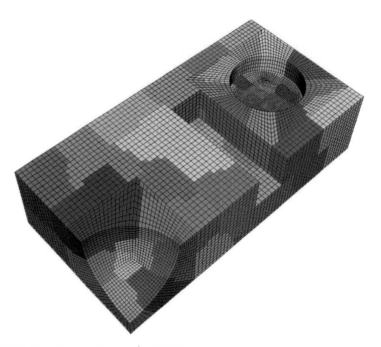

FIGURE 21.1: Example of an ALE3D mesh decomposed into domains. [Image courtesy of Bert Still (LLNL).]

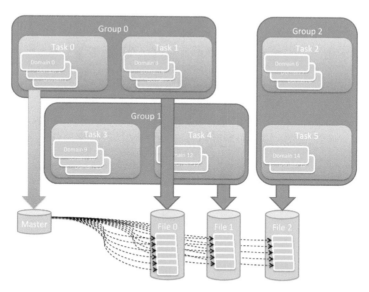

FIGURE 21.2: Example silo-based MIF-IO. There are 6 MPI tasks. Tasks 0–3 have 3 domains. Tasks 4 and 5 have 2 domains. Tasks are divided into 3 I/O groups. Task 0 creates file 0 and writes its 3 domains in 3 sub-directories in the file. Simultaneously, tasks 1 and 2 create files 1 and 2 and write their domains. There are 3 parallel streams of data from the application.

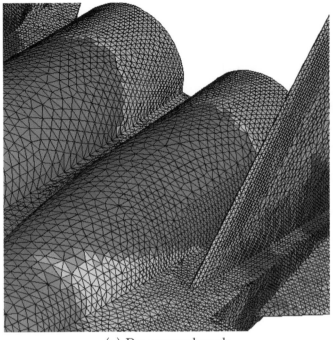

(a) Decomposed mesh

Increasing file offset

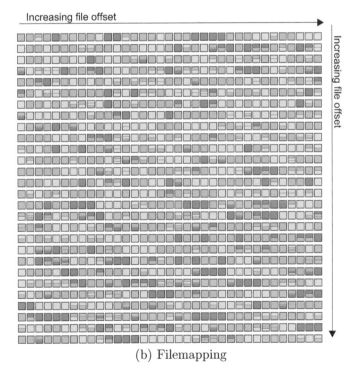

(b) Filemapping

FIGURE 30.1: Domain decomposition resulting in highly non-contiguous access pattern. Color indicates node access..

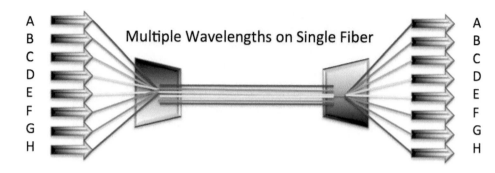

FIGURE 33.2: Wavelength division multiplexing.

Chapter 16

HDF5

Quincey Koziol

The HDF Group

Russ Rew

University Corporation for Atmospheric Research

Mark Howison

Brown University

Prabhat

Lawrence Berkeley National Laboratory

Marc Poinot

French Aerospace Laboratory

16.1	Motivation	186
16.2	History and Background	186
16.3	Design and Architecture	187
	16.3.1 The HDF5 Data Model	188
	16.3.2 The HDF5 Library	191
	16.3.3 The HDF5 File Format	192
16.4	Usage and Applications	192
	16.4.1 netCDF-4	193
	16.4.1.1 Design	193
	16.4.1.2 Applications	193
	16.4.2 H5hut	194
	16.4.2.1 Design	194
	16.4.2.2 Applications	194
	16.4.3 CGNS	195
	16.4.3.1 Design	195
	16.4.3.2 Applications	197
16.5	Conclusion	199
16.6	Additional Resources	199
	Bibliography	199

16.1   Motivation

HDF5 [13], short for "Hierarchical Data Format, version 5" is a data model, library, and file format for storing and managing data. It is designed to meet the needs of applications that push the limits of what can be addressed by traditional database systems, XML documents, or in-house data formats. Many HDF5 adopters have very large datasets, very fast access requirements, or very complex data relationships. Others turn to HDF5 because it allows them to easily share data across a wide variety of computational platforms using applications written in different programming languages. Some use HDF5 to take advantage of the many open-source and commercial tools that understand HDF5.

Similar to XML documents, HDF5 files are self-describing and allow users to specify complex data relationships and dependencies. In contrast to XML documents, HDF5 files can contain binary data (in many representations) and allow direct access to parts of the file without first parsing the entire contents.

HDF5, not surprisingly, also allows hierarchical data objects to be expressed in a very natural manner, in contrast to the tables of a relational database. Whereas relational databases support storing records in tables, HDF5 defines n-dimensional datasets where each element in the dataset may itself be a complex object. Relational databases offer excellent support for queries based on field matching, but are not well-suited for sequentially processing all records in the database or for subsetting based on coordinate-style lookup, prime use cases for HDF5's capabilities.

In-house data formats are often developed by individuals or teams to meet specific needs of a project. While the initial time to develop and deploy such a solution may be quite low, the results are often not portable, not extensible, and not high performance. In many cases, the time devoted to extending and maintaining custom data management code takes an increasingly large percentage of the project's total development effort—in effect reducing the time available for the primary objectives of the project. HDF5 offers a flexible format and powerful API backed by over 25 years of development history. Developers can leverage HDF5's capabilities and tailor them to their needs by building a thin project- or domain-specific API on top of the HDF5 API, creating the best of both worlds.

16.2   History and Background

In 1987, the Graphics Foundations Task Force (GFTF) at the National Center for Supercomputing Applications (NCSA) at the University of Illinois at Urbana–Champaign set out to create an architecture-independent software library and file format to address the need to move scientific data among the many different computing platforms at NCSA. Additional goals for the project included the ability to store and access large objects efficiently, the ability to store many objects of different types together in one container, the ability to grow the format to accommodate new types of objects and object metadata, and the ability to access the stored data from both C and Fortran applications.

Originally dubbed AEHOO (All Encompassing Hierarchical Object Oriented format), the new software and file format was ultimately called Hierarchical Data Format (HDF), and was developed as an open-source product and distributed free of charge under a University of Illinois license. The design of HDF combined ideas from a number of different formats including TIFF, CGM, FITS, and the Macintosh PICT format.

In 1996 the HDF group began a successful collaboration with the Department of Energy's (DOE) Advanced Simulation and Computing (ASC) program. The goal of ASC was to increase the computing power of DOE systems at Lawrence Livermore, Los Alamos, and Sandia National Laboratories by several orders of magnitude. This boost in computational power was clearly going to require an associated scale-up in data management capabilities—data files would be very large, written in parallel on massively parallel systems, and the data itself would be more complex than ever.

A Data Models and Formats (DMF) group, drawn from the three DOE laboratories and NCSA, set about to create a format that would address ASC's needs. HDF had many of the required features, but it didn't scale to sufficiently large files, and could not easily support parallel I/O. Like the GFTF before it, the DMF borrowed ideas and lessons learned from other formats, in particular from HDF and a format from Livermore called Array I/O (AIO), to define a new format for the project. Initially called "Big HDF," the resulting format was finally named "HDF5" because the latest release of the original HDF was HDF version 4.0.

The DOE laboratories and NCSA, with additional support from NASA, jointly developed and released the first version of HDF5 in 1998. HDF5 continues to enjoy a distinguished status as a scientific data format and library, with successful collaborations with NASA and DOE continuing to the present day.

16.3   Design and Architecture

HDF5 is designed at three levels: a data model, a software library, and a file format. The HDF5 data model consists of abstract classes, such as files, datasets, groups, datatypes, and dataspaces, that application developers use to construct a model of their higher-level concepts. As a software library, HDF5 is designed to provide applications with an object-oriented programming interface that is powerful, flexible and high performance. HDF5's file format provides a portable, backward- and forward-compatible, and extensible instantiation of the HDF5 data model.

16.3.1   The HDF5 Data Model

At the highest level, the HDF5 data model provides classes that application developers use to construct models of their domain-specific objects. The primary classes in the HDF5 data model are:

File: A container which holds HDF5 dataset and group objects. Files always contain at least one group object, the "root" group.

Dataset: A multi-dimensional array of data elements.

Group: A set of links to HDF5 dataset and group objects.

Link: A named reference to an HDF5 dataset or group object.

Attribute: User-level metadata associated with an HDF5 dataset or group.

Figure 16.1 shows an HDF5 container (typically stored as a file), with examples of the primary HDF5 object model classes. HDF5 objects in a container do not have explicit names because they can be referenced with links from multiple locations in the container's group hierarchy, so the objects discussed here are labeled numerically. Object 1 is the root group for the file, referenced with the name "/" and is shown with a set of user-defined attributes attached to it. Object 2 is a dataset, referenced with the name "/A/C" and has a single attribute attached to it. Object 3 shows a dataset object that can be reached from two different groups in the container, and can be referenced as either "/A/E" or "/B/F."

Figure 16.1 shows a sample of the power of HDF5 groups and links for structuring application information in ways that best match the application's needs. HDF5 groups can be nested to arbitrary depth and HDF5 links allow dataset or group objects to be referenced from multiple groups. This flexibility allows the creation of directed graphs, not just hierarchical structures. Although not shown in Figure 16.1, links can also "dangle" (referring to objects not yet placed in the container) or refer to objects in another container.

Groups and links provide the structure for the objects in an HDF5 container, but datasets are where an application's bulk data is stored. HDF5 datasets are multi-dimensional array objects that are stored in the container and referred to by links from one or more groups. Each dataset has metadata that describes the array dimensions, the array element type and the storage layout in the container. Figure 16.2 shows a three-dimensional dataset with 32-bit floating-point elements, stored contiguously in the container.

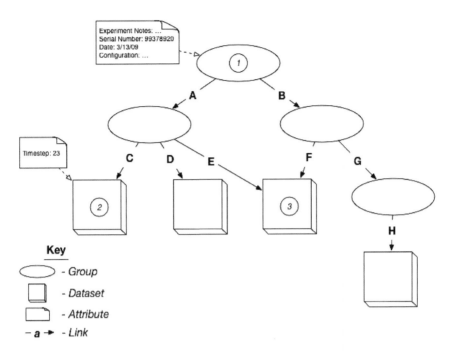

FIGURE 16.1: An example of the main objects in the HDF5 data model.

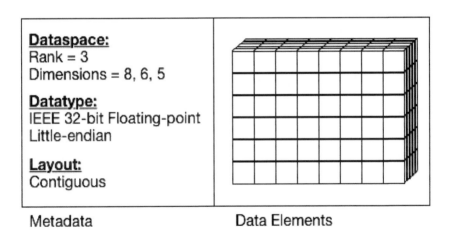

FIGURE 16.2: An overview of a simple 3D dataset's structure.

An HDF5 dataset's dataspace describes the number of dimensions of the array (or its "rank") and can range in dimensionality from 0 dimensions (a single element) up to 32 dimensions. Each dimension can be a fixed or unlimited size, and unlimited dimensions allow any edge of the array to be expanded.

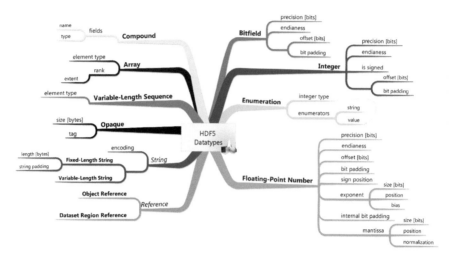

FIGURE 16.3 (See color insert): An overview of HDF5 datatypes. [Image courtesy of Gerd Heber, The HDF Group.]

The datatype of an HDF5 dataset describes the type of the element stored at each location of the array. Each element of a dataset must have the same datatype, but datatypes themselves are capable of describing very complex structures for each element. Figure 16.3 shows the categories of datatypes and some of their capabilities. Notable features include the ability to nest array, compound, and variable-length datatypes arbitrarily to create user-defined integer and floating-point types, and to reference other objects and regions of objects within the container. HDF5 datatypes give great power to the application developer, allowing them to describe their data in memory and store it in HDF5 containers without forcing them to convert the data when storing it.

The layout of an HDF5 dataset describes how elements of the array described by the dataset's dataspace and datatype are stored within the file. As part of HDF5's flexibility, dataset layouts allow for multiple optimizations, such as contiguously storing all the elements together, storing the elements for very small arrays with the dataset's metadata (for faster access), chunking an array up into regular pieces (allowing for array dimension expansion and data compression), and storing the array elements externally in another file.

Finally, HDF5 attributes allow an application to add user-defined metadata to any object in the container. Attributes are name-value pairs that can be attached to any object, with the value for each attribute being essentially a small dataset, with a datatype, dataspace, and array elements. Attributes provide the full richness of the datatypes available to datasets, but are limited in size and access operations, as they are designed to be small objects that augment a larger component in the application's data model.

The HDF5 data model provides a flexible and deep set of objects that application developers can use to store and retrieve data structures in a self-described and portable way.

16.3.2 The HDF5 Library

The HDF5 library is implemented in C, with wrappers for many other programming languages, such as FORTRAN, C++, Perl, Python, .NET, Java, and ADA—all of which call the C API routines. Although the core library is written in C, its API routines are designed in an object-oriented manner that enables simple operations to be written quickly, and still makes complex operations possible in a straightforward way.

In addition to the classes described in the data model section earlier, additional classes are available at runtime for setting properties that control the behavior of objects and operations, selecting regions of dataspaces to perform partial I/O, and a variety of classes that support infrastructure operations like error reporting and object management.

Operations that support partial I/O and property lists that control how to write data in parallel are particularly important in the high performance computing arena. Multiple processes within an MPI application that coordinate to write elements to a single HDF5 dataset can each select part of that dataset in the container and then set a "collective I/O" property when writing their information, allowing all the processes to collaboratively choose an efficient manner to write all the elements to the dataset. Other properties allow further optimizations without adding complexity to the core set of data access routines.

The listing in Figure 16.4 shows a simple program that creates an HDF5 file, creates a three-dimensional dataset of floating-point values linked from

```
/* Create a new file using default properties. */
file_id = H5Fcreate("File.h5", H5F_ACC_TRUNC, H5P_DEFAULT, H5P_DEFAULT);

/* Create a dataspace that describes the dataset's array dimensions. */
dataspace_id = H5Screate_simple(3, {8, 6, 5}, NULL);

/* Create a dataset with floating-point array elements. */
dataset_id = H5Dcreate(file_id, "/dset", H5T_NATIVE_FLOAT, dataspace_id,
                       H5P_DEFAULT, H5P_DEFAULT, H5P_DEFAULT);

/* Write elements to the dataset. */
H5Dwrite(dataset_id, H5T_NATIVE_FLOAT, H5S_ALL, H5S_ALL, H5P_DEFAULT, buf);

/* Terminate access to the objects created. */
H5Sclose(dataspace_id );
H5Dclose(dataset_id);
H5Fclose(file_id);
```

FIGURE 16.4: A simple HDF5 application.

the root group of the file (referred to as "/dset"), and writes all the elements of the array out from a memory buffer. The HDF5 programming API and its usage is extensively documented online with example code, tutorials, a user's guide, and API reference manual [14].

16.3.3   The HDF5 File Format

Based on many years of experience developing the original HDF package (now called "HDF4" [12]) and in broadly surveying many other file formats and data storage mechanisms, the HDF5 file format is designed to be portable, resilient to data corruption, and future-proof through "micro-versioning." Micro-versioning within an HDF5 file allows individual aspects of each object to be stored with a different version. This capability allows the format of individual components of objects to be incrementally extended and improved as needed, without version changes for the entire file format.

Files created by the HDF5 library are always backward compatible and are as forward compatible as possible. Backward compatibility indicates that old files continue to be able to be accessed with newer versions of the HDF5 library. Forward compatibility allows files created by later versions of the library to be read by earlier versions, to the extent possible. The HDF5 library implements this capability by storing each object in a container with the oldest micro-version of the object's components that can possibly represent the information and features requested for the object. This allows the greatest range of older released software to read files produced by newer libraries.

In a very strong sense, HDF5 files implement a file system within a container, with groups analogous to directories and datasets similar to (structured) files. As such, there are many pieces of infrastructure within an HDF5 container, such as B-trees, heaps, etc. All aspects of the HDF5 file format are described in the format specification [15], which has allowed third-party implementations of HDF5 file readers, proving the ability of HDF5 files to outlast even the current library implementation.

16.4   Usage and Applications

HDF5 is used across hundreds of science, engineering, and business domains and by thousands of applications within those domains, from high-energy physics, climate modeling, and financial market tracking to airplane flight test data recording and medical record storage. The following vignettes highlight some of the high performance computing applications of HDF5 that are most relevant to this text.

16.4.1 netCDF-4

16.4.1.1 Design

NetCDF (network Common Data Form) is a data model for array-oriented scientific data, as well as a freely distributed collection of access libraries that support the implementation of the same data model, and a machine-independent data format. Together, the interfaces, libraries, and format support the creation, access, and sharing of scientific data.

Unidata's netCDF-4 data access software supports optional use of HDF5 as a storage layer, to take advantage of features and benefits of HDF5 for high performance computing and advanced data structures. The widespread use of netCDF in archives and third-party software, the simplicity of the netCDF data model, and the increasing use of netCDF-based standard CF (climate and forecast) conventions for scientific metadata in the earth sciences motivated the development of a seperate API.

Specifying the use of the HDF5 format in netCDF-4 programs eliminates some limitations of the simpler netCDF "classic" format. The enhanced netCDF-4 data model supports user-defined types and data structures, hierarchies for organizing large groups of named data, additional primitive types, and multiple dimensions along which data may be appended. The underlying HDF5 storage layer also supports performance improvements consistent with the classic netCDF data model, such as per-variable compression, chunking, larger dataset sizes, and efficient dynamic schema changes.

Using the HDF5 format through netCDF-4 APIs for storing data and metadata results in an HDF5 file. The features of netCDF-4 are a subset of the features of HDF5, so data in the resulting file can be accessed by existing HDF5 applications. Some representational artifacts specific to the netCDF data model, such as shared dimensions, are not interpreted by HDF5 APIs.

Although every file in netCDF-4 format is an HDF5 file, there are HDF5 files that are not netCDF-4 format files, because the netCDF-4 format intentionally uses a selected subset of the HDF5 data model and file format features. HDF5 features not supported in netCDF-4 include non-hierarchical group structures, HDF5 reference types, multiple links to a data object, user-defined atomic data types, stored property lists, the HDF5 date/time type, and attributes associated with user-defined types. As a result, netCDF presents a simpler data model and API than HDF5, at the cost of sacrificing some of the power and generality of the more complex HDF5 data model and software.

Parallel I/O is supported through a common API for both netCDF-4/HDF5 and netCDF-3 classic format, the latter through access with a separate Parallel-netCDF library (see Chapter 15).

16.4.1.2 Applications

Internationally, netCDF has been especially popular among climate and ocean modelers; for example, its use (along with the CF conventions) was mandated for the last two archives of the Climate Model Intercomparison Project, associated with IPCC assessment reports. More than 100 open-source software packages provide netCDF access. NetCDF is also used in other disciplines, including chromatography, neuro-imaging, molecular dynamics, and fusion research. NetCDF data access is included with many commercial software packages, such as ESRI ArcGIS, MATLAB, and IDL.

16.4.2   H5hut

16.4.2.1   Design

Particle-based simulations running on large high performance computing systems over many timesteps can generate an enormous amount of particle- and field-based data for post-processing and analysis. Achieving high performance I/O for this data, effectively managing it on disk, and accessing it from analysis and visualization tools can be challenging, especially for domain scientists who do not have I/O and data management expertise. The H5hut [7] library is an implementation of several data models for particle-based simulations that encapsulates the complexity of parallel HDF5 and is simple to use, yet does not compromise performance.

H5hut is a veneer API for HDF5: H5hut files are also valid HDF5 files and are compatible with other HDF5-based interfaces and tools. For example, the h5dump tool that comes with HDF5 can export H5hut files to ASCII or XML for additional portability. H5hut also includes tools to convert H5hut data to the Visualization ToolKit (VTK) format and to generate scripts for the GNUplot data plotting tool.

H5hut is tuned for writing collectively from all processors to a single, shared file. Although collective I/O performance is typically (but not always) lower than that of file-per-processor, having a shared file simplifies scientific workflows in which simulation data needs to be analyzed or visualized. In this scenario, the file-per-processor approach leads to data management headaches because large collections of files are unwieldy to manage from a file system standpoint. Often a post-processing step is necessary to refactor file-per-processor data into a format that is readable by the analysis tool. In contrast, H5hut files can be directly loaded in parallel by visualization tools like VisIt and ParaView.

16.4.2.2   Applications

OPAL (Object Oriented Parallel Accelerator Library) is a tool for simulating charged-particle optics in large accelerator structures and beam lines [1]. OPAL is based on IP^2L [2] and provides a data parallel approach for particles, fields, and associated operators. Production runs of OPAL codes use several thousand cores, on the order of 10^9 simulation particles, and mesh resolutions on the order of 1024^3, which can be saved for post-run analysis using H5hut.

MC4 is a parallel particle-mesh cold dark matter (CDM) code based on MC2 [6]. MC4 currently achieves scalable parallel performance for maximum values of $N_particles = N_grid = 4096^3$ using $O(10,000)$ cores, and uses H5hut to output several terabytes of particle and field data per timestep. Work is progressing toward problem sizes of $N_particles = N_grid = 8192^3$ or even larger using $O(100,000)$ cores.

The **HDF5-FastQuery** [4] library enables multi-dimensional indexing and searching on large H5Part datasets by leveraging an efficient bitmap indexing technology called FastBit [16]. Storing bitmap indices directly in the H5hut file significantly speeds up access to subsets of multi-dimensional data, especially through range queries. This has been applied to interactive exploration of simulations of laser wakefield particle accelerators. Data from the simulation is stored with H5Part and indexed with HDF5-FastQuery. High-energy particles in the laser wakefield can then be efficiently selected by thresholding for large momenta in the direction of the beam [10].

16.4.3   CGNS

16.4.3.1   Design

In 1994, NASA, Boeing, and McDonnell Douglas started a common effort on computational fluid dynamics data standardization. In 1999 they created the *CGNS Steering Committee*, a voluntary public forum made up of international representatives from government and private industry, with the aim of gathering the CFD community on a standard for data interoperability. Today, this committee includes the main actors of CFD from the USA and Europe; they regularly meet in the framework of the *American Institute of Aeronautics and Astronautics (AIAA)* who now holds the standard as one of its recommended practices.

The CGNS standard [3] defines both a data model, the so-called SIDS (Standard Interface Data Structure), and its implementations on physical medium. The data model, a public document, is dedicated to CFD (computational fluid dynamics) computations but has enough genericity to host other CFD-coupled simulations such as CFD/CAA (Aeroacoustics) or CFD/CSM (structural mechanics). The CGNS data model handles few nodes but with a strongly typed grammar. Figure 16.5 shows a simple program that creates a CGNS file. It defines a complete set of data for computation, the definition of the equations, the flow fields and parameters, the meshes and associated topological information, and other auxiliary data.

The data model is the basis for data representation. Once an entity that the standard defines is described in the CGNS/SIDS document, it must be translated to store on a physical medium. There are three CGNS/SIDS mappings: ADF, HDF5, and Python. A mapping defines the translation between the tree data model of CGNS/SIDS and the actual nodes and set of nodes

```
GoverningEquationsType_t := Enumeration(
  GoverningEquationsTypeNull,
  GoverningEquationsTypeUserDefined,
  FullPotential,
  Euler,
  NSLaminar,
  NSTurbulent,
  NSLaminarIncompressible,
  NSTurbulentIncompressible ) ;

GoverningEquations_t< int CellDimension > :=
  {
  List( Descriptor_t Descriptor1 ... DescriptorN ) ;                   (o)

  GoverningEquationsType_t GoverningEquationsType ;                    (r)

  int[CellDimension*(CellDimension + 1)/2] DiffusionModel ;           (o)

  List( UserDefinedData_t UserDefinedData1 ... UserDefinedDataN ) ;   (o)
  } ;
```

FIGURE 16.5: A CGNS/SIDS data model definition.

on disk (ADF, HDF5) or in memory (Python). The CGNS/HDF5 mapping is the main and default implementation [11].

Mapping CGNS/SIDS to HDF5 was chosen to increase performance on dedicated platforms and to avoid maintenance on middleware. The former disk mapping was ADF, developed by McDonnell Douglas in the 1990s. This format is no longer maintained, had been designed for a single process architecture, and had almost no metadata management. The CGNS steering committee decided to keep ADF for compatibility purposes but to change the future low-level storage to use HDF5.

The implementation of the internal CGNS tree structure fit perfectly with the HDF5 tree structure. CGNS has large node contents, but most of the time there are not a lot of nodes per level (in the range of 10^2). Each node is a group, its metadata is stored as attributes, and its children are sub-groups. Some nodes may also store data as a single dataset, with a datatype of integer or floating-point values in simple or double precision, or plain characters. In case of symbolic links, the mapping software keeps track of the link information using its own attributes.

The migration to HDF5 enabled CGNS to change some already existing capabilities such as symbolic links, which are now handled in a more portable manner, and to implement new features such as the parallel access to data. Parallel access to data [5] is applicable to both application or library use. The default CGNS library, the Mid-Level Library (MLL), offers a set of functions with parallel features. The actual use of parallel HDF5 is almost completely hidden to the application writer.

Changing the CGNS implementation to use HDF5 helped focus the team's development effort on the actual details of the standard, avoiding time spent on porting or maintaining the supporting middleware. But it also should be noted that the CGNS/HDF5 mapping has made it possible to create new implementations of the mapping. As the representation to and from the CGNS data model node to its corresponding HDF5 form was public, some alternative implementations [8] have arisen.

16.4.3.2 Applications

CGNS/HDF5 is used for archival and interoperability in multi-physics simulations [9] involving computer fluid dynamics solvers. A CFD solver is a very compute-intensive application. For example, current applications in aerodynamics require a large number of points and parameters with a large number of iterations on these sets of data. The usual parallel strategy splits the configuration into separate sets of points, distributes those sets onto the processors and exchanges the required information at interfaces. The overall simulation is quite synchronous, with many barriers required to coordinate sending data from pre-processing stages to the solvers.

The file-per-processor mapping is usually split into two strategies, shown in Figure 16.6. The first strategy is used for structured meshes, where the CGNS data model defines a set of groups per processor, the application uses one file per processor, and there is no concurrent write access between processors. The second strategy is used for unstructured meshes where a CGNS group is shared by several processors and write access can be performed in parallel. Both strategies use more than one CGNS/HDF5 file, which are gathered into one or more top-level files by means of HDF5 symbolic links. With HDF5, the whole simulation file layout can be defined in advance, as the symbolic links need not to have an actual file target. This link-based approach is preferred for very large results, such as unsteady simulations that could produce hundreds of gigabytes per processor.

By now, HDF5 is widely used by CGNS pre- and post-processing tools. Most preprocessing tools are running on standalone workstations, before the simulation is submitted to the HPC cluster. The generation, modifications, and distribution of the files is performed by FORTRAN, C, or Python scripts, all manipulating HDF5 files. The post-processing is performed on dedicated workstations, using HDF5 as well in combination with third-party software coming from various well-established software companies.

The CGNS standard was first designed for archival. Now we see multiphysics applications using the CGNS standard to define a common interface and data model at the conceptual level and HDF5 as the common storage mechanism. Using HDF5 as the storage standard for simulations has helped the CFD community achieve true interoperability in the complete simulation workflow, and at the same time opens applications up to a wide range of HDF5-based tools, such as that shown in Figure 16.7.

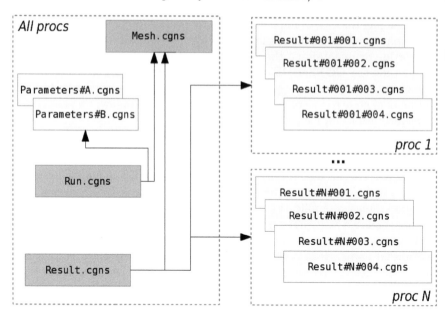

FIGURE 16.6: Typical file layout and links relationships for a parallel computation.

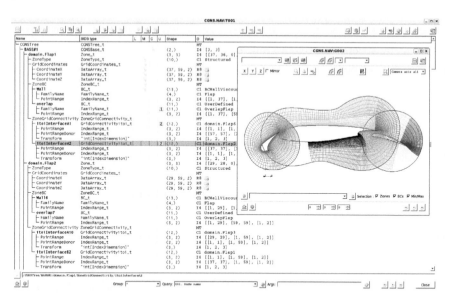

FIGURE 16.7: A graphical view of a CGNS/HDF5 file. [Image courtesy of Onera (http://www.onera.fr).]

16.5 Conclusion

Future development efforts for HDF5 include the ever-present press to improve performance, for both parallel and sequential applications. Adding capabilities to improve concurrent multi-process access to HDF5 files, particularly in a single-writer/multiple-reader scenario, is underway as well, which will enable using HDF5 in new data- and event-monitoring scenarios. The explosion in the number of compute cores available to a single application has increased pressure to make the HDF5 library multi-threaded and to support asynchronous I/O, both of which are under development. Efforts to improve fault tolerance of HDF5 files will enable recovery of files open for modification when an application crashes.

HDF5 has been under development for over 18 years and is expected to continue to grow and evolve for many more to come. Major application communities, government agencies, and large corporations rely on HDF5 for storing mission-critical data that must remain accessible for decades. As new I/O and computing paradigms emerge, such as using flash-memory for storage, shifting from synchronous to asynchronous I/O operations, and building fault-tolerant file systems for exascale computing, HDF5 continues to adapt to the ever-changing landscape in high performance computing.

16.6 Additional Resources

Further information about HDF5 can be found on its home page: `http://www.hdfgroup.org/HDF5/`. The HDF5 home page contains extensive documentation about building and using the HDF5 library and tools, example programs, tutorials, pre-built binaries, the source code repository, links to hundreds of packages that use HDF5, and information about how to access the HDF5 help desk and join the mailing list.

Bibliography

[1] A. Adelmann et al. The OPAL (Object Oriented Parallel Accelerator Library) Framework. Technical Report PSI-PR-08-02, Paul Scherrer Institut, 2008–2010.

[2] A. Adelmann. The IPPL (Independent Parallel Particle Layer) Framework. Technical Report PSI-PR-09-05, Paul Scherrer Institut, 2009.

[3] CGNS Steering Committee. Computational Fluid Dynamics General Notation System.

[4] Luke Gosink, John Shalf, Kurt Stockinger, Kesheng Wu, and E. Wes Bethel. HDF5-FastQuery: Accelerating Complex Queries on HDF Datasets Using Fast Bitmap Indices. In *Proceedings of the 18th International Conference on Scientific and Statistical Database Management*, July 2006. LBNL-59602.

[5] T. Hauser. Parallel I/O for the CGNS System. In *(AIAA Paper 2004-1088)*, 2004.

[6] K. Heitmann, P. M. Ricker, M. S. Warren, and S. Habib. Robustness of Cosmological Simulations I: Large Scale Structure. *Astrophys. J. Suppl.*, 160, 2005. [arXiv:astro-ph/0411795].

[7] Mark Howison, Andreas Adelmann, E. Wes Bethel, Achim Gsell, Benedikt Oswald, and Prabhat. H5hut: A High Performance I/O Library for Particle-Based Simulations. In *Workshop on Interfaces and Abstractions for Scientific Data Storage (IASDS '10)*, Heraklion, Crete, Greece, September 2010.

[8] M. Poinot. CGNS/HDF5 implementation.

[9] M. Poinot, C. L. Rumsey, and M. Mani. Impact of CGNS on CFD Workflow. In *(AIAA Paper 2004-2142)*, 2004.

[10] Oliver Rübel, Prabhat, Kesheng Wu, Hank Childs, Jeremy Meredith, Cameron G. R. Geddes, Estelle Cormier-Michel, Sean Ahern, Gunther H. Weber, Peter Messmer, Hans Hagen, Bernd Hamann, and E. Wes Bethel. High Performance Multivariate Visual Data Exploration for Extremely Large Data. In *SC '08: Proceedings of the 2008 ACM/IEEE conference on Supercomputing*, Austin, Texas, 2008. LBNL-716E.

[11] C. Rumsey, B. Wedan, T. Hauser, and M. Poinot. Recent Updates to the CFD General Notation System (CGNS). In *(AIAA Paper 2012-1264)*, 2012.

[12] The HDF Group. Hierarchical Data Format, version 4, 1988–2014. http://www.hdfgroup.org/products/HDF4.

[13] The HDF Group. Hierarchical Data Format, version 5, 1997–2014. http://www.hdfgroup.org/HDF5.

[14] The HDF Group. Hierarchical Data Format, version 5 Documentation, 1997–2014. http://www.hdfgroup.org/HDF5/doc.

[15] The HDF Group. Hierarchical Data Format, version 5 File Format Specification, 1997–2014. http://www.hdfgroup.org/HDF5/doc/H5.format.html.

[16] Kesheng Wu, Ekow Otoo, and Arie Shoshani. Optimizing Bitmap Indices with Efficient Compression. *ACM Transactions on Database Systems*, 31:1–38, 2006.

Chapter 17

ADIOS

Norbert Podhorszki, Scott Klasky, Qing Liu, and Yuan Tian

Oak Ridge National Laboratory

Manish Parashar

Rutgers University

Karsten Schwan and Matthew Wolf

Georgia Institute of Technology

Sriram Lakshminarasimhan

North Carolina State University

17.1	Motivation	203
17.2	Design and Architecture	204
17.3	Deployment, Usage, and Applications	205
	17.3.1 Checkpoint/Restart	205
	17.3.2 Analysis	206
	17.3.3 Code Coupling	207
	17.3.4 Visualization	208
	17.3.5 Data Reduction	210
	17.3.6 Deployment	210
17.4	Conclusion	211
	Bibliography	211

17.1 Motivation

There are two conventional strategies for writing data from applications that are run on supercomputers: a file-per-process, or a single-shared-file for all processes. However, neither of these processes scale well for large-scale applications. At the application level, it is very hard to implement a flexible I/O strategy that works well on all supercomputers. Application developers cannot be tasked with waiting and maintaining custom I/O middleware. In designing ADIOS, the primary goal was to create an I/O framework that enables scientists to create their data-driven scientific processes, and write their applications with a simple I/O programming interface. Using ADIOS takes away the burden of implementing the I/O strategy at the application level, and chooses the best-performing I/O strategy depending on the parameters of an actual run and the target storage system. Each process in an application needs only to declare what data should be moved and when, but the "how," i.e., the I/O strategy (e.g., aggregation and output file organization), is not implemented at this level. ADIOS takes care of the data movement using an I/O strategy chosen separately.

17.2   Design and Architecture

ADIOS [9] is a user-level I/O library located on top of the I/O stack. ADIOS's write API is designed to be as close to the POSIX I/O calls as possible, but without specifying what happens in the "write" call. Datasets are "opened" and "closed" and variables are "written" to them. In general, write calls only buffer the data content, and in the close call, ADIOS performs burst writes to the file system. However, the actual I/O method used in a run determines how the data is processed and transferred to the target, and if the target is a file system or something else.

The API lets the scientist express I/O in terms of variables in the code as with HDF5 or netCDF. An ADIOS dataset consists of typed, multi-dimensional arrays or simple scalars, with global dimensions defined by scalar variables (similar to netCDF dimensions) or simply by integer values. A writing process also has to declare where its array fits in a global array using offsets and local dimensions.

ADIOS methods implement different I/O strategies, like writing one-file-per-process, or a single-shared-file, or aggregating data into a certain number of files; to push data into the memory of another application using memory-to-memory transfers, or pull data from another application, and so on. The actual method for performing I/O can be selected at runtime in the application.

The ADIOS-BP file format, which is used by most file-based I/O methods, provides a self-describing data format, a log-based data organization, and redundant metadata for resiliency and performance. The log-based data organization allows for writing each process's output data into a separate chunk of the file concurrently. ADIOS contrasts logically contiguous file formats where the data in the (distributed) memory of the processes has to be reorganized to be stored on disk according to the global logical organization. ADIOS-BP however, eliminates (i) communication among processes when writing to reorder data and (ii) seeking to multiply offsets in the file by a process to write data interleaved with what is written by other processes. While local buffering by the processes exploits the best available I/O bandwidth by streaming large, contiguous chunks of data to disk, the destination format itself avoids the common bottlenecks that would hamper that performance. The many processes writing to different offsets in a file or to different files avoid each other on a parallel file system as much as possible. In most cases, each process attempts to write to a single stripe target to avoid the metadata server overhead of spanning storage targets. The read performance of this file format was shown to be generally advantageous by Lofstead et al. [10].

17.3 Deployment, Usage, and Applications

17.3.1 Checkpoint/Restart

Most applications face the I/O bottleneck when they are running at scale and need to perform checkpointing. Writing checkpoint data represents two classes of I/O challenges: write (1) large or (2) small amount of data, stored in many variables, from every process of the application. In both cases, buffering helps to decrease the amount of individual write operations, thus avoiding I/O latency and utilizing the available I/O bandwidth. In both cases, aggregation is required to decrease the number of entities hitting on the file system at the same time. ADIOS has consistently improved all large-scale applications' checkpoint writing (and reading) performance by 10–100x and thus allowed for writing checkpoint data of the size of multiple terabytes at a time with acceptable I/O overhead, as reported in Lofstead et al. [10, 11].

An application, however, does not need to run on tens of thousands of cores to experience I/O bottlenecks. For example, one application is Fine/Turbo, a Computational Fluid Dynamics (CFD) code from Numeca International, that is used in industrial engineering. This CFD simulation simulates billions of cells to get new insights in turbulent behaviors. The irregular topology of a specific simulation is partitioned into small regular 3D blocks. Its load-balancing algorithm divides up the blocks and the variables on each block among the processes so that different variables in a block have different sets of processes assigned to them. The original sequential I/O naturally could not scale up to thousands of cores. Collecting all data on a single core led to high communication overhead. Attempts to write in parallel, while retaining each variable of each block organized on the disk as a contiguous block of data, led again to too much communication between processes.

ADIOS provided the optimal solution to the writing problem. Each process dealt with its own I/O, thus completely avoiding cross-communication among the processes. The data on each process was buffered locally. Then, because of the ADIOS-BP file format, data was written into a separate segment of the output file, that is, with one write request with a single seek in the output. The original sequential I/O took 2000 seconds to complete writing (a smallish) 18 GB of output of a 500-million-cell simulation running on 1280 cores. ADIOS, with the single-shared-file approach, completed the same I/O in 60 seconds. However, scaling the application up to 8000 processes showed the limitations of the single file approach, and therefore aggregation with multiple files was finally used. With aggregation, the above example was completed in 12 seconds, and scalability of the code was maintained for larger simulations up to 3.7 billion cells.

17.3.2   Analysis

Seismography. Recent advances in high performance computing and numerical techniques have facilitated full 3D simulations of global seismic wave propagation at high resolutions. The spectral-element method (SEM) described by Tromp et al. [15] has recently gained popularity in seismology and now SEM is widely used for 3D global simulations. The Theoretical & Computational Seismology research group at Princeton University has developed the open-source SEM package SPECFEM3D_GLOBE; see Carrington et al. [3]. Their goal is to improve the models of Earth's subsurface and kinematic representations of earthquakes.

There are about 6000 earthquakes recorded as of today, with several thousand seismograms available for each earthquake. About 50 iterations of a long processing pipeline for each earthquake will be needed to achieve a highly accurate subsurface model of the whole Earth. In the pipeline, thousands of seismograms (both observed and synthetic ones) are processed and produced at each step for each earthquake while several earthquakes are processed concurrently. Observational data is provided by the IRIS (Incorporated Research Institutions for Seismology) organization but it has to be processed (cleaned and aligned) for the comparative analysis with the synthetic datasets. The current standard data format is a separate binary file for each seismogram, resulting in millions of small input files and multiples of that number of files for intermediate synthetic data. Even the largest parallel file systems cannot provide access to this many files with reasonable performance. Therefore, a new seismography data format has been developed that stores all seismograms of an earthquake in a single ADIOS file, which provides efficient access to all of them while reducing the total number of files by several orders of magnitude. This change alone allows the processing pipeline to execute on Titan, a supercomputer at the Oak Ridge Leadership Facility, using the allocated time efficiently. Previously, the processing pipeline was stalled by waiting on the reads and writes of small files.

Climate research. Climate modeling applications address one of the most pressing issues faced by our society. Numerous surveys show increasing trends in the average sea-surface and air temperatures. A promising method of predicting the future effects of climate change is to run large-scale simulations of the global climate many years into the future. In such simulations, climatologists discretize our entire globe, setting up differential equations to model

Earth's climate. These climate simulations can generate several terabytes, or even petabytes, of raw data. Such data-intensive applications present a tremendous set of challenges for computer centers that strive to accommodate, maintain, transfer, and preserve data.

Large-scale computing centers that host such applications cannot afford to frequently stall on data accesses and lose precious computing cycles. The I/O performance of scientific applications such as climate models has a great impact on the completion of scientific simulation and post-mortem data visualization and analysis. However, many applications have complex data characteristics that are not well supported by existing parallel I/O libraries, for example, applications may generate a large number of small variables. While the data is large in aggregate, each process only holds a very small amount of data for each variable. An example is one of NASA's climate and weather models named GEOS-5 (the Goddard Earth Observing System Model), a GEOS-5 simulation at a coarse resolution of half-degree generates only 3.12 GB data, but consists of 185 2D variables and 80 3D variables at a time. The number of timesteps can be configured to the order of thousands. It is challenging to provide good I/O speed for both writing and reading where large amounts of small I/O requests are expected. Moreover, it is also quite common for data post-processing to examine data along time dimensions, e.g., observing the change of temperature within one hour. However, storage data layouts currently common in use do not provide a good support for such an access pattern.

In addressing critical climate issues, climatologists and meteorologists are limited by the available spatial and temporal resolutions of the current climate and weather models. An I/O method of ADIOS was specifically designed by Tian et al. [14] to enable higher resolution in output datasets. It leverages the spatial and temporal relationships between variable data. Spatially, it aggregates and merges data chunks of the same timesteps so that fewer processes write larger blocks. Moreover, the same variable across different timesteps are merged together with time as a new dimension, which again reduces the amount of I/O requested for both writing and reading. This strategy has provided two orders of magnitude of speedup compared to simple writing (and reading) approaches.

17.3.3 Code Coupling

ADIOS DataSpaces [6] is a scalable data-staging substrate that supports advanced coordination and interaction services for extreme-scale coupled simulation workflows. It provides the abstractions and mechanisms to support flexible and dynamic inter-application coupling and interactions at runtime. It also supports asynchronous data insertion and retrieval to/from a staging area composed of a set of cores on application nodes and dedicated staging nodes. For example, in case of a simulation-visualization workflow, the simulation can output data to the staging resources at runtime using the DataSpaces put() operator, and the visualization processes can asynchronously fetch relevant portions of the data using the corresponding get() operator. Note that these operators are independent of the scale and the distribution of these interacting applications. The internal data management mechanisms in DataSpaces ensure the scalability of the distributed data storage and lookup mechanisms. The DataSpaces runtime builds on DART [5], which enables direct low-overhead, high-throughput memory-to-memory communication between the interacting nodes using Remote Direct Memory Access (RDMA).

DataSpaces implements a distributed query engine with simple and flexible query semantics to facilitate access to the data. An application component can query any data region from the global application domain, e.g., an individual, or a range of data points. Extending the query engine, DataSpaces builds higher-level data sharing and coupling abstractions to support complex and dynamic interaction and coupling patterns. Applications can query data regions on-demand, register to obtain continuous notifications of data availability, implement the publisher-subscriber programming paradigm, share and redistribute data in a decoupled manner, and move analytics code to the data.

DataSpaces consists of two main components: a client module used by the ADIOS/DataSpaces method, and a DataSpaces server module. The client library is light weight and provides an asynchronous I/O (AIO) API. It is integrated with ADIOS and the functionality is exposed through the ADIOS write/read semantics, which bundles the variables of the same output together, so that reading applications can access a set of variables of an output step consistently just like when reading from files.

ADIOS/DataSpaces is currently used in production in coupled scientific simulation workflows on large-scale supercomputers. For example, as part of the fusion simulation framework described by Docan et al. [7] (see Figure 17.1), DataSpaces enables memory-to-memory coupling between the gyrokinetic particle-in-cell edge simulation code XGC0, and the MHD code M3D-OMP. Similarly, as part of the turbulent combustion workflow by Bennett et al. [1], DataSpaces enables data coupling between the direct numerical simulations (DNS) code S3D and the data analytics pipeline.

17.3.4 Visualization

Pixie3D [4] is a magneto-hydrodynamic simulation for fusion. This simulation performs calculations in general curvilinear geometry, which is more optimal for the speed of calculations, but has to be transformed to other meshes for visualization. A separate code, Pixplot, has always been used to process the output on a small number of processes, transform, and write the data and multiple meshes in Cartesian coordinates for visualization. The three components in the visualization pipeline, the Pixie3D simulation, Pixplot transformation, and ParaView parallel visualization server, represent a typical scenario for concurrent in-transit visualization (shown in Figure 17.2). Besides the interactive visualization, a light sequential code, Pixmon, is used to extract 2D slices of

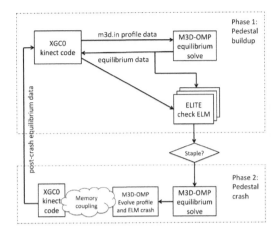

FIGURE 17.1: Coupled fusion simulation workflow using ADIOS and Data-Spaces.

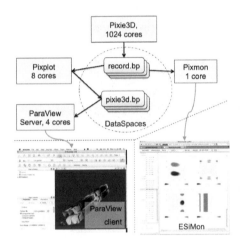

FIGURE 17.2: In-transit analysis and visualization pipeline using ADIOS.

the original output and to upload images of those slices to a web-accessible dashboard (eSiMon [13]), providing continuous and remote monitoring of the simulation.

The application codes are written as if writing data to files and reading data from files, processing one step at a time and only advancing forward in time. ADIOS allows for a seamless switch from file-based post-processing to online processing with memory-to-memory data transfers. Staging methods that transfer data directly from the memory of the producer into the memory of the consumer are best for coupling and for straight analytical pipelines (e.g., the DIMES and FlexPath methods of ADIOS). The DataSpaces model by Docan et al. [6], however, provides a virtual shared multi-dimensional space using a set of separate nodes as a "staging area." Thus multiple, parallel applications can simultaneously read a multi-dimensional array, with an arbitrary decomposition. More importantly for interactive visualizations, DataSpaces can hold as many output steps as the allocated memory can hold. Moreover, DataSpaces provides fault isolation for the application. Failures downstream in a process pipeline do not propagate to the application. More details on using ADIOS and DataSpaces for in-transit visualization can be found in the "*In Situ* Processing" chapter of the book on High Performance Visualization [2].

17.3.5 Data Reduction

Data reduction techniques with ADIOS have shown to be effective in reducing the bottleneck on I/O during simulation writes. These techniques fit well with the minimal communication principle employed by ADIOS where each process handles its own I/O. By applying compression routines locally on every process, encoding costs are effectively minimized. This also enables compression techniques to take advantage of similarity in data values within each process, typically seen with spatio-temporal scientific datasets. For example, ISOBAR [12], an *in situ* lossless compression routine specific to scientific data, demonstrated up to a 46% reduction in storage on datasets from simulations spanning various domains such as combustion (S3D), plasma (XGC1, GTS) and astrophysics (FLASH). This technique coupled with ADIOS and with the addition of interleaving allowed throughput gains proportional to the degree of data reduction.

While checkpoint/restart data, such as particle data, must be compressed losslessly, datasets that are used for analysis and visualization, such as field data, can be compressed in a lossy fashion. Unlike lossless compression, lossy compression techniques, such as wavelets-based compression (i.e., ISABELA [8], etc.) provide a multi-fold reduction in storage sizes, trading precision for storage reduction. Depending on the sensitivity of the analysis routines to errors introduced by the compression process, the end users can change the level of accuracy desired in the configuration file used by ADIOS. The configuration file can also instruct ADIOS to employ different compression routines for different variables and output groups (checkpoint/restart or analysis) without having to change the application code.

17.3.6 Deployment

ADIOS is an open-source software with a BSD license. It has been installed as central software and is supported by the Oak Ridge Leadership Facility, by the iVEC organization in Western Australia for the purpose of supporting the Square-Kilometer Array project, by the High Level Support Team (HLST) supporting EFDA (European Fusion Development Agreement) sites, and by the Engineer Research and Development Center of the U.S. Army Corps of Engineers. At other locations, application scientists install ADIOS themselves for their own applications. Many of those receive direct guidance from the ADIOS team to utilize their target system optimally.

17.4   Conclusion

ADIOS provides a scalable I/O library and has successfully improved the I/O performance of several large-scale applications. In general, it turns out that scientists are frequently limited by I/O performance, and they limit their output data accordingly. As ADIOS provides better application I/O performance, scientists are now able to write more data and thus gain more scientific insights during their analysis. With computing systems generating data at an ever-increasing rate, good application I/O is becoming harder to maintain. Approaches such as *in situ* data analysis and data reduction are becoming more mainstream. The researchers behind ADIOS are working on *in situ* and in-transit (or staging) processing capabilities with an easy-to-use API while maintaining the effectiveness of the ADIOS framework. However, one of the challenges of staging is that moving data around while the application is running interferes with the application's own communication, and thus slows the application down. Therefore, the overhead of staging processing has to be carefully identified and analyzed. ADIOS is becoming a staging framework that provides solutions for low-overhead data transfers. ADIOS's generic I/O API uses flexible programming that is portable to newer computing systems. It is also flexible in switching from file-based post-processing to *in situ* processing.

Bibliography

[1] Janine C Bennett, Hasan Abbasi, Peer-Timo Bremer, Ray Grout, Attila Gyulassy, Tong Jin, Scott Klasky, Hemanth Kolla, Manish Parashar, Valerio Pascucci, et al. Combining *In-Situ* and In-Transit Processing to Enable Extreme-Scale Scientific Analysis. In *High Performance Computing, Networking, Storage and Analysis (SC), 2012 International Conference for*, pages 1–9. IEEE, 2012.

[2] E. Wes Bethel, Hank Childs, and Charles Hansen, editors. *High Performance Visualization: Enabling Extreme-Scale Scientific Insight*. Chapman & Hall, CRC Computational Science. CRC Press/Francis–Taylor

Group, Boca Raton, FL, USA, November 2012. http://www.crcpress.com/product/isbn/9781439875728.

[3] Laura Carrington, Dimitri Komatitsch, Michael Laurenzano, Mustafa M Tikir, David Michéa, Nicolas Le Goff, Allan Snavely, and Jeroen Tromp. High-Frequency Simulations of Global Seismic Wave Propagation Using SPECFEM3D_GLOBE on 62K Processors. In *Proceedings of the 2008 ACM/IEEE conference on Supercomputing*, page 60. IEEE Press, 2008.

[4] Luis Chacón, Dana A. Knoll, and John M. Finn. An Implicit, Nonlinear Reduced Resistive MHD Solver. *J. Comput. Phys.*, 178:15–36, May 2002.

[5] Ciprian Docan, Manish Parashar, and Scott Klasky. Enabling High-Speed Asynchronous Data Extraction and Transfer Using DART. *Concurrency and Computation: Practice and Experience*, 22(9):1181–1204, 2010.

[6] Ciprian Docan, Manish Parashar, and Scott Klasky. DataSpaces: An Interaction and Coordination Framework for Coupled Simulation Workflows. *Cluster Computing*, 15(2):163–181, 2012.

[7] Ciprian Docan, Fan Zhang, Manish Parashar, Julian Cummings, Norbert Podhorszki, and Scott Klasky. Experiments with Memory-to-Memory Coupling for End-to-End Fusion Simulation Workflows. In *10th IEEE/ACM International Symposium on Cluster, Cloud and Grid Computing (CCGrid10)*, pages 293–301, May 2010.

[8] Sriram Lakshminarasimhan, Neil Shah, Stephane Ethier, Seung-Hoe Ku, C. S. Chang, Scott Klasky, Rob Latham, Robert Ross, and Nagiza F. Samatova. ISABELA for Effective *In Situ* Compression of Scientific Data. *Concurrency and Computation: Practice and Experience*, 25(4):524–540, 2013.

[9] Qing Liu, Jeremy Logan, Yuan Tian, Hasan Abbasi, Norbert Podhorszki, Jong Youl Choi, Scott Klasky, Roselyne Tchoua, Jay Lofstead, Ron Oldfield, Manish Parashar, Nagiza Samatova, Karsten Schwan, Arie Shoshani, Matthew Wolf, Kesheng Wu, and Weikuan Yu. Hello ADIOS: The Challenges and Lessons of Developing Leadership Class I/O Frameworks. *Concurrency and Computation: Practice and Experience*, pages n/a–n/a, 2013.

[10] Jay Lofstead, Milo Polte, Garth Gibson, Scott Klasky, Karsten Schwan, Ron Oldfield, Matthew Wolf, and Qing Liu. Six Degrees of Scientific Data: Reading Patterns for Extreme Scale Science I/O. In *Proceedings of the 20th International Symposium on High Performance Distributed Computing*, HPDC '11, pages 49–60, New York, NY, USA, 2011. ACM.

[11] Jay Lofstead, Fang Zheng, Scott Klasky, and Karsten Schwan. Adaptable, Metadata Rich I/O Methods for Portable High Performance I/O. In

Parallel Distributed Processing, 2009. IPDPS 2009. IEEE International Symposium on, pages 1–10, May 2009.

[12] Eric Richard Schendel, Saurabh V. Pendse, John Jenkins, David A. Boyuka, Zhenhuan Gong, Sriram Lakshminarasimhan, Qing Liu, Scott Klasky, Robert Ross, and Nagiza F. Samatova. ISOBAR Hybrid Compression-I/O Interleaving for Large-Scale Parallel I/O Optimization. In *Proceedings of the 21st ACM Symposium on High Performance Parallel and Distributed Computing (HPDC 2012)*. ACM, 2012.

[13] Roselyne Tchoua, Hasan Abbasi, Scott Klasky, Qing Liu, Norbert Podhorszki, Dave Pugmire, Yuan Tian, and Matthew Wolf. Collaborative Monitoring and Visualization of HPC Data. In *2012 International Symposium on Collaborative Technologies and Systems (CTS)*, may 2012.

[14] Yuan Tian, Zhuo Liu, Scott Klasky, Bin Wang, Hasan Abbasi, Shujia Zhou, Norbert Podhorszki, Tom Clune, Jeremy Logan, and Weikuan Yu. A Lightweight I/O Scheme to Facilitate Spatial and Temporal Queries of Scientific Data Analytics. In *Mass Storage Systems and Technologies (MSST), 2013 IEEE 29th Symposium on*, 2013.

[15] Jeroen Tromp, Dimitri Komatitsch, and Qinya Liu. Spectral-Element and Adjoint Methods in Seismology. *Communications in Computational Physics*, 3(1):1–32, 2008.

Chapter 18

GLEAN

Venkatram Vishwanath, Huy Bui, Mark Hereld, and Michael E. Papka

Argonne National Laboratory

18.1	Motivation	215
18.2	Design and Architecture	216
	18.2.1 Exploiting Network Topology and Reduced Synchronization for I/O	217
	18.2.2 Leveraging Application Data Semantics	218
	18.2.3 Asynchronous Data Staging	219
	18.2.4 Compression and Subfiling	219
18.3	Deployment, Usage, and Applications	220
	18.3.1 Checkpoint, Restart, and Analysis I/O for HACC Cosmology	220
	18.3.2 Data Staging for FLASH Astrophysics	221
	18.3.3 Co-Visualization for PHASTA CFD Simulation	222
18.4	Conclusion	223
	Bibliography	223

18.1 Motivation

While the computational power of supercomputers continues to increase with every generation, the I/O systems have not kept pace, resulting in a significant performance bottleneck. Further impeding progress, one often finds that existing I/O solutions only achieve a fraction of quoted capabilities. On the Argonne Leadership Computing Facility's (ALCF) Blue Gene/P resource, FLASH, an astrophysics simulation with a highly tuned I/O subsystem, achieves only 10% of the potential throughput. As the HPC community pushes toward larger-scale systems and the anticipated increase in the size of datasets, this situation will only become even more critical. I/O infrastructures at extreme scales face several system challenges. At the node level, one expects a deep and complex memory hierarchy, including non-volatile memory, as well as higher levels of concurrency. At the system level, leadership computing systems are being architected with higher radix interconnect topologies including the 5D torus (IBM BG/Q), dragonfly (Cray Cascade), and 6D torus (K-machine). Additionally, our community is witnessing systems designed to include burst buffer and dedicated analysis nodes. Parallel file systems deployed at supercomputing centers tend to have diverse performance characteristics for I/O patterns including a single shared file versus a file per process, due to the design and implementation of their underlying metadata and lock management mechanism. Applications need to deal with these factors, among others, in order to scale their I/O performance. To overcome these bottlenecks and help increase the scientific output of leadership facilities, GLEAN provides a topology-aware mechanism for improved data movement, compression, subfiling, and staging for accelerating I/O, interfacing to running simulations for co-analysis, and/or an interface for *in situ* analysis requiring little or no modification to the existing application code base.

18.2 Design and Architecture

has been explicitly designed to improve application performance and productivity. GLEAN users can move data out of the simulation with minimal overhead using a clean interface. The GLEAN design aims to:

- exploit the underlying network topology to speed data motion off of the supercomputer;

- provide asynchronous data I/O via staging nodes;

- develop scalable mechanisms for collective I/O by reducing synchronization requirements;

- mitigate variability in I/O performance of shared file systems using staging;

- leverage data semantics of applications;

- enable simulation-time data analysis, transformation, and reduction;

- provide non-intrusive integration with existing applications; and

- provide transparent integration with native application data formats.

Figure 18.1 provides an overview of the GLEAN infrastructure and compares the traditional mechanism used for I/O with GLEAN. The simulation running on the compute nodes may invoke GLEAN directly or transparently through a standard I/O library such as Parallel-netCDF [8] and HDF5 [6]. The data is moved out either directly to storage or to dedicated analysis/staging

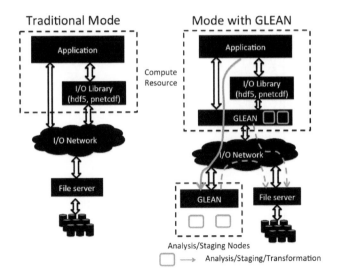

FIGURE 18.1: Relationships between GLEAN and principal components of an HPC application.

nodes. Using GLEAN, one can apply custom analyses to the data on the compute resource or on the staging nodes. This can help reduce the amount of data written out to storage. On the staging nodes, GLEAN uses MPI-IO or higher-level I/O libraries to write the data out asynchronously to storage.

GLEAN is implemented in C++ leveraging MPI and pthreads, and provides interfaces for Fortran and C-based parallel applications. It offers a flexible and extensible API that can be customized to meet the needs of the application. The following subsections describe GLEAN's design in terms of four principal features: network topology and reduced synchronization, data semantics, asynchronous data staging, compression and subfiling.

18.2.1 Exploiting Network Topology and Reduced Synchronization for I/O

As system designs continue to evolve toward heterogeneous and complex network topologies, effective ways to fully exploit their heterogeneity is becoming more critical. For example, in BG/P, the system has different networks with varying throughputs and topologies. The 3D torus interconnects a compute node with its six neighbors at 425 MB/s over each link. In contrast, the collective network is a shared network with a maximum throughput of 850 MB/s to the I/O network. The collective network is the only way to get to the I/O network in order to perform I/O. Recent supercomputing systems have a higher radix interconnect—BG/Q has a 5D torus and the K-machine

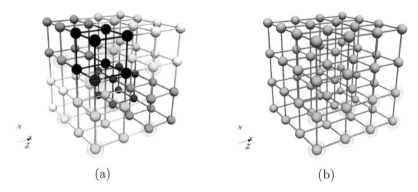

(a)   (b)

FIGURE 18.2 (See color insert): Aggregation groups formed within a set of
nodes by GLEAN (a) with aggregator nodes highlighted, and (b) aggregator
node configuration used by MPI I/O.

has a 6D torus. An important goal in GLEAN is to leverage such topologies
to move the data out of the machine as soon as possible, thereby enabling the
simulation to continue on with its computation.

MPI collective I/O uses *AllToAllv* wherein, depending on an aggregator's
rank, the aggregation traffic can cross the partition boundaries of the aggregator group. This leads to global communication and network contention.
However, GLEAN restricts the aggregation traffic within the group boundary.
This also reduces the synchronization requirements to just the processes involved in an aggregation group, typically 64 nodes for BG/P and 128 nodes
for BG/Q, instead of all the nodes as in the MPI collective I/O case. This
significantly improves performance with larger core counts by reducing the
global communication. Figure 18.2(a) shows GLEAN's selection of 8 aggregator groups formed for 64 nodes. Each group is depicted by a distinct color
(or shade of gray) and the aggregator node for the group is highlighted. For
comparison, Figure 18.2(b) shows the 8 aggregator nodes used in MPI-IO collective operations. In this case, the first 8 nodes are selected as aggregators
and highlighted. Note that the aggregation traffic in the MPI collection I/O
is global and not restricted to an aggregator group.

18.2.2   Leveraging Application Data Semantics

A key goal in designing GLEAN is to make application data semantics a
top priority. This enables GLEAN developers to apply various analytics to
the simulation data at runtime to reduce the data volume written to storage,
transform data on-the-fly to meet the needs of analysis, and enable various
I/O optimizations leveraging the application's data models. This effort has
worked closely with FLASH (see Section 18.3.2) [3], an astrophysics application used to capture FLASH's adaptive mesh refinement (AMR) data model,

and with HACC (see Section 18.3.1), a cosmology application, to capture its particle data model. The GLEAN project has also worked with PHASTA [9], an adaptive unstructured mesh data model, to support unstructured grids in GLEAN. Additionally, pNetCDF and HDF5 APIs have been mapped to relevant GLEAN APIs, thus enabling the developers to interface with simulations using pNetCDF and HDF5. These represent the common HPC simulation data models ranging from AMR grids to particles, and to unstructured adaptive meshes.

18.2.3 Asynchronous Data Staging

Asynchronous data staging refers to moving the application's I/O data to dedicated nodes, and next writing this data out to the file system asynchronously while the application proceeds ahead with its computation. A key distinguishing characteristic of GLEAN's data staging is that it leverages the data models and semantics of applications for staging instead of viewing data simply as files and/or buffers. On the staging nodes, GLEAN runs as an MPI job and communicates with the GLEAN aggregator nodes using a network abstraction layer customized to exploit the underlying interconnects. Asynchronous data staging blocks the computation only for the duration of copying data from the compute nodes to the staging nodes. The data staging serves as a burst buffer for the simulation I/O that can be written out asynchronously to the file system while the computation proceeds. Data staging also significantly reduces the number of clients seen by the parallel file system, and thus mitigates the contention including locking overheads for the file system. The data semantics enables GLEAN to transform the data on-the-fly to various I/O formats. On the staging nodes, GLEAN aims to be deployed either as an "always ON" service, run on dedicated set-aside nodes of a simulation, or co-scheduled along with the simulation. If there is insufficient memory on the staging nodes (receivers), the transfer is blocked until sufficient buffer/memory space is made available. Staging can leverage local node storage to mitigate this issue.

18.2.4 Compression and Subfiling

To reduce the amount of data written to storage and thus improve the I/O performance, GLEAN incorporates compression for I/O. The current implementation leverages Blosc [1], a blocking, shuffling, and loss-less compression library, for data compression and decompression; however, the API enables programmers to invoke their own user-defined compression libraries to achieve the best speed/compression ratio. To mitigate the overhead of the locks and metadata of parallel file systems, GLEAN's I/O mechanism incorporates subfiling [4] wherein a few large files are written out to overcome the parallel file system overheads of a single shared file and a file-per-process I/O. The number of files written out is tunable. On the ALCF Blue Gene systems, files are written out per I/O node.

18.3   Deployment, Usage, and Applications

GLEAN has been deployed on leadership computing systems at Argonne for I/O acceleration, asynchronous data staging, and *in situ* visualization for a number of diverse applications.

18.3.1   Checkpoint, Restart, and Analysis I/O for HACC Cosmology

Next-generation sky surveys will map billions of galaxies to explore the physics of the "Dark Universe." Science requirements for these surveys demand simulations at extreme scales; these will be delivered by the HACC (Hybrid/Hardware Accelerated Cosmology Code) framework [5]. GLEAN's I/O performance was integrated and evaluated with the HACC simulation. A weak scaling study was performed using a number of cores from 16,384 to 262,144 on the Mira BG/Q system with a total number of particles ranging from 2048^3 to 5012^3. The total data per rank varies between 38 MB and 57 MB—i.e., 1 to 1.5 million particles per rank. Thus, 400 GB were written at 16,000 cores and 4.8 TB of data at 256,000 cores. The performance of I/O for HACC was compared using four configurations: (1) MPI collective I/O to a single shared file; (2) subfiling with a file per I/O network; (3) using both topology-aware aggregation and subfiling; and (4) using all the three components of the framework; i.e., compression, aggregation, and subfiling. The simulation was performed for 10 steps with each I/O configuration and the maximum performance was reported for each configuration.

Various I/O configurations show different performance rates, as depicted in Figure 18.3. Subfiling yielded a 5× improvement at 16,000 cores and a 10× improvement at 256,000 cores over a single shared file. Thus, subfiling is of critical importance as it mitigates the impact of the parallel file system metadata overheads at scale. Topology-aware aggregation yields a 20% improvement over subfiling at 16K cores and up to an 80% improvement over subfiling at 256,000 cores. Thus, leveraging system topology plays an increasingly important role when scaling to larger core counts. Using compression, and thus using all three components of the I/O framework, an additional 40% increase in performance was observed over using aggregation. This is primarily due to the ability to achieve 50% compression for the HACC datasets, and thus writing less data to the storage system. Overall, by using subfiling, aggregation, and compression, a 10× improvement was observed over MPI collective I/O at 16,000 cores and a 14× improvement at 256,000 cores, achieving 130 GB/s. Thus, all three are critical to achieving scalable parallel I/O performance. The combination of compression, topology-aware data aggregation, and the subfiling mechanism improved I/O performance on the HACC application multifold. Thus, achieving optimal I/O system performance required

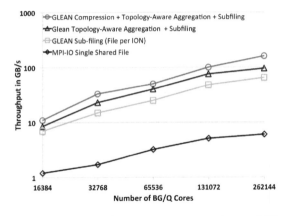

FIGURE 18.3: Efficacy of topology-aware aggregation, subfiling, and compression on the I/O performance of HACC Cosmology Simulation.

improvements to each of the components, from compute nodes to storage disks.

18.3.2 Data Staging for FLASH Astrophysics

The FLASH code [3] is an adaptive mesh, parallel hydrodynamics code developed to simulate astrophysical thermonuclear flashes in two or three dimensions, such as Type Ia supernovae, Type I X-ray bursts, and classical novae. It solves the compressible Euler equations on a block-structured adaptive mesh. FLASH provides an AMR grid using a modified version of the PARA-MESH package and a Uniform Grid (UG) to store Eulerian data.

For this study, GLEAN developers used the Sedov simulation included in the FLASH distribution. Sedov evolves a blast wave from a delta-function initial pressure perturbation [2]. The Sedov problem exercises the FLASH infrastructure (with AMR and I/O) of FLASH with the minimal use of physics solvers. It can, therefore, produce representative I/O behavior of FLASH without spending too much time in computations. The application was run in 3D with 16^3 cells per block. Each block consists of ten mesh variables, and the problem size is controlled by adjusting the global number of blocks. The study advanced four timesteps and produced I/O data at every single step so that most application runtime is spent on I/O. The I/O in each step consisted of the checkpoint files for restart purposes and plot files for analysis. A checkpoint file is the output of the complete state of a runtime application, including mesh data in double precision. A plot file is a user-selected subset of mesh variables stored in single precision. In these experiments, checkpoint I/O writes all ten mesh variables. The plot file I/O writes only selected variables of interest (in these experiments, the first, sixth, and seventh variables).

The performance of GLEAN was evaluated for two standard FLASH output streams (checkpoint and plot data) on the Intrepid BG/P system. Working closely with the FLASH developers, GLEAN was designed to have an API to capture the data semantics of FLASH including the AMR hierarchy. To interface with FLASH, pNetCDF was transformed into the appropriate GLEAN API calls. By setting an environment variable that is passed to the flash executable when the job is launched with pNetCDF, one can use GLEAN with FLASH. Thus, GLEAN is able to integrate with FLASH without any modifications to the FLASH simulation code. On the staging nodes (Eureka), GLEAN can be configured to write data out asynchronously using either pNetCDF, or transformed on-the-fly to HDF5 and written out. This is possible because GLEAN captures the data semantics of FLASH. By incorporating asynchronous data staging, a multifold improvement was achieved in the I/O performance for FLASH at 32,000 cores on the BG/P system [10].

18.3.3 Co-Visualization for PHASTA CFD Simulation

The PHASTA code [9] performs computational fluid dynamics (CFD) using a finite element discretization that uses a large-eddy-simulation-based turbulence model. PHASTA uses an adaptive, unstructured tetrahedral grid. The number and locality of elements changes frequently, based on solution characteristics and load balancing. Grid and field structures are stored in dynamically allocated memory, due to frequent updates.

GLEAN's success is described by the application's ability to enable the simulation-time analysis and the visualization of PHASTA running on 128,000 cores of Intrepid (32 racks) with ParaView [7] running on 80 data-staging Eureka nodes. To achieve this, GLEAN developers worked closely with PHASTA developers to capture the unstructured tetrahedral mesh data model. Additionally, to facilitate visualization of the PHASTA data using ParaView, GLEAN supports ParaView's visualization meshes. On Eureka, GLEAN was able to transform PHASTA's staged data into ParaView's mesh format on-the-fly. ParaView is a highly common visualization toolkit on leadership-class systems. Simulations can now use ParaView and GLEAN to visualize data at runtime.

Two additional scaling studies for co-visualization of the PHASTA simulation with ParaView [10] include a 416-million-element and a 3.32-billion-element case study. For the 416-million-element case of PHASTA on 32 Intrepid racks consisting of about 20 GiB, GLEAN was able to transfer this data in about 0.6*s*, achieving around 34 GiBps. For the 3.32 billion elements (about 160 GB) using 32 racks and 80 Eureka nodes, GLEAN achieved around 41 GiBps. GLEAN enabled PHASTA developers to visualize a live simulation on 128,000 cores.

18.4 Conclusion

The performance mismatch between the computing and I/O components of current-generation HPC systems has made I/O the critical bottleneck for scientific applications. It is therefore crucial that software take every advantage available in moving data between compute, analysis, and storage resources as efficiently as networks will allow. Currently available mechanisms often fail to perform as well as the hardware infrastructure will allow, suggesting that improved optimization and perhaps adaptive mechanisms deserve increased study.

The GLEAN infrastructure was developed to improve I/O performance on supercomputers. The GLEAN infrastructure hides significant details from the end user, while at the same time providing them with a flexible interface offering the fastest path to their data and in the end, scientific insight. GLEAN provides a mechanism to leverage topology-aware data movement for accelerating I/O, interface to run simulations for co-analysis, and an interface for *in situ* analysis with minimal modifications to the existing application code base. It has been deployed on production facilities and demonstrated to scale on 768,000 cores.

Bibliography

[1] F. Alted. Why Modern CPUs Are Starving and What Can Be Done About It. *Computing in Science and Engg.*, 12(2):68–71, March 2010.

[2] FLASH User Guide. http://flash.uchicago.edu/website/.

[3] B. Fryxell, K. Olson, P. Ricker, F. X. Timmes, M. Zingale, D. Q. Lamb, P. MacNeice, R. Rosner, and H. Tufo. FLASH: An Adaptive Mesh Hydrodynamics Code for Modelling Astrophysical Thermonuclear Flashes. *Astrophysical Journal Supplement*, 131:273–334, 2000.

[4] Kui Gao, Wei-keng Liao, Arifa Nisar, Alok Choudhary, Robert Ross, and Robert Latham. Using Subfiling to Improve Programming Flexibility and Performance of Parallel Shared-File I/O. In *Proceedings of the 2009 International Conference on Parallel Processing*, ICPP '09, pages 470–477, Washington, DC, USA, 2009. IEEE Computer Society.

[5] Salman Habib, Vitali Morozov, Hal Finkel, Adrian Pope, Katrin Heitmann, Kalyan Kumaran, Tom Peterka, Joe Insley, David Daniel, Patricia Fasel, Nicholas Frontiere, and Zarija Lukić. The Universe at Extreme

Scale: Multi-Petaflop Sky Simulation on the BG/Q. In *Proceedings of the International Conference on High Performance Computing, Networking, Storage and Analysis*, SC12, pages 4:1–4:11, Los Alamitos, CA, USA, 2012. IEEE Computer Society Press.

[6] HDF Group. HDF5: Hierarchical Data Format. http://www.hdfgroup.org/HDF5.

[7] Kitware. ParaView. http://www.paraview.org/.

[8] Jianwei Li, W. Liao, Alok Choudhary, Robert Ross, Rajeev Thakur, William Gropp, Rob Latham, Andrew Siegel, Brad Gallagher, and Michael Zingale. Parallel netCDF: A High Performance Scientific I/O Interface. In *ACM/IEEE Conference on Supercomputing*, Phoenix, AZ, Nov. 2003.

[9] O. Sahni, M. Zhou, M. Shephard, and K. Jansen. Scalable Implicit Finite Element Solver for Massively Parallel Processing with Demonstration to 160K Cores. In *Proceedings of the Conference on High Performance Computing Networking, Storage and Analysis*, pages 1–12, Portland, Oregon, 2009. ACM.

[10] Venkatram Vishwanath, Mark Hereld, Vitali Morozov, and Michael E. Papka. Topology-Aware Data Movement and Staging for I/O Acceleration on Blue Gene/P Supercomputing Systems. In *Proceedings of 2011 International Conference for High Performance Computing, Networking, Storage and Analysis*, SC '11, pages 19:1–19:11, New York, NY, USA, 2011. ACM.

Part IV

I/O Case Studies

Chapter 19

Parallel I/O for a Trillion-Particle Plasma Physics Simulation

Surendra Byna, Prabhat

Lawrence Berkeley National Laboratory

Homa Karimabadi

University of California, San Diego

William Daughton

Los Alamos National Laboratory

19.1	Abstract	227
19.2	Science Use Case	228
19.3	I/O Challenges	229
19.4	Software and Hardware	229
	19.4.1 Hardware Platform	229
	19.4.2 Software Setup	230
19.5	Parallel I/O in VPIC	230
19.6	Performance	232
	19.6.1 Tuning Write Performance	232
	19.6.2 HDF5 Tuning	233
	19.6.3 Tuning Lustre File System and MPI-I/O Parameters	233
19.7	Conclusion	236
19.8	Acknowledgments	236
	Bibliography	236

19.1 Abstract

As magnetic field lines break apart and reconnect, collisionless magnetic reconnection releases an explosive amount of energy. Such a reconnection plays an important role in a variety of astrophysical applications involving both hydrogen and electron-positron plasmas. Furthermore, collisionless magnetic reconnection is the dominant mechanism that enables plasma from solar winds to enter the Earth's magnetosphere.

A full-resolution magnetosphere simulation is an exascale computing problem. As an inherently multi-scale problem, reconnection is initiated as a small-scale problem around individual electrons that eventually leads to a large-scale reconfiguration of a magnetic field. Recent simulations have revealed that electron kinetic physics is not only important in triggering reconnection [6, 5, 7, 10, 14, 11, 15], but also in its subsequent evolution. This finding suggests a need for modeling details of electron motion, which poses severe computational challenges for 3D simulations of reconnection.

The advent of petascale computers together with advances in particle simulations are now enabling scientists to conduct simulations that are a thousand times larger than the previous state of the art. Recent simulations of collisionless magnetic reconnection used a highly optimized particle code called VPIC [1]. The increased computational capability is providing scientists with the first glimpse of details of collisionless reconnection in 3D. This chapter focuses on large data management and analysis challenges, and demonstrates the effectiveness of using a larger two-trillion-particle run conducted at the National Energy Research Scientific Computing center (NERSC) located at the Lawrence Berkeley National Laboratory.

19.2   Science Use Case

Computational plasma physicists are generally interested in understanding the structure of high-dimensional phase space distributions. For example, in order to understand the physical mechanisms responsible for producing magnetic reconnection in a collisionless plasma, it is important to characterize the symmetry properties of the particle distribution, such as agyrotropy [13]. Agyrotropy is a quantitative measure of the deviation of the distribution from cylindrical symmetry about the magnetic field. Another question of significant practical importance in studies of magnetic reconnection is the characterization of energetic particles. Particle properties of interest include spatial location (x, y, z), energy, and projection of velocity components on the directions parallel and perpendicular to the magnetic field $(U_\parallel, U_{\perp,1}, U_{\perp,2})$.

The main scientific questions addressed in this experiment are as follows:

- Analysis of highly energetic particles:

    - Are the highly energetic particles preferentially accelerated along the magnetic field?
    - What is the spatial distribution of highly energetic particles?

- What are the properties of particles near the reconnection hot spot (the so-called X-line)?

> — What is the degree of agyrotropy in the spatial vicinity of the X-line? In other words, is the density plot of the $U_{\perp,1}$ vs. $U_{\perp,2}$ components highly asymmetrical?

While these questions can be addressed to some extent for smaller-scale 2D and 3D simulations involving millions or billions of particles, it is challenging to address these questions when the number of particles reach beyond hundreds of billions or trillions. Hampered by the lack of scalable tools, physicists have largely ignored the particle data, used some form of sub-sampling, or relied on coarser gridded data for their analysis. The two-trillion-particle study was the first to offer flexible technical capabilities for analyzing trillion-particle datasets.

19.3 I/O Challenges

The main challenges with the trillion-particle VPIC simulation are managing the sheer volume of data. The VPIC simulation writes a significant amount of data at a user-prescribed interval. In the simulation of two trillion particles (including one trillion ions and one trillion electrons), three different datasets were stored: particle datasets, field and hydro datasets, and checkpoint datasets. The particle dataset for a given timestep comprises about one trillion electrons. The data size of each electron particle is 32 bytes, representing various particle properties. The number of particles increases as the simulation progresses. In our simulation, the datasets written in each timestep varied between 30 TB to 42 TB of data. The simulation wrote the particle dataset at 10 timesteps and the total particle data size was about 335 TB. The field dataset includes information such as electric and magnetic field strength, and the particle dataset includes information about the particle's position, momentum, and energy. The field dataset per timestep is relatively small, on the order of tens of gigabytes. Overall, the total amount of data after finishing the simulation was approximately 490 TB, including field data and checkpoint data. Another challenge discussed in Section 19.3 explains a scalable strategy to store terabytes of data produced by a simulation running on hundreds of thousands of cores.

19.4 Software and Hardware

19.4.1 Hardware Platform

Hopper is a Cray XE6 system located at NERSC consisting of 6,384 compute nodes, each containing two 12 core AMD 2.1-GHz MagnyCours processors. Each compute core has a peak performance of 8.4 Gflops/s resulting in a system with a peak performance of 1.28 PFlops. All but 384 compute nodes have 32 GB of memory while the remaining larger nodes have 64 GB of memory creating a system with over 217 TB of memory. It employs the Gemini interconnect with a 3D torus topology.

Hopper has two identical local Lustre parallel file systems: /scratch and /scratch2; each has a peak performance of 35 GB/s and a capacity of 1.1 PB. The Lustre file system is made up of an underlying set of I/O servers and disks called Object Storage Servers (OSSs) and Object Storage Targets (OSTs), respectively. Each /scratch file system has 26 OSSs and 156 OSTs. When a file is created in /scratch it is "striped" or split across a specified number of OSTs. The default stripe count on Hopper is 2 and the default stripe size is 1 MB.

19.4.2   Software Setup

The study used Cray's MPICH2 library (xt-mpt 5.1.2) for running VPIC. The I/O module used HDF5 version 1.8.8 and the particle data is written with H5Part version 1.6.5, along with Cray's MPI-I/O implementation. H5Part is a veneer API built on top of HDF5 for improving the ease of use for writing particle data.

19.5   Parallel I/O in VPIC

VPIC uses 20,000 MPI processes, where each MPI process spawns 6 OpenMP threads to perform computations.[1] An overview of the VPIC simulation setup on Hopper is shown in Figure 19.1. Each OpenMP thread runs on a CPU core and the total amount of CPU cores used in this simulation is 120,000. The figure also shows MPI-I/O aggregators to collect data from multiple MPI domains before writing data to the Lustre file system.

To write the particle data, the study uses an extension of parallel HDF5 called H5Part [8]. Parallel HDF5 has demonstrated competitive I/O rates on modern computational platforms [9]. The H5Part extension to HDF5 improves the ease of use in managing large particle counts. H5Part is a veneer API for HDF5: H5Part files are also valid HDF5 files and are compatible with other HDF5-based interfaces and tools. By constraining the use case to particle-based simulations, H5Part is able to encapsulate much of the complexity of implementing effective parallel I/O in HDF5. That is, it trades off HDF5's

---

[1] In subsequent discussion, "MPI process" is referred to as an "MPI domain" in order to highlight the fact that each MPI process has multiple OpenMP threads.

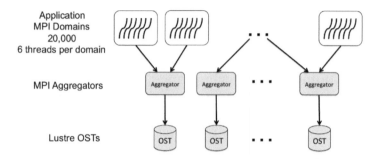

FIGURE 19.1: Configuration of the VPIC simulation using MPI and OpenMP threads for computation. Parallel I/O uses MPI-IO in collective buffering mode and the Lustre parallel file system.

flexibility and complexity in supporting arbitrary data models for ease of use with a specific, particle-based data model.

Using a small set of H5Part API calls, parallel HDF5 I/O was quickly integrated into the VPIC codebase. The simple H5Part interface for writing VPIC particle data is outlined in the following lines of code:

```
h5pf = H5PartOpenFileParallel (fname, H5PART_WRITE |
                  H5PART_FS_LUSTRE, MPI_COMM_WORLD);
H5PartSetStep (h5pf, step);
H5PartSetNumParticlesStrided (h5pf, np_local, 8);

H5PartWriteDataFloat32 (h5pf, "dX", Pf);
H5PartWriteDataFloat32 (h5pf, "dY", Pf+1);
H5PartWriteDataFloat32 (h5pf, "dZ", Pf+2);
H5PartWriteDataInt32   (h5pf, "i",  Pi+3);
H5PartWriteDataFloat32 (h5pf, "Ux", Pf+4);
H5PartWriteDataFloat32 (h5pf, "Uy", Pf+5);
H5PartWriteDataFloat32 (h5pf, "Uz", Pf+6);
H5PartWriteDataFloat32 (h5pf, "q",  Pf+7);

H5PartCloseFile (h5pf);
```

The H5Part interface opens the particle file and sets up the attributes, such as the timestep information and the number of particles. The H5PartWrite···() calls wrap the internal HDF5 data writing calls.

The H5Part interface opens the file with MPI-I/O collective buffering and Lustre optimizations enabled. Collective buffering breaks the parallel I/O operations into two stages. The first stage uses a subset of MPI tasks to aggregate the data into buffers, and the aggregator tasks then write data to the I/O servers. With this strategy, fewer nodes communicate with the I/O nodes, which reduces contention. The Lustre-aware implementation of Cray MPI-I/O sets the number of aggregators equal to the striping factor such that the stripe-sized chunks do not require padding to achieve stripe alignment [4]. Because of the way Lustre is designed, stripe alignment is a key factor in achieving optimal performance.

19.6　Performance

19.6.1　Tuning Write Performance

Performance of parallel I/O depends on multiple software layers of the parallel I/O stack. A contemporary parallel I/O software stack with HDF5 as the high-level I/O library, MPI-I/O as the middleware layer, and Lustre as the parallel file system is shown in Figure 19.2. Each layer offers tunable parameters for improving performance, and hopes to provide reasonable default settings for the parameters.

Tuning HDF5, MPI-I/O, and Lustre parameters was an important part of achieving the I/O performance goals. This study modified the implementation of HDF5 version 1.8.8 to disable the file size verification process. For Lustre, this study varied the stripe count and the stripe size. The stripe count is the number of OSTs used in writing contiguous chunks of data and the stripe size is the size of the contiguous chunk. As mentioned earlier, the Lustre-aware implementation of Cray MPI-I/O sets the MPI-I/O collective buffering parameters. In this implementation, the number of MPI-I/O aggregators is equal to the stripe count, and the size of the collective buffer is equal to the stripe size.

Tuning I/O for the VPIC simulation typically requires running the simulation multiple times while varying the values of tunable parameters. However,

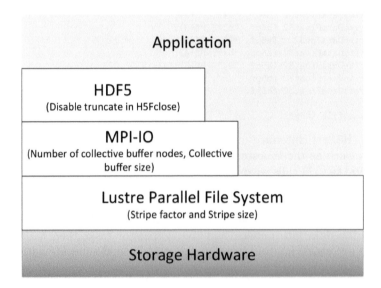

FIGURE 19.2: Parallel I/O stack and the parameters tuned and modifications made in the study's effort.

VPIC is a computationally intensive application, and it is impractical to run the entire code repeatedly, and at scale for tuning. Instead, the study developed a simplified parallel I/O kernel, called VPIC-IOBench. The kernel uses the same H5Part calls shown in Section 19.5 for writing VPIC particle data. VPIC-IOBench disables the simulation component of the VPIC code and uses random data. The kernel contains the full data volume generated by the code with a slightly simplified pattern. In VPIC-IOBench, each MPI process writes an equal number of particles to a shared file, whereas in a VPIC simulation, each MPI domain writes a slightly varying (up to 15%) number of particles. The amount of data the kernel writes is proportional to the number of MPI processes.

19.6.2 HDF5 Tuning

When a HDF5 file is closed, the `H5Fclose` function ensures that the size of the file matches its allocated size. HDF5 tracks the size of the file for two reasons: to detect external file modification/corruption (i.e., from something other than the HDF5 library modifying/corrupting the file), and to allocate space within the file for changes to the file's structure. HDF5 currently verifies the file's size by truncating the file (using a POSIX or MPI operation) to the size of the allocated space within the file. This truncate-based verification step initiates several metadata server operations that degrade performance significantly. Disabling the file's size verification in some cases will likely make the file unreadable. For example, if the truncate operation during `H5Fclose` would actually extend the file (instead of truncating it), but does not occur (because of disabling truncate), data will be double allocated in the file, causing corruption later. If the truncate was actually truncating the file (instead of extending it), it is less of a problem—space in the file will be leaked, but the file will still be readable. The file's size verification was disabled for performance.

In all the datasets, disabling truncate did not affect the ability to read the files. The HDF5 library source code (version 1.8.8) was modified to disable the file size verification process, which improved performance of writing files by a factor 3–5X. The impact of disabling the file size verification is shown in Figure 19.3. The plot shows improvement of the I/O bandwidth of VPIC-IOBench over a range of MPI processes counts, where each MPI process writes 32 MB of data. A better alternative to simply disabling the truncate call is to track the valid section of the file by adding more metadata to the file format. This optimization will soon be a part of upcoming HDF5 release allowing all parallel HDF5 applications to more productively use HDF5 for I/O.

19.6.3 Tuning Lustre File System and MPI-I/O Parameters

To tune MPI-I/O and Lustre layers, the study extracted VPIC's I/O kernel into a benchmark, named VPIC-IOBench. During the study, a series of tests

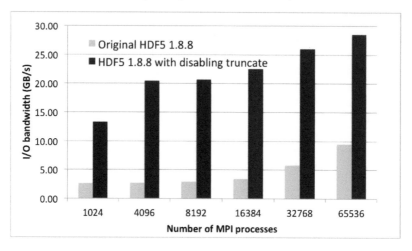

FIGURE 19.3: Performance improvement with patching HDF5 truncate.

were conducted with VPIC-IOBench using 8,000 tasks, and varied the stripe count from 64 OSTs to the maximum of 156 and the stripe size from 1 MB to 1 GB. The Cray Lustre-aware, MPI-I/O implementation varies the MPI-I/O collective buffer aggregators and their buffer size to match the corresponding stripe count and stripe size. Prior experiments indicated that the attainable data rate did not increase with stripe counts beyond 144. The last few OSTs did not add any performance. Finally, 144 OSTs with a stripe size 64 MB were chosen.

The results of a scaling study for 1,000 to 128,000 MPI tasks are shown in Figure 19.4. This is a *weak* scaling study in that the number of particles per task was constant at eight million. These experiments use the modified HDF5 library that has the patch for disabling file size verification when an HDF5 file closes. As the number of MPI tasks increases, the I/O rate becomes greater. With fewer MPI tasks running on a highly shared system, such as Hopper, interference from I/O activity of other jobs can reduce the attained I/O rate. At the scale of 128,000 cores, VPIC-IOBench occupies 85% of Hopper, which reduces the opportunity for interference from other jobs sharing the I/O system. The 128,000 task instance writes about 32 TB of data, and Figure 19.4 shows that at that scale, the delivered I/O performance is about 27 GB/s, which compares favorably with the rated maximum on Hopper of about 35 GB/s. It is also comparable with the best rates achieved with a *file per process* (*fpp*) model. The trillion-particle VPIC simulation uses the same values for Lustre striping as those used after tuning the VPIC-IOBench kernel. As shown in Figure 19.5, writing each of the eight variables by the simulation achieves peak I/O rate of the file system on Hopper.

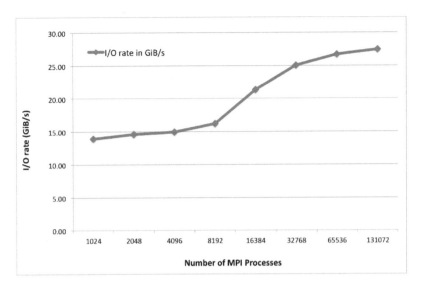

FIGURE 19.4: VPIC-IOBench weak scaling study. Shows I/O performance with increasing number of processes writing data to a HDF5 file using H5Part.

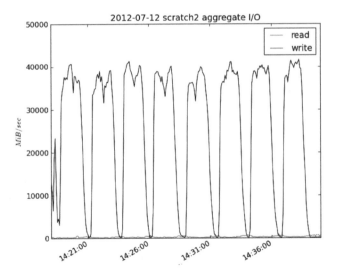

FIGURE 19.5: Performance of writing a single HDF5 file of 34 TB to Lustre. The eight peaks correspond to writing the eight variables of particle data, using all the available file system bandwidth. After writing each variable, synchronization occurred. Overall, the achieved I/O performance was 78% of the peak performance.

19.7　Conclusion

This study successfully undertook an unprecedented trillion-particle simulation on 120,000 cores on Hopper. The fully functional simulation produced 30 TB to 42 TB of data on a per-timestep basis resulting in major I/O challenges. While the study utilized a well-tuned production I/O stack consisting of HDF5, Cray MPI-IO, and Lustre, the study faced and addressed a number of issues at scale. Terabytes of data were successfully written to a single file on the Lustre file system using the available peak bandwidth. This performance was comparable with the *fpp* model, where each MPI process writes data into one file. The *fpp* model is often considered the gold standard for writing large data to parallel file systems. The study also analyzed the particle datasets, which led to various scientific discoveries answering the science objectives mentioned in Section 19.2. More details of analysis and visualization of the data are available in works by Byna et al. [2, 3, 12].

19.8　Acknowledgments

Contributions of this study and chapter also come from V. Roytershteyn, K. Wu, O. Rübel, J. Chou, K-W. Lin, A. Uselton, Y. He, and D. Knaak. This work is supported by the Director, Office of Science, Office of Advanced Scientific Computing Research, of the U.S. Department of Energy under Contract No. DE-AC02-05CH11231. This research used resources of the National Energy Research Scientific Computing Center (NERSC). The authors would like to thank NERSC and Cray staff for troubleshooting I/O issues on Hopper. We would also like to thank members of the HDF Group for their advice on HDF5 I/O optimizations, and Burlen Loring for his advice and support.

Bibliography

[1] K. J. Bowers, B. J. Albright, L. Yin, B. Bergen, and T. J. T. Kwan. Ultrahigh Performance Three-Dimensional Electromagnetic Relativistic Kinetic Plasma Simulation. *Physics of Plasmas*, 15(5):7, 2008.

[2] Surendra Byna, Jerry Chou, Oliver Rübel, Prabhat, Homa Karimabadi, William S. Daughton, Vadim Roytershteyn, E. Wes Bethel, Mark Howison, Ke-Jou Hsu, Kuan-Wu Lin, Arie Shoshani, Andrew Uselton, and

Kesheng Wu. Parallel I/O, Analysis, and Visualization of a Trillion-Particle Simulation. In *Proceedings of the International Conference on High Performance Computing, Networking, Storage and Analysis*, SC '12, pages 59:1–59:12, 2012.

[3] Surendra Byna, Andrew Uselton, Prabhat, David Knaak, and Yun He. Trillion Particles, 120,000 cores, and 350 TBs: Lessons Learned from a Hero I/O Run on Hopper. In *Proceedings of the Cray User Group meeting 2013*, CUG 2013, 2013.

[4] Getting Started with MPI I/O. `http://docs.cray.com/books/S-2490-40/S-2490-40.pdf`.

[5] W. Daughton, V. Roytershteyn, H. Karimabadi, L. Yin, B. J. Albright, B. Bergen, and K. J. Bowers. Role of Electron Physics in the Development of Turbulent Magnetic Reconnection in Collisionless Plasmas. *Nature Physics*, 7:539542, 2011.

[6] W. Daughton, J. D. Scudder, and H. Karimabadi. Fully Kinetic Simulations of Undriven Magnetic Reconnection with Open Boundary Conditions. *Physics of Plasmas*, 13, 2006.

[7] J. Egedal, W. Daughton, and A. Le. Large-Scale Electron Acceleration by Parallel Electric Fields during Magnetic Reconnection. *Nature Physics*, 8:321324, 2012.

[8] Mark Howison, Andreas Adelmann, E. Wes Bethel, Achim Gsell, Benedikt Oswald, and Prabhat. H5hut: A High Performance I/O Library for Particle-Based Simulations. In *Proceedings of 2010 Workshop on Interfaces and Abstractions for Scientific Data Storage (IASDS10)*, Heraklion, Crete, Greece, September 2010. LBNL-4021E.

[9] Mark Howison, Quincey Koziol, David Knaak, John Mainzer, and John Shalf. Tuning HDF5 for Lustre File Systems. In *Proceedings of 2010 Workshop on Interfaces and Abstractions for Scientific Data Storage (IASDS10)*, Heraklion, Crete, Greece, September 2010. LBNL-4803E.

[10] H. Karimabadi, W. Daughton, and J.D. Scudder. Multi-Scale Structure of the Electron Diffusion Region. *Geophys. Res. Lett.*, 34, 2007.

[11] A. Klimas, M. Hesse, and S. Zenitani. Particle-in-Cell Simulation of Collisionless Reconnection with Open Outflow Boundary Conditions. *Physics of Plasmas*, pages 082102–082102-9, 2008.

[12] Kuan-Wu Lin, Jerry Chou, Surendra Byna, and Kesheng Wu. Optimizing FastQuery Performance on Lustre File System. In *Proceedings of the 25th International Conference on Scientific and Statistical Database Management*, SSDBM 2013, 2013.

[13] J. D. Scudder, R. D. Holdaway, W. S. Daughton, H. Karimabadi, V. Roytershteyn, C. T. Russell, and J. Y. Lopez. First Resolved Observations of the Demagnetized Electron-Diffusion Region of an Astrophysical Magnetic-Reconnection Site. *Phys. Rev. Lett.*, 108:225005, Jun 2012.

[14] M. Shay, J.F. Drake, and M. Swisdak. Two-Scale Structure of the Electron Dissipation Region during Collisionless Magnetic Reconnection. *Phys. Rev. Lett.*, 99, 2007.

[15] Roytershteyn V., W. Daughton, H. Karimabadi, and F. S. Mozer. Influence of the Lower-Hybrid Drift Instability on Magnetic Reconnection in Asymmetric Configurations. *Phys. Rev. Lett.*, 108:185001, 2012.

Chapter 20

Stochastic Simulation Data Management

Dimitris Servis

AutoForm Development GmbH

20.1	Background	239
20.2	Science Use Case	240
20.3	The I/O Challenge	241
20.4	Using HDF5 in Industrial Stochastic Simulations	243
	20.4.1 Data Model and Versioning	244
	20.4.2 VFL and Filters	244
	20.4.3 Encryption	244
	20.4.4 Robustness	244
	20.4.5 Fragmentation	245
	20.4.6 Process and Thread Synchronization	245
20.5	A (Near) Efficient Architecture Using HDF5	245
20.6	Performance	247
20.7	Conclusion	248

20.1 Background

The Finite Element Method (FEM) is one of those tools that made it early into industrial applications and in particular the simulation of engineering systems. In the early 1990s there was already enough academic work on using FEM as well as niche and high-end industrial applications. It was the time when general-purpose FEM software was becoming ubiquitous but processing power was still in small supply. Soon, processing power started catching up and it was possible to simulate structures with millions of elements, yet it was so difficult to manipulate and process this information because software was not equally able to scale and was too general purpose. Meanwhile, the industry started seeing value in using FEM as it promised to reduce the cost of expensive physical testing and modeling. Special-purpose software emerged, aiming at solving specific problems in a way that industrial users could understand and customers could measure cost savings and quality improvements.

It also became painfully understood that complex natural phenomena cannot be modeled so easily, common cause variation being one of the main reasons. Models can be improved but neglecting variation renders the correlation to physical findings arbitrary. Hence, the industry is now at a point where it begins to embrace the concept of stochastic simulation: a single simulation is no longer adequate, but a number of well-designed simulations are needed to capture the behavior of the physical process rather than a single realization.

20.2 Science Use Case

Stochastic simulations call for the computation of several realizations of a process and then processing the results in order to extract conclusions about the relationship of input and output, and based on different levels of assumptions, about process performance and robustness as well as higher-level meta-modeling. This section is concerned with the particular application of stochastic stamping simulations the automotive industry. Automotive stamping is the process of deforming flat sheets of material (usually steel or aluminum) into car body parts using a hydraulic press. The flat sheet is cut in blanks, and clamped and pressed against dies that are milled to represent the desired shape. Usually this is a cold process; however, recently there is increased application of hot forming.

The process is heavily influenced by the variation of material properties, blank geometry and position, thickness, rolling angle, forces exerted by the press, shape and strength of the clamping arrangements, tribological aspects, to name at least those that may be controlled in practice. Varying such parameters, in fact encoding the stochastic understanding of these variables, the stochastic simulation yields valuable information on the behavior of the production process.

However, a stochastic simulation is also used to model the design process. Instead of an iterative design, based on successive changes and trial and error, the designer of the dies might use stochastic simulations to encode her understanding of the design process variables. In such a case, the number of variables and possibilities is infinite. The designer may choose to vary every single geometric detail she thinks might affect performance against the set of criteria that assist the decision making of when a tool is ready to be released for milling. Clearly, the number of simulations the automotive engineer needs to perform has now multiplied. Not only does she need to assess the performance of the dies in production, but also perform stochastic simulations to take decisions on the design of the dies. More than one stochastic simulation is therefore needed for many processes, while a single engineer designs 20 or more die sets at the same time, in a department with multiple engineers. Obviously this simulation load needs to be performed in parallel and one increasingly finds vast computing resources in the simulation centers of automotive OEMs and their suppliers alike. Industrial customers have invested and continue to invest in hardware, and expect software vendors to make the best use of it so as to improve the Return on Investment (ROI) and reduce the Total Cost of Ownership (TOC). For example, as microprocessor manufacturers are not producing faster CPUs anymore but rather ones with multiple cores, customers expect software to use multiple threads efficiently.

20.3   The I/O Challenge

These changes in the modus operandi of industrial customers are reflected on a broad set of requirements on the data access, manipulation, and storage, what could collectively be called simulation data management. Such requirements, imposed on software vendors, have in turn increased the non-functional requirements to the persistence systems used:

1. Data should never be lost. The "last known good version" should always be accessible. More often than not, the development of die set geometries is laborious and very costly to repeat. Delays in design also cause delays in downstream processes, only to increase the costs.

2. Data should be accessible from normal users in the form of files. These files are often manipulated by customer processes that back up, compress, delete them, or other processes like Product Lifecycle Management (PLM) software that treats files like product assets, providing auditing and tracking, load-balancing systems like Platform LSF, Condor, or others. Furthermore, user account restrictions apply to the creation and manipulation of files and the directories in which they reside.

3. Allow access to files from multiple threads and multiple processes: appropriate coordination so that there is no data loss or corruption and so that the hardware is optimally exploited. Parallel processes, either on the same machine or on a network, need to access data using different patterns; simulation software, as a data producer, creates new data structures in a serial manner for a single simulation; processing software, as the main data consumer, needs to have access to simulation data in a lateral manner, spanning multiple simulations.

4. Files should be accessed efficiently on network drives using drive mapping or other means that allow shared storage areas to use similar paths as local storage media. Accessing files on shared storage areas increases complexity as processes from different platforms access network file systems in different manners.

5. Minimize file size. Stochastic simulations tend to produce multi-gigabyte files, and as their use is expanding, the file size is not expected to stabilize. For FEM applications, the file size depends on the size of the FE meshes that are produced by simulation processes and the number of results per mesh. For highly nonlinear problems like the ones discussed in this section, the number of timesteps and the level of mesh refinement can be extremely high. This is multiplied by the number of simulations stored in a single file, which in turn depends on the number of parameters that the user is varying. But in a time of cheap hardware, the requirement of minimizing file size might appear irrelevant. For industrial users however, storage economics is a complicated matter. It is not uncommon for the TCO/terabyte/year to be equal to $15,000 or more if all cost items are factored in, such as labor costs, backup, redundancy, servers, floor space, software licenses, etc. Some IT departments are also using Total Cost of Data Ownership (TCDO), which considers the actual amount of data stored per terabyte, factoring in the cost of waste (usable and unallocated and allocated but not used space), RAID, and backup overhead costs. The TCDO of 1 TB of data/year may be multiple times higher than the TCO of 1 TB of storage/year.

6. Use industry standards. Avoid niche and untested platforms and systems. Industrial customers avoid things they cannot manage and that, upon failure, will disrupt their processes. Custom-made solutions are rare and, when present, their lifetime is surprisingly long. Customers prefer not to use exotic solutions such as file systems or parallel access patterns that are not fully supported by existing software vendors or well known by their own IT. Otherwise, the cost of failure can be extremely high.

Apart from the customer requirements, the Voice of the Customer—there are additional requirements emanating from the software vendors—the Voice of the Business:

1. Use proprietary formats. As much as data is valuable for customers, software vendors do not like competitors to build software on top of that data. Most software vendors use proprietary file formats that, to some extent, conceal the structure of the data in the file.

2. Allow for different persistence concepts. Modern software architectures have departed from the typical Plain Old Data Structure (POD) type of data models. The advent of Object-Oriented Programming (OOP) has introduced extensive and complicated relationships between data. OOP is combining the data and the methods to manipulate the data in one object entity. Modern software systems often require large networks of objects that represent specific and limited concepts. Such networks develop to graphs with cyclic dependencies. Collecting the data for persistence from such graphs is not trivial.

3. File size should scale without significantly affecting access performance. It is expected that files can have a wide variation in size. On the other hand, performance should not vary in a proportional manner. For example, accessing time of the same amount of information from a 1-GB and a 100-GB file should be comparable.

4. Reduce the dependence on third-party software. Similar to the customers, software vendors want to avoid the complexity of multiple software facilities that are outside of their control but they still need to support in the eyes of their customers. Furthermore, when third-party software is used, and Open Source Software (OSS) in particular, changes to the source code should be limited to the minimum.

This list of requirements is limited to the ones that are relevant for the discussion in this section.

20.4   Using HDF5 in Industrial Stochastic Simulations

There aren't many software systems available that can fit the bill. Many software vendors devise their own solutions, in essence, reinventing the wheel. Such homebrewed solutions provide a lot of flexibility and control but also increase development and maintenance costs. They encompass a limited set of requirements available at the time of development and notoriously fail to scale or adapt to different business and data models. Another potential danger is that these solutions are tightly linked to the client code. The lack of appropriate interfaces makes it even more difficult to exchange parts of the code. In other cases, vendors use systems that are not well suited for the purpose. Database management or other general-purpose data management systems have failed in the past to deliver. There is a compromise between I/O performance and access granularity which deteriorates as datasets increase in size.

HDF5 is a potentially strong contender in this arena. It is one of the few libraries to advertise its ability to handle large datasets and its high-end industrial and academic provenance makes it appealing, or at least to some extent promising that it can be useful for resolving simulation data management problems. Indeed, HDF5 is versatile and simple to be used for storing simulation data. The in-file data model, and the ability to arrange data and fine tune the access granularity and layout on disk, makes it possible for different clients to access data without sharing data models, providing adequate I/O performance. However, a parallel I/O implementation fulfilling the requirements of industrial customers faces some significant challenges. In the following, some areas where HDF shines or fails are outlined.

20.4.1 Data Model and Versioning

One of the biggest strengths of HDF5 is that the data model lies in the file. What is more important, there is forward and backward compatibility with files generated by the library. This allows a very flexible view of the data when considering parallel access to the file. As a rule of thumb, programs should use the HDF5 format to store data that other programs should read. The common data model is stored in the file and it is easy to explore and consume. For simulation data, this is crucial as it allows different access patterns to be implemented. Each program can access the same data without sharing the same business. Furthermore, the same program between versions can freely change its business and still be able to access any file version. In case data need not be shared between programs, a process may store proprietary data in the same file alongside shared data. Or, if it needs to have more granular access to its own data, it can still use the HDF5 format. This flexibility accommodates a broad array of use cases and serves multiprocess access and versioning very well.

20.4.2 VFL and Filters

The HDF5 library leaves enough open ends for extending it and more can be devised, as will be shown later. Two of the most interesting open ends are the Virtual File Layer (VFL) and the filters. Exploiting VFL, one may implement different modifiers and storage support drivers for data. For example, a terminal VFL driver that stores HDF5 objects in RAM can be used for platform-independent large data attachments in combination with Inter Process Communication systems. Filters can also be used for encryption, compression and other data manipulations. Another open-ended facility of HDF5 is the definition of new data types and conversion between data types. This feature allows for optimal performance when storing data using different precision than the one allowed by the memory data type.

20.4.3 Encryption

The openness of HDF5 is its blessing and its curse. For commercial applications, data encryption is often imperative. However, HDF5 allows anyone with access to a computer and HDFView to look at data, manipulate it, and export it. This is a major shortcoming and software vendors need to devise workarounds to restrict access to their data.

20.4.4 Robustness

HDF5 really shines when everything goes well. However, more often than not, when something goes wrong, HDF5 fails in different ways, from making files inaccessible to crashing processes. In most cases, the underlying reasons do not justify the effects. One of the easiest ways to render a file unreadable and crash a process is writing to a nearly full disk. In the case of stochastic simulations, it is often impossible to predict the exact amount of disk space that the simulation will need. In case there is not enough space, customers loose days of work and CPU cycles.

20.4.5 Fragmentation

In the cases where the files are no created for warehousing, the same file will be used to run simulations multiple times. This results in data being deleted and rewritten. HDF5 does not provide the means to efficiently recover the free space in the file, often leading to excessive fragmentation and increased TCDO.

20.4.6 Process and Thread Synchronization

HDF5 does not provide any means to synchronize processes. Processes are free to access a file and the results are undefined. Furthermore, opening a file from synchronized processes using file locking on open handles does not ensure that after a process has written additional data to the file, the file view of other processes can still access all the data before the write. Thread synchronization is an issue with HDF5 and it is not trivial to ensure that it always works. Further, there are cases where static symbol in the library cause anything from memory leaks to crashes.

20.5   A (Near) Efficient Architecture Using HDF5

Considering all the pros and cons of the HDF5 library, it is a relatively good platform to implement a persistence system for parallel computing, within the described context. It does, nevertheless, need a lot of additional development, exploitation of open ends, and extensive stress and starvation testing, to ensure the quality levels that industrial users require. Figure 20.1 shows an architecture that describes how HDF5 can be used to allow efficient access to files from multiple processes and threads in a parallel computing environment of stochastic FE simulations. The intimidating nature of this figure is indicative of the amount of work that is needed to get HDF5 to deploy its greatness as a tool for large dataset I/O.

At the lowest level, before accessing OS I/O functions, there is an obscure component designated "detours." This is a component that exploits the nature of VFL drivers, which is that the driver itself is a set of function pointers. A malicious user of the library could detour these functions to his own functions

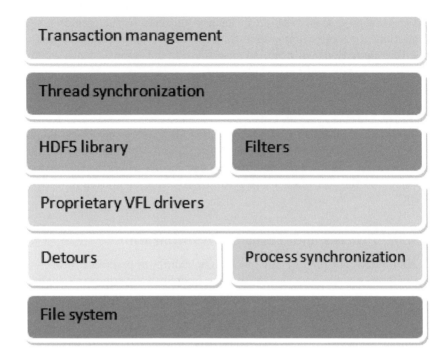

FIGURE 20.1: An architecture for efficient stochastic simulation data management using HDF5.

and implement any kind of behavior before and after the actual calls to original the HDF5 functions. This way, the behavior of an existing VFL driver could be modified without actually modifying the code of the HDF5 library, thus minimizing the need to patch the library every time a new version is made available. One advantage of this approach is detouring the functions that open and close files. This function can then be replaced with a function that locks the file handle right after it has been acquired and unlocks it directly before closing it. The process synchronization module provides appropriate file locking mechanisms that enforce synchronization between processes on different operating systems. Other potential uses of this technique include "fixing" bugs of the library without actually touching it. For example this way it is possible to rectify HDF5 shortcomings that render a file unreadable when a disk is full.

Proprietary VFL drivers are required to implement data manipulation at higher or terminal level, for example, a driver for writing to the RAM instead of the disk. These drivers are used by the HDF5 library alongside the filters module, in order to implement encryption, compression, and lossy or lossless data type–aware transformations.

Thread synchronization ensures that each process accesses a file through the same file driver and all threads of the process share that file driver. The file driver concept also implements thread access policies. Each file driver allows write access to one thread at a time, but may allow read access to multiple threads.

Finally, at the top level of the architecture, transactions are defined and managed. These, in principle, use the Data Access Object (DAO) pattern. A DAO implements a set of transactions through its methods. Each transaction needs to lock a file context, perform the transaction, and release the file context. This ensures that thread and process synchronization policies from lower levels are respected. At this level, there is also a facility to bundle DAO transactions together in a single composite transaction. This ensures that consecutive transactions that assume data presence reported by previous transactions do not get surprised if another process deleted that data. It also ensures that the overhead of opening, locking, and closing files, along with refreshing HDF5 structures, is needed only once.

20.6   Performance

Despite the complexity of the proposed architecture, practical application shows good performance in terms of file access, especially over networks, and increased robustness of the HDF5-based persistence implementation. Performance in this context is measured in terms of user perceived performance, user experience, comparison to other applications, and user expectations from a particular action, so measurements are quite dependent on the application and its interaction with the user.

The absence of figures and numbers in this section underpins that it is particularly difficult to offer quantified results regarding performance in such use cases. The reason is that the factors that determine performance are numerous and adverse. Internally, the system attempts to write from different processes data generated in or required from different threads in different access patterns. While simulation processes or proxies write simulation data in the file, other processes read this data across multiple simulations to perform their own tasks while threads of these processes probe for statuses, write or read logging information, etc. The system needs to respond efficiently to all kinds of transactions of different sizes. Externally, the system is installed on disparate logical and physical environments. Customers may use any kind of configuration to run a stochastic simulation: files can be local or on a file server; network systems can be of any kind with often detrimental effects in process coordination; different mixes of machines need to access the file; different job schedulers such as LSF, Condor, and others are used to submit jobs; network latency is not predictable; all kinds of processes may interfere, from antivirus, to backup demons, to SVN. Notably, these all happen in environments outside the direct reach of the software vendor. The same use case which runs brilliantly in one configuration fails notoriously in another.

The definition of performance in this case is what the user considers good or bad. The anecdote of adding a progress bar when the performance is poor becomes a painful reality. However, users have a pretty clear idea of what to expect from the system in terms of performance. Qualitative and quantitative surveys are used to define good or bad performance of user actions, and these become the benchmark of any performance improvements and continuously monitoring that performance does not deteriorate.

20.7 Conclusion

The aim of this section was to show that HDF5 can be used in industrial HPC applications effectively, respecting the requirements that force implementations not to use special arrangements and custom-made solutions based on a particular computational site. Despite the shortcomings, the HDF5 format and library have the potential to improve their market position in the area of black box, low-risk, and conservative software applications. The optimistic bottom line is that in the end, it works. HDF5 format is possible to use in such industrial use cases effectively and efficiently. The HDF5 library offers the knobs and open ends to adjust it for the different uses.

Chapter 21

Silo: A General-Purpose API and Scientific Database

Mark Miller

Lawrence Livermore National Laboratory

21.1	Canonical Use Case: ALE3D Restart and VisIt Visualization Workflow	250
21.2	Software, Hardware, and Performance	251
21.3	MIF and SSF Scalable I/O Paradigms	252
21.4	Successes with HDF5 as Middleware	256
21.5	Conclusion	257
	Bibliography	258

This chapter presents results and lessons learned in developing and using Silo [4]. Silo is neither an application nor an application-specific I/O framework or library. Instead, Silo is a general-purpose application programming interface (API) and I/O library for reading and writing a variety of scientific computing data objects to HDF5 files.

Silo supports several mesh types including gridless, structured, unstructured, arbitrary, adaptive (AMR), and solid model (CSG) meshes. It supports piecewise-constant and piecewise-linear variables (e.g., fields) defined on the node, edge, face, or volume elements of such meshes as well as the decomposition of meshes into subsets including boundaries, materials, and part assemblies.

Although Silo is a serial library, key features enable it to be applied effectively and scalably in parallel.

There is no specific science application to motivate Silo's development or use. Silo was developed to address a fundamental software engineering challenge. That is, to spur the development of common tools by enabling storage, sharing and exchange of data among diverse scientific computing applications through a common API and database.

This chapter illustrates the use of Silo by describing a canonical use case. The chapter will use as examples the ALE3D multi-physics simulation, the VisIt visualization application, the Lustre file system, and the way Silo is used to store and exchange data between these components.

21.1 Canonical Use Case: ALE3D Restart and VisIt Visualization Workflow

ALE3D [7] is a multi-physics application utilizing arbitrary Lagrangian-Eulerian (ALE) techniques. It models fluid and elastic–plastic response on unstructured grids of hexahedra. ALE3D integrates a variety of multi-physics capabilities through an operator-splitting approach including heat conduction, chemical kinetics with species diffusion, incompressible flow, and a wide range of material and chemistry models. Fully featured ALE3D simulations have been run with good scaling behavior up to as many as 128,000 MPI [5] tasks.

ALE3D uses Silo to produce restart files, plot files, time-history files, and mesh-to-mesh linking files. Restart files are used to restart ALE3D after execution has been terminated. Plot files are used in visualization and analysis. Time-history files capture high time-resolution data at specific user-defined points. Mesh-to-mesh linking files are produced periodically when workflows require ALE3D solution data to be integrated and exchanged with applications modeling other physical phenomena.

For restart and plot files, the key data objects ALE3D writes to the files are the main mesh, the material composition of the main mesh, and key physical variables (e.g., fields) defined on the main mesh such as pressure, velocity, mass, flux, etc.

The main mesh is an unstructured cell data (UCD) mesh; an arbitrary arrangement of connected 3D hexahedral mesh elements (see Figure 21.1). For computation in a distributed, scalable parallel setting, the main mesh is decomposed into pieces called domains ranging in size from 2.5 to 25 and typically 10 thousand mesh elements. To reduce communication in parallel computation, neighboring domains typically contain copies of each other's elements along their shared boundaries. In Silo parlance, these copies are called ghost elements.

The total number elements in the main mesh is a commonly used metric for the scale or size of the problem being simulated. As problem size increases, typically the number of domains increases but the size of each domain (e.g., per-domain element count) remains roughly the same. When I/O performance and scaling is studied, the focus is on those Silo objects the application produces whose size varies with problem size.

Once decomposed, the main mesh is forevermore stored and exchanged via Silo in its decomposed state. All tools and applications used in Silo-enabled HPC workflows are designed to interact with the data in its decomposed state. In fact, all applications are designed so that any single MPI task can manage multiple domains simultaneously. For example, given a mesh decomposed into 60 domains, both ALE3D and VisIt can run one domain per task on 60 MPI tasks, 2:1 on 30 tasks, 3:1 on 20 tasks, or even 3:1 on 12 together with 4:1

FIGURE 21.1 (See color insert): Example of an ALE3D mesh decomposed into domains. [Image courtesy of Bert Still (LLNL).]

on 6 of 18 total tasks. This gives applications great flexibility in allocating compute resources.

21.2 Software, Hardware, and Performance

In a typical HPC workflow, ALE3D will run for hours to days on tens of thousands of MPI tasks, producing restart files about once per hour and plot files perhaps several times per hour on the Lustre file system. Users will run VisIt on approximately one-tenth the compute allocation used for ALE3D to visualize and perform sanity checks as the simulation proceeds.

Silo is a serial I/O library. Therefore, when ALE3D writes a restart file, it first determines the number of Silo files to be used to store all the domains of the main mesh: call this number N. N is selected completely independently of the number of MPI tasks and domains. A good choice for N is to match the number of independent I/O pathways available from compute nodes to the file system. Typically, this number is between 8 and 1024 depending on problem size and the compute and file system resources involved.

ALE3D groups MPI tasks into N groups and each group is responsible for creating one of the N files. At any one moment, only one MPI task from each group has exclusive access to the file. Hence, I/O is serial within a group. However, because one task in each group is writing to its group's own file, simultaneously, I/O is parallel across groups. Within a group, access to the group's file is handled in a round-robin fashion. The first MPI task in the group creates the file and then iterates over all domains it has. For each domain, it creates a sub-directory within the file (e.g., a separate namespace for Silo objects) and writes all the Silo objects (the main mesh domain, the material composition of the domain, the mesh variables defined on the domain) to that directory. It repeats this process for each domain. Then, the first MPI task closes the Silo file and hands off exclusive access to the next task in the group. That MPI task opens the file and iterates over all domains in the same way. Exclusive access to the file is then handed off to the next task. This process, shown in Figure 21.2, continues until all processors in the group have written their domains to unique sub-directories in the file.

After all groups have finished writing their Silo files, a final step involves creating a master Silo file which contains special Silo objects (called multi-block objects) that point at all the pieces of mesh (domains) scattered about in the N files.

Setting N to be equal to the number of MPI tasks, results in a file-per-process configuration, which is typically not recommended for users. However, some applications do indeed choose to run this way with good results. Alternatively, setting N equal to 1 results in effectively serializing the I/O and is certainly not recommended. For large, parallel runs, there is a sweet spot in the selection of N which results in peak I/O performance rates. If N is too large, the I/O subsystem will likely be overwhelmed; setting it too small will likely underutilize the system resources. This is illustrated in Figure 21.3 for different numbers of files and MPI task counts.

21.3 MIF and SSF Scalable I/O Paradigms

This approach to using Silo for scalable, parallel I/O was originally developed in the late 1990s by Rob Neely, a lead software architect on ALE3D at the time. This approach is sometimes called "Poor Man's Parallel I/O." It and variations thereof have since been adopted and used productively through several transitions in orders of magnitude of MPI task counts from hundreds then to hundreds of thousands today.

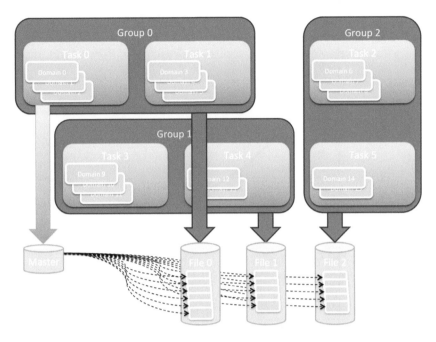

FIGURE 21.2 (See color insert): Example silo-based MIF-IO. There are 6 MPI tasks. Tasks 0–3 have 3 domains. Tasks 4 and 5 have 2 domains. Tasks are divided into 3 I/O groups. Task 0 creates file 0 and writes its 3 domains in 3 sub-directories in the file. Simultaneously, tasks 1 and 2 create files 1 and 2 and write their domains. There are 3 parallel streams of data from the application.

During this same period of time, R&D efforts in scalable, parallel I/O largely focused on the case of concurrent I/O to a single, shared file. There has long been the belief that concurrent I/O to a single shared file is the best way to achieve truly scalable I/O. By contrast, these approaches are sometimes called "Rich Man's Parallel I/O" because the underlying software subsystems support parallel I/O to a single shared file, natively.

The key distinction between the Poor Man's and Rich Man's approaches is the need for applications to manage distribution of data among multiple files. For this reason, it is technically appropriate to refer to these two approaches as Multiple Independent File (MIF) and Single Shared File (SSF) parallel I/O.

There are a large number of advantages to MIF-IO over SSF-IO.

1. MIF-IO is a much simpler programming model because it frees developers from having to think in terms of collective I/O operations. The code to write data from one MPI task doesn't depend on or involve other tasks. For large multi-physics applications where the size, shape, and

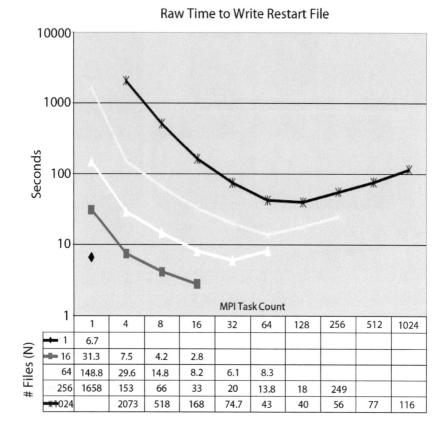

MPI Task Count									
1	4	8	16	32	64	128	256	512	1024
6.7									
31.3	7.5	4.2	2.8						
148.8	29.6	14.8	8.2	6.1	8.3				
1658	153	66	33	20	13.8	18	249		
	2073	518	168	74.7	43	40	56	77	116

FIGURE 21.3: Variation in ALE3D I/O performance as the number of file parts is varied. [Image courtesy of Rob Neely (LLNL).]

even existence of data can vary dramatically among MPI tasks, this is invaluable in simplifying I/O code development.

2. MIF-IO alleviates any need for global-to-local and local-to-global remapping upon every exchange of data between the application and its file.

3. In-transit compression is easier to apply in a MIF-IO setting because processors are freed from having to coordinate changes in data sizing as it is moved to the file.

4. For MIF-IO, good performance demands very little in the way of extra/advanced features from the underlying I/O hardware and file system. A relatively dumb file system can get it right and perform well.

5. Application-controlled throttling of I/O is easily supported in a MIF-IO setting because the number of concurrent operations is explicitly controlled. This can help to avoid overloading the underlying I/O subsystems.

6. MIF-IO is consistent with the way leading-edge commercial "big data" I/O in map-reduce operations is handled. Datasets are broken into pieces and stored in the file system as a collection of shards and different numbers of parallel tasks can process different numbers of shards.

With minor variations, the process by which ALE3D writes plot files is completely analogous to restart files. However, the application will often enable some "in-transit" transformations on data destined for plot files that it would otherwise not perform for restart files. This can include transformations from double to single precision, the addition of ghost zone layers enveloping domains, the inclusion of domain spatial and variable extents as well as both lossless and lossy compression. In earlier systems where computations were performed on Crays and visualizations on SGIs, Silo would also perform transformations from Cray to SGI floating point representations.

Nonetheless, both restart and plot files, because they are Silo files, are still visualizable by VisIt. Plot files are designed to be a little more convenient and optimized for visualization in VisIt, while restart files are optimized for restarting ALE3D.

When VisIt [6] reads a Silo restart or plot file, it starts by opening the master file. From that file, VisIt's metadata server determines all of the objects in the file, their names and types, and then populates VisIt's GUI menus based upon what it finds in the files. There are a number of interesting aspects to how VisIt manages data distributed across multiple files. What is most relevant here is that VisIt essentially piggy-backs its parallel processing paradigm on top of the parallel decomposition already provided by the data producer.

Like ALE3D, VisIt can process multiple domains on each MPI task. When the user starts VisIt, she specifies a suitable number of MPI tasks to use. VisIt then automatically assigns domains to tasks (it has a number of different algorithms for doing this depending on various factors). Each task then uses information from the master file to determine which file(s) contain the domains it needs and then opens those files and reads the relevant domains from them.

If the data producer bothered to write per-domain spatial and variable extents, VisIt can use such information to accelerate various operations. For example, to display a slice of a mesh, VisIt can exclude from processing any domain whose spatial extents do not intersect the slice. Likewise, when displaying iso-surfaces, VisIt can exclude from consideration any domain whose variable extents do not contain the iso-values of interest.

21.4 Successes with HDF5 as Middleware

Silo is built on top of and uses the HDF5 library. Because of this, it is possible to alter the manner in which Silo uses HDF5 without having to alter applications above it. We have used this to advantage on numerous occasions to address various file system performance and reliability issues. Examples of some of those capabilities are briefly described here.

1. Application-level checksumming: To address file system reliability issues, a checksumming capability in HDF5 was enabled. As Silo applications write data, the data is checksummed by HDF5 while in transit to the file. No attempt to detect errors during write is made. However, checksums are also computed and compared upon read. In the event of a checksum error on read, the application may attempt to re-read the data. However, repeated read failures generally indicate an error most likely occurred during write and the data is corrupted.

2. Mesh-aware compression: To experiment with advanced compression techniques that can take advantage of mesh structure to optimize data locality during compression, we added the compression algorithms as HDF5 filters. This enables the compression to be applied in transit as the data is written from the Silo application. We have used these compression methods to improve I/O performance and reduce file sizes for certain cases by as much as $5\times$.

3. Block-based Virtual File Driver (VFD): To address file system performance issues, a custom VFD designed to optimize I/O for BG/Q class systems. The VFD coalesces I/O requests from Silo applications and separates I/O for small objects (Silo metadata) from larger objects (application raw data). It breaks a file into large blocks consisting entirely of either metadata or raw data and keeps an application-specified number of blocks cached in memory at any one time. An LRU algorithm is used to preempt cache blocks to disk when new blocks are needed. This VFD has demonstrated $30-50\times$ performance improvements on BG/Q systems. Results are illustrated in Figure 21.4.

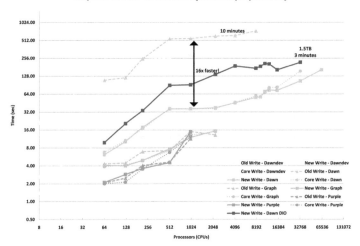

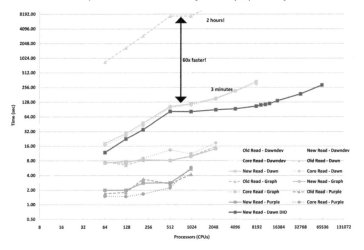

FIGURE 21.4: Comparison of MIF-IO write and read performance on 3 ASC systems (Purple [3], Dawn [1] and Graph [2] and improvement in I/O performance with block-based VFD. [Image courtesy of Michael Collette (LLNL).]

21.5   Conclusion

Silo was developed to address a software engineering challenge: to enable the development of common tools with which applications can share and exchange diverse scientific datasets. As a serial library, Silo has nonetheless demonstrated scalable performance for many HPC applications (ALE3D, Kull, Overlink, PMesh, Ares, and VisIt are some examples) using the MIF-IO parallel I/O approach. MIF-IO has demonstrated good performance to 100,000 tasks and is currently in process of being scaled to 1,000,000 cores. MIF-IO has a number of advantages over SSF-IO making its application very attractive in HPC workflows involving diverse and disparate datasets with dramatic variation in size, shape, and existence of data across MPI tasks. Silo's success is due in large part to the performance and capabilities available in HDF5.

Bibliography

[1] ASC Dawn Machine. `https://computing.llnl.gov/tutorials/bgp/#Hardware`, 2010.

[2] LLNL Graph Machine. `https://computing.llnl.gov/?set=resources&page=SCF_resources#graph`, 2012.

[3] ASCI Purple Machine. `https://asc.llnl.gov/computing_resources/purple/`, 2010.

[4] Silo User's Guide: Version 4.7.1. `https://e-reports-int.llnl.gov/pdf/382967.pdf`, 2009.

[5] Marc Snir, Steve Otto, Steven Huss-Lederman, David Walker, and Jack Dongarra. *MPI-The Complete Reference, Volume 1: The MPI Core.* MIT Press, Cambridge, MA, USA, 2nd. (revised) edition, 1998.

[6] Bethel W., Childs H., and Hansen C. *High Performance Visualization: Enabling Extreme-Scale Scientific Insight.* Chapman and Hall/CRC, 2012.

[7] Futral W.S., Dube E., Neely J.R., and Pierce T.G. Performance of ALE3D on the ASCI Machines. In *Nuclear Explosives Code Development Conference*, 1999. `https://e-reports-ext.llnl.gov/pdf/234827.pdf`.

Chapter 22

Scaling Up Parallel I/O in S3D to 100-K Cores with ADIOS

Scott Klasky, Gary Liu, Hasan Abbasi, and Norbert Podhorszki

Oak Ridge National Laboratory

Jackie Chen and Hemanth Kolla

Sandia National Laboratories

22.1	Science Use Case	259
22.2	Software and Hardware	260
	22.2.1 ADIOS-BP	261
	22.2.2 Staged Write Method	262
	22.2.3 Group-Based Hierarchical I/O Control	262
	22.2.4 Aggregation and Subfiling	263
	22.2.5 Index Generation	266
	22.2.6 Staged Read Method	266
	22.2.7 Staged Opens	266
	22.2.8 Chunking	267
	22.2.9 Limitations	268
22.3	Conclusion	269
	Bibliography	269

22.1 Science Use Case

Combustion is at the heart of the energy conversion process in most transportation and power generation systems, and is likely to remain so for the foreseeable future. Combustion invariably occurs in turbulent environments, which involves a complex coupling between fluid dynamics, chemical kinetics and molecular transport phenomena. This coupling is a multi-scale process which makes it very critical to understand the fine-scale phenomena in order to design effectively for desired large-scale operating characteristics. First principles–based Direct Numerical Simulations (DNS) is one methodology of simulating turbulent combustion where all the continuum scales are sufficiently resolved. However, the multi-scale nature implies that DNS of turbulent combustion is not feasible without high performance computing. Even with petascale capabilities, DNS of turbulent combustion has only been able to achieve conditions that are one generation removed from those in real devices, which makes it essentially an exascale-class problem. Nonetheless, petascale DNS provide a wealth of information and fundamental insight in canonical configurations that is invaluable in developing and assessing models which enable engineering design of combustion systems such as internal combustion engines and gas turbine combustors.

S3D [2], developed at Sandia National Laboratories, is a massively parallel DNS code used to perform simulations of gas-phase turbulent combustion using explicit high-order finite difference numerics. The petascale simulations performed by S3D typically generate massive amounts of data to provide sufficient information spanning a broad range of spatio-temporal scales. This can be illustrated using the recent S3D simulation of a reacting transverse jet in a vitiated cross-flow. This configuration is relevant in gas-turbine combustors that employ secondary fuel injection downstream of a primary combustion zone to enable variable load operating conditions. In such a configuration, the thermo-acoustics of the system are a serious concern and the simulation was designed, in conjunction with experimental research at Georgia Institute of Technology, to study the stability characteristics of the transverse jet. Topics being investigated include (i) what are mechanisms of flame stabilization and how are they affected by the vitiated conditions of the cross-flow, (ii) is the transverse jet convectively unstable or globally unstable, (iii) how does the heat release by the chemical reactions influence the stability of the jet, and (iv) how is the mixing between the jet and cross-flow influenced by the jet instability and how does it couple with the flame stabilization?

The simulation corresponds to a three-dimensional rectangular Cartesian domain comprised of 4.68 billion grid points. The state vector consisted of 18 variables representing the full thermo-chemical state of a synthesis gas reacting system which results in approximately 84 billion degrees of freedom. The simulation was performed on 100,000 cores of the "Edison" system at NERSC and it periodically saves the full state (every 600 timesteps) to disk for post-processing and analysis. The file size of each of these snapshots is 674 GB, and a total of 300 snapshots were saved making the total amount of data generated equal to nearly 200 TB. During simulation, the I/O challenge was to minimize the impact of storing 674-GB snapshots on the overall runtime. However, during the post-processing and analysis, the disk storage and memory requirements are obviously very large since all 300 snapshots need to be processed upon (not always simultaneously).

22.2   Software and Hardware

File formats used in many conventional I/O libraries such as HDF5 and NetCDF4 require data to be written contiguously on disk. This is a natural organization for serial programs where the entire dataset is contained within a single process. However, for parallel programs, datasets (e.g., a multi-dimensional array) are likely scattered across multiple processors. In order to make data logically contiguous on disk, extensive communication must occur among MPI processes either to aggregate data chunks on a single process or to exchange write offsets to enable collective, non-overlapping writes. As scientific codes are scaled up, this involves many "all-to-one" or "all-to-all" collectives and will be a significant performance bottleneck. Meanwhile, scientific simulations often do calculations and I/O in an iterative manner (i.e., for timesteping). For a contiguous file format, appending to an existing dataset can be a very costly operation. It requires heavy data shuffling on disk and the rewriting of substantial file metadata.

22.2.1   ADIOS-BP

Keeping these limitations in mind, we designed ADIOS-BP, which adopts an alternative approach, i.e., a non-contiguous, log-based file format. Choosing the format to be non-contiguous allows BP to scale extremely well to hundreds of thousands of cores. There are two main factors behind the performance advantage that this format brings. First, the non-contiguity allows each MPI processor to perform I/O in a more independent fashion, significantly reducing (if not eliminating) collective communications. Each processor outputs its local buffer, along with header information such as indexes and data dimensionality, independently to a file. It completely eliminates the MPI communication step that two-phase I/O involves to make data appear contiguous on disk. In a non-contiguous file format like ADIOS-BP, "all-to-one" data shuffling is not required. Additionally, non-contiguity makes file system lock contention much easier to resolve, particularly when the subfile technique is applied. The key elements are briefly explained in the ADIOS-BP file format:

- *Process Group:* One of the major concepts in ADIOS-BP format is "process group" or PG. The ADIOS-BP file format consists of a series of PG entries and the ADIOS-BP file footer, see Figure 22.2. Each process group is the entire self-contained output from a single process and is written out independently into a contiguous disk space.

- *Footer:* One known limitation of the NetCDF4 format is that the file contents are stored in a header that is exactly big enough for the information provided at file creation. Any changes to the length of that data will require moving data. To avoid this cost, a foot index is employed instead. The version identifier and the offset are placed at the beginning of the index as the last few bytes of the file, making it simple to find the index information and to add new and different data to the files without affecting any data already written. The variable's index table is composed of the total count of variables in the ADIOS-BP file, the size of the variable's index table, and a list of variable records. Each record contains the size of the record and the basic metadata to describe the variable. The metadata include the name of the variable, the name of the group the variable is associated with, the data type of the variable, and a series of characteristic features. More details can be found in the ADIOS manual [5].

22.2.2   Staged Write Method

The idea behind the staged write method is to first, perform bulk writes as large as we can, using aggressive buffering and aggregation strategy. This is done by aggregating data from two levels: within a single processor and among a subset of processors (i.e., group). Second, further eliminate contentions in the parallel file system and MPI collective communication. The aggregated data will be written out in multiple subfiles, with each group outputting one file. Each subfile is striped on a single storage target and therefore writes can be done independently from other groups. The design specifics are highlighted next.

22.2.3   Group-Based Hierarchical I/O Control

The group-based hierarchical I/O control scheme, see Figure 22.1, divides all MPI processes into sub-groups based upon the individual MPI rank, to avoid the overhead of doing MPI collective among all processors. Suppose an MPI process can be denoted as P_i where $0 \leq i < N$ and N is the total number of MPI processors. The number of subfiles that we are going to generate is M and, without losing generality, we also assume N is a multiple of M. Therefore, the number of processes that each group contains is N/M and hence, for group G_i, the processes that it contains is $[P_{N/M \cdot i}, P_{N/M \cdot (i+1)-1}]$. Each group is assigned a group coordinator (i.e., aggregator), which is responsible for managing data sent from all the members in the group G_i and writing them to disk in group. It also serves to collect an index from its members during index generation. Note that only the aggregator processor in each group issues writes to the file system, thereby significantly reducing the write contentions. Similarly, to generate a metadata file which describes the entire datasets that are scattered across all subfiles, a global coordinator will be chosen, e.g., P_0. Note that more complex leader election algorithms can be adopted here to balance load across all processes and is left for future study. All processes within G_i write to a single subfile, thereby completely avoiding interference from other groups. Overall group-based I/O control is designed to eliminate bottlenecks and therefore achieve scalability. The number of groups is specified as an external parameter in ADIOS XML file. By and large, the selection of the number is a tradeoff between (1) aggregation (subject to memory constraints) and (2) utilization of as many storage targets as possible to improve concurrency.

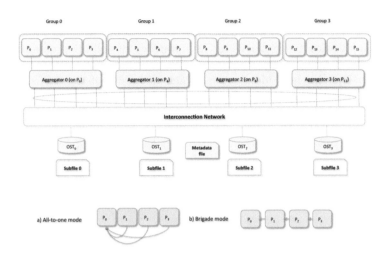

FIGURE 22.1: Group-based hierarchical I/O control for ADIOS. This hierarchical control enables ADIOS to efficiently write out small data chunks from S3D.

22.2.4   Aggregation and Subfiling

There are two levels of data aggregation underneath ADIOS write calls. This is intended to make the *final* data as large as possible when being flushed to disk, and as a result, expensive disk seeks can be reduced. At the first level, data are aggregated in memory within a single MPI processor among all variables output by the adios_write statement, i.e., a write-behind strategy. For the example below, variable *NX, NY* and *temperature* in the adios_write statement will all be copied to ADIOS internal buffer, the maximum size of which can be configured through the ADIOS XML file, instead of being flushed out to disk. This is a well-known technique being used by other I/O libraries, such as IOBUF and the FUSE file system. Meanwhile, the second level of aggregation occurs between a sub-set of processors. This is to further deal with the situation that each processor has a relatively small amount of data to output (after the first-level aggregation). An good example is combustion S3D code [2, 3]. In a typical 96,000-core S3D run on JaguarPF, each processor outputs under 2 MB. Clearly, in this case, many small writes to disk hurt I/O performance. One can argue that, to make data further larger, using MPI collectives to exchange bulk data between processors can be costly. Here we postulate four reasons in favor of aggregation techniques. (1) Interconnect in the high-end computing systems are becoming faster and faster. For example, the latest Cray Gemini interconnect can sustain up to 20 GB/s [1]. (2) The issue with doing the MPI collective operation in MPI-IO is not the sheer volume of data to exchange. Instead, the dominating factor that slows down application performance is the frequency of collective operations and possibility of lock contention. Earlier work [4] shows that MPI_Bcast is called 314,800 times in the Chimera run, which take 25% of the wall clock time. (3) The collective operation in ADIOS is done in a very controlled manner. All MPI processors are split into sub-groups and aggregation is done within a sub-communicator. Therefore, the interference between groups is minimized. Meanwhile, indexes are also generated first within a group and then sent by all the aggregator processors to a root processor (e.g., rank 0) to avoid global collectives. (4) Most of today's computing resources such as Jaguar Cray XT5 use multicore CPU, and aggregation among the cores within a single chip is inexpensive as the cost is close to that of the *memcpy()* operation.

Listing 22.1: Example ADIOS code.

```
adios_open (&adios_handle, "analysis", filename, "w", &
    comm);
adios_write (adios_handle, "NX", &NX);
adios_write (adios_handle, "NY", &NY);
adios_write (adios_handle, "temperature", t);
adios_close (adios_handle);
```

Within a group, an aggregator gathers the buffered PGs from all of its members, provided that there is sufficient memory on the aggregator processor. Depending on the communication pattern, an aggregator can either perform all-to-one communication (i.e., MPI_Gather()) or brigade-like communication (see Figure 22.1). For the former case, all members send data addressed directly to the aggregator processor. For the latter case, a member sends its data to its upstream processor. As a result, while an aggregator writes data from one member, data from another member will be moved closer. Therefore, the communication cost can be minimized. The idea of brigade aggregation is to overlap MPI communication with disk I/O and achieve streaming-like I/O. Next, each aggregator writes out all data that it receives to a subfile. The subfile is striped on a single OST (Object Storage Target) to minimize the potential write lock contention between aggregators. A global metadata file is also written out from P_0 to make reading data subfiles possible.

One challenge of *one file per process* (N-N) is the overwhelming metadata pressure resulting from the simultaneous creation of tens of thousands of files. And *one file* (N-1) pattern often results in unaligned access across file system boundaries, which in turn causes write lock contention among processors. The aggregation scheme offers a flexible N-M pattern that overcomes the drawbacks from both N-N and N-1 via a reduced number of files and larger writes.

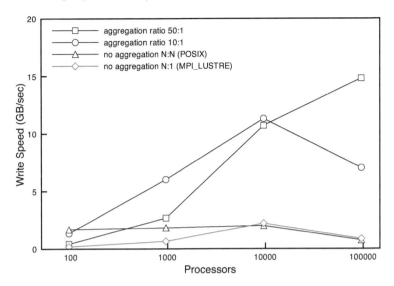

FIGURE 22.2: S3D write performance scaling as application size is increased. Note the change in best performance from 10:1 aggregation to 50:1 aggregation as application size hits 96,000 cores.

To evaluate the staged write performance, we ran S3D on JaguarPF varying from a 96-core run to a 96,000-core run in a weak scaling configuration (see Figure 22.2). Each data point in the figure is the average of the results collected in ten consecutive runs. Clearly, N-N and N-1 with no aggregation can only achieve a few GB/s for all the runs. POSIX is quite good for the smallest 96-core run but the write speed decreases as the run scales up. MPI_LUSTRE is an I/O method in ADIOS that writes out one file with the Lustre stripe aligned. Its write performance versus POSIX improves slightly as the number of cores increases. However, at the 96,000-core run, the performance drops due to heavy contention. For 10:1 ratio aggregation, the speed is much improved versus no aggregation schemes but also with a significant drop at the 96,000-core run. The reason is that, with 10:1 ratio, the number of subfiles generated in the 96,000-core job overwhelms the metadata server (similar to POSIX) and file open/close takes a much longer time to finish. We subsequently increased the ratio to 50:1. Although it has lower performance (due to the fact that it didn't fully utilize all the OSTs because of the lower number of aggregators) than 10:1 at low core count, at 96,000-core run, it yields a much higher throughput than the 10:1 ratio.

22.2.5　Index Generation

An aggregator in each group is responsible for generating local indexes for each subfile and the aggregator in the first group (P_0) also generates indexes in the metadata file. This is done by performing a two-round of collective communications (using sub-communicator) among all processors in order to improve scalability. First, every rank builds indexes locally and then sends its portion of the indexes to its aggregator. Once the aggregator receives the data, it populates the data structures for the process groups (PG), variables and attributes. These are used to create the footer for the local file. All aggregators then send their indexes to the highest level aggregator (P_0), which writes out a combined global metadata file for the entire cohort.

22.2.6　Staged Read Method

The subfiling technique can greatly improve write performance, however, it poses new challenges for reading data. Without carefully managing metadata operations such as *MPI_File_open()* or POSIX *open()*, subsetting data can be very expensive, particularly for operations such as planar access. Suppose there are M MPI processors and N subfiles on disk and each MPI rank needs to read in a arbitrary plane from a multi-dimensional array, which can be scattered across all subfiles. There will be $M * N$ file opens simultaneously issued to Lustre metadata server, which can be overwhelming. Figure 22.3 shows the metadata operation cost that measures the open() and close() time. It is clear that as the run is scaled up, the metadata cost increases quickly. Now for a typical S3D post-processing run, say a 2400-core post-processing job reads in data across subfiles dumped out by a 96,000-core computation job. Depending on the access pattern, it may issue 4 million file opens. Assuming each file open takes 0.5 *ms*, the metadata operation alone will take around 40 minutes. The staged read method aims to tackle the issue by performing staged file operations, in which only selected MPI processors open/close files. I/O chunking is another technique used here to achieve bulk reads, similar to MPI-IO, and details are discussed next.

22.2.7　Staged Opens

Staged opens bring two major advantages to read operations: They effectively alleviate the "large metadata/footer" problem mentioned early. As scientific simulations scale up and more analytical data, such as statistics and indexes will be eventually included in the future, file metadata (such as header, footer) will continue to expand regardless of individual file formats. Loading the entire metadata section in before any read/write operation is a common practice in many parallel I/O libraries. Therefore, as the metadata grows and cannot be fit into the memory of a compute core, more advanced metadata management are needed. We can resolve this issue either by adopting a *lazy*

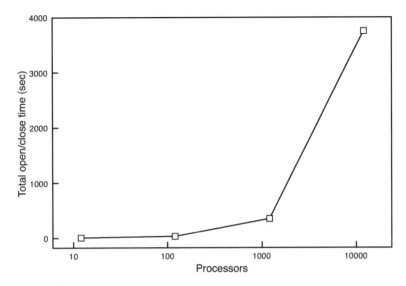

FIGURE 22.3: Metadata operation cost scaling with increasing number of writers. As applications cross 10,000 cores, the time spent in metadata operation becomes untenable.

read approach, i.e., reading the minimum metadata that is required and the rest only when necessary. The downside is that accessing a single dataset in a file is "two-pass" operation with suboptimal performance. Another option is to make only a subset of processors load in metadata so that for systems such multi-core cluster where memory is shared among several cores, it reduces total memory consumption for metadata. More importantly, by calling open/-close only at aggregators, it also reduces the number of metadata operations, which is very beneficial to both users and file system.

22.2.8   Chunking

To avoid excessive small read requests, chunking is used here to achieve bulk reads. This is done by merging read requests into larger ones at the aggregator side. For a non-contiguous file format, chunking is particularly useful to speed up reading as data is not contiguously stored on disk and disk seeks are otherwise needed to jump from one position to another. An aggregator first collects all read requests issued from its group members. The read request message includes information such as data address and size. Namely, for a non-aggregator processor, the *adios_read_var()* call simply saves read parameters such as the *adios group handler*, *start*, *count*, and *buffer address*, without doing any actual I/O access. In the *adios_fclose()* call, the processor then packs all parameters into a read request and sends to its aggregator

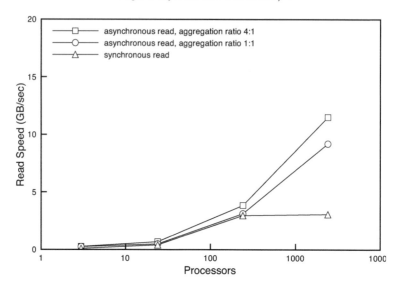

FIGURE 22.4: S3D read performance scaling. Asynchronous read demonstrates much better performance than synchronous reads as application scales up. Higher aggregation ratio also demonstrates better performance.

processor. Next, the aggregator processor parses the received message and then sorts all requests by their address (i.e., *file idx* and *offset*). *file idx* is the subfile ID and *offset* is the file offset within a subfile. If a set of requests fall into a window of certain size (e.g., 64 MB), a single read request that accommodates the entire request set will be issued to the file system. The aggregator subsequently extracts the portion that was requested and sends it back to its member via MPI messaging. The staged read performance is shown in Figure 22.4. We can see the staged read (i.e., asynchronous read) outperform synchronous read substantially, about 3–5 times at 96,000-core runs. At low core counts, the three techniques achieve largely the same performance due to the relatively high cost of staged read.

22.2.9   Limitations

Staged read is essentially a type of "delayed read" technique, in which memory buffers that are passed into the adios_read_var() call becomes valid *only* after file close, i.e., the adios_fclose() call. This will restrict the technique from being used in certain applications where a few variables must first be read in before others, for example, sizing/dimension data. Luckily, in ADIOS-BP, we store the scalar values directly in metadata and their values are available immediately after file open, thereby avoiding the problem to some degree. Another disadvantage is that chunk reading might increase the overhead in some cases since there is junk data that must be read in along with requested data. In future storage systems with SSDs (solid-state drive) where disk seek is inexpensive, this staged read approach might not be the best solution and this is left for future study.

22.3 Conclusion

S3D offers a challenging I/O problem at scale, a problem that ADIOS is able to tackle in a compelling and usable manner. The obstacles faced in scaling up I/O performance for S3D are general obstacles that many applications will face. By combining aggregation, subfiling, and chunking techniques, ADIOS provides a solution that can be generalized for many I/O problems. The comparison of the N-M I/O pattern to N-1 and N-N patterns provides a higher-level view of the file system limitations in current platforms.

The key advantages of staged I/O are three-folded. First, it effectively aggregates small I/O accesses into large chunks and hence eliminates disk seek operations. By allowing only a subset of MPI processors to perform I/O operations to the storage system, it further avoids lock contention for writing. On the other hand, it significantly reduces the cost of metadata operations such file open and close for reading and memory consumption. This scheme is implemented as a stand-alone I/O method inside the ADIOS framework so that existing ADIOS applications can benefit from it without source code change.

This approach underlies the philosophy of the ADIOS platform. The service-based approach of ADIOS allows the development of new techniques and methods that can be easily shared with the I/O community at large, providing new insights into I/O performance for a vast variety of applications.

Bibliography

[1] Cray XE6 Brochure. http://www.cray.com/Assets/PDF/products/xe/CrayXE6mBrochure.pdf.

[2] J. Chen, A. Choudhary, B. de Supinski, M. DeVries, E.R. Hawkes, S. Klasky, W. K. Liao, K. L. Ma, J. Mellor-Crummey, N. Podhorszki, R. Sankaran, S. Shende, and C. S. Yoo. Terascale Direct Numerical Simulations of Turbulent Combustion Using S3D. *Computational Science and Discovery*, 2(1):015001, 2009.

[3] E.R. Hawkes, R. Sankaran, J.C. Sutherland, and J.H. Chen. Direct Numerical Simulation of Turbulent Combustion: Fundamental Insights Towards Predictive Models. *Journal of Physics: Conference Series*, 16(4):65–79, Winter 2005.

[4] Jay Lofstead, Fang Zheng, Scott Klasky, and Karsten Schwan. Adaptable, Metadata Rich I/O Methods for Portable High Performance I/O. In *Proceedings of IPDPS'09, May 25-29, Rome, Italy*, 2009.

[5] ADIOS Manual. `http://www.olcf.ornl.gov/center-projects/adios/`.

Chapter 23

In-Transit Processing: Data Analysis Using Burst Buffers

Christopher Mitchell, David Bonnie, and Jonathan Woodring

Los Alamos National Laboratory

23.1	Motivation	271
23.2	Design/Architecture	273
23.3	Systems Prototypes Related to Burst Buffers	274
23.4	Conclusion	275
	Bibliography	275

23.1 Motivation

With the progressive march toward ever larger and faster HPC platforms, the HPC community is seeing a discrepancy between the aggregate bandwidth of the compute node's capability to send data to storage and the bandwidth available on traditional parallel file systems, utilizing hard drives, to ingest this data. Rather than purchasing additional disks to increase bandwidth (beyond what is required for capacity requirements), the concept of a burst buffer has been proposed to impedance match the compute nodes to the parallel file system [4]. A burst buffer is an allocation of solid-state storage that is capable of absorbing a burst of I/O activity that can then be slowly drained to a parallel file system while computation resumes within the running application. The original design intent of such a system was to handle the I/O workload commonly seen in the checkpoint/restart process, which many current HPC applications use to handle faults. In checkpoint/restart, the application pauses operation and then proceeds to write the state of the entire application's memory space to a formatted file on disk such that the current application state can be reconstructed should a future failure occur. This process is periodic in nature, but places considerable strain on the I/O subsystem for the several seconds to minutes it takes to complete.

Since a checkpoint/restart dump contains the state of the application at a given point in time, and placing it in a burst buffer temporarily positions the

TABLE 23.1: Comparison of analysis execution methods.

	In situ	In Transit	Post-Processing
Analysis Execution Location	Within Simulation	Burst Buffer	Separate Application
Data Location	Within Simulation Memory Space	Within Burst Buffer Flash Memory	On Parallel File System
Data Reduction Possible?	YES: Can limit output to only analysis products.	YES: Can limit data saved to disk to only analysis products.	NO: All data saved to disk for future use.
Interactivity	NO: Analysis actions must be pre-scripted to run within simulation.	LIMITED: Data is not permanently resident in flash and can be removed to disk.	YES: User has full control of what to load and when to load data from disk.
Analysis Routines Expected	Fast-running analysis operations, statistical routines, image rendering.	Longer-running analysis operations bounded by the time until drain to file system. Statistics over simulation time.	All possible analysis and visualization routines including interactive exploration of the rendered dataset.

data for fast access, an opportunity becomes available to perform data reductions, data analysis, and/or scientific visualization. Analyzing simulation data in the burst buffer while it is in flight to the parallel file system is known as "in-transit" analysis. This is in contrast to both traditional post-processing analysis and emerging *in situ* analysis. A post-processing workflow requires the user to reload the requisite data from the parallel file system to perform the analysis functions desired, independently of the simulation application itself. *In situ* analysis is another emerging option to perform analysis that integrates the analytics routines directly into the simulation, and processes the data while it is still resident in the simulation's memory space. Each technique has its own set of benefits and drawbacks, as shown in Table 23.1, which ultimately implies that a combination of these techniques will be employed going forward.

23.2   Design/Architecture

For in-transit processing to succeed, the I/O subsystem and software stack must be designed to accommodate the execution of the analysis operations to be performed on the in-flight data. These accommodations are built on top of a base HPC system with burst buffers installed for checkpoint/restart capability. In such a system, the compute nodes communicate with the parallel file system by routing I/O requests over the high-speed fabric to an I/O node, which routes the request onto a storage network where the storage resides. This generalized setup can take many forms depending on the make and model of the system in question. One potential setup is illustrated in Figure 23.1 The burst buffer subsystem is installed either internal to or connected to the I/O nodes of such a system, and takes the form of a pool of solid-state non-volatile memory. This pool absorbs the bursts of I/O traffic and through the I/O node, has the ability the drain the content to disk for permanent storage, much like a cache in a RAID controller buffers write requests to the attached disks.

However, when in-transit processing of data is desired, the burst buffer's configuration must be augmented to accommodate more than just buffering of data in-flight to the parallel file system. In this scenario, the burst buffer flash pool must be associated with directly attached compute capability, RAM, and cross–burst buffer communication links. Essentially, a place to execute the desired analysis code is needed with the intent that it have high-bandwidth

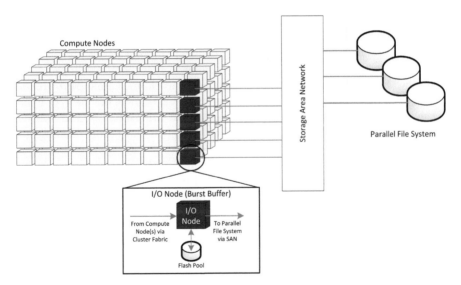

FIGURE 23.1: Potential system diagram for a supercomputer with burst buffers.

access to the stored data in the burst buffer. The cross–burst buffer communication allows for the analysis application running to perform global operations across all data stored within a set of storage pools. An example of this would be computing the average ocean temperature across all stored grid points stored in all burst buffers assigned to the job.

In addition to the hardware changes, software capability is also required to make in-transit data analysis a success. First, a standard API for invoking analysis operations in the burst buffer subsystem is needed. This API should be simulation agnostic and serve as a piece of middleware that each application leverages. Second, a standardized way for simulation applications to communicate the current status of their I/O operations to the burst buffer processing elements is needed. This communication not only serves to notify the burst buffers as to what data is being sent down (which timestep, which variables, etc.) but also to alert the analysis application as to when all of the data is present on the burst buffers and available for operation. This communication could take the form of either flags in the file's metadata or explicit communication over the network.

23.3 Systems Prototypes Related to Burst Buffers

One initial prototype that sets the stage for using burst buffers in modern HPC systems is called "Overlapped Checkpointing with Hardware Assist" [6]. In the overlapped checkpointing system, the I/O nodes in an HPC system are configured with a RAM disk or some type of fast non-volatile storage (what is now flash in current implementations) running PVFS and mounted onto the compute nodes. Applications wishing to checkpoint are linked with a shim header, which intercepts MPI-IO's open and close commands to redirect the write path from the parallel file system to the storage on the I/O nodes. Daemons on the I/O nodes in turn handle the drain of the data from the local storage pool to the actual expected path on the parallel file system. This concept allows applications to write data to storage quickly and return to computation while the storage system handles the data's safe transfer to disk asynchronously. This idea has morphed into the current idea for a burst buffer as outlined in studies by Grider et al. and Liu et al. [4, 5] where flash pools are connected to the I/O nodes and software integration is much more refined.

Argonne National Laboratory's GLEAN system [7, 8] (also see Chapter 18) is a framework designed to provide *in situ* and in-transit storage and processing services. Using GLEAN, application data can be migrated to staging nodes within the HPC system and processed in-transit, all while maintaining the application's data structure semantics. This has allowed, for example, one demonstration of GLEAN where the PHASTA computational fluid dynamics code was interfaced with a running instance of ParaView on an associated visualization cluster and the visualization produced while the simulation was running (see Section 18.3.3).

Similarly, the Adaptable I/O System (ADIOS) library has been extended to allow for data to be "staged" to a set of nodes where processing can be performed before sending the final dataset to storage [1, 9]. In such a setup, the I/O library provides the application with a mechanism to move the data to storage by way of a staging node where the I/O library can invoke user-supplied analysis or data transformation (such as converting the data to a specific format like HDF5) libraries. A similar concept was introduced with ActiveSpaces [3], which provides a mechanism that allows for data to be processed through a staging node on the way to persistent storage. Additional details on ADIOS are discussed in Chapter 17.

One final prototype of in-transit analysis is a collaboration between Los Alamos National Laboratory and EMC to develop a prototype system consisting of a burst buffer connected between a cluster and a Lustre parallel file system [2]. In this demonstration, a simulation of the fluid dynamics of a wind turbine model was run such that as timesteps were dumped to the burst buffer, a ParaView instance was run to produce a visualization at each timestep. Comparing the runtime of the tests, it was clear that by overlapping the visualization process with the simulation execution, time-to-results was reduced. This reduction was approximately 33% off of the runtime when using burst buffers as compared to the same run without the benefit of their use.

23.4   Conclusion

In-transit processing of data is a natural extension of placing burst buffers into HPC systems. With data being held close to a processing element in fast storage (flash in this case), the ability to analyze the data before it is sent to slower rotating storage provides a significant potential for decreased time to results for users. The prototype systems discussed in this chapter are examples of some of the initial work conducted to explore this potential and develop effective systems to leverage in-transit analysis in HPC systems. As no current HPC system has a burst buffer in production use, this technique of in-transit processing will undoubtedly evolve as technology changes in the years ahead.

Bibliography

[1] Hasan Abbasi, J. Lofstead, Fang Zheng, K. Schwan, M. Wolf, and S. Klasky. Extending I/O through High Performance Data Services. In

Cluster Computing and Workshops, 2009. CLUSTER '09. IEEE International Conference on, pages 1–10, 2009.

[2] J. Bent, S. Faibish, J. Ahrens, G. Grider, J. Patchett, P. Tzelnic, and J. Woodring. Jitter-free Co-processing on a Prototype Exascale Storage Stack. In *Mass Storage Systems and Technologies (MSST), 2012 IEEE 28th Symposium on*, pages 1–5, 2012.

[3] C. Docan, M. Parashar, J. Cummings, and S. Klasky. Moving the Code to the Data: Dynamic Code Deployment Using ActiveSpaces. In *Parallel Distributed Processing Symposium (IPDPS), 2011 IEEE International*, pages 758–769, 2011.

[4] G. Grider. Exascale FSIO: Can We Get There? Can We Afford To? In *7th IEEE International Workshop on Storage Network Architecture and Parallel I/O*, May 2011.

[5] N. Liu, J. Cope, P. Carns, C. Carothers, R. Ross, G. Grider, A. Crume, and C. Maltzahn. On the Role of Burst Buffers in Leadership-Class Storage Systems. In *Mass Storage Systems and Technologies (MSST), 2012 IEEE 28th Symposium on*, pages 1–11, 2012.

[6] C. Mitchell, J. Nunez, and J. Wang. Overlapped Checkpointing with Hardware Assist. In *Cluster Computing and Workshops, 2009. CLUSTER '09. IEEE International Conference on*, pages 1–10, 2009.

[7] V. Vishwanath, M. Hereld, V. Morozov, and M.E. Papka. Topology-Aware Data Movement and Staging for I/O Acceleration on Blue Gene/P Supercomputing Systems. In *High Performance Computing, Networking, Storage and Analysis (SC), 2011 International Conference for*, pages 1–11, 2011.

[8] V. Vishwanath, M. Hereld, and M.E. Papka. Toward Simulation-Time Data Analysis and I/O Acceleration on Leadership-Class Systems. In *Large Data Analysis and Visualization (LDAV), 2011 IEEE Symposium on*, pages 9–14, 2011.

[9] Fang Zheng, H. Abbasi, C. Docan, J. Lofstead, Qing Liu, S. Klasky, M. Parashar, N. Podhorszki, K. Schwan, and M. Wolf. PreDatA: Preparatory Data Analytics on Peta-Scale Machines. In *Parallel Distributed Processing (IPDPS), 2010 IEEE International Symposium on*, pages 1–12, 2010.

Part V

I/O Profiling Tools

Chapter 24

Overview of I/O Benchmarking

Katie Antypas and Yushu Yao

National Energy Research Scientific Computing Center, Lawrence Berkeley National Laboratory

24.1	Introduction	279
24.2	I/O Benchmarking	280
24.3	Why Profile I/O in Scientific Applications?	283
24.4	Brief Introduction to I/O Profilers	283
24.5	I/O Profiling at NERSC	284
	24.5.1 Application Profiling Case Studies	284
	24.5.1.1 Checkpointing Too Frequently	285
	24.5.1.2 Reading Small Input Files from Every Rank	286
	24.5.1.3 Using the Wrong File System	286
24.6	Conclusion	287
	Bibliography	287

24.1 Introduction

For users of HPC systems, I/O remains a challenge in achieving high performance on large-scale parallel systems. There are numerous reasons for I/O bottlenecks. First, an I/O subsystem may be undersized for a particular HPC compute partition. A great challenge for HPC centers is how much budget to devote to components of a system. The balance of the I/O partition to the compute partition depends on the system's workload as well as the scheduling policies. Second, depending on how a system is architected, concurrent applications could be sharing limited I/O resources, leading to lower performance. I/O subsystem resources that could produce increased latencies and reduced bandwidth with multiple concurrent applications include contention in I/O nodes, network components, metadata servers, spinning disk, amongst others. Last, how a user reads and writes data can greatly affect application performance (also discussed in Chapters 19–23). A user performing I/O, in a non-optimal manner may see low performance because of these operations. An application that performs many small writes may run into lock contention in a block-based file system while an application that tries to open many files concurrently may suffer from reduced metadata performance.

There are a number of techniques that application developers and HPC system administrators can use to assess the performance of an application or the I/O subsystem. This chapter introduces I/O benchmarking, file system monitoring, and I/O profiling for these purposes.

24.2   I/O Benchmarking

To measure a system's I/O capabilities, the HPC community has long used I/O benchmarks to measure performance. Benchmarks vary in complexity and purpose, but in general, the goal is to mimic a workload in a simple way, or to test and stress certain aspects of the file system [19].

At HPC centers, I/O benchmarks are used to test and accept new systems. They are also used to investigate reports of low performance and to find bottlenecks in the file system.

I/O workloads run at HPC centers include a variety of access patterns and interfaces [19, 13]. Within the DOE Office of Science user community, applications use the POSIX, MPI-IO, HDF5, and netCDF interfaces. Some of these applications write to and read from single shared files while others use a file-per-processor format. Furthermore, applications display a variety of access patterns from large block, append-only writes, to small block bursty I/O patterns, to reading large input files [21].

Figure 24.1 shows some of the common access patterns that result from moving data between memory and a file. In the simplest case, the data is contiguous in both memory and the file. Alternatively, the data could be contiguous in memory, but not in the file; contiguous in the file, but not in memory; or contiguous in neither. The reasons for different I/O access patterns in different scientific applications vary widely. A developer may choose a specific data structure because it is most optimal for a particular computational algorithm, but may choose a different data layout in the file to facilitate post-processing and analysis.

With such a variety of I/O patterns, it is difficult for a single I/O benchmark to represent a complex multi-user environment, so instead, synthetic I/O benchmarks are used to test and isolate specific I/O components in a storage subsystem or to measure a distinct I/O pattern [19]. Many of the existing I/O benchmarks do not reflect a complex HPC workload, either because they only test POSIX APIs or because they only measure serial I/O performance.

The IOR [7] benchmark is one of the most flexible benchmarks because simple input parameters can control different I/O APIs such as POSIX, MPI-IO HDF5, and Parallel-NetCDF. Parameters also control whether output is a single shared file or multi-file. Additionally, a user can control the size of

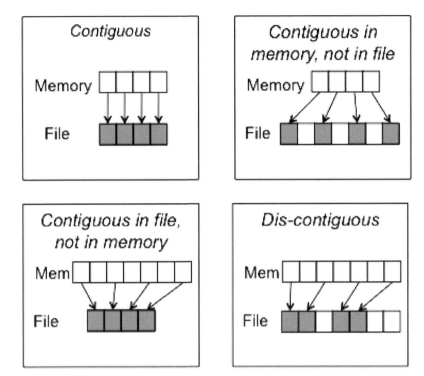

FIGURE 24.1: Application access patterns for moving data between memory and a file.

writes and reads, the amount of data read and written, and whether the data is strided or sequential in a file.

At NERSC, the IOR benchmark is used for procuring and testing new systems, as well as measuring the performance of the file system over the lifetime of a system. A number of different IOR tests are used to gauge the performance and health of the file system. Tests include small block I/O, where an I/O transaction size (the amount of data transferred to disk at a given time) is significantly less than the lock size on the file system. This measures the file system's capabilities aggregating small transactions, as well as measuring lock contention overhead. The small block I/O tests are performed using different I/O APIs, namely POSIX file-per-processor I/O, in addition to MPI-IO. Running the same test, but only altering the I/O API allows overhead from MPI-IO to be measured. These same tests are performed using large block I/O where the I/O transaction size is equal to or greater than the lock size of the file system, typically 1–4 MB.

The IOR benchmark returns the aggregate write and read rate in the output of the test. These numbers can also be verified by monitoring the performance of the file system. Figure 24.2 shows the activity on the Franklin XT-4 file system when the IOR benchmark is run. In this example, the IOR benchmark achieves a write rate of over 9 GB/s while the read test achieves a rate of 6 GB/s. This benchmark was run on a production system and so the smaller blue and red points indicate other I/O occurring on the system. File system monitoring is measured by the Lustre Monitoring Tool (LMT) [21], which measures server-side I/O activity.

Ideally, I/O benchmarks would be run on a dedicated system with no other users or applications on the system. Running in isolation negates the effect of contention from other applications and yields more predictable, repeatable tests with lower variability. But running in a dedicated mode for a long period of time can be impractical for HPC centers that have a responsibility to keep a system available to its users. In this case, the benchmarker must perform tests on a system running other applications, which could be affected by other users on the system [21]. If possible, benchmark runs should avoid being scheduled at the same time as other I/O-intensive jobs. This may be impossible, in which case a benchmark should be run enough times to determine when the benchmark performance is lowered as a result of contention.

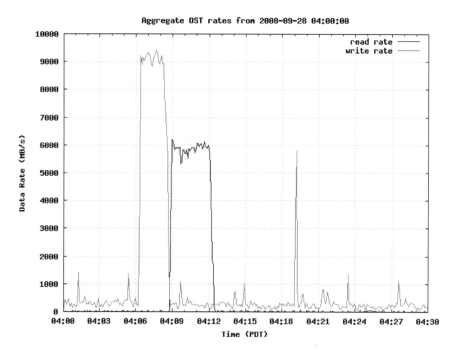

FIGURE 24.2: Franklin XT-4 file system activity during an IOR run. The IOR benchmark achieves a write rate of over 9 GB/s while the read test achieves a rate of 6 GB/s.

While some benchmarks, like IOR, can be adjusted to mimic a specific application [19], a single synthetic benchmark has not been used to represent a diverse complex workload. In I/O benchmarking, there is a trade-off between the simplicity of the benchmark and what it represents.

In order to understand the I/O characteristics of a specific application or a more complex workload, applications need to be profiled individually.

24.3   Why Profile I/O in Scientific Applications?

In order achieve optimal performance on HPC systems, users profile applications to understand an application's characteristics. Profiling an application can inform the user about such metrics as the top routines where time is spent, MPI overhead, and cache misses. In the HPC community, there are a number of tools for profiling applications such as IPM [5], HPC toolkit [4], Valgrind [11], as well as a number of vendor-provided solutions such as Vtune [6] from Intel, Craypat [1] from Cray, and the IBM profiler from IBM.

Profiling I/O in applications can be just as important. With the I/O and data needs of the HPC community expanding, and as more time is spent in application I/O, it is even more important to profile application I/O. Non-optimal I/O can provide significant bottlenecks to performance. There are a number of reasons to do I/O profiling in an application. The first is simply to understand the amount of time an application is spending doing I/O. If after profiling an application, it is found that an application is spending very little time doing I/O, then a user can focus his or her time optimizing other parts of the code. On the other hand, if an application is spending a significant amount of time doing I/O, then a user knows this is an area to target to improve an application's performance.

I/O profilers can provide a wealth of information to the developer of a code, such as the amount of data read and written, the rate at which data is read and written, and the distribution of write and read sizes. Armed with this information, an application developer can change an applications I/O pattern to improve performance.

24.4   Brief Introduction to I/O Profilers

While the mechanisms of different I/O profilers may vary, at their core they must in some way intercept the I/O calls (trace) in an application and record and output the data. A number of tools have been produced especially for the tracing of I/O operations in large-scale parallel applications, such as LANL-Trace [3], HPCT-IO [18], IOT [17], etc. Some of the general-purpose tools can also trace I/O information in additional to MPI calls and CPU activities, such as FPMPI [2], Jumpshot [22, 15], TAU [20] (see Chapter 25), IPM [16] (see Chapter 26), STAT [12], etc. Most of these tools produce a log containing the time series of I/O operations. The logs are useful for understanding the I/O behavior of each process. However, due to the size of the log, the overhead of these are usually large, so they are suited for debugging jobs. Darshan (see Chapter 27) is also an I/O tracing profiler. Darshan only gives aggregate information over time, so the log files are much smaller than other tools and the overhead is very low. For this reason, Darshan can be enabled for a compute system by default to capture the I/O of every job. However, Darshan does not provide I/O behavior over time, which limits the depth of the I/O knowledge.

24.5   I/O Profiling at NERSC

At NERSC the Darshan tool is used to characterize I/O on the Hopper Cray XE6 system [10]. Darshan captures MPI-IO calls using the PMPI interface [9] and captures POSIX-I/O calls using the GNU linker's wrap argument [14]. NERSC staff and Darshan developers have worked together to make Darshan usable to a wide number of users by loading the Darshan module by default. A user simply needs to relink his or her application in order to for Darshan to instrument the application. The primary purpose of profiling by default is to give users feedback on their I/O behavior, so that they can improve the I/O efficiency to achieve more meaningful calculation within a certain allocation. Darshan output is collected and put on a website for the user to see. The Darshan output displayed on the website includes:

- I/O size in megabytes read and written,

- I/O rate in megabytes per second,

- percentage of application time spent in I/O, and

- distribution of write and read sizes.

24.5.1   Application Profiling Case Studies

NERSC has used the Darshan tool to identify and help users who may be performing I/O in a less than optimal way. This section selects three of the most representative case studies to show how Darshan has been used to find possible I/O application problems.

24.5.1.1   Checkpointing Too Frequently

In the case where the user is writing a checkpoint file about every 90 minutes, all I/O activity is represented by the benchmark tests (as shown in Figure 24.4). The write I/O is achieving a high rate, as indicated by the periodic blue dots, however, the user is checkpointing very frequently and spent 80% of time on I/O (Figure 24.3). Based on the mean time between failure of the Hopper system, the user could be checkpointing once every 8 to 10 hours, reducing the amount of time spent in I/O.

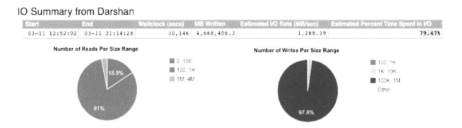

FIGURE 24.3: Darshan statistics of a job that is checkpointing too frequently.

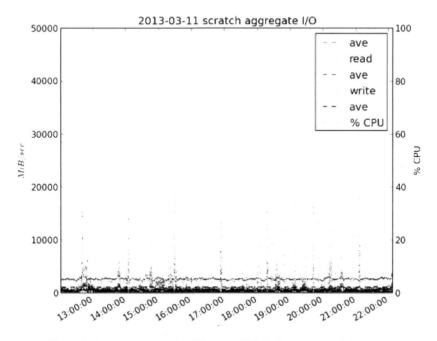

FIGURE 24.4: Activities on the Hopper XE-6 file system during a user run. The user is frequently checkpointing, causing the I/O activity to be high.

Total Wall-Clock Time

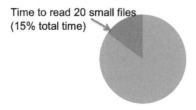

FIGURE 24.5: A job spent 15% of wall time reading 20 small input files.

24.5.1.2　Reading Small Input Files from Every Rank

In the second use case, an application using over 50,000 compute cores is reading 20 small input files of around 1 KB each. This results in a large amount time spent in opening the files as each of the 50,000 cores opens each of the 20 input files. The result is that 15% of total application wall-clock time is spent reading the 20 input files.

The user was advised to instead have a single MPI task open up each of the 20 input files and broadcast the contents of the file to the other 50,000 tasks.

24.5.1.3　Using the Wrong File System

In the last case, a user is spending a large (33%) of wall-clock time writing a small amount of I/O. As the Darshan results show, the application wrote only 640 MB, but achieved a rate of only 110 KB/s and spent 33% of time in I/O. On further investigation using more detailed Darshan logs, NERSC staff found the application was writing a file using 40,000 cores using the MPI-IO interface to the NERSC home file system. The home file system at NERSC is not configured for high-bandwidth I/O and is instead optimized for compiling the applications. The user was advised to instead write the output file to the larger "scratch" Lustre [8] file system. The Figure 24.6, shows the dramatic improvement when the user switched to a high performing file system. The

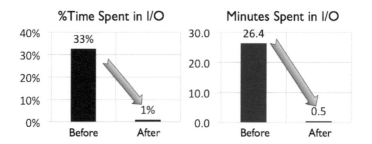

FIGURE 24.6: Using the wrong file system can greatly impact the job performance.

amount of time spent in I/O fell from over 26 minutes to 30 seconds, less than 1% of application runtime.

24.6 Conclusion

In summary, in order to get optimal performance from a complex I/O subsystem, it is useful to do I/O benchmarking and I/O application profiling. Benchmarking allows an HPC analyst to understand the performance of an I/O subsystem, while I/O profiling shows an application developer details about an application's I/O patterns that can illuminate how to improve performance.

Bibliography

[1] CrayPat Performance Tool. http://www.nersc.gov/users/software/debugging-and-profiling/craypat/.

[2] FPMPI-2 Fast Profiling Library for MPI. http://www.mcs.anl.gov/research/projects/fpmpi/WWW/.

[3] HPC-5 Open Source Software Projects: LANL-Trace. http://institute.lanl.gov/data/software/.

[4] HPC Toolkit. http://hpctoolkit.org/.

[5] Integrated Performance Monitoring (IPM). http://ipm-hpc.sourceforge.net/.

[6] Intel VTune Toolset. http://software.intel.com/en-us/intel-vtune-amplifier-xe.

[7] IOR Project Website. http://sourceforge.net/projects/ior-sio/.

[8] Lustre File System. http://wiki.lustre.org/.

[9] MPI Standard Profiling Interface. http://www.open-mpi.org/faq/?category=perftools.

[10] NERSC Hopper Cray XE6 System. http://www.nersc.gov/users/computational-systems/hopper/.

[11] Valgrind. http://valgrind.org/.

[12] D.C. Arnold, D.H. Ahn, B.R. De Supinski, G.L. Lee, B.P. Miller, and M. Schulz. Stack Trace Analysis for Large-Scale Debugging. In *Parallel and Distributed Processing Symposium, IPDPS 2007. IEEE International*, pages 1–10, 2007.

[13] Philip H. Carns, Robert Latham, Robert B. Ross, Kamil Iskra, Samuel Lang, and Katherine Riley. 24/7 Characterization of Petascale I/O Workloads. In *CLUSTER*, pages 1–10. IEEE, 2009.

[14] Philip H. Carns, Y. Yao, K. Harms, R. Latham, Robert B. Ross, and K. Antypas. Production I/O Characterization on the Cray XE6. In *CUG2013*, Napa Valley, CA, May 9, 2013 2013.

[15] A. Chan, W. D. Gropp, and Ewing L. Lusk. An Efficient Format for Nearly Constant-Time Access to Arbitrary Time Intervals in Large Trace Files. *Sci. Programming*, 16:155–165, 2007.

[16] Karl Fürlinger, Nicholas J. Wright, and David Skinner. Performance Analysis and Workload Characterization with IPM. In *Parallel Tools Workshop*, pages 31–38, 2009.

[17] Philip C. Roth. Characterizing the I/O Behavior of Scientific Applications on the Cray XT. In *Proceedings of the 2nd International Workshop on Petascale Data Storage: Held in Conjunction with Supercomputing '07*, PDSW '07, pages 50–55, New York, NY, USA, 2007. ACM.

[18] S. Seelam, I-Hsin Chung, Ding-Yong Hong, Hui-Fang Wen, and Hao Yu. Early Experiences in Application Level I/O Tracing on Blue Gene Systems. In *IEEE International Symposium on Parallel and Distributed Processing, IPDPS 2008*, pages 1–8, 2008.

[19] Hongzhang Shan, Katie Antypas, and John Shalf. Characterizing and Predicting the I/O Performance of HPC Applications Using a Parameterized Synthetic Benchmark. In *Proceedings of the 2008 ACM/IEEE conference on Supercomputing*, page 42. IEEE Press, 2008.

[20] Sameer S. Shende and Allen D. Malony. The Tau Parallel Performance System. *Int. J. High Perform. Comput. Appl.*, 20(2):287–311, May 2006.

[21] A. Uselton, K. Antypas, D.M. Ushizima, and J. Sukharev. File System Monitoring as a Window into User I/O Requirements. In *Proceedings of the 2010 Cray User Group Conference*, 2010.

[22] Omer Zaki, Ewing Lusk, and Deborah Swider. Toward Scalable Performance Visualization with Jumpshot. *High Performance Computing Applications*, 13:277–288, 1999.

Chapter 25

TAU

Sameer Shende and Allen D. Malony

University of Oregon

25.1	Abstract	....	289
25.2	Features	....	290
	25.2.1	MPI-IO Instrumentation	291
	25.2.2	Runtime Preloading of Instrumented Library	291
	25.2.3	Linker-Based Instrumentation	291
	25.2.4	Instrumented External I/O Libraries	292
25.3	Success Stories	....	292
25.4	Conclusion	....	294
	Bibliography	....	294

25.1 Abstract

I/O performance is becoming a key bottleneck in many cases at the extreme scale. As the volume of data and application reads and writes increases, it is important to assess the scalability of I/O operations as a key contributor to overall application performance. Optimizing I/O performance presents unique challenges for application developers and performance measurement and analysis tools, as it often involves an integration of multiple techniques to observe performance and create integrated I/O performance views from multiple I/O layers. Furthermore, reasoning about how to improve I/O performance necessarily involves understanding its relationship to the application behavior as a whole. The TAU Performance System [4, 7] is an integrated performance profiling and tracing toolkit that provides flexible support for performance instrumentation of both the application and the I/O layers.

25.2   Features

Observing the performance of the I/O operations requires instrumentation to be inserted in the library layers of the I/O software stack, including commonly used I/O interfaces such as POSIX I/O and MPI-IO. However, characterization of I/O performance must also be done with respect to an application context in order to fully understand overall performance impact. TAU can gather performance data from the application and I/O layers to create a unified performance perspective that shows program context information alongside I/O statistics. It does so by instrumenting both the application source code and the intercepting calls from the I/O layers using wrapper libraries.

Application source code written in a variety of HPC languages (e.g., C, C++, Fortran, UPC) can be instrumented by TAU's compiler scripts using the Program Database Toolkit (PDT) [2] source analysis technology. The PDT-based tau_instrumentor tool inserts code into the application at selected points for performance measurement. PDT can also be used to interpret library header files for purposes of *wrapping* the interface routines with interposition code that intercept library calls in the application, performs measurements, and invokes the library operation. The TAU wrapping capability is applied to create wrappers for MPI-IO and POSIX I/O. In fact, these wrapped libraries are distributed with TAU. Additional tools, such as the tau_gen_wrapper [5], are provided to automate the creation of external wrapper libraries for other I/O libraries such as HDF5. By capturing events from several layers of wrapped libraries, TAU is able to observe the flow through these calls and associate routine parameters captured (e.g., file ID, I/O data size) with timing measurements to produce metrics such as the bandwidth of read and write operations for each file. TAU can further attribute I/O costs to specific code regions without modifying the source code of the application.

More specifically, TAU supports the following techniques for intercepting I/O calls:

- MPI-IO instrumentation,

- preloading of instrumented libraries,

- linker-based instrumentation, and

- instrumented external libraries.

Each of these techniques is described in more detail in the following subsections.

25.2.1 MPI-IO Instrumentation

The MPI message-passing libraries provide a name-shifted interface that permits tools, including TAU, to intercept calls using the profiling message-passing interface (PMPI) name-shifted interface. TAU additionally uses this support to create a wrapper library for MPI-IO calls (e.g., `MPI_File_read`) that internally calls the name-shifted interface (e.g., `PMPI_File_read`). Like before, the wrappers can examine the arguments that flow through the I/O calls to compute volume and bandwidth of individual I/O operations. In addition to TAU, this instrumentation technique is used in a wide variety of HPC tools including Scalasca [9], VampirTrace [6], Score-P [8], mpiP [1], and Integrated Performance Monitoring (IPM) (see Chapter 26). However, library interposition through name-shifted interfaces is only available as a technique if such interfaces are implemented in the library. This is not the case with POSIX I/O.

25.2.2 Runtime Preloading of Instrumented Library

Many HPC operating systems such as Linux, Cray Compute Node Linux (CNL), IBM Blue Gene Compute Node Kernel (CNK), and Solaris permit preloading of a library in the address space of an executing application specifying a shared object (DSO) in an environment variable (`LD_PRELOAD`). It is possible to create a tool based on this technique that can intercept all I/O operations by means of a wrapper-library where the POSIX I/O calls are redefined to call the global routine (identified using the `dlsym` system call) internally. Preloading instrumented libraries is a powerful technique implemented by the runtime linker and is used in TAU [4] and VampirTrace [6]. While it can resolve all POSIX-I/O calls and operates on un-instrumented executables, it only supports dynamic executables. Static executables are used by default on IBM Blue Gene and Cray XE6 and XK6 systems, although dynamic executables may be created using the `dynamic` command line flag. A different technique will be necessary to support static binaries.

25.2.3 Linker-Based Instrumentation

A linker can redirect references to a wrapped routine when it is invoked with a special flag on the command line (`-Wl,-wrap,function_name`). In this case, the application does need to be re-linked to use the wrapped library, but this instrumentation technique overcomes the limitation of the previous approach provided by the runtime linker and may be used with both static and dynamic executables. TAU has applied this approach to instrument POSIX I/O calls by creating a wrapper library. Since the number of wrapped routines that may be present in a library might be potentially large, listing each routine on the linker's command line can interfere with predefined system limits for command line length. Instead, a linker may read a file that contains wrapped symbol names and expand these internally to construct the appropriate command line. TAU's compiler scripts have been updated to automatically add the necessary flags to the linker command line when the user sets a special I/O instrumentation flag (-optTrackIO) in the TAU_OPTIONS environment variable. Section 25.3 describes this approach in greater detail with regards to GCRM profiling.

25.2.4   Instrumented External I/O Libraries

When a user needs to evaluate the time spent in un-instrumented I/O libraries, such as HDF5 (see Chapter 16) and other system libraries, it is important to be able to generate custom user-directed wrapper libraries. These wrapper libraries may be pre-loaded at runtime or re-linked to create an instrumented binary using linker-based instrumentation as described above. However, manually building these libraries may prove to be cumbersome. TAU automates the creation of these wrapper libraries using the tau_gen_wrapper tool.

25.3   Success Stories

The Global Cloud Resolving Model (GCRM) [3] models climate on the entire globe at a horizontal grid spacing of at least 4 km, and a vertical dimension on the order of 256 layers resulting in over 10 billion cells. A single cell-based variable written in single precision will require approximately 43 GB of disk storage. Corner data will require 85 GB and edge data 128 GB. A single snapshot of history data will require 1.8 TB of storage as currently configured. Climate scientists will want to write data as frequently as possible (down to the order of minutes) while maintaining an I/O cost below 10% of the overall simulation. Obviously, the efficiency of the I/O is a critical requirement. Understanding and optimizing the behavior of the I/O system for an application is difficult for several reasons. First, there are several layers in the I/O stack, some of which are proprietary software. Second, there are many options for controlling these layers varying from optional arguments, to hints, or to alternative APIs. Third, there are often multiple implementations of some of the layers.

Profiling all the layers of the GCRM I/O is necessary in order to determine where the true bottlenecks reside. TAU provides the capabilities both to look deep into the various API layers and to organize and analyze the numerous configurations under evaluation. For instance, application phases could be profiled, and read and write bandwidths were evaluated for each phase. Figure 25.1 shows the data for each file and read operation collected by TAU. Here we see how the MPI-IO layer internally calls the POSIX I/O layer. Figure 25.2 shows the peak I/O bandwidth and I/O volume for read calls on each

TAU: ParaProf: Context Events for: node 29 – zgrd_hopp2_40_r5_craylib_dio_allf.xml

Name	Total	NumSamples	MaxValue	MinValue	MeanValue	Std. Dev.
▸ .TAU application						
▸ GIO_IO::GIO_OPEN [{io_netcdfx.pp.F90} {138,3}-{157,23}]						
MPI-IO Read Bandwidth (MB/s)		78	0.082	0	0.022	0.026
MPI-IO Write Bandwidth (MB/s)		89	12.297	0.003	1.867	2.222
▸ MPI_File_read()						
▾ MPI_File_read_at()						
▾ read()						
Bytes Read	543,103	891	4,096	8	609.543	1,038.442
Bytes Read <file=./cloud_ice_19010101_000000.nc>	13,407	22	4,096	8	609.409	1,053.463
Bytes Read <file=./cloud_water_19010101_000000.nc>	13,409	22	4,096	8	609.5	1,053.417
Bytes Read <file=./divergence_19010101_000000.nc>	13,381	22	4,096	8	608.227	1,053.845
Bytes Read <file=./graupel_mmr_19010101_000000.nc>	13,409	22	4,096	8	609.5	1,053.417
Bytes Read <file=./grid.nc>	39,017	71	4,096	8	549.535	798.746
Bytes Read <file=./heat_flux_vdiff_19010101_000000.nc>	13,433	22	4,096	8	610.591	1,053.112
Bytes Read <file=./exner_lfc_19010101_000000.nc>	13,362	22	4,096	8	607.364	1,054.049
Bytes Read <file=./geopotential_19010101_000000.nc>	13,409	22	4,096	8	609.5	1,053.453
Bytes Read <file=./heating_sw_19010101_000000.nc>	13,438	22	4,096	8	610.818	1,053.071
Bytes Read <file=./heating_sw_cs_19010101_000000.nc>	13,441	22	4,096	8	610.955	1,053.002
Bytes Read <file=./heating_latent_19010101_000000.nc>	13,442	22	4,096	8	611	1,052.979
Bytes Read <file=./heating_lw_cs_19010101_000000.nc>	13,441	22	4,096	8	610.955	1,053.002
Bytes Read <file=./heating_lw_19010101_000000.nc>	13,438	22	4,096	8	610.818	1,053.071
Bytes Read <file=./prec_frz_19010101_000000.nc>	12,006	18	4,096	8	667	1,086.515
Bytes Read <file=./pressure_19010101_000000.nc>	13,387	22	4,096	8	608.5	1,053.751
Bytes Read <file=./prec_tot_19010101_000000.nc>	12,006	18	4,096	8	667	1,086.515
Bytes Read <file=./mass_19010101_000000.nc>	13,386	22	4,096	8	608.455	1,053.856
Bytes Read <file=./ke_19010101_000000.nc>	13,388	22	4,096	8	608.545	1,053.857
Bytes Read <file=./olr_19010101_000000.nc>	12,014	18	4,096	8	667.444	1,086.415
Bytes Read <file=./qsn_tend_micro_19010101_000000.nc>	13,446	22	4,096	8	611.182	1,052.939
Bytes Read <file=./qgr_tend_micro_19010101_000000.nc>	13,446	22	4,096	8	611.182	1,052.939
Bytes Read <file=./qrw_tend_micro_19010101_000000.nc>	13,446	22	4,096	8	611.182	1,052.939
Bytes Read <file=./qcw_tend_micro_19010101_000000.nc>	13,446	22	4,096	8	611.182	1,052.939
Bytes Read <file=./qci_tend_micro_19010101_000000.nc>	13,446	22	4,096	8	611.182	1,052.939

FIGURE 25.1: I/O profile for GCRM shows the bytes read for each file using MPI-IO read operations.

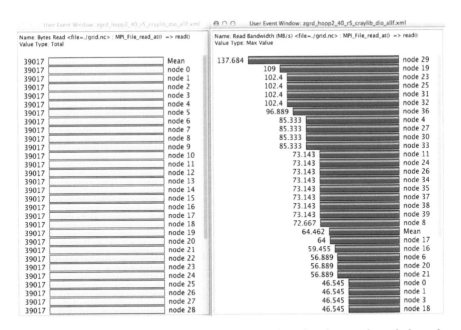

FIGURE 25.2: Peak I/O bandwidth observed and volume of read data for GCRM on different MPI ranks.

MPI rank. For a full description of the problem, please refer to Shende et al.'s work [5]. Here, TAU can help evaluate an application's I/O performance by transparently intercepting the I/O calls using a wrapper interposition library.

25.4 Conclusion

Understanding the performance of software packages in combination with the applications in which they are used requires an ability to capture important events and performance data at the library interfaces. This is particularly true for I/O. Here, several techniques for creating wrapper libraries were presented with the TAU performance system. These techniques were then demonstrated for tracking I/O that was performed by the GCRM application on a Cray XE6 system. This work has been instrumental in improving I/O performance in the GCRM application.

Bibliography

[1] J. Vetter and C. Chambreau. mpiP: Lightweight, Scalable MPI Profiling. http://mpip.sourceforge.net, 2014.

[2] K. Lindlan, J. Cuny, A. D. Malony, S. Shende, B. Mohr, R. Rivenburgh, and C. Rasmussen. A Tool Framework for Static and Dynamic Analysis of Object-Oriented Software with Templates. In *Supercomputing Conference (SC 2000)*, 2000.

[3] D. Randall, T. Ringler, R. Heikes, P. Jones, and J. Baumgardner. Climate Modeling with Spherical Geodesic Grids. *Computing in Science and Engineering*, 4:32–41, 2002. http://kiwi.atmos.colostate.edu/gcrm/.

[4] S. Shende and A. Malony. The TAU Parallel Performance System. *International Journal of High Performance Computing Applications*, 20(2, Summer):287–311, 2006. ACTS Collection Special Issue.

[5] S. Shende, A. D. Malony, W. Spear, and K. Schuchardt. Characterizing I/O Performance Using the TAU Performance System. In D. Bailey, R. Lucas, and S. Williams, editors, *Advances in Parallel Computing. Applications, Tools, and Techniques on the Road to Exascale Computing*, volume 22, pages 647–655. IOS Press, New York, 2010.

[6] T.U. Dresden, ZIH. VampirTrace. http://www.tu-dresden.de/zih/vampirtrace, 2014.

[7] University of Oregon. TAU Performance System. `http://tau.uoregon.edu`, 2014.

[8] VI-HPS. Score-P. `http://www.score-p.org`, 2014.

[9] F. Wolf, B. Wylie, E. Ábrahám, D. Becker, W. Frings, K. Fürlinger, M. Geimer, M. Hermanns, B. Mohr, S. Moore, M. Pfeifer, and Z. Szebenyi. Usage of the SCALASCA Toolset for Scalable Performance Analysis of Large-Scale Parallel Applications. In *Proc. of the 2nd HLRS Parallel Tools Workshop*, pages 157–167, Stuttgart, Germany, July 2008. Springer.

Chapter 26

Integrated Performance Monitoring

David Skinner

National Energy Research Scientific Computing Center, Lawrence Berkeley National Laboratory

26.1	Design and Features	297
26.2	Success Stories	301
	26.2.1 Chombo's ftruncate	301
	26.2.2 MADBENCH and File System Health	302
	26.2.3 Buffer Size	303
	26.2.4 HPC Workload Studies	304
26.3	Conclusion	305
	Bibliography	306

Application performance is usually tested as part of a benchmark or controlled characterization study. Conducted by tools experts, the applications are assessed in an "off-line" or non-production environment. In practice [6], the performance delivered by an application over the duration of many executions can vary in uncontrolled and significant ways. A properly load-balanced code and input deck can be easily, and often severely, bottle-necked by minor changes in input, concurrency, and execution environment. Many of these "minor" changes are too easy to arrive at through natural adjustments of scientific need or resource availability, which is the motivation behind the Integrated Performance Monitoring (IPM) framework to measure and improve *in-vivo* HPC application performance as it happens in a production computing setting.

26.1 Design and Features

The IPM framework tests application performance in a production-like environment to assesses application performance realistically and accurately. IPM has been used in the context of individual work on codes [1], for HPC system procurements [9], and metering workloads' sustained performance at

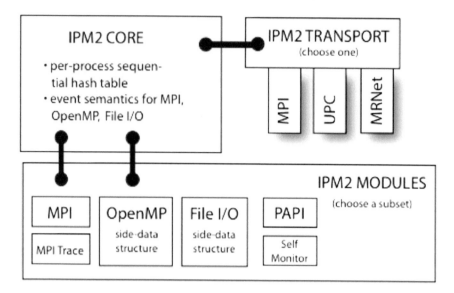

FIGURE 26.1: IPM's core framework collects performance events from IPM modules and transports them via the parallel interconnect to provide an application-level performance profile. Modules are topical and selectable at runtime.

a computing facility [4] level. The basis for such monitoring derives from the hardware performance monitoring (HPM) tools [7] that pre-date widespread need for I/O monitoring. For the present purposes, the former cases are discussed more than the latter and specifically on the topic of I/O. IPM has a modular structure and monitors compute cores and messaging traffic topologies.

The modules of the framework in Figure 26.1 all share a lightweight hashing scheme that maps a large space of potential application events, each keyed by a 128-bit event signature, into a small memory footprint (2–4 MB) event table. For each event ID, a minimal set of timings and counts are maintained and reported when the application completes. The hashing scheme is designed for fast inserts to minimally perturb the running application both in terms of CPU and memory overhead, as shown in Figure 26.2. The overall design of IPM is intended to introduce a small [2], predictable, and scale-free perturbation on application performance.

Figure 26.3 shows the text output from IPM, which by default takes the form of a high-level overview of application performance that includes aggregate I/O performance.

The POSIX interface is, on modern architectures, a reasonable point to reliably intercept and monitor I/O communication between the application and disk. On the post-IBM AIX HPC architectures, even complex POSIX

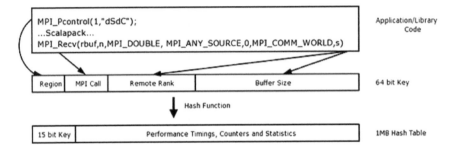

FIGURE 26.2: IPM's profiling uses double-open address hashing to map the space of possible events into an inventory of observed events. A 128-bit binary vector encodes the signature of the event based on the details described. Storage of the performance data inventory is optimized for speed and small memory footprint.

```
##IPM2#################################################################
# command    : ./a.out
# start      : Sun Mar 14 16:55:39 2010    host       : nid01829
# stop       : Sun Mar 14 17:04:33 2010    wallclock  : 533.12
# mpi_tasks  : 2048 on 1024 nodes          %comm      : 29.41
# omp_thrds  : 6                           %omp       : 50.63
# files      : 12                          %i/o       : 12.09
# mem [GB]   : 2774.44                      gflop/sec  : 418.58
#
#            :        [total]      <avg>          min          max
# wallclock  :    1091671.57      533.04       532.99       533.12
# MPI        :     321034.43      156.76       109.03       239.23
# I/O        :     131947.08       64.43        11.83       113.87
# OMP        :     552665.28      269.86       205.07       305.36
# OMP idle   :      48262.98       23.57        21.30        27.40
# %wall      :
#   MPI      :                     29.41        20.45        44.88
#   OMP      :                     50.63        38.47        57.28
#   I/O      :                     12.09         2.22        21.36
# #calls     :
#   MPI      :      76235998       37224        37223        37320
# mem [GB]   :       2774.44        1.35         1.35         1.36
#
#                           [time]      [count]      <%wall>
# OMP_PARALLEL           552665.28    131439989        50.63
# MPI_Allreduce          247648.04     14438400        22.69
# fread                   69813.27      5488640         6.40
# ...
#######################################################################
```

FIGURE 26.3: Text output from an application run with IPM. The I/O performance is given in aggregate for the entire job—25% of the 152 core hours is spent in I/O. Maxima and minima across tasks is also reported with MPI tasks spending between 2 and 21% of wall time in I/O.

```
FILE* fopen          int fseek            size_t fread         size_t fwrite
FILE* fdopen         void rewind          int getc             int ungetc
FILE* freopen        int fgetpos          int fgetc            ssize_t write
int fclose           int fsetpos          ssize_t read         int creat
int fflush           long ftell                                int truncate
int close            off_t lseek                               int ftruncate
int open             off64_t lseek64                           int truncate64
int open64                                                     int ftruncate64
```

FIGURE 26.4: The POSIX and MPI-IO calls profiled by IPM's I/O module.

operations such as `mmap` are often correctly intercepted by POSIX library calls as they communicate through system calls to the kernel. IPM intercepts POSIX I/O and reports performance profiles through its standard *double open address hashing* technique. An inventory of I/O conducted during execution with data volumes and timings are reported when execution is complete. A pre-configured list of POSIX calls supported by IPM is prototyped in the file ipm.h.

A C library (preloaded or linked) is used to instrument execution. This can be connected to the execution and/or compile time environment through modules or user environment customization. When adopted by user communities or HPC user facilities, IPM provides a barometer for sustained application performance delivered in the actual context of using the computer as a tool for science. A shared log directory collects the body of performance profiles, each with its own XML file. Parsing one or more XML files is done with the IPM _parse utility or a wide variety of custom parsers and report generators. There are scalability concerns here as part of a data collection strategy. Very large numbers of files and time spent in XML parsing are often the first limits to be stretched. Large-scale data analytics have a role in HPC performance engineering in addition to their main concerns in physics, chemistry, and biology, for example.

It is important to recognize that IPM modules may be nested hierarchically. The MPI-IO layer will often invoke POSIX calls for the I/O transactions to the file system. IPM intercepts and reports both layers. This can provide corroborating evidence of I/O performance loss but must be recognized so as to not double count the reported I/O volume and times.

IPM's feature set for I/O includes

- aggregate I/O performed by a parallel job;

- task-level I/O including each POSIX call and each buffer size transacted; and

- minimum, maximum, and average time spent in each task level I/O.

This is essentially the I/O *parts list* along with the rough cost for each part. For an individual task without "complex" I/O, this provides a code-level view of the I/O strategy. Across tasks, it demonstrates the success of that strategy given contention and load imbalance. Detection of load imbalance is in practice often the primary source of I/O performance loss. Root causes for this imbalance include many-to-few I/O strategies, file system striping, and congestion of I/O due to overlapping I/O operations. I/O performance losses, balanced or not, are sometimes due to the transfer (buffer) sizes of I/Os being so small that transactional overheads are high, or due to synchronous locking I/O operations.

When the I/O load is balanced across tasks, the next question is whether the sustained rates are achieving the I/O rates that the storage system is expected to deliver. If not, then what is the underlying cause of the loss? In some cases the loss is due to the strategy, and in others cases is due to resource scheduling or contention that lies outside the application's control. Defensive I/O strategies are thus sought as much as absolutely optimal strategies. I/O hangs are a notorious source of vexation among HPC enthusiasts and the notions of defense extends to the lower ends of performance. Most HPC I/O goes unmonitored and this is likely a rich area for investigation to guide future data science architectures [5].

There is much to be gained from continued research in this area. As exascale architectures emerge, the pathways from compute core to disk will become more complex as will their performance. It is interesting to consider architectural simulation in the design and provisioning of such systems. Given a body of existing I/O profiles, can one map these into a performance estimate as to what would be possible on a proposed architecture? To what degree can we construct useful models for the design of future I/O systems [3]?

To make actionable decisions about I/O it is important to build models from profiles that are tightly integrated with application performance as it happens. The following sections draw from HPC application I/O scenarios observed at NERSC using IPM.

26.2 Success Stories

26.2.1 Chombo's ftruncate

Chombo's `ftruncate` is a simple case study that shows why profiling is best done in a production setting. Figure 26.5 shows a wide range of I/O tuning techniques applied by HPC experts to the Chombo code. The dominant increase in I/O bandwidth is attributable to removing an extraneous POSIX call from the production-deployed parallel I/O libraries. A profiling interface that captures either the application's I/O activity, the operating system's, or preferably both is often enough to reveal which type of I/O and/or which system resources drive the time spent in I/O. In some cases the improvements listed above took place in how the middleware is used and in other cases changes were made directly to the middleware. For instance, the `remove`

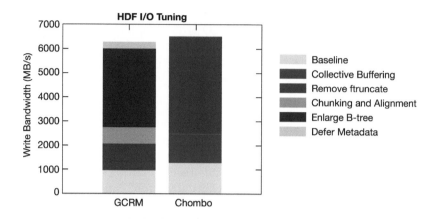

FIGURE 26.5: Steps required to improve performance of writes in HDF-based MPI codes.

`ftruncate` optimization removed a POSIX `ftruncate` call from the HDF code, which caused negligible problems at smaller concurrencies but quickly became a bottleneck in the neighborhood of 1024 tasks. In general, the nature of the optimizations is to re-organize the I/O into forms that match the file system's optimal block size and to align file offsets along those blocks.

26.2.2 MADBENCH and File System Health

I/O performance is a characteristic of applications and the shared resources on which the applications run. In some cases, "out" performance is not a specific concern of the application performance but instead at the file system of the HPC system level. In March of 2009 reports of file system performance loss on Franklin (a Cray XT4 at NERSC) were investigated using IPM. This was not a controlled experiment but I/O performance profiles were measured as steps were taken to improve the I/O rates by adaptation of the file system layout (number of OSS I/O nodes) and upgrades to the file system software versions. Figure 26.6 looks inside the I/O performance before and after those changes and shows the improvement in particular in I/O read rates in the out-of-core MADBENCH solver code. In this case, monitoring I/O does not fully explain the cause of performance loss but does point to the source of performance loss in the application (the read step) and also improves confidence in understanding the impact of steps to improve it.

There is a great deal to be learned from the statistical properties of I/O transaction times. Viewing the file system as a black box, one can develop strategies around concurrency and I/O middleware solely on the basis of the shifts in performance. A detailed mechanistic understanding of the file system is also a useful approach to engineering better I/O performance, but we

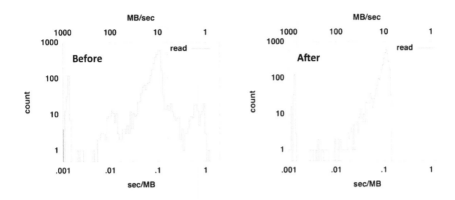

FIGURE 26.6: Histograms of MADBENCH parallel reads (same transaction size in all cases) before and after tuning the parallel file system. Slow reads (long timings) have been mitigated.

leave HPC system monitoring questions largely aside here. By profiling the application's POSIX layer alone, a great deal of file system health data can be gathered.

26.2.3 Buffer Size

The choice of transaction (buffer) size for I/O in many codes is a complicated function of concurrency, input/problem specifics, and file syetem tunables. In general, larger I/Os will show better performance but collective I/O (MPI-IO collectives), I/O middleware (such as netCDF and HDF5), and other application specifics can obscure the actual transaction sizes behind higher-level I/O operations. Obtaining a transaction size profile from IPM is straightforward and in many cases reveals the general overall I/O picture. A standard performance engineering practice is to aggregate I/O where possible to increase the granularity of the larger block sizes that HPC file systems are often tuned for.

IPM produces an inventory of buffer sizes during execution for I/O calls along with their *minimum, maximum,* and *average* times to completion, along with the number of transactions. These buffer sizes may easily be compared to the file system block size to determine if the I/O is latency-limited or making full use of the file system bandwidth.

While we state the importance of buffer size in modern HPC workloads, this is difficult in the context of single application runs. For this reason we suggest that the IPM approach be applied in the broader context of HPC workloads.

26.2.4   HPC Workload Studies

The previous examples look at individual performance issues. But in the broader context, an HPC workload that runs on a shared computing resource requires analysis of many such profiles [11]. This allows one to closely connect I/O performance to the sustained performance at the HPC system level. When all applications in a workload are profiled, a convenient first step is to segment the workload into distinct applications or similar applications by the I/O and messaging functions invoked by each code. Figure 26.7 shows 1053 jobs run on the Magellan cluster at NERSC. Of course, not all codes invoke all functions, and the invoked calls provide a reasonable first step toward classification of applications.

Jobs showing identical or similar function-level profiles can then be examined side by side to identify patterns in I/O performance bottlenecks. There is value in mentioning that a production-integrated approach is one part of transitioning the HPC performance tools community away from well-controlled singleton performance experiments in favor of a streaming data analytics viewpoint that seeks the same goal of making I/O fast. Clustering and classification of *in-vivo* I/O measurements is a different paradigmatic perspective than that of performance/cost models built on independent parallel flows. There are many ways for applications as actually run by scientists to

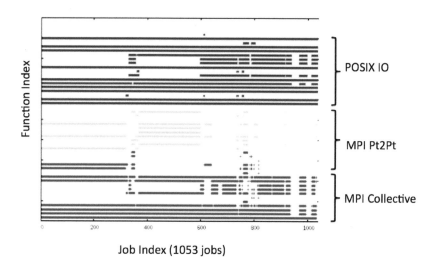

Job Index (1053 jobs)

FIGURE 26.7: Large numbers of jobs in a workload may be difficult to identify by name or other job metadata. The 1053 jobs profiled above can be examined from a workload perspective by examining the calls each job invokes. In the figure above, functions are given an ordinal index that groups calls by MPI, MPI Collective, and POSIX I/O.

diverge from their sketches as benchmarks. That this is observed in the few systemwide profiling studies conducted on production HPC is an indication that the performance tools community may do well to shift its perspective to one of sustained performance in a production setting.

In order to target workload-level improvements in I/O, it is useful to prioritize the opportunities for analysis by their contribution to the overall core hours expended by the workload. One such prioritization is given in Figure 26.7 where a treemap organized by core hours vs. user and concurrency clarifies that some profiles are worth more attention than others. Both function-level profiles and user-concurrency pairs do not conclusively segment the workload by distinct applications. In practice on production machines, such as those at NERSC, one can often find clear I/O performance patterns using such filters. Performance profile classes that are sufficiently similar and persist across many jobs point to I/O strategies that need to be improved at the application level or in user environment settings. Figure 26.4 shows such a single code run on 128 tasks by a single user. The I/O strategy shows persistent load imbalance between MPI ranks with some tasks transacting substantially more I/O than others. In other IPM case studies, several many-to-few and many-to-one I/O strategies were identified with less than optimal I/O rates.

26.3 Conclusion

Profiling I/O through the interception of POSIX-I/O calls provides a scalable and generalizable path to understanding application I/O performance. Examples of using IPM for this purpose demonstrate some commonly encountered aspects of I/O worth consideration to improve performance. This technique is shared by other tools like TAU (see Chapter 25), Darshan (see Chapter 27), among others; and the performance analysis is generalizable to other tools that provide trace or profiles of POSIX calls. Root causing I/O performance with a single tool can be complex. Some approaches involving [10, 8] simultaneous profiling of application and file system have been explored to allow more conclusive determination of I/O in relation to file system capabilities. For I/O bottlenecks that have their origin within an application or that arise from persistent contention for I/O can often be addressed without a specific root cause. Profiling POSIX-I/O calls can, as demonstrated in the above examples, provide sufficient visibility into I/O performance to improve performance. By addressing sources of load imbalance and scalable I/O, better strategies can be implemented for applications and workloads. IPM focuses on achieving such I/O performance gains in the context of production HPC applications and workloads, because computers should be fast for a reason.

Bibliography

[1] Julian Borrill, Jonathan Carter, Leonid Oliker, David Skinner, and Rupak Biswas. Integrated Performance Monitoring of a Cosmology Application on Leading HEC Platforms. In *Parallel Processing, 2005. ICPP 2005. International Conference on*, pages 119–128. IEEE, 2005.

[2] Karl Fürlinger, Nicholas J. Wright, and David Skinner. Performance Analysis and Workload Characterization with IPM. In *Tools for High Performance Computing 2009*, pages 31–38. Springer, 2010.

[3] Ioan Raicu, Ian T. Foster, and Pete Beckman. Making a Case for Distributed File Systems at Exascale. In *Proceedings of the third international workshop on Large-scale system and application performance*, pages 11–18. ACM, 2011.

[4] Lavanya Ramakrishnan, Piotr T. Zbiegel, Scott Campbell, Rick Bradshaw, Richard Shane Canon, Susan Coghlan, Iwona Sakrejda, Narayan Desai, Tina Declerck, and Anping Liu. Magellan: Experiences from a Science Cloud. In *Proceedings of the 2nd International Workshop on Scientific Cloud Computing*, pages 49–58. ACM, 2011.

[5] Hongzhang Shan, Haoqiang Jin, Karl Fuerlinger, Alice Koniges, and Nicholas J. Wright. Analyzing the Effect of Different Programming Models upon Performance and Memory Usage on Cray XT5 Platforms. In *Cray User's Group Meeting 2010*, Edinburgh, May 2010.

[6] David Skinner and William Kramer. Understanding the Causes of Performance Variability in HPC Workloads. In *Workload Characterization Symposium, 2005. Proceedings of the IEEE International*, pages 137–149. IEEE, 2005.

[7] Dan Terpstra, Heike Jagode, Haihang You, and Jack Dongarra. Collecting Performance Data with PAPI-C. In *Tools for High Performance Computing 2009*, pages 157–173. Springer, 2010.

[8] Andrew Uselton, Katie Antypas, Daniela Ushizima, and Jeffrey Sukharev. File System Monitoring as a Window into User I/O Requirements. In *Proceedings of the 2010 Cray User Group Meeting, Edinburgh, Scotland*, 2010.

[9] Andrew Uselton, Mark Howison, Nicholas J. Wright, David Skinner, Noel Keen, John Shalf, Karen L. Karavanic, and Leonid Oliker. Parallel I/O Performance: From Events to Ensembles. In *Parallel & Distributed Processing (IPDPS), 2010 IEEE International Symposium on*, pages 1–11. IEEE, 2010.

[10] H. Wartens and Jim Garlick. LMT-The Lustre Monitoring Tool.

[11] Vincent M. Weaver, Dan Terpstra, Heike McCraw, Matt Johnson, Kiran Kasichayanula, James Ralph, John Nelson, Phil Mucci, Tushar Mohan, and Shirley Moore. PAPI 5: Measuring Power, Energy, and the Cloud. In *Performance Analysis of Systems and Software (ISPASS), 2013 IEEE International Symposium on*, pages 124–125. IEEE, 2013.

Chapter 27

Darshan

Philip Carns

Argonne National Laboratory

27.1 Features 309
27.2 Success Stories 311
27.3 Conclusion 313
      Bibliography 314

Darshan is an application-level I/O characterization tool that captures production-level I/O behavior with minimal overhead. Darshan does not record a complete trace of all I/O system calls. It instead gathers compact access pattern statistics for each file opened by the application. These statistics are reduced, compressed, and aggregated into a single log file that summarizes the I/O activity and access patterns of the application as a whole. Although this summary data does not offer the same fidelity as a traditional tracing or profiling tool, it can be collected with negligible overhead and no source code modification. This combination of features makes it possible not only to instrument full-scale application runs, but also to transparently deploy Darshan for the automatic characterization of all production jobs on a leadership-class HPC system. Darshan characterization data can be used for a variety of purposes ranging from performance tuning of specific applications [6, 7, 8] to analysis of trends in system-wide I/O behavior [1, 2].

Although Darshan is designed for system-wide deployment, it can also be installed and used by individual end users as well. The runtime component of Darshan consists of a set of user-space libraries and compiler wrappers to simplify development environment integration. The command line utility component of Darshan includes tools to interpret application logs and produce graphical summaries for high-level analysis.

27.1 Features

The initial motivation for the Darshan project was to gain a better understanding of production I/O behavior by performing system-wide workload studies. Previous system-wide workload studies [9] were very influential in HPC I/O research but no longer reflected the scale, architecture, and scientific application diversity of present-day systems. Collecting data on large-scale present-day systems required the development of efficient, non-intrusive instrumentation methods. This led directly to the following core design goals for Darshan: transparent integration with the user environment and negligible impact on application performance, and reliability.

Darshan operates in the user-space as an interposition library in order to collect per-application statistics without source code modifications. As with many other HPC profiling tools, Darshan leverages the MPI profiling interface in conjunction with either link-time wrappers for statically linked executables or preloaded libraries for dynamically linked executables. Static instrumentation can be enabled system-wide using MPI compiler script functionality, while dynamic instrumentation can be enabled system-wide using environment variables. End users do not need to change their work flow in either case.

The Darshan function call wrappers intercept POSIX and MPI-IO functions, as well as a few key HDF5 and PNetCDF functions. The wrappers are used to gather information, such as operation counters (such as `open`, `read`, `write`, `stat`, and `mmap`); datatypes and hint usage; access patterns in terms of alignment; sequentiality; access size; and timing information including cumulative I/O time and intervals of I/O activity. (A full description of counters can be found in the Darshan documentation [5].) Darshan does not issue any communication or storage operations to manage characterization data while the application is running. Each process is instrumented independently using a bounded amount of memory. When the application shuts down, the results are then aggregated, compressed, and stored persistently. Darshan uses a combination of MPI reduction operations, collective I/O, and parallel Zlib compression to reduce overhead and minimize log file size.

The command line utility component of Darshan includes tools to parse and analyze log files produced by the runtime library. Figure 27.1 shows an example of output produced by `darshan-job-summary`, a utility that summarizes the I/O behavior of a job. This example was chosen from production logs captured on the Mira IBM Blue Gene/Q system operated by the Argonne Leadership Computing Facility (ALCF). The "I/O Operation Counts" graph in the upper right corner indicates that the MPI-IO collective buffering optimization [10] was enabled; there is a large discrepancy between the number of MPI-IO collective write calls and the number of POSIX write calls. The "Most Common Access Sizes" table confirms that the majority of the POSIX write operations were 16 MB in size, which corresponds to the collective buffer size used by MPI-IO. The bottom graph indicates that the application was divided into subsets of processes that wrote data in different time intervals.

The Darshan command line utilities also include tools to anonymize identifying information, such as file names and executable names, within log files. This capability makes it possible to release Darshan characterization data to

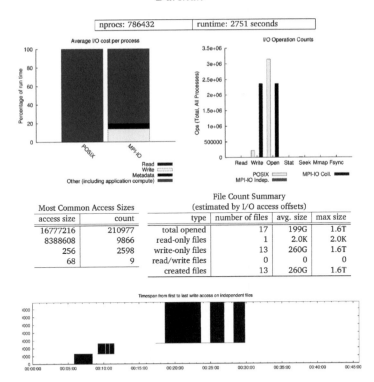

FIGURE 27.1: Screenshot showing excerpts from the `darshan-job-summary` utility included with Darshan. This example summarizes the I/O behavior of a 786,432-process turbulence simulation that wrote over 3 TB of data.

the community. The ALCF I/O Data Repository [3] is a notable example. It provides public access to nearly 200,000 log files collected on the Intrepid Blue Gene/P system at the ALCF.

27.2 Success Stories

Darshan can fundamentally change the approach to I/O performance engineering on systems where it is deployed. When an I/O performance problem is observed, scientists and I/O experts can immediately refer to the Darshan report for initial diagnosis. This often eliminates the need for additional profiling runs (costly in CPU time) or manual source code inspection (costly in manpower).

Historic collections of Darshan characterization data can also be used to study trends in system usage as well, as illustrated in this section with example

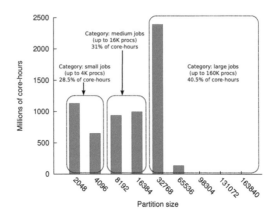

FIGURE 27.2: Histogram of the number of core hours consumed by Darshan-instrumented jobs in each partition size on Intrepid. The histogram bins are further categorized into small, medium, and large sizes for subsequent analysis.

data collected on the ALCF Intrepid Blue Gene/P system. Intrepid is a 557-teraflop system containing 163,840 compute cores, 80 TB of RAM, and 7.6 PB of storage. More information about Intrepid and its I/O subsystem can be found in Chapter 4. Darshan has been used to automatically instrument MPI applications on Intrepid since January 2010. In this case study, five months of Darshan log files are analyzed from January 1, 2013 to May 30, 2013. Darshan instrumented 13,613 production jobs from 117 unique users over this time period.

The jobs instrumented by Darshan in the first five months of 2013 ranged in size from 1 process to 163,840 processes, offering an opportunity to observe how I/O behavior varies across application scales. Figure 27.2 shows a histogram of the number of core hours consumed by Darshan-instrumented jobs in each of the 9 available partition sizes on Intrepid. The most popular partition size in terms of core-hour consumption contains 32,768 cores. The jobs can be split into three comparably sized, broader categories for further analysis; however, 28.5% of all core hours were in partitions of size 4,096 cores or smaller, 31% of all core hours were in partitions of size 8,192 or 16,384, and 40.5% of all core hours were in partitions of size 32,768 or larger.

Figure 27.3 shows the total amount of data read and written by jobs in each partition size category. All three categories are dominated by write activity with one notable exception: the small job size category is dominated by a single climate application labeled as "Climate user A." This application accounted for a total of 776.5 TB of read activity and 31.1 TB of write over the course of the study by reading as much as 4.8 TB of netCDF data in each job instance. The other notable trend evident in Figure 27.3 is that smaller jobs accounted for a larger fraction of the I/O usage on the system than larger jobs.

Figure 27.4 illustrates the prevalence of two key I/O characteristics across job size categories. The first is file-per-process file usage. A job was defined

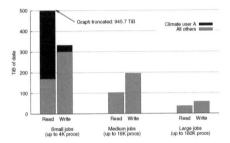

FIGURE 27.3: Total amount of data read and written by Darshan-instrumented jobs in each partition size category on Intrepid.

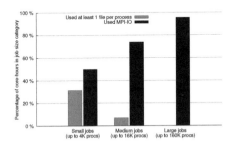

FIGURE 27.4: Prevalence of key I/O characteristics in each partition size category on Intrepid.

as having a file-per-process access pattern if it opened at least N files during execution, where N is the number of MPI processes. Such jobs account for 31% of all core hours in the small job size category, but they do not appear at all in the large job size category. Another job was defined as using MPI-IO if it opened at least one file using MPI_File_open(). In contrast to the file-per-process usage pattern, MPI-IO usage increases with job scale, going from 50% for small jobs up to 96% for large jobs. The decline in file-per-process access patterns and the increase in MPI-IO usage suggest that large-scale applications are using more advanced I/O strategies in order to scale effectively and simplify data management.

27.3   Conclusion

The Darshan I/O characterization tool has demonstrated that it is possible to instrument leadership-class production applications with negligible overhead. Since its initial development in 2009 [4], it has been in production on multiple large-scale HPC systems, including the IBM Blue Gene/P systems, IBM Blue Gene/Q systems, and Cray XE6 systems. Darshan enables both targeted investigation of key applications, as well as broad system studies. Key challenges for the future are to further expand the scope of such instrumentation without compromising efficiency and to develop more sophisticated tools to leverage data produced by Darshan.

Bibliography

[1] P. Carns, K. Harms, W. Allcock, C. Bacon, S. Lang, R. Latham, and R. Ross. Understanding and Improving Computational Science Storage Access through Continuous Characterization. *ACM Transactions on Storage (TOS)*, 7(3):8, 2011.

[2] P. Carns, Y. Yao, K. Harms, R. Latham, R. Ross, and K. Antypas. Production I/O Characterization on the Cray XE6. In *Proceedings of the Cray User Group Meeting 2013 (CUG 2013)*, 2013.

[3] Philip Carns. ALCF I/O Data Repository. Technical report, Argonne National Laboratory (ANL), 2013.

[4] Philip Carns, Robert Latham, Robert Ross, Kamil Iskra, Samuel Lang, and Katherine Riley. 24/7 Characterization of Petascale I/O Workloads. In *Proceedings of 2009 Workshop on Interfaces and Architectures for Scientific Data Storage*, September 2009.

[5] Darshan Documentation. http://www.mcs.anl.gov/research/projects/darshan/documentation/, 2013.

[6] Jing Fu, Misun Min, R. Latham, and C.D. Carothers. Parallel I/O Performance for Application-Level Checkpointing on the Blue Gene/P System. In *The Workshop on Interfaces and Abstractions for Scientific Data Storage (IASDS) in Conjunction with the 2011 IEEE International Conference on Cluster Computing*, pages 465–473, 2011.

[7] Rob Latham, Chris Daley, Wei-keng Liao, Kui Gao, Rob Ross, Anshu Dubey, and Alok Choudhary. A Case Study for Scientific I/O: Improving the FLASH Astrophysics Code. *Computational Science & Discovery*, 5(1):015001, 2012.

[8] Ning Liu, Jing Fu, Christopher D. Carothers, Onkar Sahni, Kenneth E. Jansen, and Mark S. Shephard. Massively Parallel I/O for Partitioned Solver Systems. *Parallel Processing Letters*, 20(04):377–395, 2010.

[9] Nils Nieuwejaar, David Kotz, Apratim Purakayastha, Carla Schlatter Ellis, and Michael Best. File-Access Characteristics of Parallel Scientific Workloads. *IEEE Transactions on Parallel and Distributed Systems*, 7(10):1075–1089, October 1996.

[10] Rajeev Thakur, William Gropp, and Ewing Lusk. Data Sieving and Collective I/O in ROMIO. In *The Seventh Symposium on the Frontiers of Massively Parallel Computation*, pages 182–189. IEEE, 1999.

Chapter 28

Iota

Mark Howison

Brown University and Lawrence Berkeley National Laboratory

Prabhat and Surendra Byna

Lawrence Berkeley National Laboratory

28.1 Features 317
28.2 Success Stories 318
28.3 Conclusion 320
      Bibliography 321

28.1 Features

Iota is a lightweight tracing tool for diagnosing poorly performing I/O operations to parallel file systems, especially Lustre. It collects complete traces of POSIX I/O calls with minimal overhead, and has been tested to scale to 110,052 MPI tasks and 1.5 TB of data. Iota is freely available under a non-commercial license from:

https://bitbucket.org/mhowison/iota

As the storage systems and the parallel file systems that service super-computers become more complex, it is increasingly important to have finely tuned tracing tools for investigating poor I/O performance. The POSIX I/O layer is often informative because it is the interface between user-space code (either the application itself or a middle-ware library like MPI-IO or HDF5) and a kernel-space parallel file system.

Iota has similar aims to Darshan (Chapter 27, [3]), but adds two missing features: recording of complete traces, rather than aggregates, which allows for more flexibility in post-processed analyses; and integration with the Lustre API to capture stripe parameters and OST assignment of files opened on Lustre file systems.

Like Darshan, Iota traces are buffered in memory to avoid many small writes to the trace file (in ASCII for human readability). Darshan limits the buffer's footprint by storing only aggregate values instead of a complete traces of all I/O activity.

Iota offers two alternative methods for limiting the footprint during tracing, while still collecting complete traces:

- *subsetting*, which restricts tracing to a subset of files specified by a wildcard pattern in an environment variable;

- *flushing*, which flushes the trace buffer to file at 1 MB intervals, but requires writing one such file per MPI task. On Lustre file systems, the trace file is opened with stripe count 1 and stripe size 1 MB. Flushing has the added benefit that some tracing information may be available even if the program aborts in the middle of a run.

Unlike Darshan, Iota is not intended for use as an automated, center-wide collection tool (c.f. Carns et al. [2]). Runs with pathological I/O could create significant buffering overhead and cause the run to fail; for instance, an I/O pattern with one billion 1 KB writes from a single MPI task would create about 32 GB of buffered string data for that task. However, even this pathological case could be handled by Iota if the *flushing* mechanism is used. Thus, Iota is best used for targeted profiling tasks with careful selection of tracing parameters (for examples of targeted I/O profiling, see Uselton et al. [5]).

Iota supports both runtime and linktime interposition of POSIX I/O functions in the GNU C library. For runtime interposition of dynamically linked executables, Iota redefines each function and calls the `dylib` function with `RTLD_NEXT` to locate the next (e.g., system) symbol for that function name. For linktime interposition of dynamically or statically linked executables, Iota uses the GNU linker's `--wrap` feature and defines a `__wrap_*` variant for each function.

Iota supports both MPI and non-MPI executables. In MPI mode, initialization and finalization are accomplished by redefining the `MPI_Init` and `MPI_Finalize` functions and calling into the standard MPI profiling interface (`PMPI_Init` and `PMPI_Finalize`). In non-MPI mode, the GNU linker's `constructor` and `destructor` function attributes provide similar hooks. In both modes, Iota measures the elapsed time of POSIX I/O calls with the high-precision `gettimeofday` timer.

28.2   Success Stories

We have tested Iota at scale with stand-alone I/O kernels from three scientific applications: a climate simulation, the Global Cloud Resolving Model (GCRM), and a plasma simulation, VORPAL, both described previously by Howison et al. [4]; and a second plasma simulation, VPIC, described by Byna et al. [1]. File sizes ranged from 15 GB to 1.5 TB.

All results were collected on NERSC's Cray XE6 system, Hopper, which has 6,384 twenty-four-core nodes with 32 GB of memory each. It features a Gemini interconnect with a 3D torus topology, and a Lustre parallel file system with 156 Object Storage Targets (OSTs) and an advertised peak bandwidth of 35 GB/s. The OSTs are backed by 26 Object Storage Servers (OSSs), which share 13 LSI 7900 disk controllers. Lustre router nodes in the Gemini interconnect forward I/O requests from the Hopper compute nodes to the OSSs through a separate QDR InfiniBand interconnect.

Iota's overhead, as a percentage of overall runtime, remained low even as the runs scaled up to 110,052 MPI tasks (see Figure 28.1). We expect that tracing of real applications should incur even less overhead, since our test applications are all I/O benchmarks that do nothing but issue I/O calls.

We ran Iota in *gather* mode (instead of *flushing* mode) to validate the feasibility of gathering the entire trace to the root task for output to a single file. The results showed that gathering the trace accounted for very little of the overhead (see Figure 28.1). After further investigation, we found considerable variation in the overhead for calls into the Lustre API to obtain striping information. This is likely due to the design of the Lustre file system, with its centralized metadata server.

In all cases, no MPI tasks used more than the initial 2 MB allocated to buffer the string data for the trace entries. In MPI_Finalize, the root task allocated a buffer as large as the final trace output, which ranged from 1.8 MB to 139 MB across the test runs. In practice, we expect that the application has freed its allocated memory before finalizing, so that additional memory is available for Iota at this point.

Figures 28.2 and 28.3 show examples of the plots we can generate when complete traces are available for post-processing.

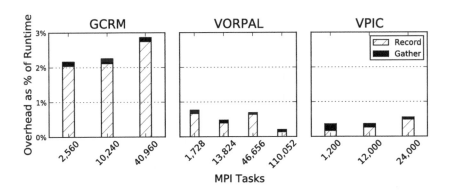

FIGURE 28.1: Overhead of the Iota library, tested with three I/O benchmarks.

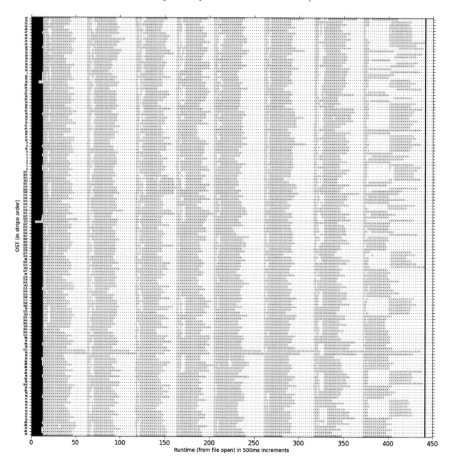

FIGURE 28.2: Horizontal bar charts for each OST show the spatial-temporal pattern of writes in the 12,000 core VPIC run. Writes appear clustered by the 8 distinct timesteps in the output file.

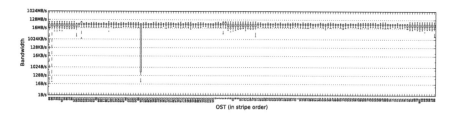

FIGURE 28.3: Box and whisper plots show the distribution of write bandwidths to each OST in the 1,728 core VORPAL run. OST 126 had an abnormal number of low-bandwidth writes in the B/s and KB/s range.

28.3 Conclusion

Our application of Iota to I/O kernels demonstrate that complete tracing of POSIX I/O calls is possible for petascale MPI applications. In addition, by querying Lustre metadata during tracing, we can reconstruct the mapping of I/O operations to individual OSTs when post-processing the traces.

Bibliography

[1] Surendra Byna, Jerry Chou, Oliver Rübel, Prabhat, Homa Karimabadi, William S. Daughton, Vadim Roytershteyn, E. Wes Bethel, Mark Howison, Ke-Jou Hsu, Kuan-Wu Lin, Arie Shoshani, Andrew Uselton, and Kesheng Wu. Parallel I/O, Analysis, and Visualization of a Trillion-Particle Simulation. In *International Conference for High Performance Computing, Networking, Storage and Analysis (SC12)*, Salt Lake City, UT, USA, November 2012.

[2] Philip Carns, Kevin Harms, William Allcock, Charles Bacon, Samuel Lang, Robert Latham, and Robert Ross. Understanding and Improving Computational Science Storage Access through Continuous Characterization. *ACM Transactions on Storage*, 7(3), October 2011.

[3] Philip Carns, Robert Latham, Robert Ross, Kamil Iskra, Samuel Lang, and Katherine Riley. 24/7 Characterization of Petascale I/O Workloads. In *Workshop on Interfaces and Abstractions for Scientific Data Storage (IASDS '09)*, New Orleans, LA, USA, September 2009.

[4] Mark Howison, Quincey Koziol, David Knaak, John Mainzer, and John Shalf. Tuning HDF5 for Lustre File Systems. In *Workshop on Interfaces and Abstractions for Scientific Data Storage (IASDS '10)*, Heraklion, Crete, Greece, September 2010.

[5] Andrew Uselton, Mark Howison, N.J. Wright, David Skinner, Noel Keen, John Shalf, K.L. Karavanic, and Leonid Oliker. Parallel I/O Performance: From Events to Ensembles. In *IEEE International Symposium on Parallel & Distributed Processing (IPDPS '10)*, Atlanta, GA, USA, April 2010.

Part VI

Future Trends

Chapter 29

Parallel Computing Trends for the Coming Decade

John Shalf

Lawrence Berkeley National Laboratory

29.1   Technology Scaling 326
     29.1.1   Classical Scaling Period (1965–2004) 326
     29.1.2   End of Classical Scaling (2004) 326
     29.1.3   Toward Data-Centric Computing (2014–2022) 328
29.2   Implications for the Future of Storage Systems 329
29.3   Conclusion 331
     Bibliography 331

The broader technology industry has come to depend on the rapid, predictable, and cheap scaling of computing performance and storage density. For decades, exponentially increasing capability could be procured at roughly constant annual cost, and that expectation has permeated computing resource planning and decision making. For the past twenty years, we have become accustomed to a very steady technological progression where improvements in silicon lithography (Moore's Law) have translated directly into improved computing and storage speed, density, and energy efficiency. All of our assumptions about how to program these systems implicitly assume the progression will continue unabated. In 2004, however, a confluence of events changed forever the architectural landscape that underpinned our current assumptions about what to optimize for when we design new algorithms and applications. Storage technologies must be refactored to handle massive parallelism, the severe constraints on the energy cost of data movement, and reduced reliability. Furthermore, this confluence of factors presents a more fundamental challenge to the traditional POSIX semantics that underpinned parallel file system design for the past few decades.

29.1 Technology Scaling

29.1.1 Classical Scaling Period (1965–2004)

In 1965, Gordon Moore famously observed that the number of components on an integrated circuit had been doubling every year since the introduction of this technology in 1959.[1] Shrinking the dimensions on an integrated structure also made it possible to operate the structure at higher speed for the same power per unit area, so that computing functionality would improve exponentially with time at roughly constant cost per generation. This latter observation is commonly referred to as *Dennard Scaling* because it was formalized and extended in Robert H. Dennard of IBM.[2] From 1965 to approximately 2004, Dennard Scaling enabled exponential increases in the serial computing performance over a period of three decades. This offered a compelling benefit in that software could remain relatively stable and still execute substantially faster with every new technology generation. As a result, most of the commercial software infrastructure is designed for serial computation. Throughout this period, parallel computing remained a fringe activity, conducted in the national laboratories, universities, and a few leading companies.

These scaling trends are primarily associated with computing technology, but also directly relate to improvements in storage technology as we move forward. Disk storage densities are primarily limited by the superparamagnetic limit, but with vertical recording methods, the size of the magnetic recording head for a disk unit is closely related to Moore's law improvements in fabricating these devices at smaller scale. As the industry moves away from magnetic disk technologies, FLASH and other solid-state storage technologies also depend upon the same lithographic advances used to improve logic density so that they can improve storage density. The improvements in lithographic density underpin storage density and cost improvements for the past two decades.

29.1.2 End of Classical Scaling (2004)

Although Moore's Law has continued to enable us to increase logic and storage densities at historical rates (as shown in Figure 29.1), by 2004 it was no longer feasible to scale voltage down with lithographic feature size due to physical limits relating to the underlying materials' characteristics. As a

---

[1]This is the source of what is commonly referred to as *Moore's Law*, which first appeared in Gordon E. Moore, "Cramming More Components onto Integrated Circuits," *Electronics* 38 (8): 114–117, April 19, 1965.

[2]This observation is commonly referred to as Dennard Scaling because it was formalized and extended in Robert H. Dennard et al. "Design of Ion-Implanted MOSFET's with Very Small Physical Dimensions," *IEEE Journal of Solid-State Circuits* SC-9 (5): 256–268, October 1974.

35 YEARS OF MICROPROCESSOR TREND DATA

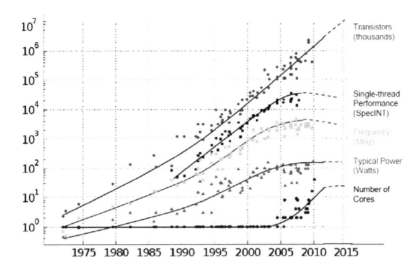

Original data collected and plotted by M. Horowitz, F. Labonte, O. Shacham, K. Olukotun, L. Hammond and C. Batten
Dotted line extrapolations by C. Moore

FIGURE 29.1: The effect of the end of Dennard Scaling on microprocessor performance, power consumption, and architecture.

result, the favorable power scaling Moore and Dennard observed has been lost, clock rates have consequently plateaued, and single-processor computational performance has therefore stagnated (also shown in Figure 29.1). With the end of voltage scaling, power has become the dominant constraint for future computing. The challenges posed by improving performance pervade all design choices in building future processor and storage technology from 2004 forward, which will be explored in more detail in Chapter 33.

Since single-processing core performance no longer improved with each generation, performance could be improved, theoretically, by packing more cores into each processor. This multicore approach continues to drive up the theoretical peak performance of the processing chips, and we are on track to have chips with thousands of cores by 2020 [1]. This increase in parallelism via core count is clearly visible in the black trend line in Figure 29.2. This is an important development in that programmers outside the small cadre of those with experience in parallel computing must now contend with the challenge of making their codes run effectively in parallel. Parallelism has become everyone's problem and this will require deep rethinking of the commercial software and algorithm infrastructure. The changes portend a move toward unprecedented levels of parallelism that fundamentally challenge POSIX data

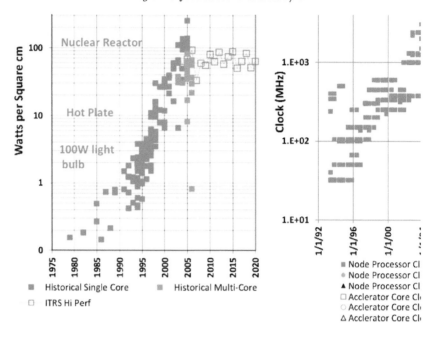

FIGURE 29.2: The Power and Clock Inflection point in 2004. Unable to continue reductions in supply voltages, we saw a nearly exponential rise in chip thermal density—approaching that of a nuclear reactor by 2004. To avoid melting the chip, the industry was forced to abandon historical increases in clock frequency. By 2008, the trends in clock frequency growth across the industry had leveled off when chips reached their thermal density limits, which leads to exponential rise in parallelism to continue historical performance improvements.

consistency semantics and current approaches to maintaining reliability of storage systems. The challenges to I/O system design that are posed by this exponential rise in parallelism will be treated in more detail in Chapter 31.

29.1.3   Toward Data-Centric Computing (2014–2022)

Since the loss of Dennard Scaling, a new technology-scaling regime has emerged. Due to the laws of electrical resistance and capacitance, the intrinsic energy efficiency for a fixed-length wire does not improve appreciably as it shrinks down with Moore's law improvements in lithography, as shown in Figure 29.1. In contrast, the power consumption of transistors continues to decrease as their gate size (and hence capacitance) decreases. Since the energy efficiency of transistors is improving as their sizes shrink, and the energy efficiency of wires is not improving, the point is rapidly approaching where

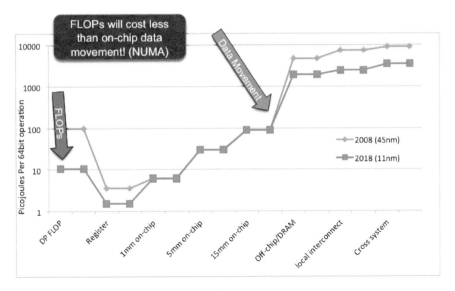

FIGURE 29.3: The energy consumed by data movement is starting to exceed the energy consumed by computation.

the energy needed to move the data exceeds the energy used in performing the operation on those data.[3] (See Figure 29.3.)

By 2018, further improvements to compute efficiency will be hidden by the energy required to move data to the computational cores on a chip. The current computing infrastructure is built on the premise that computing is the most expensive component. In the current era, computing is cheap and ubiquitous, whereas data movement dominates energy costs. This overturns basic assumptions about programming and portends a move from a *computation-centric* paradigm to a *data-centric* paradigm for programming future systems [2]. The severe constraints in data movement are also driving the industry toward alternative technologies for data communication such as optics and silicon nanophotonics that integrate optical technologies directly onto silicon chips.

29.2   Implications for the Future of Storage Systems

Data-Centric Computing and Non-POSIX I/O: Whereas current models focus on equal partitioning of computation and moving the data to

[3]This observation is explained in more detail in D. A. B. Miller and H. M. Özaktas, "Limit to the Bit-Rate Capacity of Electrical Interconnects from the Aspect Ratio of the System Architecture," *Journal of Parallel and Distributed Computing* 41, 4252 (1997).

the processing elements, data-centric models provide facilities to describe how the data is laid out on the system and apply the computation to the data where it resides (*in situ*). There are numerous software-based approaches being pursued that enable data to be operated upon where it was produced, or while in transit. Even more aggressive technological approaches try to embed computing capability into the storage devices. This includes everything from embedding intelligence directly into disk systems such as the Netezza, to the re-emergence of processor-in-memory and processor-near-memory technologies. Chapter 30 explores the fact that all of these innovative solutions are fundamentally orthogonal to the standard POSIX view of I/O consistency, and open the door to new object-storage approaches that obey a more transactional or "functional language" semantics to preserve consistency and correctness.

Data Movement: The data movement challenges may also accelerate development of nanoscale optical/photonic solutions. Although much of our data transmission within a datacenter still uses wires, the intrinsic resistance of the material used by "wires" (electrical connections of some form) limits any solution involving electrons. The principal problem is that the energy consumed to transmit a bit is proportional to the distance it must travel (due to the resistance of the metal used to conduct the electricity). Copper is as good a conductor as can be expected for a common material at room temperature. For communications (wire replacement), photonics has the benefit of having energy costs that are nearly independent of the distance that data travels, whereas the standard electrical wires have a strong distance-dependent energy cost. Therefore, photonic technology has enormous potential to overcome the fundamental limitation of wire resistance, if they can overcome the challenge of improving the efficiency of laser light sources.

Photonics offers huge bandwidth density improvements. Whereas an electrical communication channel can only carry one signal, multiple wavelengths of light can share the same optical conduit without interference using Wave Division Multiplexing (WDM). Photonics will play an essential role in overcoming limits of wires and break through the boundary of on-chip and off-chip communications costs, and cost/distance relationships [3]. The implications for dense wave division multiplexing (DWDM) using photonic device technology for interconnects is explored in more detail in Chapter 32.

Resilience: Lastly, nanoscale components with aggressive scaling in voltages, currents, photons, etc. can raise energy efficiency, but the probability of failures, and more critically soft errors, will also rise. Creating systems that are inherently resilient to both hard and soft failures is perhaps the most daunting challenge for exascale computing. Worse yet, we depend on our storage systems as the "safe location" to recover application state for the most commonly used application resilience methods, so the requirements for the resilience of storage systems are far higher than that of the compute devices to which they are connected.

Much current computer architecture research is focused on dealing with soft errors in the datapath (logic soft errors) as well as the traditional challenges faced in memories. Many emerging nanoscale memory devices rely on different physical mechanisms than charge storage and may provide interesting opportunities to "harden" critical parts of a datapath or memory to upset events. Furthermore, they are non-volatile and can enable processors to become tolerant of sudden power supply interruptions. This can be exploited to reduce the power-down and power-up transients of processors, allowing them to be idled with their supplies turned off at short intervals. The challenges to reliability for future device technologies are discussed in detail in Chapter 31.

29.3 Conclusion

The changes to underlying technology characteristics result in fundamental re-evaluation of computer architecture where decisions have been largely based on previous component technology limitations. The new technology offers new features that would fundamentally change long-standing architectural choices that are deeply ingrained in the current computer industry. Foundational computer architecture decisions are based on physical constraints of the underlying components used to implement the architecture. Our challenge is to reconceptualize computer architecture and storage models for technology that will need to be developed for the next 10+ years.

Bibliography

[1] John Morrison John Shalf, Sudip S. Dosanjh. Exascale Computing Technology Challenges. In *VECPAR*, pages 1–25, 2010.

[2] P. Kogge and J. Shalf. Exascale Computing Trends: Adjusting to the "New Normal" for Computer Architecture. In *Computing in Science and Engineering 15*.

[3] D. A. B. Miller. Device Requirements for Optical Interconnects to Silicon Chips. In *Proceedings of the IEEE 97*, pages 1166–1185, 2009.

Chapter 30

Storage Models: Past, Present, and Future

Dries Kimpe and Robert Ross

Argonne National Laboratory

30.1 The POSIX Era 334
30.2 The Current HPC Storage Model 335
    30.2.1 The POSIX HPC I/O Extensions 335
    30.2.2 MPI-IO 337
    30.2.3 Object Storage Model 337
30.3 Post POSIX 338
    30.3.1 Prior Work 338
    30.3.2 Object Abstractions in HPC 339
    30.3.3 Namespaces 341
30.4 Conclusion 341
    Bibliography 342

The storage component of HPC systems, like most components in these systems, is built of parts borrowed from other communities and markets. Early in the development of HPC systems it was recognized that a globally accessible storage system was desirable, and the HPC community converged on the use of the Portable Operating System Interface for UNIX (POSIX) I/O model as its *de facto* standard: a globally accessible directory tree holding files that each contain a stream of bytes of user data, with a strong consistency model enforcing immediate (global) visibility of updates.

As systems have grown in scale, supporting this model has become increasingly problematic, both in terms of performance and in terms of reliability. In this chapter we will discuss the POSIX model, how the HPC community has worked to adapt the POSIX model over time to meet its needs, and alternative models that are emerging from current research.

30.1 The POSIX Era

The POSIX I/O standard was developed by the IEEE and is currently defined as part of "IEEE Std 1003.1-1988" [13] (often referred to as "POSIX.1-1998." There have been numerous updates and corrections since; the latest version (at the time of this publication) was IEEE Std 1003.1-2013 [1]. The first version of the POSIX standard was developed when a single computer operating system managed its own (local) file system, and issues of concurrent access were limited to the processes running on that operating system. Since all file accesses went through a single operating system on a single machine, enforcing strict consistency semantics was relatively easy. Likewise, data (and metadata such as current file size or last access time) could easily be cached, lowering the cost of accurately tracking last access, update time, and file size. This is reflected in the design of the API. For example, when retrieving the list of files in a directory, the `readdir` function only retrieves file names; to obtain extra information (such as file size), a call to `fstat` needs to be made for each file found. In a time when disks were local and uniquely accessed by a single computer and metadata could easily be cached, the cost of performing these extra calls was minimal. However, fast forwarding to modern times, where file systems are often remote (i.e., exported by file servers) and shared between multiple client computers, each call requires a round trip to a remote server. Likewise, caching is no longer straightforward as remote invalidation is required to keep cache contents consistent. In this environment, the cost of providing a single global, consistent view of the file system becomes exceedingly large.

Another problem with the POSIX model is that it forces a single, high-level data storage model for all applications, with associated costs, regardless of whether the semantics of the model are appropriate or not for the application at hand. For example, data can only be stored in a file. Each file has metadata such as file size and last access time, that are globally visible and consistent across all clients, whether an application requires this information or not. Likewise, each file needs to be in a directory. Creating a file in a directory is an atomic operation, with immediate global visibility. Because of this, file creation in a distributed file system can be highly synchronizing and consequently fundamentally unscalable.

Thus, while many distributed applications use more scalable methods internally for both I/O and data organization, POSIX offers no possibility of relaxing its strict rules, needlessly limiting application scalability. To mitigate this, numerous groups have developed additional layers that provide new organizational models and reorganize access prior to interacting with POSIX storage, many of which have been discussed previously in this book, and enhancements to POSIX to address scalability limitations have been proposed.

30.2 The Current HPC Storage Model

Considering the high cost (during development as well as at runtime) of implementing full POSIX I/O compliance in a distributed environment, it should not come as a surprise that some file systems instead aim to be *mostly* compliant. For example, the NFS client emulates the common unlink-after-open approach of creating temporary files by renaming the file with the goal of later removing those files (something which does not always succeed). Attribute consistency is another area where NFS is not fully compliant. In the default mode, client-side caching is used to improve performance and reduce server load. However, this means that full POSIX attribute consistency is not provided. In addition, there is no guaranteed, portable method to enforce consistency. Some of these issues are being addressed in newer versions (v4) of the NFS protocol.

In many cases, the POSIX semantics are unnecessarily strict, and consequently most applications continue to function correctly even on these mostly POSIX-compliant file systems. Thus the current HPC storage model aims to work around the POSIX shortcomings by adjusting or breaking POSIX where necessary and leveraging new software layers to optimize I/O before it hits the POSIX interface. Simultaneously, new storage concepts are being deployed *below* the POSIX API that have potential for larger benefits to HPC storage.

30.2.1 The POSIX HPC I/O Extensions

POSIX HPC I/O extensions [9] were designed to improve performance of POSIX I/O in large-scale HPC environments. Software running on these systems differs from most other software in that on HPC systems, many processes, distributed over many nodes, work *collectively* on a problem. Specifically, focusing on I/O operations, this means many processes on many nodes are opening the same file(s) concurrently. Since HPC applications tend to be more synchronized as well, often all of the operations performed on these files (such as open) will be issued within a short time interval, leading to very high and bursty metadata workloads on the file system.

Since POSIX file handles are only valid on the local node, in a distributed environment—despite accessing the same file—each node is required to open the file. This causes each individual node to traverse the directory hierarchy to locate the requested file, causing high metadata overhead at the (remote) file system. The POSIX HPC extensions seek to reduce this load by allowing a single node to open the file and then *export* some representation of the resulting file handle (for example, containing a direct pointer to the enclosing directory) to other nodes (openg function), which then convert the exported handle directly to a file handle (sutoc function) without having to perform a full open call.

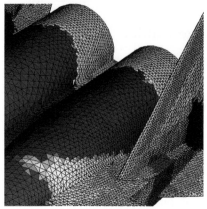

(a) Decomposed mesh   (b) File mapping

FIGURE 30.1 (See color insert): Domain decomposition resulting in highly non-contiguous access pattern. Color indicates node access.

HPC applications also tend to differ in how files are accessed. Often, a computational problem is partitioned between a set of nodes working on a single problem. For example, in the case of a weather simulation application, the three-dimensional region for which the weather is computed is sliced into multiple pieces and distributed among the nodes. When a part of a higher-dimensional region gets mapped to a single-dimensional file (when each node writes its portion of the simulated region to disk) a highly non-contiguous access pattern emerges. This is demonstrated in Figure 30.1, which shows a detailed 3D mesh (a), where color indicates the partitioning across nodes, and the resulting mapping to a one-dimensional file (b).

Unfortunately, the standard POSIX functions do not offer a way of expressing an I/O operation that is non-contiguous in the file (non-contiguous in memory is supported through the `readv` family of functions), forcing the application programmer to issue many small contiguous I/O requests instead, leading to severely reduced I/O performance. The `readx` and `writex` functions, proposed by the POSIX HPC extensions, aim to resolve this by offering functionality to describe an I/O transfer which can be non-contiguous in memory as well in the file.

The POSIX HPC I/O extensions also enable relaxing the rather strict POSIX I/O consistency semantics. For example, a new open flag is proposed, O_LAZY. The effect of this flag is to reduce the consistency scope of data and metadata to the scope of the process or local node, as opposed to all nodes mounting the same file system. When system-wide consistency is required, an application can call `lazyio_propagate` to propagate modifications to other processes or node, and `lazyio_synchronize` to invalidate any locally cached data or metadata.

Other extensions include functionality to retrieve both directory contents and associated file metadata, as well as the ability to retrieve only a subset of the file metadata. The latter avoids forcing the file system to compute updated values for all file attributes, some of which (e.g., file size) can be very costly to obtain.

Adoption and support for the POSIX HPC extensions has been minimal. However, a number of calls similar to the `openg` and `sutoc` functions proposed in the POSIX I/O extensions have made it into the Linux kernel: `name_to_handle_at` and `open_by_handle_at`. These functions were added in May 2011 in Linux kernel version 2.6.39.

30.2.2   MPI-IO

The MPI standard is widely used to program HPC systems. In version 2 of this standard, support for file I/O (MPI-IO) was added. Being designed for distributed computing environments, the MPI-IO model provides a more suitable API for HPC applications. For example, non-contiguous accesses are directly supported (through the use of *MPI datatypes*), and default data consistency is more relaxed, and formally defined. MPI-IO also defines *collective* I/O operations, enabling many optimizations such as group open, which offers similar functionality to the `openg` POSIX HPC extension call.

However, since MPI-IO is frequently built on top of POSIX I/O functionality, many of the issues described in Section 30.1 resurface. Whenever possible, MPI-IO uses file system specific calls (for example, through the use of `ioctl`) to work around some of the POSIX limitations, but these calls are non-standard and often vary even between versions of the same file system. Widespread adoption of the POSIX HPC extensions would provide MPI-IO with a portable method to obtain the same effect. When specialized support is not available for the underlying file system, MPI-IO is limited to POSIX functionality, including the inability to communicate relaxed data consistency requirements. Consequently, MPI-IO performance is highly variable from system to system [12], causing some application and library developers to avoid MPI-IO all together.

30.2.3   Object Storage Model

In 1998, Gibson et al. [10] proposed a new storage interface, called Network Attached Secure Disk (NASD), proposing to replace the low-level sector access by an object-based access API allowing a client to access an object (typically by numerical identifier) and offset within that object, while the device itself controls the mapping of the object data to the disk platters. The NASD work influenced the design of the ANSI T10 Object-based Storage Device (OSD) standard. This work does not aim to replace the POSIX-I/O functionality; instead it is intended to offer a basic building block on which other, high-level I/O functionality can be built. In a sense, these form a replacement for plain disks. OSDs differ in that they typically offer byte access granularity (as opposed to sector granularity). The OSD implements the storage operations (data transfer and layout), without defining any policy.

Many parallel file system implementations today, while exporting a mostly POSIX-compliant model to their clients, internally access local storage using an object storage model similar to the T10 standard [6, 7, 19, 18]. Unfortunately, as seen with MPI-IO, these object storage abstractions are frequently built on top of an existing local POSIX file system. This means potential efficiency gains (for example, in avoiding directory overhead) are often not fully realized. At least one reason for this insistence on building on top of POSIX is that no other data storage model comes close in terms of availability and portability.

Luckily, some alternatives are now starting to appear. Seagate, a well-known American data storage company, recently commercialized a disk drive which exposes storage only as object storage API, as opposed to exposing low-level sectors, as is still common for disk drives. A widely adopted standardized object-based access method for low-level storage could finally provide libraries and applications an equivalent solution providing the portability of POSIX with the flexibility to define their own access semantics (consistency) and grouping structures (directories or alternatives).

30.3   Post POSIX

Currently, the POSIX model for storage still dominates in HPC. However, there is increasing use of libraries such as PnetCDF and HDF5 that provide alternative data models to users. These libraries create an opportunity for storage system designers: new underlying storage models can be deployed by mapping these libraries directly onto the new storage model, avoiding the need to support the POSIX model at all.

Thus, the HPC community may be at the cusp of a "post-POSIX" era where new HPC storage models appear in production systems. When considering what the storage model(s) in this era might look like, two needs are evident. First, highly parallel applications (and the libraries that support them) need to store multiple, concurrent streams of data and organize these conveniently. Second, with the explosion of data that is occurring, new methods for identifying data of interest are increasingly important.

30.3.1   Prior Work

Of course, while production HPC systems have primarily provided POSIX storage access, software products outside of HPC and research in the HPC community have pointed to a number of viable alternative models. This section will discuss a few, more relevant examples.

The IBM Virtual Storage Access Method (VSAM) model [15], defined in the 1970s, provides a number of features that would be compelling in an HPC system. Data is stored as records of potentially variable length with multiple fields. Data items can be referenced with a key, with a record number, or the file can be directly accessed with byte offsets. Multiple dataset organizations are provided to cater to specific use cases.

While most users do not realize it, the Microsoft New Technology File System (NTFS) also provides an interesting alternative model in the form of *alternative data streams* [5]. This functionality allows for multiple streams of data to be associated with the same file name. A default data stream holds standard "POSIX-style" data, while a colon notation is used to define and access additional named streams under the same file name.

This model of multiple streams associated with a single file name is not unique to NTFS, and in fact the approach has appeared in HPC parallel file systems research as well. The Galley parallel file system [16], developed in the 1990s, supported a concept of *subfiles*. In their model, a set of subfiles were created at the time a file was created that mapped to underlying storage devices. These subfiles then contained a set of *forks* where each could hold an array of bytes (like a normal POSIX file). The authors showed how upper software layers could map astronomical data into this organization.

The Vesta parallel file system [8] was developed at IBM in the 1990s specifically for HPC. Vesta exposes a 2D structure for files, with *physical partitions* holding sequences of records. Physical partitions are similar to subfiles in the Galley model and are meant to map to storage nodes. This provides a notion of parallelism of access that has been adopted by current research in the area.

30.3.2 Object Abstractions in HPC

Work in object-based file systems set the stage for one possible alternative: providing direct access to storage objects. Researchers are investigating how to expose an object abstraction while maintaining the existing namespace abstraction. In this model, a directory entry refers to a collection of objects, each individually accessible.

The "End of Files" (EOF) [11] project is one such example. Goodell et al. developed a prototype atop PVFS [7] that allows for a static set of objects to be associated with a directory entry. Conceptually, this is best thought of as the file system no longer owning the distribution of data into objects, but rather delegating this to higher-level software layers. This approach exposes the natural unit of concurrency (i.e., the object) and provides multiple data streams that may be used by upper layers for organizational purposes.

Figure 30.2 shows how the PnetCDF (Chapter 15) library maps netCDF datasets to a POSIX file (left) or to the EOF object model (right). In the POSIX file mapping, PnetCDF lays out variables across the single file byte

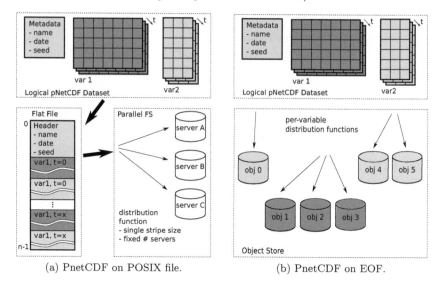

(a) PnetCDF on POSIX file.   (b) PnetCDF on EOF.

FIGURE 30.2: Mapping of PnetCDF dataset to (a) POSIX file, or (b) EOF objects.

stream. One complication of this process is *record variables*, which have one dimension of undefined length. In the netCDF standard, $n - 1$ dimension subsets of these variables are interleaved at the end of the file in order to reduce the overall file size. This organizational choice is problematic for high performance access, as it leads to noncontiguous I/O.

In the EOF object model, distinct objects are used to hold metadata and the data corresponding to variables. The PnetCDF library becomes responsible for mapping multidimensional variables into one or more objects. This simplifies data layout, especially for record variables that can now be mapped into distinct object sets without need for interleaving.

The Intel Storage and I/O Fast Forward project [2, 4] is similarly looking at how high-level data models can be mapped onto exascale storage architectures. The Intel activity includes three sub-projects: looking at how HDF5 (Chapter 16) can target object storage back ends; examining how PLFS (Chapter 14) and I/O Forwarding Software Library (IOFSL) [3] can be adapted to manage burst buffers to optimize data layout on object storage backends; and developing a prototype Distributed Application Object Storage (DAOS) system, building on Lustre (Chapter 8) including a distributed transaction capability.

The transaction capability is one unique feature of the Intel prototype I/O stack and is built on top of a versioning capability at the DAOS level. This capability allows for transactions with Atomicity, Consistency, Isolation, Durability (ACID) properties when data moves from burst buffer to persistent storage. Transactions are similarly supported at the burst buffer layer, and the augmented HDF5 library takes advantage of these to ensure consistent transitions of a given dataset.

Another interesting feature of the Intel Fast Forward work is the manner in which burst buffers are integrated into the overall system. I/O nodes that manage local NVRAM export three distinct data models for use by application libraries: a blob object (i.e., a byte stream), a keyword-value object, and an array object. All are used within HDF5, and the I/O node is responsible for mapping transactions on these constructs into operations on DAOS objects. This issue of translations between abstractions at various levels of the I/O stack is critical, and often overlooked.

30.3.3　Namespaces

Despite hierarchical file systems being declared as dead [17], this model of data organization still dominates in HPC. While both the EOF and Intel Fast Forward projects provide alternative organizations for data, neither makes radical changes to the way we organize and reference named entities.

What seems most likely is that the role of providing namespaces for HPC applications will be taken over by upper layers of the HPC storage stack, layers such as HDF5, PnetCDF, and others, with storage systems instead providing a richer building-block abstraction on which these namespaces are constructed.

What is even less clear is how search-like capabilities will be integrated into the HPC storage stack. Activities such as hFAD [17] and Spyglass [14] have provided some insight, but ultimately HPC search is about application data structures — not something that the low-level storage system is necessarily even aware of. Perhaps active storage advances will be what ultimately enable application-oriented searches to be executed local to storage where they can be performed efficiently.

30.4　Conclusion

The POSIX storage model has been a cornerstone of HPC systems for decades. As a result of its success, HPC system providers have been slow to adopt alternatives to the well-understood POSIX file model, but the increasing use of I/O libraries such as HDF5 and PnetCDF by scientific codes have eliminated many long-standing dependencies on the antiquated POSIX model and provided new ways for science teams to interact with storage.

Research has identified a number of promising alternative models, and the community seems ready to embrace a new model. New additions in the storage hierarchy, such as the inclusion of nonvolatile memory in the storage system, have further disrupted the status quo. With current storage systems struggling to keep pace, the timing could not be better.

Bibliography

[1] IEEE Std 1003.1, 2013 Edition. http://www.unix.org/version4/ieee_std.html.

[2] Intel Fast Forward Storage and I/O Program Documents. Technical report, Intel, 2013.

[3] Nawab Ali, Philip Carns, Kamil Iskra, Dries Kimpe, Samuel Lang, Robert Latham, and Robert Ross. Scalable I/O Forwarding Framework for High Performance Computing Systems. In *IEEE International Conference on Cluster Computing (Cluster 2009)*, New Orleans, LA, September 2009.

[4] Eric Barton. Fast Forward I/O and Storage. Keynote at the 7th Parallel Data Storage Workshop (PDSW), November 2012.

[5] Hal Berghel and Natasa Brajkovska. Wading into Alternate Data Streams. *Commun. ACM*, 47(4):21–27, April 2004.

[6] Peter J. Braam. The Lustre Storage Architecture. Technical report, Cluster File Systems, Inc., 2003.

[7] Philip H. Carns, Walter B. Ligon III, Robert B. Ross, and Rajeev Thakur. PVFS: A Parallel File System for Linux Clusters. In *Proceedings of the 4th Annual Linux Showcase and Conference*, pages 317–327, Atlanta, GA, October 2000. USENIX Association.

[8] Peter F. Corbett and Dror G. Feitelson. The Vesta Parallel File System. *ACM Transactions on Computer Systems*, 14(3):225–264, August 1996.

[9] Marti Bancroft DOD, NRO John Bent DOE, NNSA LANL, Gary Grider DOE, James Nunez DOE, Ellen Salmon NASA, Lee Ward DOE, and NNSA SNL. High End Computing Interagency Working Group (HECIWG) Sponsored File Systems and I/O Workshop HEC FSIO 2011.

[10] Garth A. Gibson, David F. Nagle, Khalil Amiri, Jeff Butler, Fay W. Chang, Howard Gobioff, Charles Hardin, Erik Riedel, David Rochberg, and Jim Zelenka. A Cost-Effective, High-Bandwidth Storage Architecture. *SIGPLAN Not.*, 33(11):92–103, October 1998.

[11] David Goodell, Seong Jo Kim, Robert Latham, Mahmut Kandemir, and Robert Ross. An Evolutionary Path to Object Storage Access. In *Proceedings of the 7th Parallel Data Storage Workshop*, Salt Lake City, UT, November 2012.

[12] William D. Gropp, Dries Kimpe, Robert Ross, Rajeev Thakur, and Jesper Larsson Träff. Self-Consistent MPI-IO Performance Requirements

and Expectations. In *Recent Advances in Parallel Virtual Machine and Message Passing Interface*, pages 167–176. Springer, 2008.

[13] IEEE. *2004 (ISO/IEC). IEEE/ANSI Std 1003.1, 2004 Edition. Information Technology—Portable Operating System Interface (POSIX®)—Part 1: System Application: Program Interface (API) C Language*. IEEE, New York, NY USA, 2004.

[14] Andrew W. Leung, Minglong Shao, Timothy Bisson, Shankar Pasupathy, and Ethan L. Miller. Spyglass: Fast, Scalable Metadata Search for Large-Scale Storage Systems. *FAST*, 9:153–166, 2009.

[15] Dave Lovelace, Rama Ayyar, Alvaro Sala, and Valeria Sokal. VSAM Demystified (Second Edition). Technical Report SG24-6105-01, IBM International Technical Support Organization, September 2003.

[16] Nils Nieuwejaar and David Kotz. The Galley Parallel File System. *Parallel Computing*, 23(4):447–476, June 1997.

[17] Margo I. Seltzer and Nicholas Murphy. Hierarchical File Systems Are Dead. In *HotOS*, 2009.

[18] Sage A. Weil, Scott A. Brandt, Ethan L. Miller, Darrell D. E. Long, and Carlos Maltzahn. Ceph: A Scalable, High Performance Distributed File System. In *Proceedings of the 7th USENIX Symposium on Operating Systems Design and Implementation*, pages 307–320, 2006.

[19] B. Welch, M. Unangst, Z. Abbasi, G. Gibson, B. Mueller, J. Small, J. Zelenka, and B. Zhou. Scalable Performance of the Panasas Parallel File System. In *Proceedings of the 6th USENIX Conference on File and Storage Technologies (FAST)*, pages 17–33, 2008.

Chapter 31

Resilience

Gary Grider and Nathan DeBardeleben

Los Alamos National Laboratory

31.1   Present 346
    31.1.1   Getting the Correct Answer 347
31.2   Future 348
31.3   Conclusion 350
    Bibliography 351

The term "resilience" has become an overarching term that describes the reliability of both software and hardware in the high performance computing field. Resilience came about, during a philosophical shift away from merely tolerating faults and toward being able to ride through failure. While there certainly are examples of resilience, particularly in hardware, there are relatively few examples of true resilience at higher levels of the software/hardware stack.

For many reasons, resilience is a key challenge for future supercomputing systems. System reliability is intricately tied to the scale of hardware and software components. Reliability has become a bigger problem as systems scale to use petascale and exascale, and the predicted component counts for systems of the future will only exacerbate this issue. Secondly, performance, power, and reliability are interrelated and while strict requirements are being set for performance (i.e., "exaflop") and power (i.e., 20 MW), reliability requirements are somewhat less constrained. Furthermore, decreases in supply voltage come with a decrease in reliability [9].

While current supercomputers almost exclusively address reliability through some form of checkpointing, there is concern that future HPC systems will need more elaborate tools to achieve resilience. However, rather than force system reliability to some unachievable goal, there remains hope for moving from the current systems that still tolerate faults to those that are truly resilient to failure.

31.1   Present

Application fault tolerance on today's systems is almost exclusively handled through defensive I/O checkpointing. Checkpointing (also discussed in Chapters 19 and 23) is by and large the only reliable (albeit expensive) means of recovering from application interrupts.

For the most part, applications that run on current supercomputers are unable to handle any failure of any of the components being used by that application. This means that an application running across 10,000 nodes of a supercomputer will entirely fail when one node experiences an unrecoverable memory error. Imagine if your car broke down every time it hit a pot hole! That is what today's applications are like.

Obviously there are exceptions to this extreme brittleness. While there are certainly interesting and promising research approaches to move the field beyond this mode of computation, they have yet to gain enough traction to see widespread deployment. These techniques range from new programming languages, models, and paradigms to hardware-assisted fault avoidance and recovery.

HPC systems today are almost exclusively built out of commodity components. Some systems will have small portions that are proprietary: a custom compute node kernel, an ultra-high-speed network, a co-processor, etc. However, by and large, the systems are assembled out of the same components that are used by consumers at home with slight improvements. One example of such an improvement is server-grade dual in-line memory modules, or DIMMs (with advanced error protection).

As individual system components are designed to be reliable for a consumer, each piece is expected to last around five years. However, when you take many hundreds of thousands of parts and assemble them together into a world-class supercomputer with requirements that the system be stable and compute accurately, problems arise.

Large-scale supercomputing centers are usually somewhat shy about sharing failure rates on these systems, but on the largest supercomputers of today, the *application mean time between failure* (AMTBF) is on the order of 8–24 hours. This means that an application running across the entire machine will see an interrupt one to several times a day *unless it can ride through failure*. As aforementioned, today's applications largely cannot do so, and hence checkpointing to prepare for this impending failure becomes imperative.

There are a myriad of *metrics around supercomputer reliability* (MTBF, system MTBF, application MTBF, mean uptime, mean time to repair, etc.). While the HPC resilience community has released definitions of these terms before [1, 10], not everyone is in full agreement. As such, not everyone measures these metrics the same way and it can be difficult to compare numbers from different data centers.

31.1.1 Getting the Correct Answer

When people talk about supercomputer reliability they have, historically, almost exclusively spoken of faults that cause detectable errors. Examples include a node crashing due to an unrecoverable memory error, a crash of a software middleware or hardware driver, a power glitch that causes a machine to halt, or an unreachable file system (for whatever reason) when an application tries to use it. Each of these examples have detectable signatures that cause a change in the application. In most examples, this simply causes the application to fail, and data needs to be recovered from a recent checkpoint.

These are not the only types of faults on systems. Indeed, there are faults that make undetectable changes to a computation. Like all faults, these can be transient, intermittent, or permanent. Transient faults are usually caused by environmental effects, such as cosmic radiation and alpha particles emitted by radioactive impurities in the electronics packaging. Intermittent faults are often the effect of temperature or voltage extremes and variations. These effects can sometimes grow into permanent failures.

All of these effects can and do cause computing hardware to perform incorrectly. In the case of data storage, particularly in memory (main memory, caches, registers, etc.), most supercomputers today employ advanced error correction codes. These codes can identify and correct a large number of these errors. However, as the amount of memory on supercomputers has grown, so has the required complexity of these error correction codes such that a non-negligible amount of energy is expended to ensure correctness. Still, some data corruption will slip past these codes and the extreme scale of today's systems continues to make that increasingly likely. Additionally, it is possible that computational logic can corrupt results.

Supercomputers are used in a wide range of application spaces. While those applications undoubtedly require different levels of precision, it is important to understand that supercomputers (and indeed, all computers) cannot be viewed as entirely reliable digital machines. Instead, users must check the integrity of their calculations in as many ways as possible.

One such way that is gaining in popularity is *algorithm-based fault-tolerance* (ABFT). This technique embraces fundamental algorithmic changes that allow an application to check for correctness and recompute corrupted data. Examples of this are few and far between and due to the nature of ABFT, there is little that can be generalized across different classes of applications. As such, ABFT may find use only in a portion of supercomputing application fields while others require some more special techniques.

Luckily, on current systems, data corruption appears to be rare. By the very nature of the faults being undetectable it is likely that the HPC community does not have an accurate understanding of data corruption rates.

The fundamental reason the HPC community is not seeing complex and innovative systems for dynamically adapting to failures is that the problem has not, to date, been large enough to warrant serious investment in resilience, although this may be changing in the near future.

31.2 Future

Several reports [2, 7, 12] state the increasing need for resilient, high performance computing systems as HPC continues to strive for larger and larger supercomputer deployments. Different groups of leaders in the HPC resilience field have issued reports [6, 5, 8, 11, 3] on the challenges, opportunities, and suggested approaches to field a reliable supercomputer in the exascale timeframe.

As component counts of future systems continue to grow to staggering numbers, so do the reliability concerns. Leadership-class supercomputers in the 2020 timeframe are likely to contain between 32 and 100 petabytes of main memory, a $100\times$ to $350\times$ increase compared to the 2012 levels [2]. If implemented in DRAM DIMMs, the amount of DIMMs alone on a machine of this scale will make failure rates (both due to hard and soft faults) extremely challenging. Similar increases are expected in the amount of cache memory (SRAM) on future systems.

Several studies [2, 12], suggest that without aggressive engineering, crude projections show that an exascale supercomputer will have a failure every 10–50 minutes. Clearly, saving a checkpoint for an application at scale, consuming much of the supercomputer's main memory, is a serious challenge in that tens of minutes timeframe. Engineering approaches are certainly possible, however they are likely to be costly and it is unlikely to align well with commodity desktop or server demands. Therefore, there is great potential for innovative approaches to resilience in this timeframe so that the HPC community is not forced to pay for fault-hardened expensive hardware.

Figure 31.1 shows a prediction of different types of errors and how they will increase as the process technology scales [5]. In particular, this shows that the amount of soft-error-related faults in the logic latches is predicted to rise. Although not included in this figure, there is also a great deal of uncertainty about the aging effects in new process technology.

Additionally, as the industry continues to drive down power usage by moving to near-threshold voltage, it is expected that power-related error rates will also rise. Figure 31.2 shows that, historically, as process technology has scaled downward, each new generation has become less susceptible to soft errors when voltage was also scaled downward [9]. Even though this trend is promising, there appears to at least be *some* effect from voltage scaling and that will probably continue.

To ensure correct operation, all circuits should operate within their specific environmental envelope at all times, over the operational life of the machine.

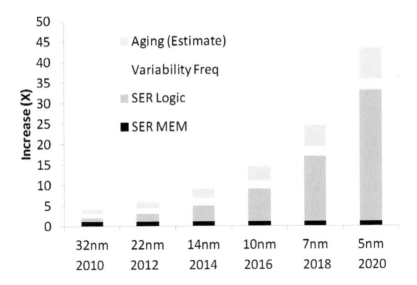

FIGURE 31.1: Estimates of the relative increase in error rates as a function of process technology. [Image courtesy of Report from the Inter-Agency Workshop on HPC Resilience at Extreme Scale [5].]

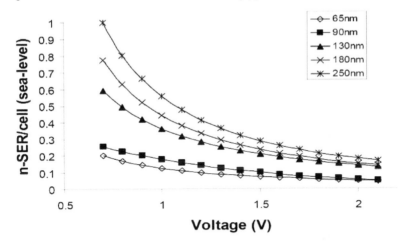

FIGURE 31.2: Relationship between soft errors and voltage scaling through several process technology generations. [Image courtesy of Kaul, Himanshu, et al. [9].]

Normally, those specifications include average and transient voltages, as well as temperature and other physical variables. With the inherent growth of complexity in advanced dynamic power management, the number of special, at-the-limit cases in environmental specifications grows very rapidly; therefore the risk of incorrect operation due to transients which explore these corner cases grows. Recent experience justifies concerns about these risks, which are already showing up as root causes of intermittent errors in large-scale machines.

One area of research with great potential impact is to break the reliance on tightly coupled applications that are unable to handle faults in any used software or hardware component. This is sometimes referred to as local failure causing global failure and restart. Instead, approaches that focus on allowing portions of a calculation to fail while other portions continue (perhaps at a reduced accuracy) become important. Certainly, there is much more research to be conducted in this area as the most widely used parallel programming paradigm, MPI, does not readily facilitate this. Furthermore, application developers will need to be trained to design algorithms for this new style of computation.

The notion of localizing failures is closely related to the concept of containment domains (CDs) [4]. CDs are essentially a form of transactional computing brought to HPC programming. In this programming model, users "contain" regions of an application by describing different failure domains. Then, an advanced compiler and/or runtime system can perform many reliability-related tasks transparently for the user, such as voting for correctness and rollback. CDs seem to show promising results and are likely to appear in some form in future programming paradigms that target reliable computation.

31.3　Conclusion

HPC resilience is a problem that is growing in importance and recognition with the size of the HPC systems themselves. Today, system interruptions are a nuisance that can be addressed (at non-negligible cost) through defensive checkpointing. Experts in government, industry, and academia believe the rate of failures is increasing to the point that in the near future system failure will no longer be the exception. As such, checkpointing is unlikely to be the only way to address application reliability on future systems.

Furthermore, future systems are likely to become *less* reliable with respect to application correctness. The HPC community will see more emphasis put on user applications that can check a calculation for correctness. They will also see new programming techniques built around defining reliable and unreliable portions of an application and accompanying hardware that can take advantage of multiple levels of fidelity.

Resilience represents a great opportunity to develop applications that can be agile, and adapt to unreliable hardware and software components. There will be more opportunities available to develop hardware and software solutions that address other HPC challenge areas as more resilient applications are developed.

Bibliography

[1] Algirdas Avizienis, J-C Laprie, Brian Randell, and Carl Landwehr. Basic Concepts and Taxonomy of Dependable and Secure Computing. *Dependable and Secure Computing, IEEE Transactions on*, 1(1):11–33, 2004.

[2] Keren Bergman, Shekhar Borkar, Dan Campbell, William Carlson, William Dally, Monty Denneau, Paul Franzon, William Harrod, Kerry Hill, Jon Hiller, et al. Exascale Computing Study: Technology Challenges in Achieving Exascale Systems. Defense Advanced Research Projects Agency Information Processing Techniques Office (DARPA IPTO), Tech. Rep, 2008.

[3] Franck Cappello, Al Geist, Bill Gropp, Laxmikant Kale, Bill Kramer, and Marc Snir. Toward Exascale Resilience. *International Journal of High Performance Computing Applications*, 23:374–388, November 2009.

[4] Jinsuk Chung, Ikhwan Lee, Michael Sullivan, Jee Ho Ryoo, Dong Wan Kim, Doe Hyun Yoon, Larry Kaplan, and Mattan Erez. Containment Domains: A Scalable, Efficient, and Flexible Resilience Scheme for Exascale Systems. In the *Proceedings of SC12*, November 2012.

[5] John Daly et al. Inter-Agency Workshop on HPC Resilience at Extreme Scale. http://institute.lanl.gov/resilience/docs/Inter-AgencyResilienceReport.pdf, February 2012.

[6] Nathan DeBardeleben, James Laros, John Daly, Stephen Scott, Christian Engelmann, and Bill Harrod. High-End Computing Resilience: Analysis of Issues Facing the HEC Community and Path-Forward for Research and Development. http://institute.lanl.gov/resilience/docs/HECResilience.pdf, December 2009.

[7] Jack Dongarra et al. The International Exascale Software Project Roadmap. *International Journal of High Performance Computing Applications*, 25:3–60, February 2011.

[8] Al Geist et al. Fault Management Workshop Final Report. http://science.energy.gov/~/media/ascr/pdf/program-documents/docs/FaultManagement-wrkshpRpt-v4-final.pdf, June 2012.

[9] H. Kaul, M. Anders, S. Hsu, A. Agarwal, R. Krishnamurthy, and S. Borkar. Near-Threshold Voltage (NTV) Design: Opportunities and

Challenges.   In *Design Automation Conference (DAC), 2012 49th ACM/EDAC/IEEE*, pages 1149–1154, 2012.

[10] Jean-Claude Laprie. Dependable Computing: Concepts, Limits, Challenges. In *FTCS-25, the 25th IEEE International Symposium on Fault-Tolerant Computing-Special Issue*, pages 42–54, 1995.

[11] M. Snir, R. W. Wisniewski, J. A. Abraham, S. V. Adve, S. Bagchi, Pavan Balaji, J. Belak, P. Bose, F. Cappello, B. Carlson, Andrew A. Chien, P. Coteus, N. A. DeBardeleben, P. Diniz, C. Engelmann, M. Erez, S. Fazzari, A. Geist, R. Gupta, F. Johnson, Sriram Krishnamoorthy, Sven Leyffer, D. Liberty, S. Mitra, T. S. Munson, R. Schreiber, J. Stearley, and E. V. Hensbergen. Addressing Failures in Exascale Computing. *International Journal of High Performance Computing Applications*, May 2014, vol. 28, no. 2, 129–173.

[12] The JASONs. Technical Challenges of Exascale Computing. *JSR-12-310*, April 2013.

Chapter 32

Multi/Many Core

Ramon Nou, Toni Cortes

Barcelona Supercomputing Center

Stelios Mavridis, Yannis Sfakianakis, and Angelos Bilas

Foundation for Research and Technology—Hellas

32.1	Introduction	353
32.2	Storage I/O at Present	354
32.3	Storage I/O in the Near Future	355
32.4	Challenges and Solutions	356
	32.4.1 NUMA Effects	356
	32.4.2 Improving I/O Caching Efficiency	357
	32.4.3 Dynamic I/O Scheduler Selection	359
32.5	Conclusion	360
	Bibliography	360

32.1 Introduction

With current trends moving toward large multicore servers as building blocks for HPC and data centers, storage I/O is becoming an increasing concern for application scaling and performance. The main contributing factors that lead to this landscape are: (a) technology that allows and dictates building large multicore servers; (b) servers that are built as shared memory systems that run a single instance of the operating system for convenience and market size purposes; (c) with the advent of "big data" problems, applications that tend to become more and more data intensive; and (d) fast storage devices that allow such systems to operate at high input/output operations per second (IOPS). Therefore, a major trend for both HPC and data centers is toward using large shared servers as infrastructure components for computation.

Large, shared servers and data-intensive applications pose significant challenges for the storage I/O path. I/O requests need to traverse multiple layers in the operating system, storage controllers, and the devices themselves. The operating system in general and the Linux kernel in particular have not been designed to handle large amounts of concurrency in the I/O path, nor to handle large numbers of IOPS. Moreover, memory management and synchronization become more difficult to handle due to the more complex memory hierarchies, NUMA levels, and system interconnects. In addition, mixing multiple I/O streams due to the high levels of concurrency creates patterns that lead traditional magnetic hard disks (HDDs) and modern solid-state disks (SSDs) to operate inefficiently. Overall, modern server platforms are becoming larger, more heterogeneous, with a much wider range of memory access and synchronization costs, and they are required to support higher degrees of concurrency at the I/O level.

This chapter will focus briefly on three I/O problems on multicore servers:

- NUMA effects. Buffer placement and affinity of processes and memory buffers can result in large variations in performance and can limit scalability.

- Efficiency of I/O caching. I/O caching is an important function of the I/O path in the operating system kernel. Modern multicore servers can improve the efficiency of the I/O cache by trading CPU via deduplication.

- I/O scheduling. A single scheduler will not work well for diverse workloads in modern systems, and systems can dynamically choose a scheduler from the current existing choices in the operating system kernel, by considering all I/O requests.

Some of these problems are illustrated on real systems, along with general mitigating approaches, using a custom-designed kernel I/O stack that provides new mechanisms for managing affinity, buffer management, synchronization, and scheduling in the I/O path.

The rest of this chapter is organized as follows: Section 32.2 discusses challenges in the storage I/O, Section 32.3 presents ideas about the future, Section 32.4 provides solutions to improve the I/O stack, and finally, Section 32.5 summarizes observations and predictions with concluding remarks.

32.2 Storage I/O at Present

Currently, storage I/O faces new challenges. Until recently, storage I/O was primarily limited by the storage devices themselves, as HDDs were the main limiting factor for the number of IOPS and the I/O throughput a server could sustain. As such, the main goal of the host-level I/O path has been to reduce the number of I/O operations, e.g., by properly managing metadata.

However, with the advent of new storage device technologies, such as SSDs, modern multicore servers can operate at a performance regime that is two orders of magnitude higher in terms of IOPS and one order of magnitude higher in terms of throughput. At this regime, bottlenecks shift from the devices to the host I/O path and reveal many of the shortcomings of today's I/O path design in the operating system kernel.

Modern systems introduce significant complexity due to the non-uniform memory architectures they employ. The I/O path and all the buffers and structures it uses are shared across all contexts that perform I/O. Therefore, access to memory results in poor locality. NUMA effects result in both high overheads and poor scalability as well.

Multicore systems present additional opportunities for improved I/O performance by trading CPU for memory efficiency. The dynamic random access memory (DRAM) I/O cache is most important for reducing the number of I/O operations, e.g., by absorbing metadata I/O operations and allowing devices to serve mostly data I/O operations. More efficient use of the I/O cache can significantly improve I/O performance.

In addition, modern servers and applications typically use a large number of contexts, e.g., threads, that issue I/O requests. However, large numbers of outstanding requests typically result in mixed patterns that degrade device performance. Jung et al. [7], explain that even with modern SSDs, small and non-sequential I/Os result in significantly lower than nominal device performance. Therefore, the scheduler will play an increasingly important role, as workloads become more diverse.

32.3   Storage I/O in the Near Future

Current technology trends stipulate that the number of cores will be increasing and that the persistent I/O hierarchy will include additional types of non-volatile devices besides SSDs and HDDs. In this landscape, all issues discussed will intensify and multiple aspects of today's I/O path in the operating system kernel will need to be redesigned to satisfy future I/O requirements as Shoaib Akram et al. show [1]. At a high level, some solutions will be introduced for the following:

- Dealing with NUMA servers

- Improving the efficiency of DRAM caching

- Dealing with mixed I/O patterns

Generally, the I/O path is designed as a shared resource. This approach, although it is flexible and provides a convenient single-system image, it does not scale as the number of cores and the required levels of I/O performance increase. Therefore, in the future, the I/O path is expected to be redesigned to allow for a higher degree of isolation between independent streams of I/O requests at all layers. For instance, I/O requests originating from different contexts should be kept separate while traversing the I/O hierarchy, to avoid generating mixed I/O patterns.

32.4   Challenges and Solutions

This section discusses an initial approach to improve the current I/O path with respect to each problem listed in Section 32.3.

32.4.1   NUMA Effects

At present, a typical server implements a non-uniform memory architecture with at least two NUMA nodes. The results of running a flexible I/O (FIO) tester [3] on a standard 8-core Intel machine with two sockets and relatively uniform memory accesses is shown in Figure 32.1. The workload used consists of 4-KB random read requests with one to eight application threads. The two curves correspond to two runs: one that takes into account the affinity between threads and the memory they allocate, and a base execution that does not. After four application threads, where both system sockets are occupied with threads, the performance of the base execution deteriorates up to 21% compared to the one that takes affinity into account.

Figures 32.2 and 32.3 display results for both FIO and interleaved-or-random benchmarking (IOR) [8], an MPI-based benchmark that emulates checkpoint patterns on a 64-core AMD server with eight NUMA nodes organized in four sockets. This system exhibits pronounced non-uniformity in

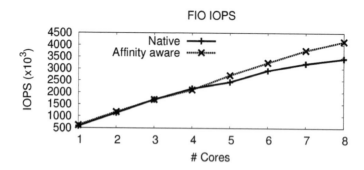

FIGURE 32.1: FIO read IOPS (4-KB random requests) of native (XFS file system) with and without proper placement. Performance of the base execution deteriorates by at most 21%.

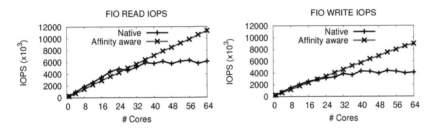

FIGURE 32.2: FIO read and write IOPS (4-KB random requests) of native with and without proper placement in a 64-core machine.

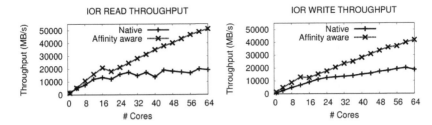

FIGURE 32.3: IOR read and write throughput (4-KB requests) of native with and without proper placement in a 64-core machine.

memory access overhead compared to smaller-scale systems. The same effect is visible in this system as well, especially when more than one socket is shared by application threads.

One approach to resolve this problem is to collocate threads and buffers used for I/O. However, policies used should not interfere with the CPU's scheduler policy to spread active threads over all server resources. Current system software lacks mechanisms and policies to achieve this goal in the I/O path transparently.

As a proof-of-concept, the I/O path redesign using custom Linux kernel modules addresses the NUMA effects. A custom file system provides hints to the CPU scheduler, and a DRAM cache creates separate memory pools to cache pending I/O. The file system and the cache assign CPU cores and memory buffers from a single socket to application threads. Figures 32.2 and 32.3 show that custom I/O stacks are able to improve I/O throughput up to 84% for random reads, 118% for random writes, 167% for sequential reads, and 123% for sequential writes.

32.4.2 Improving I/O Caching Efficiency

Given the rate of data growth, modern applications tend to access larger amounts of persistent storage. Therefore, the efficiency of I/O caching is

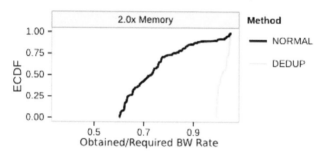

FIGURE 32.4: Using on-memory deduplication provides extra performance without any administration cost (i.e., installing a new file system).

becoming more important. Deduplication is a technique that has been mainly used to reduce the size of data in various cases, such as in file systems (ZFS [11]), virtual machines (KVM, XEN [5], VMware [12]), and special tagged memory zones (KSM [2]). However, using deduplication to improve I/O caching by effectively increasing the size of the I/O cache incurs significant CPU overhead due to the cost of deduplication techniques. On the other hand, with the increasing number of cores, it makes sense to examine related trade-offs when trading CPU cycles to improve the cache hit ratio and to achieve better I/O performance.

Deduplication is a powerful tool such that along with NUMA-aware algorithms and adaptive CPU partitioning, latency and overheads can be significantly reduced. The results indicated in Figure 32.4 confirm that using deduplication in the case of a VM's file server improves I/O performance by 30% as Jin et al. [6] show, offering better quality of service while using the same hardware.

An important aspect of trading CPU efficiency for I/O efficiency is to ensure that the CPU cycles being used are not stolen from running applications. Ideally, only idle resources should be used to perform I/O-related tasks, such as deduplication. To examine this issue, a framework [10] was designed that is able to dynamically assign CPUs to I/O or application tasks. The framework sends tasks to idle cores (including GPUs) and partitions them in two categories: cores that run specialized tasks and cores that run application tasks. The framework is able to dynamically decide the number of cores that should be used for executing I/O-related tasks. As there is no monotonic relation between performance obtained and cores used, all possible partitions should be examined to find the best one, for example, using Berry et al.'s Armed Bandit [4] technique. Figure 32.5 shows that any static CPU partitioning can degrade performance significantly, while using a dynamic algorithm allows executing I/O tasks and keeping application performance above 90%.

Overall, the preliminary investigation shows that performing I/O-related tasks in parallel without hurting application performance, can lead to better I/O performance.

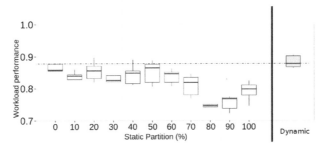

FIGURE 32.5: Assigning cores to I/O processes may increase the performance of the system [10].

32.4.3   Dynamic I/O Scheduler Selection

Device I/O schedulers play an important role in I/O performance. With multicore servers, the notable difference from the past is that I/O patterns tend to become more diverse due to more application contexts issuing I/O requests. This issue is becoming more involved with the widening range of device performance characteristics, e.g., with the introduction of SSDs. As a result, systems today employ a number of I/O schedulers, each being tailored for a set of workloads or devices. However, selecting the right scheduler for a workload is a difficult problem and therefore, administrators and users tend to not use any scheduler at all.

One approach to addressing this issue is to dynamically choose the right scheduler by continuously observing and analyzing the current I/O pattern. To explore this direction, a prototype system was developed that chooses the most appropriate I/O scheduler based on pattern matching in the data flow of the operating system and the devices. This is called the IOAnalyzer [9]. The I/O data flow is compared online, building a database of I/O patterns → {I/O scheduler, I/O performance}. Once there is enough information, the IOAnalyzer selects the most appropriate I/O scheduler in a proactive way.

The workflow of the IOAnalyzer is discussed as follows and is displayed in Figure 32.6. First, data about the I/O performance, the actual I/O scheduler, and the I/O trace from the kernel are gathered, then this data is compared to previously stored traces from the running system. If there is a match, the IOAnalyzer looks for the most beneficial I/O scheduler for the next probable workload; if not, the gathered information is stored. If there is a hit and there is not enough information about which scheduler will be the best, IOAnalyzer forces an arbitrary scheduler to complete the information. The learning phase is short and the performance improvement compared to the worst scheduler is very high (a 2–5 time speedup on I/O). As it is an online system, statistics are updated continuously to learn new patterns and overcome system modifications (i.e., aging).

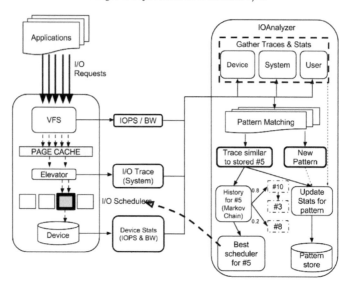

FIGURE 32.6: IOAnalyzer captures I/O traces and statistics and compares this with previous traces in order to find which is the most beneficial scheduler for the near future.

32.5   Conclusion

As the number of cores increases in modern multicore servers, several issues arise for the I/O path. In this chapter, three such issues were briefly examined: NUMA effects, I/O cache efficiency, and I/O scheduler selection. Early investigation shows that these three areas will require a significantly better understanding of the problems ahead and new mechanisms in the I/O path to ensure the scalability of I/O performance.

Bibliography

[1] Shoaib Akram, Manolis Marazakis, and Angelos Bilas. Understanding Scalability and Performance Requirements of I/O Intensive Applications on Future Multicore Servers. In *MASCOTS*, pages 171–180, 2012.

[2] Andrea Arcangeli, Izik Eidus, and Chris Wright. Increasing Memory Sensity by Using KSM. In *OLS '09: Proceedings of the Linux Symposium*, pages 19–28, July 2009.

[3] Jens Axboe. Flexible I/O Tester. https://github.com/axboe, 2005.

[4] Donald A. Berry and Bert Fristedt. Two arms, one arm known. In *Bandit Problems*, Monographs on Statistics and Applied Probability, pages 83–135. Springer Netherlands, 1985.

[5] Diwaker Gupta, Sangmin Lee, Michael Vrable, Stefan Savage, Alex C. Snoeren, George Varghese, Geoffrey M. Voelker, and Amin Vahdat. Difference Engine: Harnessing Memory Redundancy in Virtual Machines. *Commun. ACM*, 53(10):85–93, October 2010.

[6] Keren Jin and Ethan L Miller. The Effectiveness of Deduplication on Virtual Machine Disk Images. In *Proceedings of SYSTOR 2009: The Israeli Experimental Systems Conference*, page 7. ACM, 2009.

[7] Myoungsoo Jung and Mahmut Kandemir. Revisiting Widely Held SSD Expectations and Rethinking System-level Implications. In *Proceedings of the ACM SIGMETRICS/International Conference on Measurement and Modeling of Computer Systems*, SIGMETRICS '13, pages 203–216, New York, NY, USA, 2013. ACM.

[8] William Loewe and Tyce McLarty. Parallel File Systems Benchmark. https://github.com/chaos/ior, 2003.

[9] Ramon Nou, Jacobo Giralt, and Toni Cortes. Automatic I/O Scheduler Selection through Online Workload Analysis. In *2012 9th International Conference on Ubiquitous Intelligence & Computing and 9th International Conference on Autonomic & Trusted Computing (UIC/ATC)*, pages 431–438. IEEE, 2012.

[10] Ramon Nou, Jacobo Giralt, and Toni Cortes. DYON: Managing a New Scheduling Class to Improve System Performance in Multicore Systems. In *Proceedings of the 1st Workshop on Runtime and Operating Systems for the Many-Core Era (ROME'13)*, Best paper award, 2013.

[11] Oracle Solaris ZFS Deduplication. http://hub.opensolaris.org/bin/view/Community+Group+zfs/dedup, 2013.

[12] Carl A. Waldspurger. Memory Resource Management in VMware ESX Server. In *Proceedings of the 5th ACM/USENIX Symposium on Operating System Design and Implementation*, 2002.

Chapter 33

Storage Networks and Interconnects

Parks Fields and Benjamin McClelland

Los Alamos National Laboratory

33.1 Current State of Technology 363
33.2 Future Directions 365
33.3 Challenges and Solutions 366
33.4 Conclusion 367
      Bibliography 367

33.1 Current State of Technology

At present, HPC facilities primarily use Ethernet and IB interconnect technologies, although Cray and IBM have deployed some larger systems with a proprietary interconnect. In the June 2013 Top500 list [8], 40.2% of the systems use InfiniBand (DDR/QDR/FDR) as the interconnect, 43% use a combination of 1 GigE and 10 GigE, 4.2% use the Cray interconnect (Seastar/Gemini/Aries), 2% are proprietary, and 10% are custom interconnects. The remaining 4.2% of the proprietary interconnects that are not using Cray on the Top500 are from IBM and other countries like China and Japan who are developing their own interconnects. The custom category includes interconnects like the tofu network found on the Fujitsu machine. InfiniBand has proven itself over the years for small- and medium-size clusters. But due to scalability concerns, the DOE National Laboratories have avoided using IB for their largest capability machines.

The InfiniBand networks are usually created with a Fat Tree topology, but there are some exceptions. For example, REDSKY at Sandia National Lab was implemented with a 3D torus [7]. Sandia contributed much work and software to the routing algorithm to make sure that the network was deadlock free and avoided credit loops. Silicon Graphics International Corp. has used a HyperCube topology in some of the larger IB machines. The IB network has choices for routing algorithms, such as Fat Tree, Up-Down, Min-Hop, LASH, and DOR [9].

The IB market is primarily composed of two vendors, Mellanox and QLogic. Mellanox supplied chips to other companies including Voltaire.

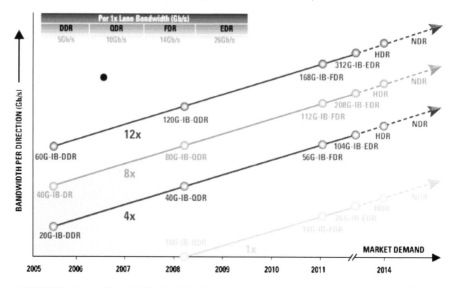

FIGURE 33.1: The IBTA's InfiniBand roadmap from 2005 to 2014. [Image courtesy of InfiniBand Trade Association.]

Recently, Intel bought the QLogic IB team and their intellectual property (IP) for IB and is currently selling the QDR hardware [2].

IB has a very good install base and has a significant open source software community. IB is following various portions of the IB Trade Association (IBTA) roadmap as seen in Figure 33.1. The IB vendors have rarely implemented IB 12× preferring the 4× path, as it is easier to implement and more profitable. The IB community has slowed its original aggressive bandwidth pace and adjusted to market demand.

There are many cluster vendors integrating Ethernet as the primary interconnect. Because Gigabit Ethernet is so cheap, many companies use it where bandwidth and latency between nodes is not as important. Many companies sell clusters with 10 GigE as the primary interconnect also. Chip makers such as Broadcom and Fulcrum created low-latency Ethernet chips that only add a few nanoseconds per hop. Gnodal is an Ethernet company that has chosen to design its own ASIC, which handles congestion very well. There are Remote Direct Memory Access (RDMA) implementations that function over Ethernet including RDMA over Converged Enhanced Ethernet (RoCEE) and Internet Wide Area RDMA Protocol (iWARP). However, due to bandwidth and latency issues when there is congestion, the DOE National Labs have not adopted this technology as a cluster interconnect.

Originally developed by Cray and then purchased by Intel in 2012, the Aries interconnect was the fastest interconnect as of 2013. The Aries network is PCIe-based but only available on a Cray built node. In 2012 Cray sold the interconnect IP and hardware team to Intel with the ability to continue integrating machines with the Aries interconnect [1]. As mentioned earlier, Intel acquired a few companies such as Cray hardware, the QLogic IB team, and Fulcrum in 2012 and 2013, but they do not currently offer any new interconnect technology.

33.2 Future Directions

The scale of future clusters at the DOE National Laboratories will force a change in interconnect technology. As clusters scale for a scientific workload, communications quickly become the bottleneck. On very large-scale clusters, the cost of interconnects and cost of power will drive technology requirements. The PCIe interface performance is not increasing as fast as processors or networks. PCIe Gen 3 is widely used today with no clear date of release for PCIe Gen 4 on the horizon.[1]

Many of the future interconnects for large-scale machines in the 2017 or the later time frame are expected to be based on silicon photonics technology. Every major processor vendor is expected to be looking at how to implement this type of network by then. The development of this technology is primarily driven by lower power and higher bandwidth requirements. The 2008 DARPA Exascale report speculates 1.5–2.0 pJ/bit for an exascale interconnect [4]. Extrapolated to the expected size of an exascale machine, the projected energy requirements would be on the order of 2–4 MW. The current target for an exascale machine is 20 MW of total power, so it is unlikely that the interconnect will be able to consume 20% of the total allocated power budget. There are several technologies in development to mitigate this problem. Some examples of these technologies include 3D chip stacking technology as well as on-package and on-die solutions, which require significantly less power. The Fast Forward and Design Forward DOE programs have listed a minimum of 400 GB/s node interface performance requirements [3]. This requires technology advances in several areas. With current technology evolution, the speed of the basic has to increase to reach these higher speeds. An alternative to a very fast single pipe is to do what telecommunications companies have done for years, which is to use wavelength division multiplexing (WDM), as shown in Figure 33.2. WDM allows for parallel communications channels over a single physical optical fiber links utilizing discrete ranges of light wavelengths. WDM can be implemented as CWDM (coarse WDM), which is up to 8 wavelengths, or DWDM (dense WDM), which can be up to 64–80 wavelengths. With this type of technology, data movement costs can be reduced. Networking for exascale systems will be moving to mostly optical connections in network interface cards (NIC), switches, and routers. There has been a recent emergence of vendors selling

---

[1]PCIe releases are announced at PCISIG.com.

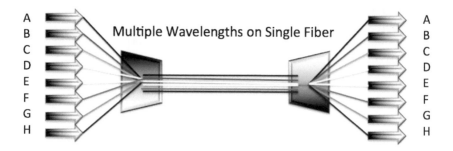

FIGURE 33.2 (See color insert): Wavelength division multiplexing.

all-optical switches, including Accipiter systems, Calient Technologies, and Huawei. The optical industry is already changing and growing to meet the needs of HPC.

One technical design detail that remains outstanding is if the optical switches will be all optical or a combination of optical and electrical (also known as O-E-O). Along with this new technology there has to be a lot of innovation with integrating wavelength multiplexing into an enhanced small form-factor pluggable (SFP+) or another similar-size form factor. This enables many ports on the line card of a switch or a couple of ports on a chip, motherboard, or NIC, which lowers the cost of the total solution.

The file system storage network has to be a cost-efficient design while continuing to meet the storage and archival needs of the platforms. This network relies on streaming bandwidth performance to file systems and typically does not have the messaging rate requirements of a cluster interconnect. The current cost-competitive network for ports and overall bandwidth is IB, even if used solely for TCP/IP communications across the IB network. IB lacks functioning as a truly enterprise network, but serves as a dedicated secondary cluster storage network quite well. The use of an external-to-the-cluster storage network allows for easier access from multiple clusters to a shared file system. Technologies such as LANL's Parallel Scalable Backbone [5] (see Chapter 6) and Lustre's Fine Grained Routing [6] minimize the cross-sectional bandwidth required for the storage network when designing a network with multiple core switches.

33.3   Challenges and Solutions

As with any new technology there are risks. DOE is trying to manage these risks through the Fast Forward and Design Forward programs. The exascale

HPC community is concerned about how much bandwidth will be available off of the chip and how many processors or threads will be required to effectively utilize the network interfaces. The trend with General-Purpose Graphics Processing Units (GPGPUs), Intel Phi processors, and ARM processors is to have many interfaces but individually lower performing processing cores. With lower performing processor cores, it is yet to be determined as to what will be required to saturate the links of such high-bandwidth networks.

The supporting infrastructure networks, such as the storage networks, are unlikely to be implemented with the advanced technology required for a future cluster interconnect primarily due to costs. This brings up a concern regarding the compatibility from the cluster environment to the external support networks. Not only is functionality a requirement, but also minimizing costs of working with the external networks with minimal additional specialty hardware.

33.4 Conclusion

Because of the expected scale of future clusters, reliability is a concern with potential new technology. Vendor integration of future technologies will determine the reliability impacts to the system. Some effective ways to increase system reliability might be to reduce the number of components, such as combining processors and network functionality, as well as broadening the install community to create community support.

Regardless of the risks, the most promising future technology for cluster interconnect at this point is silicon photonics due to the increased bandwidth capabilities and reduced power and complexity. These attributes could be the fundamental design criteria for scaling to an exascale platform.

Bibliography

[1] Intel Acquires Industry-Leading, High Performance Computing Interconnect Technology and Expertise. http://newsroom.intel.com/community/intel_newsroom/blog/2012/04/24/intel-acquires-industry-leading-high-performance-computing-interconnect-technology-and-expertise.

[2] Intel Augments Networking Portfolio with Best-in-Class High Performance Computing Fabric Technology. http://www.intel.com/content/www/us/en/high-performance-computing/infiniband-products.html.

[3] FastForward R&D Draft Statement of Work. `https://asc.llnl.gov/fastforward/rfp/04\_FastForward\_SOW\_FinalDraftv3.pdf`, 2009.

[4] Keren Bergman, Shekhar Borkar, Dan Campbell, William Carlson, William Dally, Monty Denneau, Paul Franzon, William Harrod, Kerry Hill, Jon Hiller, et al. Exascale Computing Study: Technology Challenges in Achieving Exascale Systems. *Defense Advanced Research Projects Agency Information Processing Techniques Office (DARPA IPTO), Tech. Rep*, 2008.

[5] Hsing-Bung Chen, Gary Grider, and Parks Fields. A Cost-Effective, High Bandwidth Server I/O Network Architecture for Cluster Systems. In *IPDPS*, pages 1–10. IEEE, 2007.

[6] David A Dillow, Galen M Shipman, Sarp Oral, and Zhe Zhang. I/O Congestion Avoidance via Routing and Object Placement. Technical report, Oak Ridge National Laboratory (ORNL); Center for Computational Sciences, 2011.

[7] Stephen Todd Monk, Mahesh Rajan, Marcus R Epperson, James Alan Schutt, Matthew Paul Bohnsack, Douglas W Doerfler, and John Hunt Naegle. HPC Top 10 InfiniBand Machine: A 3D Torus IB Interconnect on RREDSKY. Technical report, Sandia National Laboratories, 2010.

[8] Top500. Top500 List: June 2013. `http://www.top500.org/list/2013/06/`, 2010.

[9] Andrew Lumsdaine Torsten Hoefler, Timo Schneider. Optimized Routing for Large-Scale InfiniBand Networks. `http://htor.inf.ethz.ch/publications/img/hoefler-ib-routing-slides.pdf`.

Chapter 34

Power Consumption

Matthew L. Curry, H. Lee Ward, and David Martinez

Sandia National Laboratories

Jill Gemmill and Jay Harris

Clemson University

Gary Grider

Los Alamos National Laboratory

Anna Maria Bailey

Lawrence Livermore National Laboratory

34.1	Introduction		370
34.2	Power Use in Recent and Current Supercomputers		370
	34.2.1	Red Sky	371
	34.2.2	Cielo	371
	34.2.3	Palmetto	373
	34.2.4	Dawn	374
	34.2.5	Overall Survey Results	374
	34.2.6	Extrapolation to Exascale	377
34.3	How I/O Changes at Exascale		377
	34.3.1	Introducing More Asynchrony in the File System	378
		34.3.1.1 The Burst Buffer	378
		34.3.1.2 Sirocco: A File System for Heterogeneous Media	378
	34.3.2	Guarding against Single-Node Failures and Soft Errors	379
34.4	Conclusion		380
	Bibliography		381

34.1   Introduction

Many institutions are working toward building exascale[1] computers by 2018–2021. Along the road to exascale, there will likely be inflection points where current strategies for many aspects of a computing system (programming models, resilience and serviceability, power delivery and management, and mass storage) will no longer be adequate, and new strategies will have to be adopted. Thought leaders in all of these areas are working to ensure that we can effectively use exascale machines when they arrive.

Perhaps the largest looming barrier to exascale computing is the potential power consumption of a machine. The most power-efficient machine at the time of this writing can accomplish about 4.5 GFLOPS/W [1]. To be viable, an exascale machine will have to be able to perform 50 GFLOPS/W [30]. Researchers are scrutinizing every subsystem to ensure that no power is being wasted.

Secondary storage is receiving significant attention for two major reasons. First, the cost of moving a block of data from disk to memory is comparatively immense. Moving a byte from disk to main memory requires 100–1000× more energy than moving a byte from RAM to a CPU cache [20], disregarding network activity necessary for HPC I/O. Second, many HPC applications perform significant I/O in the form of bulk synchronous checkpointing, where the application stops computing to form a restart file on persistent storage. For applications to make acceptable progress, these (often large) checkpoints should be performed in a small fraction of the total computation time. This implies that the I/O system has to appear fast to the user, while consuming a comparatively reasonable amount of power.

This chapter begins by describing the state of power use of past and present production supercomputers at a variety of sites. Following, the chapter will extrapolate today's typical architecture and methods to exascale. Finally, this chapter describes recent and ongoing innovations that have the potential to improve I/O power use for exascale machines.

34.2   Power Use in Recent and Current Supercomputers

Historically, system researchers have not emphasized power consumption for HPC storage systems specifically. Instead, power metrics were gathered in aggregate, which included storage, compute, networking, and often cooling in the same figure. To the authors' knowledge, the following subsections discuss the largest survey of power use in HPC storage systems to date. At the time of

---

[1] 10^{18} floating point operations per second (FLOPS).

the surveys, these storage systems were important production machines used daily on important problems. Portions of this survey appeared in a previous paper by Curry et al. [13].

34.2.1 Red Sky

Red Sky is the premier capacity compute platform at Sandia National Laboratories, New Mexico. When combined with Red Mesa, a machine of the same architecture hosted at Sandia for the National Renewable Energy Laboratory (NREL), it ranked 16th on the June 2011 TOP500 list, having achieved 433.5 TFLOPS [3]. One of the machine's notable features is its interconnect topology, as it is the first Infiniband machine organized as a 3D torus [19]. It is composed of Sun X6275 blades, each containing two Intel X5570 processors and 12 GB of RAM. The storage nodes are nearly identical to the compute nodes, save connections to storage, and are in the same racks. Red Sky hosts 3 PB of raw storage organized as Linux software RAID 6 arrays. These provide the storage for several Lustre file systems.

Red Sky is designed to be split between two modes of operation simultaneously: classified and unclassified. The unclassified partition of the machine, was configured to be about 83% of the nodes in Red Sky, or about 54% of the nodes in Red Sky and Red Mesa combined [29]. This portion of the machine (called Red Sky UC from here forward) includes a 750-TB Lustre file system for scratch, and two other 18-TB Lustre file systems for home and project directories. Power consumption is projected for this portion of the machine, as it is intended to be a reasonable partition that can be used independently.

Three racks (one compute, two storage) were measured and extrapolated to the size of Red Sky UC, which contains 40 racks of compute and six racks of storage. Several times throughout a 14-hour period, the power use was read directly from the compute rack's power distribution unit, and the draw of the disk cabinets was measured directly from the circuit panel board. The compute rack consumed between 23.2 and 27.2 kW, while the two storage racks together consumed a steady 16 kW throughout the test period. Figure 34.1 shows power use as extrapolated to the full size of Red Sky UC. It can be predicted that 928–1088 kW are consumed by compute and I/O nodes, while 48 kW are consumed by disks. This implies that 4.2–4.8% of the machine's power is used for disks.

34.2.2 Cielo

Los Alamos National Laboratory and Sandia National Laboratories, through the Alliance for Computing at Extreme Scale (ACES), procured, operate, and use Cielo, the primary capability computing platform for both labs [5]. Cielo is hosted at Los Alamos National Laboratory. Cielo was measured as the sixth most powerful supercomputer on the June 2011 TOP500

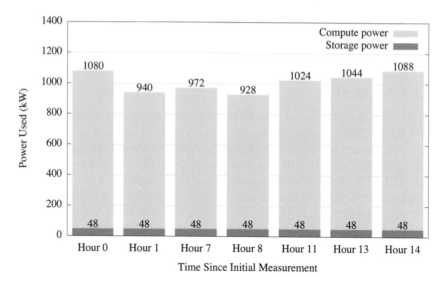

FIGURE 34.1: Predicted power use for Red Sky UC.

list, having achieved 1.11 PFLOPS [3]. The compute section of Cielo, a Cray XE6, has 8,944 dual-socket nodes, populated with 2.4-GHz eight-core AMD Magny-Cours processors, with 32 GB of DDR3 memory per node [33]. At the time of measurement, Cielo was connected to a 10-PB Panasas storage system that managed hardware-accelerated RAID 6 arrays with eight disks each.

There were other machines in the same building that used an enterprise storage model; i.e., there was a another shared 10-PB high-speed parallel file system that was available to several machines. At the time of measurement, this included Roadrunner, a 1-PFLOPS heterogeneous platform that contained IBM Cell processors [17]; and 800 TFLOPS of capacity compute clusters. The SAN is known as PaScalBB, and is a high-bandwidth 10 GigE fabric [10]. Together, all of the clusters and storage form the secure environment at Los Alamos National Laboratory, which was comprised of approximately 3.5 PFLOPS of compute and 20 PB of storage at the time of measurement.

The power use of compute and storage were measured by reading the power draw directly from the power distribution units several times throughout the course of a normal working day, when the utilization was high. Cielo uses, on average, 4.4% (306 kW compared to 6.7 MW) of its power for disks, SAN, and I/O servers. The entire secure computing environment in aggregate (including Cielo) uses 2.4% (400 kW compared to 16.5 MW) for those components.

TABLE 34.1: Types of compute nodes in Clemson University's Palmetto cluster.

Make/Model	CPU	RAM	Qty
Sun X6250	Intel Xeon L5420	32 GB	430
IBM dx340	Intel Xeon E5410	16 GB	340
Dell PE1950	Intel Xeon E5410	12 GB	258
Dell PE1950	Intel Xeon E5345	12 GB	257
Sun X2200	AMD Opteron 2356	16 GB	256
HP DL165	AMD Opteron 6176	48 GB	70
Sun X4150	Intel E5410	16 GB	10
HP DL580	Intel Xeon X7542	512 GB	6
Sun X4600	AMD Opteron 8220	256 GB	1
HP DL980	Intel Xeon X6560	2 TB	1

34.2.3 Palmetto

Palmetto is Clemson University's largest compute cluster. It represents a successful instantiation of the condominium model of supercomputing, where users contribute funds for hardware to secure time on the platform [4]. This model creates a varied mix of hardware that can participate in computations. Palmetto is used to run a large number of applications, including molecular dynamics, econometrics, network simulation, biophysics, genomics, and combustion codes. The measured configuration achieved the 96th slot on the June 2011 TOP500 list with a score of 92 TFLOPS [3].

Table 34.1 shows a list of all machines within the cluster at the time of measurement, sorted by quantity. A small number of large-RAM nodes were purchased for specific applications, and are not included in the general availability pool of resources. Nodes are connected to a Myrinet fabric.

Palmetto's storage hardware included 32 Dell R510 servers with Dell PERC H700 controllers. Each controller ran a RAID 5 array with five 1-TB disks, with a total usable space of 256 TB. An OrangeFS scratch file system [28] of 115 TB occupied this space, with the remainder unused. A further 360 TB of data storage was provided by three Data Direct Networks (DDN) arrays: two DDN 6620s with sixty 2-TB disks apiece that host home and project directories; and one unused DDN 9550 with five trays, each containing forty-eight 500-GB disks [22]. The DDN 6620 units were configured with Oracle's StorageTek Storage Archive Manager (SAM) [27]. Two Sun F5100 servers with eighty 22-GB flash disks each were used for SAM metadata.

To measure the power use of Palmetto, each power distribution unit was sampled every two hours. During this period, June 20 through June 27, 2011, Palmetto was approximately 50% loaded [11]. Figure 34.2 shows that Palmetto's storage power use ranges between 4.9% and 6.1% of the total machine's consumption throughout the testing period, or 20 to 24 kW total.

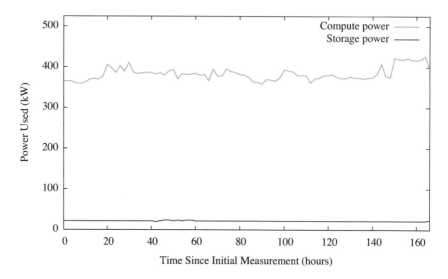

FIGURE 34.2: Power use for Palmetto and its storage infrastructure.

Meanwhile, total compute power draw ranged from 359 to 427 kW. During higher utilization periods, it is likely that the compute power draw is higher, thus reducing the proportion of power used by storage.

34.2.4 Dawn

Dawn is a 500-TFLOPS 147,456-core Blue Gene/P machine that was procured as a code-development and scaling platform for Sequoia [6]. It is connected to a storage cluster called Dusk, which contains 8400 10000-RPM 400-GB disks, connected to 56 DDN S2A 9900 controllers. The disks are organized into 8+2 RAID 6 arrays, with 15 arrays per Lustre object storage server. Internally to Dusk, there is an Infiniband network for data movement, along with an Ethernet management network. Dusk is connected to Dawn via 10 GigE.

Power data was automatically collected from Dawn and Dusk through July 2011, at 15-minute and 30-minute intervals, respectively. Figure 34.3 shows the power use of Dawn and Dusk during July 2011. There was a gap in Dusk's data collection of about 24 hours, which is visible in Figure 34.3.

34.2.5 Overall Survey Results

Figure 34.4 shows the proportion of system power used by disks in several machines. For the majority of scenarios presented, disk infrastructure uses

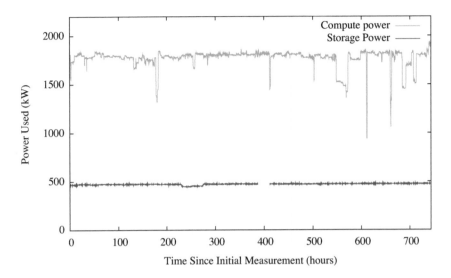

FIGURE 34.3: Absolute power use of Dawn over a one-month time period.

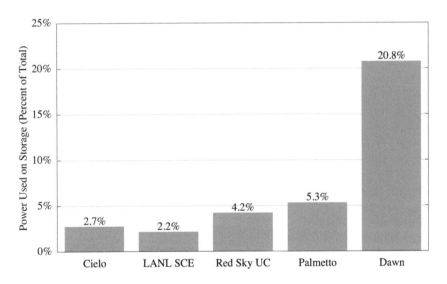

FIGURE 34.4: The percent of power used for disks and associated systems, by machine.

between 2.2% and 5.3% of the total system power. This is almost an insignificant amount of power use, and is lower than the inefficiencies in the power distribution feed system of a particularly efficient data center [21]. It is safe to say that I/O power use is not a problem in most systems today.

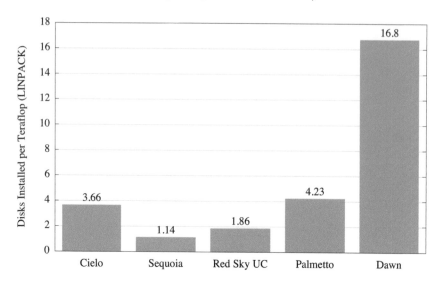

FIGURE 34.5: The number of disks installed in each system per teraFLOP of compute power, by machine.

Notably, Dawn uses more than one fifth of its power for storage. Dawn's storage system contains a comparatively large number (8,400) of small, high-RPM disks to form its file system. In comparison, Red Sky uses only 1,500 slower disks, even though it is has comparable compute performance. Figure 34.5 shows that, per TFLOP of compute capacity, Dawn has a large number of disks installed.

Dawn is included as an indication of the aforementioned "inflection points" to come. In June 2009, when Dawn was introduced to the TOP500 list, it was the largest known Blue Gene machine being run outside of Lawrence Livermore National Laboratory with Lustre. The other Blue Gene/P systems in the Top 10 ran IBM's GPFS, with Intrepid using 7,680 disks [2], a very similar number to Dawn's 8,400. Livermore was already experienced in running Lustre against its 212,992-core Blue Gene/L, where it saw disk accesses similar to random I/O even when giving sequential workloads from each core [7]. Extra disks (with high-rotation speed for reduced latency) provided more performance under this undesirable access pattern. It seems this performance problem has been solved, as Sequoia (also shown in Figure 34.5) has a much lower disks-to-teraFLOP ratio [31].

The data strongly show that storage systems consume much less power than compute nodes. Figure 34.5 shows the power use data for each machine, normalized by the LINPACK [14] score for each platform. The proportion of power consumed by storage is remarkably similar among the machines sampled (excepting Dawn), between 0.17 and 0.31 kW/TFLOPS. In comparison, computation uses up to 6.7 kW/TFLOPS. As mentioned before, Palmetto was lightly loaded at the time of measurement, so its power consumed per TFLOP of capability is artificially low.

34.2.6 Extrapolation to Exascale

At 30 kW/PB, Cielo stands as a machine that has extremely efficient power use for I/O and infrastructure. However, without a change of strategy, an exascale storage system may consume too much power. To understand why, a common workload is analyzed for large-scale machines: checkpointing. One rule of thumb is that an application should spend less than 5% of its execution time writing checkpoints to storage. With today's disks, this necessitates that the system purchaser buys enough disks to provide necessary bandwidth. The storage space obtained from the purchase is often far in excess of what is otherwise required in a scratch file system.

This assumption will also be true in the future. The first exascale machine is estimated to have at least 32 PB of RAM [30]. Disks are projected to hold 29.52 TB, and have a bandwidth of 384.2 MB/s [18]. The system is expected to require 320 PB to 1 EB of storage space [30]. Disregarding fault tolerance measures like RAID, the capacity can be satisfied with 10,847 to 33,898 disks. However, to provide necessary bandwidth to accept a checkpoint every hour, the system will need to provide at least 106.7 TB/s of bandwidth. This requires over 277,633 disks, with over 8 EB of capacity! Holding power per disk constant to the survey finds that this machine would require about 13 MW of power, or 65% of the exascale system's power budget, *without* extra capacity and bandwidth for fault tolerance.

Clearly, there will have to be some change from business as usual to achieve acceptable performance for exascale workloads. One cannot satisfy exascale bandwidth requirements as outlined above by checkpointing directly to disks. The next sections explore evolutionary storage technologies, revolutionary storage technologies, and application technologies that will allow future workloads to be reasonably satisfied on an exascale machine.

34.3 How I/O Changes at Exascale

Between now and the deployment of the first exascale machine, there will be a point where it will be economically impossible to build a large, homogeneous file system that meets both bandwidth and storage requirements for bulk synchronous checkpoint workloads. The implication is that the file system's form must change, the application's fault characteristics must change, or both. This section explores methods in both areas.

34.3.1   Introducing More Asynchrony in the File System

Asynchronous I/O (AIO) is a method of allowing computation and I/O to be performed simultaneously, potentially improving the utilization of a system's resources and reducing the execution time of a task. AIO is most effective when provided with hardware support, application design, and operating system support. This is often the case in stand-alone workstations, but many HPC applications running at large scales are coupled, which causes resource contention to affect the efficiency of the application. AIO directly incurs network traffic while the application is executing, which can introduce delays in completing synchronizing actions like halo exchanges, collectives, etc.

Another, perhaps more significant, issue with using AIO in HPC applications is memory pressure. A bulk synchronous checkpoint is typically going to write a significant proportion of the application's memory to disk. Applications often run more efficiently when using more memory, but AIO requires holding the checkpoint's buffers until they have been moved off-node. This extra memory use has the potential to reduce the application's overall effectiveness to the point that AIO would cause the application to run slower.

One possible solution to these problems is to add asynchrony to the portions of the parallel file system running outside of the compute node, in the form of off-node buffer caches. There are at least two major projects that aim to implement this concept: the Burst Buffer project, and the Sirocco file system.

34.3.1.1   The Burst Buffer

The burst buffer (see Chapter 23) may be the most widely discussed hardware I/O accelerator within the storage system research community. The burst buffer is a high-bandwidth, flash-based storage server that is placed between the compute nodes and disk-based storage servers, acting as an initial destination for data being written to disk. Because flash has a much higher write bandwidth than disk, an application can checkpoint quickly to the burst buffer, then continue computing. The burst buffer can then orchestrate a slow data migration to disk-based storage before the next checkpoint interval, creating a storage system that can satisfy bursty write workloads like bulk synchronous checkpointing. Previous estimates, through anticipated capacities and bandwidths, show that an exascale storage system that supports checkpoint restart would only consume approximately 6.6% of an anticipated exascale power budget [13].

34.3.1.2   Sirocco: A File System for Heterogeneous Media

Sirocco [12] is a file system that is inspired by peer-to-peer systems. It is intended for pre-exascale machines and beyond. The core of its design is based on a small number of fundamental ideas about how a client and a server should behave in a scalable system. These include:

- Clients that may autonomously choose which servers receive writes based on quality of service.

- Servers that may move and replicate data autonomously to improve fault tolerance.

- Servers that may come and go quickly, due to failure or temporary instantiation.

- Clients that should be cooperative to help enforce consistency.

In short, Sirocco provides a self-organizing system that allows local decision making in clients and servers to yield a self-tuning, reliable file system.

Sirocco enables self-organization by exposing the characteristics of each server's storage to the storage system. Heterogeneous media is quickly becoming the norm in HPC systems, so tiered solutions (including the Burst Buffer) are being proposed to manage it. Sirocco is implemented as a large victim cache, with ejections targeted from less reliable storage to more reliable storage automatically, without global knowledge of tiering. This is enabled by resource discovery, where a storage node will seek more reliable nodes as targets for ejections. It is adaptive because the targets are not fixed, and can be eschewed for targets that provide better service (including if the original target ceases to operate).

The implication is that Sirocco clients can automatically use faster targets as burst buffers for checkpoints, or even use temporary servers running on compute nodes as RAM-backed stores. These ephemeral RAM-backed nodes can be started on demand, and relinquished when they finish bleeding checkpoints to disk.

Sirocco is currently under active development, and is being used as a vehicle to investigate several research areas like data location [32] and fault-aware message passing [15]. Sirocco is an effort of the Advanced Storage Group (ASG), which includes Argonne National Laboratory, Clemson University, the University of Alabama at Birmingham, and Texas A&M University.

34.3.2 Guarding against Single-Node Failures and Soft Errors

In some circumstances, checkpoint I/O consumes a significant proportion of an application's runtime. Oldfield et al. measured compute jobs on three HPC platforms at 131,072 processes, and found that each spent about half of their time checkpointing, with optimal checkpoint frequency being about every twenty minutes [26]. This is an artifact of applications experiencing total failure upon a single node failure, whether permanent or transient. If a job can continue after a single node failure, then checkpointing can be done less frequently.

Checkpoints, in part, guard against unexpected application failure, which can be caused by non-permanent faults (i.e., soft errors). Cosmic-ray-induced neutrons are a well-known source of soft errors in memory, having been extensively studied in at least one large supercomputer [23]. There are several hardware-based strategies for mitigating soft errors in memory, but each has its own trade-offs in terms of effectiveness, power consumption, and speed [25]. Exascale systems are expected to demonstrate that soft errors will become common, and that designers should help mitigate soft errors in software.

Soft errors do not discriminate, and can manifest in application software or system software. Application researchers are actively seeking modifications to their algorithms and data structures that allow applications to successfully continue in the face of soft errors [8]. System software researchers are surveying operating systems for important data structures that require hardening, such that soft errors will not cause a node to crash [9].

Library-based fault tolerance is also an option. Scalable Checkpoint Restart (SCR) is an I/O library that provides a range of local checkpoint strategies to applications [24]. Its main goal is to enable a node in a job to checkpoint to one or more other nodes, allowing an application to recover from failure of individual nodes in a job. It is designed to work with on-node storage, which could be a RAM disk, spinning disk, flash, NVRAM, etc.

Another library-based approach includes rMPI [16]. rMPI uses replicated computations, a proven method of ensuring operability of mission-critical systems. By implementing MPI calls to ensure message ordering and state maintenance between replicas, it allows an application to transparently benefit from redundant computations. Although a job using rMPI uses at least twice as many cores as compute ranks, the overhead can be reasonable. For very large jobs, the decreased checkpoint and restart activity can yield appreciable speed-ups over a non-replicated job running an equal number of nodes, while simultaneously reducing potential load on an I/O system.

34.4   Conclusion

It is widely known that the projected power envelope for an exascale computer will be extremely limiting. All subsystems are being investigated for potential inefficiencies, including storage. This chapter presents the widest survey of storage power use in HPC systems, which shows that today's storage systems are not generally significant users of power. However, extrapolating potential disk sizes and storage requirements to exascale systems shows that today's methods of constructing and using storage will be completely inadequate from a power perspective.

Fortunately, there are several technologies under development that serve to reduce the demands on I/O systems for bulk synchronous checkpoints. These include methods of using fast, off-node storage as temporary buffers that move data to disk-based storage, like the Burst Buffer; and a reconceptualization of storage as a swarm of storage nodes and clients that work in a self-organized manner to ensure data safety and performance, embodied by Sirocco. These technologies can enable legacy applications to attain high-bandwidth periodic checkpointing to the file system with power use proportional to today's systems.

Other techniques that emphasize client behavior are also available that can reduce overall demands on the I/O system. These methods reduce the frequency of checkpointing, allowing longer running checkpoints to take proportionally similar amounts of application time to complete. By making jobs more reliable, and guarding against the most common types of faults, defensive I/O load on the system can be dramatically reduced.

These solutions, applied individually and together, significantly increase the capabilities of limited disk-based I/O systems. Bringing these technologies to effective use will allow HPC platforms to generate impactful research results for well into the exascale era.

Bibliography

[1] The Green500 list. http://green500.org/.

[2] Intrepid/Challenger/Eureka File Systems. https://www.alcf.anl.gov/user-guides/intrepid-challenger-eureka-file-systems.

[3] TOP500 Supercomputer Sites. http://www.top500.org/.

[4] Pawan Agnihotri, Vijay K. Agarwala, Jeffrey J. Nucciarone, Kevin M. Morooney, and Chita Das. The Penn State Computing Condominium Scheduling System. In *Proceedings of the 1998 ACM/IEEE Conference on Supercomputing (CDROM)*, Supercomputing '98, pages 1–23, Washington, DC, USA, 1998. IEEE Computer Society.

[5] James Ang, Doug Doerfler, Sudip Dosanjh, Scott Hemmert, Ken Koch, John Morrison, and Manuel Vigil. The Alliance for Computing at the Extreme Scale. In *Proceedings of the Cray Users Group 2010*, 2010.

[6] Blaise Barney. Using the Dawn BG/P System. https://computing.llnl.gov/tutorials/bgp/.

[7] Brian Behlendorf. Sequoia's 55PB Lustre+ZFS Filesystem. Lustre User Group 2012, http://www.opensfs.org/wp-content/uploads/2011/11/LUG12_ZFS_Lustre_for_Sequoia.pdf, April 2012.

[8] Patrick G. Bridges, Kurt B. Ferreira, Michael A. Heroux, and Mark Hoemmen. Fault-Tolerant Linear Solvers via Selective Reliability. June 2012. arxiv:1206.1390 [math.NA].

[9] Ron Brightwell, Ron Oldfield, Arthur B. Maccabe, and David E. Bernholdt. Hobbes: Composition and Virtualization as the Foundations of an Extreme-Scale OS/R. In *Proceedings of the Workshop on Runtime and Operating Systems for Supercomputers*, June 2013.

[10] H.-B. Chen, Parks Fields, and Alfred Torrez. An Intelligent Parallel and Scalable Server I/O Networking Environment for High Performance Cluster Computing Systems. In *Proceedings of the International Conference on Parallel and Distributed Processing Techniques and Applications (PDPTA)*, 2008.

[11] Clemson University. Cluster Statistics for Palmetto. `http://cluster-usage.clemson.edu/`.

[12] Matthew L. Curry, Ruth Klundt, and H. Lee Ward. Using the Sirocco File System for High-Bandwidth Checkpoints. Technical Report SAND2012-1087, Sandia National Laboratories, February 2012. Available at `http://prod.sandia.gov/techlib/access-control.cgi/2012/121087.pdf`.

[13] Matthew L. Curry, H. Lee Ward, Gary Grider, Jill Gemmill, Jay Harris, and David Martinez. Power Use of Disk Subsystems in Supercomputers. In *Proceedings of the 6th Parallel Data Storage Workshop*, 2011. `http://www.pdsi-scidac.org/events/PDSW11/resources/papers/pdsw17-curry.pdf`.

[14] Jack J. Dongarra, Piotr Luszczek, and Antoine Petitet. The LINPACK Benchmark: Past, Present, and Future, August 2003. *Concurrency Computat.: Pract. Exper.*, 15: 803-820. doi: 10.1002/cpe.728.

[15] Matthew S. Farmer, Anthony Skjellum, Matthew L. Curry, and H. Lee Ward. The Design and Implementation of SSM: A Single-Sided Message Passing Library Based on Portals 4.0. Technical Report UABCIS-TR-2012-01242012, Department of Computer and Information Sciences, University of Alabama at Birmingham, 115A Campbell Hall, 1300 University Blvd, Birmingham, Alabama 35294-1170, 2012.

[16] Kurt Ferreira, Jon Stearley, James H. Laros, III, Ron Oldfield, Kevin Pedretti, Ron Brightwell, Rolf Riesen, Patrick G. Bridges, and Dorian Arnold. Evaluating the Viability of Process Replication Reliability for Exascale Systems. In *Proceedings of 2011 International Conference for High Performance Computing, Networking, Storage and Analysis*, SC '11, pages 44:1-44:12, New York, NY, USA, 2011. ACM.

[17] D. Grice, H. Brandt, C. Wright, P. McCarthy, A. Emerich, T. Schimke, C. Archer, J. Carey, P. Sanders, J.A. Fritzjunker, S. Lewis, and P. Germann. Breaking the Petaflops Barrier. *IBM Journal of Research and Development*, 53(5):1:1–1:16, 2009.

[18] Gary Grider. Exa-scale FSIO. HEC-FSIO workshop presentation. `http://institute.lanl.gov/hec-fsio/workshops/2010/presentations/day1/Grider-HECFSIO-2010-ExascaleEconomics.pdf`, August 2010.

[19] Stephanie Holinka. Red Sky at Night, Sandia's New Computing Might. *Sandia Lab News*, 61(24), December 2009. `http://www.sandia.gov/LabNews/ln12-18-09/labnews12-18-09.pdf`.

[20] Bruce Jacob, Spencer Ng, and David Wang. *Memory Systems: Cache, DRAM, Disk*. Morgan Kaufmann, 2008.

[21] Du-Hwan Kim, Taesik Yu, Hyosung Kim, Hyungsoo Mok, and Kyung-Seok Park. 300V DC Feed System for Internet Data Center. In *Proceedings of the IEEE Eighth International Conference on Power Electronics and ECCE Asia (ICPE ECCE 2011)*, pages 2352–2358, June 2011.

[22] Randall Martin. Personal communication, September 2011.

[23] S.E. Michalak, K.W. Harris, N.W. Hengartner, B.E. Takala, and S.A. Wender. Predicting the Number of Fatal Soft Errors in Los Alamos National Laboratory's ASC Q Supercomputer. *Device and Materials Reliability, IEEE Transactions on*, 5(3):329–335, 2005.

[24] Kathryn Mohror, Adam Moody, Greg Bronevetsky, and Bronis R. de Supinski. Detailed Modeling and Evaluation of a Scalable Multilevel Checkpointing System. *IEEE Transactions on Parallel and Distributed Systems*, 99(PrePrints):1, 2013.

[25] M. Nicolaidis. Design for Soft Error Mitigation. *Device and Materials Reliability, IEEE Transactions on*, 5(3):405–418, 2005.

[26] R. A. Oldfield, S. Arunagiri, P. J. Teller, S. Seelam, M. R. Varela, R. Riesen, and P. C. Roth. Modeling the Impact of Checkpoints on Next-Generation Systems. In *Mass Storage Systems and Technologies, 2007. MSST 2007. 24th IEEE Conference on*, pages 30–46, 2007.

[27] Oracle Corporation. Sun QFS Software. `http://www.oracle.com/us/products/servers-storage/storage/storage-software/storage-archive-manager/overview/index.html`.

[28] Orange File System. `http://www.orangefs.org/`.

[29] Red Sky Hardware Environment. Sandia internal resource. Archived copy available upon request.

[30] John Shalf, Sudip Dosanjh, and John Morrison. Exascale Computing Technology Challenges. In *Proceedings of the 9th International Conference on High Performance Computing for Computational Science*, VEC-PAR'10, pages 1–25, Berlin, Heidelberg, 2011. Springer-Verlag.

[31] Marc Stearman. Installation of LLNLs Sequoia File System. Cray User's Group 2012. `http://www.opensfs.org/resources/presentations/`, April 2012.

[32] Zhiwei Sun, Anthony Skjellum, Lee Ward, and Matthew L. Curry. A Lightweight Data Location Service for Nondeterministic Exascale Storage Systems. *ACM Transactions on Storage*, 2014. To appear.

[33] Bob Tomlinson, John Cerutti, and Robert A. Ballance. Cielo Computational Environment Usage Model. Technical Report LA-UR 10-07492, Los Alamos National Laboratory, June 2011. `http://www.lanl.gov/orgs/hpc/cielo/docs/CieloUsageModel.pdf`.

Index

Accelerated Strategic Computing
    Initiative (ASCI), 52, 68
active file management, 47, 115
adaptive mesh refinement (AMR),
    218
ADIOS, 203, 260
ADIOS-BP, 204, 261
aggregation, 263
Alliance for Computing at Extreme
    Scale (ACES), 371
asynchronous data staging, 219
asynchronous I/O (AIO), 216, 378

blocking I/O, 159
Blue Waters, 17
burst buffer, 174, 271, 341, 378
byte-range locks, 112

Ceph, 338
CF Metadata Conventions, 193
CFD, 195
CGNS standard, 195
checkpointing, 174, 205, 370, 380
checksumming, 256
Chombo, 301
Cielo, 371
CNFS, 110
code coupling, 207
collective I/O, 163
combustion, 259
compression, 219, 256
Computational Fluid Dynamics
    (CFD), 205
containment domains (CDs), 350
Cray
    XE6, 18
    XK7, 18

Craypat, 283

DAOS, 340
Darshan, 46, 283, 309, 317
data analytics, 271
data direct network, see DDN
data model, 244
DataSpaces, 207
Dawn, 374
DDN, 36, 373
Design Forward, 366
Direct Numerical Simulation, 259
distributed lock manager, 111
distributed locking, 110
distributed object-based storage, 92
DMAPI, 115
Dusk, 374

Edison, 6, 260
Ethernet, 363
Exascale, 370
extendible hashing, 113

Fast Forward, 366
file domain, 164
file systems, 92, 104, 117
file-per-process, 29, 252
filesets, 114
finite element modeling, 239
FLASH, 218
Flash memory, 378
FPMPI, 283
FUSE, 263

Gemini, 18
General Parallel File System, see
    GPFS
GEOS-5, 207

GLEAN, 216
Global Cloud Resolving Model (GCRM), 318
Globus, 27
GPFS, 9, 39, 41, 52, 67, 107, 108, 376
    GPFS file placement optimizer, 110
    GPFS Native RAID, 114

H5hut, 194
H5Part, 230
HACC, 219
Hadoop, 129
HDF5, 29, 62, 73, 179, 185, 216, 230, 243, 280, 310, 340
HDF5-FastQuery, 195
heterogeneous media, 379
high availability, 111
Hopper, 6, 230, 318
HPC facilities
    Argonne Leadership Computing Facility (ALCF), 33
    Texas Advanced Computing Center, 79
    Livermore Computing Center, 51
    Los Alamos National Laboratory, 65
    National Center for Supercomputing Applications, 17
    National Energy Research Scientific Computing (NERSC) Center, 5
HPCT-IO, 283
HPSS, 11, 25, 26

I/O
    I/O benchmarking, 280
    I/O hint, 157, 165
    I/O instrumentation, 290
    I/O interception, 290, 310
    I/O middleware, 155, 232
    I/O profiling, 283, 309, 319
    I/O software stack, 177

I/O tracing, 317
in-transit analysis, 271
in-transit visualization, 208
independent I/O, 160
Infiniband (IB), 363
Integrated Performance Monitoring (IPM), 283, 297
interconnects, 363
Interlagos, 18
Intrepid, 34, 376
IOAnalyzer, 359
IOBUF, 263
IOFSL, 340
IOR, 22, 280
IOT, 283
Iota, 317
ISABELA lossy compression, 210
ISOBAR lossless compression, 210

job mean time to interrupt (JMTTI), 70
Jumpshot, 283

key-value stores, 92

LANL-Trace, 283
LNET, 8
LNet, 18
lock token, 111
Lustre, 21, 53, 80, 92, 233, 317, 338, 371
    LNet, 93
    Lustre Distributed Lock Manager (LDLM), 93, 96
    Lustre Lite, 68
    Lustre Monitoring Tool (LMT), 281
    Lustre Networking, 93
    Lustre networking, 93
    Lustre Object Storage Device (OSD), 92
    Lustre RPC, 94
    Lustre Commit-On-Share (COS), 103

MADBENCH, 302

magnetic reconnection, 228
many-core, 353
MapReduce, 129
metadata server (MDS), 98
metanode, 112
Mira, 35
MPI, 155, 262, 318
MPI file view, 161
MPI-IO, 44, 73, 155, 217, 230, 280,
        310, 337
multicore, 353

namespaces, 341
NASD, 337
near-threshold voltage (NTV), 348
NERSC Global Filesystems (NGF), 6
netCDF, 29, 179, 193
netCDF classic format, 193
Network Shared Disk, 109
network topology, 217
network-attached storage (NAS), 136
Non-Volatile Random-Access
        Memory (NVRAM), 137,
        341
nonblocking I/O, 159
NTFS, 339
NUMA, 356
NVIDIA
    K20X, 18
    Kepler, 18

object storage device (OSD), 97
Object Storage Model, 337
object storage targets (OSTs), 8
one-file-per-process I/O, 157
OneFS, 135
operating system, 104, 117
OrangeFS, 119, 373
OSD, 337

Palmetto, 373
Panasas, 372
PanFS, 338
Parallel I/O stack, 156, 232
Parallel Log-structured File System,
        see PLFS

Parallel Virtual File System, *see*
        PVFS
Parallel-NetCDF (pNetCDF), 177,
        216, 280, 310, 339
ParaView, 194, 208, 222, 275
PaSCalBB, 372
PHASTA, 219
plasma physics, 227
PLFS, 73, 169, 340
Poor Man's Parallel I/O, 252
portability, 178
POSIX, 43, 73, 92, 120, 170, 280,
        310, 317, 333
    POSIX file model, 334
    POSIX HPC Extensions, 335
    POSIX I/O, 157, 204
POSIX I/O, 29
power consumption, 369
power efficiency, 369
profiling, 294
PVFS, 39, 43, 119, 338, 339

Red Sky, 371
Redundant Array of Independent
        Tapes (RAIT), 26
Remote Direct Memory Access
        (RDMA), 208
replicated computations, 380
resilience, 345
resource partitioning, 357
Rich Man's Parallel I/O, 253
rMPI, 380
Roadrunner, 372
ROMIO, 163

S3D, 260, 263
Scalable Checkpoint Restart (SCR),
        62, 380
scheduling, 359
self-describing file format, 177
Sequoia, 54, 374
Serializer/Deserializer (SerDes), 365
SILO, 62
Silo, 249
Simple Linux Utility for Resource
        Management (SLURM), 84

Sirocco, 378
soft errors, 379
software-defined storage, 169
Sonexion, 21
spectral-element method (SEM), 206
staging, 216
Stampede, 79
STAT, 283
stochastic simulations, 240
storage area networks (SANs), 9, 67,
        363
storage pools, 114
subfiling, 219, 263

TAU, 283, 289
Tivoli storage managers (TSM), 67
TOP500, 372
two-phase I/O, 164

UFS, 139
unstructured grids, 219
user-defined policies, 114

Valgrind, 283
versioning, 244
Virtual File Driver (VFD), 62, 256
Virtual File Layer, 244
virtualization, 169
VisIt, 194, 255
visualization, 208, 271
VORPAL, 318
VPIC, 227, 318
VSAM, 339
Vtune, 283

ZFS, 54

T - #0338 - 071024 - C50 - 234/156/19 - PB - 9780367378233 - Gloss Lamination